Im

UNIVERSITY OF
GLOUCESTERSHIRE

NORMAL LOAN

Knowledge for Policy: Improving Education through Research

Edited by

Don S. Anderson and Bruce J. Biddle

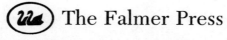 The Falmer Press

(A member of the Taylor & Francis Group)
London · New York · Philadephia

UK   The Falmer Press, 4 John St, London WC1N 2ET
USA   The Falmer Press, Taylor & Francis Inc., 1900 Frost Road, Suite
        101, Bristol, PA 19007

First published 1991

British Library Cataloguing in Publication Data
Knowledge for policy: improving education through research.
  1. Social sciences. Research
  I. Anderson, Don S.   II. Biddle, Bruce J.
  300.72

  ISBN 1-85000-822-1
  ISBN 1-85000-823-X pbk

Library of Congress Cataloging in Publication Data
Knowledge for policy: improving education through research/
  Don S. Anderson & Bruce J. Biddle (editors).
     p.   cm.
  Includes indexes.
     ISBN 1-85000-822-1: — ISBN 1-85000-823-X (pbk.):
     1. Education—Research—United States.   2. Education—
  Research—Great Britain.   3. Social sciences—Research—
  United States.   4. Social sciences—Research—Great Britain.
  I. Anderson, Don, 1926–   .   II. Biddle, Bruce J.
  (Bruce Jesse), 1928–   .
  LB1028.25.U6K58   1991
  370'.78073—dc20   90-46269
                                                        CIP

Typeset in 10.5/12 pt Caladonia by
Graphicraft Typesetters Ltd., Hong Kong

*Printed in Great Britain by Burgess Science Press, Basingstoke
on paper which has a specified pH value on final paper
manufacture of not less than 7.5 and is therefore 'acid free'.*

Contents

Contents

Contents

Preface

Once upon a time there was a national meeting of educational researchers where the President addressed the members. He spoke of the practical usefulness of research in education. That is what presidents are supposed to do, and this man (who was a distinguished scholar) did it very well, and the audience was pleased. Now it so happened that invited to the same meeting was a former President (equally distinguished). He addressed the members saying, educational research was not useful, indeed we should not expect it to be useful, because research was for advancing knowledge, not for solving problems. Yet another distinguished scholar told the members that educational research was shallow and its methods were flawed. And a fourth said research in education frustrated reform because it served only the needs of the powerful.

It also happened that we were at that meeting, and we listened to these conflicting messages and, like the members, were puzzled. We heard the first speaker and were reassured. He said that our vocation was an honourable calling, of use to the community. Like the other learned professions, it harnesses intellect and morality for disinterested service to the public. Our vocation, the President said, was to apply our special skills to the solution of problems which beset those concerned with education, be they political leaders, administrators of school systems, principals of schools, or teachers in the classroom. But each of the other scholars who spoke cast doubt. The second said that social research was not meant to solve problems, the third questioned the quality of our research efforts, the fourth challenged our basic morality.

So puzzled, we began to ponder and debate the inconsistencies of these messages and the ways in which they confronted the optimisms of our youths — for, like many others, we were initiated in PhD programs where it was assumed that social research could rescue Western civilization. Of necessity, most of our communication has been carried out across the ocean that usually divides us. But over time, we have also made several visits to each other's campus and have explored many facets of this complex topic. Finally, we began to write a monograph on the nature of social research and the ways in which it interacts with policy and practice — a task to which we hope soon to bring closure.

In the course of our work we have made many summaries and have indexed many cards from hundreds of thoughtful articles, chapters, and books. These we have continued to shuffle this way and that, according to their questions and viewpoints. Then one day a colleague, believing perhaps that our monograph would never be finished, suggested that we should edit a volume of the best works on the topic. Since we knew of no other collection that remotely represented the diversity of available insights, we took up the suggestion.

At first we had thought to tackle all realms of social science and their impact. When cold reality intervened, we chose to concentrate on the institution we know best, so that, with one or two exceptions, all of the selections we have chosen focus on education. But even this restriction left us the task of choosing 25 contributions from a massive literature.

First, we allocated all candidates for inclusion to one of the four parts we had planned for this book. With multiple contenders, we were influenced by length, clarity, and ways in which selections fit together. We also tried to keep in mind the needs of various potential readers, not only the social researcher and scholar, but also the policy maker puzzled by the fact that research does not always seem relevant, the administrator trying to improve his or her system or school, the teacher committed to an excellent classroom, the student of education trying to make sense of it all.

We also tried for some national balance in our selections but were defeated. American scholars have simply written far more about the puzzle than any others. (At times, their concern about the nature of social research and its impact seems to be a national obsession.) Inevitably many excellent works had to be omitted. The names of persons responsible for many of these may be found in our index.

Most of the selections we have included were abridged, so we consulted with all authors concerning our intentions. Most authors were agreeable to their work being included, and many applauded the endeavour. Some suggested improvements and these led to exchanges and revisions.

In most cases we have indicated abridgments and the inclusion of words that did not appear in the original source using ellipses and square brackets. In all cases, we have followed the spelling conventions of the original source, whether it was British or American usage. We have also recast citations and references into the standard forms used today in most social science publications and have excised most footnotes and endnotes. We have not, however, changed earlier uses of language in selections that were conventional at the time but would now be considered sexist. To do so would have required considerable rewriting and introduced distortion in some selections. This of course does not mean that the authors or editors condone what is now recognized as sexist language.

The book begins with an introductory essay in which we conceptualize issues, argue substantive theses, and discuss each selection briefly. It then continues in four parts. Part 1, 'Can Social Research Have an Effect?', reprints selections both critical and enthusiastic about research impact and reviews problems inherent in social research. Part 2, 'Models for Social Research', includes contributions arguing severally for 'positivistic', 'basic', 'applied', and 'alternative' approaches to social research. The selections in Part 3, 'Knowledge Generation and Knowledge Distribution', discuss communication between the research domain and the domains of policy and action in education. Selections in Part 4, 'Research, Ideology, and Educational Impact', provide illustrations of social research impact and discuss the social and ideological contexts in which impact occurs.

Many persons helped with this enterprise. In Canberra at the Australian National University, Norma Chin, May McKenzie, and Maureen Wiechert keyed in copy accurately where scanners failed, and Elizabeth Owen composed the indexes with help from Norma Chin. Most of the manuscript work at the University of Missouri, in Columbia, was done by Patricia Shanks, although she was ably assisted, from time to time, by Billye Adams, Kathy Craighead, LeeAnn Debo, Scot Heidbrink, Teresa Hjellming, and Sandy Juergensmeyer. Finally, we owe many debts to Barbara Bank for encouragement, professional advice, and timely suggestions.

Our collaboration in this project was facilitated by installing fax boards in our computers which have enabled us to swap files across the Pacific at high speed and for less than the cost of a postage stamp. This work has been the product of equal collaboration, which means that we are equally responsible for its strengths and (perish the thought) its weaknesses. We would have preferred that our names appear side by side throughout the work, but given practical limitations, DSA appears as the first-listed editor, and BJB's name appears first for our introductory essay.

DSA   BJB
Canberra   Columbia
June 1990

Acknowledgments

We are grateful to all authors and to the following organizations for permission to reprint materials that originally appeared in the indicated sources.

American Educational Research Association
FINN, C.E., Jr. (1988). What ails education research. *Educational Researcher, 17*(1), 5–8 [Chapter 3].
SHAVELSON, R.J. and BERLINER, D.C. (1988). Erosion of the education research infrastructure: A reply to Finn. *Educational Researcher, 17*(1), 9–12 [Chapter 7].
WINEBURG, S.S. (1987). The self-fulfillment of the self-fulfilling prophecy. *Educational Researcher, 16*(9), 28–37 [Chapter 24].

American Psychological Association
GERGEN, K.J. (1973). Social psychology as history. *Journal of Personality and Social Psychology, 26*(2), 309–320 [Chapter 12].

American Society for Public Administration
WEISS, C.H. (1979). The many meanings of research utilization. *Public Administration Review, 39*(5), 426–431 [Chapter 14].

Authors
HOROWITZ, I.L. and KATZ, J.E. (1975). *Social Science and Public Policy in the United States* (pp. 125–146). New York: Praeger [Chapter 20].
KOGAN, M. and ATKIN, J.M. (1982). *Legitimating Education Policy: The Use of Special Committees in Formulating Policies in the U.S.A. and U.K.* (Project Report No. 82–A17, pp. 1–17, 82–97). Stanford, CA: School of Education, Center for Educational Research at Stanford [Chapter 21].

Harvard Educational Review
COHEN, D.K. and GARET, M.S. (1975). Reforming educational policy with applied social research. *Harvard Educational Review*, 45(1), 17–43 [Chapter 11].

D.C. Heath and Company
CAPLAN, N. (1977). 'A minimal set of conditions necessary per the utilization of social science knowledge in policy formulation at the national level. In C.H. WEISS (Ed.), *Using Social Research in Public Policy Making* (pp. 183–197). Lexington, MA: D.C. Heath [Chapter 16].

Holt, Rinehart, and Winston
KERLINGER, F.N. (1979). *Behavioral Research: A Conceptual Approach* (pp. 1–18, 279–305). New York: Holt [Chapter 8].

LaTrobe University Press
SELLECK, R.J.W. (1989). The Manchester Statistical Society and the foundation of social science research. In D. STUCKLEY (Ed.), *Melbourne Studies in Education: 1987–88* (pp. 53–63). Bundoora, Victoria: La Trobe University Press. A version of this selection also appeared in *Australian Educational Researcher*, 16(1), 1989 [Chapter 25].

National Academy of Education
GETZELS, J.W. (1978). Paradigm and practice: On the impact of basic research in education. In P. SUPPES (Ed.), *Impact of Research on Education: Some Case Studies* (pp. 477–517). Washington, DC: National Academy of Education [Chapter 9].

National Academy Press
COMMITTEE ON BASIC RESEARCH IN THE BEHAVIORAL AND SOCIAL SCIENCES. (1982). *Behavioral and Social Science Research: A National Resource* (pp. 93–102). Washington, DC: Commission on Behavioral and Social Sciences, National Research Council [Chapter 2].

Pergamon Press
COLEMAN, J.S. (1984). Issues in the institutionization of social policy. In T. HUSEN and M. KOGAN (Eds.), *Educational Research and Policy: How Do They Relate?* (pp. 131–141). Oxford: Pergamon Press [Chapter 10].
POSTLETHWAITE, T.N. (1984). Research and policy making in education: Some possible links. In T. HUSEN and M. KOGAN (Eds.), (1984). *Educational Research and Policy: How Do They Relate?* (pp. 195–206). Oxford: Pergamon Press [Chapter 17].

Acknowledgments

Routledge
THOMAS, P. (1985). *The Aims and Outcomes of Social Policy Research* (pp. 97–114). London: Croom Helm [Chapter 19].

Sage
ALKIN, M.C., DAILLAK, R., and WHITE, P. (1979). *Using Evaluations: Does Evaluation Make a Difference?* (pp. 223–261). Beverly Hills, CA: Sage [Chapter 23].

BLALOCK, H.M., Jr. (1984). *Basic Dilemmas in the Social Sciences* (pp. 13–36). Beverly Hills, CA: Sage [Chapter 5].

COOK, T.D. (1985). Postpositivist critical multiplism. In R.L. SHOTLAND and M.M. MARK (Eds.), *Social Science and Social Policy* (pp. 21–62). Beverly Hills, CA: Sage [Chapter 4].

GUBA, E.G., and LINCOLN, Y.S. (1989). *Fourth Generation Evaluation* (pp. 80–109). Newbury Park, CA: Sage [Chapter 13].

KNOTT, J. and WILDAVSKY, A. (1981). If dissemination is the solution, what is the problem? In R.F. RICH (Ed.), *The Knowledge Cycle* (pp. 99–136). Beverly Hills, CA: Sage [Chapter 18].

WEISS, C.H. (1980). Knowledge creep and decision accretion. *Knowledge: Creation, Diffusion, Utilization, 1*(3), 381–404 [Chapter 15].

UNESCO
LEVIN, H.M. (1978). Why isn't educational research more useful? *Prospects, 8*(2), 157–166 [Chapter 6].

John Wiley and Sons
KAMIN, L. (1981). Some historical facts about IQ testing. In H.J. EYSENCK and L. KAMIN, *The Intelligence Controversy* (pp. 90–97). New York: John Wiley & Sons [Chapter 22].

Williams and Wilkins
CARTWRIGHT, D. (1949). Basic & applied social psychology. *Philosophy of Science, 16*, 198–208 [Chapter 1].

Introductory Essay

Social Research and Educational Change

Bruce J. Biddle and Don S. Anderson

For countless years governments have used social research knowledge in order to advance national purposes. During a period of national emergency Moses was instructed by his superior officer to count the inhabitants of the Israelite nation and classify them according to age, race, sex, and medical fitness (Numbers: Chapter 1). In the nineteenth century, Horace Mann (then Commissioner of Education for the State of Massachusetts) began collecting statistical data to promote educational change (Travers, 1983), and the Manchester Statistical Society was formed in England for the purposes of advancing education and the welfare of the working classes [R.J.W. Selleck, Chapter 25].

As in these earlier times, a good deal of social research is supported by authorities today in the hope that it will contribute to the improvement (as they define it) of social life or the advancement of national purposes. But, unlike their predecessors, modern producers and consumers of social research also are plagued with doubt about its efficacy. Within the academy controversies have arisen concerning the nature of social research. Within the bureaucracy social research is often criticized by consumers who are impatient with research pace or frustrated when major research efforts are not in accord with political agendas. And researchers are dismayed with challenges to governmental support for social research in recent years.

What then can we conclude about the relation between social research and its effects? Does social research generate useful knowledge? If so, what is the nature of that knowledge? Does that knowledge have an impact? And if it does, how does that knowledge get from producers to consumers, who are those consumers, and for what purposes do they use that knowledge?

These issues are the core concerns of this book. As it happens, interest in these issues is widespread, and they have been addressed by hundreds of talented authors in the past two decades. From this sizeable literature we have chosen 25 selections which have insightful things to say about the nature of social research and its impact. These selections take different stances, however, and in this introductory essay we provide a framework for understanding their insights.

Before addressing this topic, we should say what we mean by social research, and why our coverage is mainly about education. The terms research and social science are used in many ways. Dictionaries give both a broad and a narrow meaning for 'research'. In its broad sense, research denotes any investigatory activity, thus it might include (among other things) philosophical inquiry, textual exegesis, or self-exploration via meditation. Although this broad meaning is useful elsewhere, we choose in this book to stress the narrower sense in which research is used to denote disciplined empirical investigation or inquiries which gather and interpret evidence.

Similarly, 'social' research can be conceived to apply to all disciplines that concern themselves with the affairs of interacting beings including (among others) the fields of law, archaeology, and ethology. Although these uses may also be needed in other contexts, we choose here to restrict usage to the core social disciplines whose research has had the greatest impact on education — social psychology; sociology; anthropology, and occasionally history, political science, and economics.

When we speak of *social research*, then, we have in mind the empirical investigations characteristic of the core social sciences. Although restrictive, this definition still covers a lot of territory. It includes — for example — experiments with human subjects, social surveys, observational research; ethnographic studies; public-opinion polls; analyses of census and other records assembled by governments; historical research with archival documents; studies that are commissioned by private-interest groups; basic, applied, and evaluation research; inexpensive research that is conducted by isolated scholars or educators; complex studies with huge samples and massive funding; and intensive research on but a single person or social context.

Social research is now a large and costly enterprise in industrialized countries. It is sponsored from many sources: the private sector, through grants from foundations, governments, or public authorities, and the salaries of university faculty who both teach and do research. Most expensive social research is supported through grants and contracts from governments, and this, as we shall see, can be the tail that wags the research dog, influencing the questions that are asked and the methods that are used. Grant and contract support must compete with other legitimate needs for tax dollars, and much of it is awarded with the expectation that social research will contribute to social betterment (as defined by the sponsor), preferably in the short run. But, whatever the funding source, much social research is widely assumed to be for 'improving' social life. In this regard, social research is seen differently from a good deal of research in the natural sciences, say astronomy or physics. All forms of disciplined research are thought to generate knowledge, but much of research in the natural sciences is thought to be generated by curiosity alone. In contrast many persons assume that social research as we have defined it should be for improving the human condition and be driven by both curiosity and practical goals.

Our second limitation concerns the decision to focus this book on *education*. This decision was made for several reasons: social research has differing effects in different institutions, the two of us are familiar with education, education is important, and a large literature on social research impact in education is already available. Nevertheless, the decision to focus on education means that this book centres on the effects of social research within a specific institutional context.

By comparison with other institutions, education in most countries: is massive in size, is largely supported by public funds, has a sizeable bureaucracy, serves a vulnerable client population, has low professional status, has complex and often contradictory goals, has diffuse effects which are hard to assess, and is often politicized. These features tend to generate a unique arena for social research impact. To illustrate, education has a large number of interest groups (or 'stakeholders') who are involved in setting its policies and procedures. These interest groups include, at a minimum: *politicians, administrators in governments, policy advisors in governments, district and school administrators, teachers, teachers' unions, parents, school boards, citizen groups representing specific interests, teacher educators, educational researchers, industries with needs for trained employees, foundations and vendors pushing educational innovations,* and (lest we forget) *pupils*. Educational systems differ in the ways in which they accommodate the interests of these various groups and in their procedures for making policy, and each of these groups may have needs for access to social research knowledge.

To take another illustration, modern educational systems are subject to repeated calls for change or 'reform'. Most of these calls reflect the interests of specific groups, most calls involve assumptions about the potential effects of innovations, and in most cases those assumptions are not backed by research. (To illustrate, reformers of the past few years have urged such innovations as a career-ladder system for teachers' salaries or a longer school year. It is argued that such innovations will generate higher levels of pupil achievement, but little research has yet appeared that would support such arguments.) In short, the 'radical' notion of supporting calls for educational reform with research knowledge seems not yet popular among many reformers.

One might think this a problem, but evidence also suggests that over the years most calls for reform have had but little effect on educational practice (see Elmore and McLaughlin, 1988; Cuban, 1990). This does not mean that education is static. On the contrary, it clearly evolves in response to ideological and bureaucratic pressures and is occasionally swept by fads — some, like open learning or programmed instruction,

3

masquerading as research-generated innovations. However, educational systems generally seem to have a robust capacity for resisting pressures for change. More than one study has shown that policy decisions by educational leaders have but little impact within schools (see, for example, Popkewitz, Tabachnick, and Wehlage, 1982). But this also suggests that the deck might be stacked against those who seek evidence for the impact of social research in education. (If educational systems successfully resist other pressures for change, why should they not also resist research-generated pressures?) Nevertheless, evidence of research impact in education is abundant — indeed, the selections we have chosen for this book provide many examples of such effects.

Nevertheless, controversies have also erupted concerning the nature of research on education, and educational research has also come under attack for its presumed lack of relevance. Why have such controversies and attacks arisen?

Enthusiasms and Denigrations

Industrialized civilizations value and support research in the natural sciences because of its perceived benefits and despite its destructive potentials. Support is also sometimes extended to research in the social domain. National governments collect massive census and economic data in the hope that they will be useful. Social research was argued as an aid for social planning by advocates ranging from Adam Smith to Karl Marx, Emile Durkheim, the Fabians, and the American Pragmatists. Recent enthusiasm for social research can be traced to World War II and its aftermath, however. Large-scale investigations of propaganda, morale, and individual abilities had been useful during a time of war, and social research came to be regarded as an essential part of postwar social reconstruction. Thus Dorwin Cartwright, writing in 1949, could assert that "In the acute social crisis of our time many people are turning to social science for the solution of our social problems" [Chapter 1].

Nevertheless, support for social research remains a minute fraction of that for the natural sciences. Within the United States, support for social research on 'practical' problems appeared in various agencies in the 1940s and 1950s, but funding for 'basic' social research was not authorized in the National Science Foundation until 1960. Similarly, within Australia, support appeared first for research in the physical and biological sciences, but in the early 1950s the federal government established a major facility for natural and social research, now known as the Institute for Advanced Studies, charged with investigating subjects of importance to the nation. Systematic support for social research was not formalized in Britain until 1966, when it was established under the aegis of the Social Science Research Council. Despite these advances, support for social research has been tepid, and advocacy groups such as the Committee on Basic Research in the Behavioral and Social Sciences [R.M. Adams, N.J. Smelser and D.J. Treiman, Chapter 2], have often felt a need to argue that "Federal investment in basic research in the behavioral and social sciences ... is an investment in the future welfare of the nation."

Doubts about the value of social research efforts have been particularly strong in education. In part, this scepticism may have been fuelled by exaggerated claims for research effects. To illustrate, Patricia Graham, at that time Director of the National Institute of Education in Washington, stated that "As an intrinsic part of all our research and development programs, we will find ways to eliminate the effect of a student's race, culture, or income on the quality of education received and on the achievement level attained" (*ASA Footnotes*, 1978). But such uncritical enthusiasm had, by the end of the 1970s, been largely replaced by pessimism. Thus, a prominent researcher in the United States has recently asked:

> Is the vast majority of the variance in educational effectiveness inexplicable in terms of the influences that we can currently measure and control? Is it likely to remain so for at least the span of our professional lives? ... Should our empirical policy studies be based on the assumption that the conditions that make schooling effective are either in practice unknown, unmeasurable, too numerous, or too labile to be controlled by persons at any significant distance from the essential nexus of learning, namely a pupil's brain and a tutor? I am inclined to believe that the answer to each of these questions is "yes". (Glass, 1979)

Within Britain, the Permanent Secretary to the Department of Education and Science declared:

> I have to say, of course, that the great thing about research is that a part of it is rubbish and another part ... leads nowhere and is really indifferent; it is, I am afraid, exceptional to find a piece of research that really hits the nail on the head and tells you pretty clearly what is wrong or what is happening or what should be done.... People say they have done some research when they really mean they have stopped to think for three minutes. (Pile, 1976)

And a former university professor, in 1988 an Assistant Secretary in the U.S. Department of Education, complained:

> To put it simply, our labors haven't produced enough findings that Americans can use or even see the use of. Over the past two

decades, there has been a goodly amount of systematic inquiry and a flood of studies, reports, and recommendations, yet our education system has by many measures worsened. [Chester E. Finn, Jr., Chapter 3]

Moreover, these doubts have been accompanied by a downturn in government support for social (and educational) research accompanied — at least in the United States and Britain — by some vitriolic rhetoric.

What lies behind these negative attitudes towards the usefulness of social research? A surprising range of answers has been proposed for this question. Perhaps the simplest answer is that some social (and particularly educational) research is flabby, weak, poorly conceived, or inappropriate for solving social problems [Finn, Chapter 3]. A more sophisticated answer sees social research as often associated with social reform efforts involving intervention in the public sector, hence to be an anathema to conservative governments [Thomas D. Cook, Chapter 4]. Furthermore, advocates and ideologues already 'know' the proper solutions for human problems, and for them research is irrelevant, except perhaps to legitimate predetermined opinions. Other answers are associated with inherent problems within social research [Hubert M. Blalock, Jr., Chapter 5]; recent attacks upon 'positivism' among social researchers [Cook, Chapter 4]; and inadequate support for sustained social research efforts [Richard Shavelson and David Berliner, Chapter 7]. And still another is based on the observation that social researchers and users live in separate worlds that are difficult to link [Henry M. Levin, Chapter 6]. (In brief, the researchers' world is slower paced and tends to be focused on the complex details of research methods, findings, and interpretations. In contrast, the user lives in a world of practical demands and conflicts — where decisions must often be made quickly, whether or not research has anything to say about the topic.)

In the final analysis, however, it appears that doubts about social research are based more on hearsay than reality. Evidence abounds that social research has substantial impact, and summaries of some of its effects within education appear in many of the essays reprinted in this book. To paraphrase Mark Twain, current rumours about the ineffectiveness of social research seem to be grossly exaggerated. Why have such rumours appeared, and why are they so widely believed?

In this essay we argue that such rumours are based, in part, on misunderstandings about the nature of social research and the ways in which its knowledge can affect institutions such as education. In brief, a good deal of mischief has been created by a 'simple' model for research impact which has it that social research generates facts — i.e., definitive 'findings' or 'results' — and that such facts enable users to make unfettered decisions which will improve social life. To illustrate, some enthusiasts have thought that research on teaching can generate definitive findings about the effects of teacher behaviour on pupil achievement and that this information can be applied in ways which will inevitably improve classroom teaching.

To say the least, this model seems inappropriate for thinking about social research and its effects (see Biddle, 1987). It implies a naive view of the research process and ignores the various forms of knowledge that social research can generate. It also assumes that social research knowledge is always made available to users and that those users inevitably employ that knowledge in ways that improve the social scene. And it assumes that the field of application is politically sterile — devoid of value alternatives, the wheeling and dealing of interest groups, and the multitudinous trade-offs which characterize action in real life situations. It is widely espoused, however, and disenchantment seems to appear when the expectations it engenders are not fulfilled. If this 'simple' model is misleading, what might a more realistic model look like?

Conceptions of Social Research

We begin with the social research process. How should social research be conceived, how does it generate knowledge, and what is the nature of that knowledge?

Traditional or positivist answers to these questions are based on models for social research which are concerned with quantitative measurement, deductive reasoning, and causal relations among variables. As outlined by Fred N. Kerlinger [Chapter 8], social research is seen as similar to one version of research procedures in the natural sciences. Like them, it conducts disciplined enquiries in the real world, thus generates knowledge which is more valid than knowledge based on ideology, hearsay, superstitions, intuitions, or limited personal experience. And like them, it is based on the canons of objectivity and empiricism, explores event occurrences through surveys, and confirms causal relations by means of manipulative experiments which enable events to be predicted.

The model as outlined by Kerlinger is popular among psychologists but places limits on one's realm of study, particularly when experimentation is involved. After all, one normally cannot manipulate gender, social class, or the ethnicity of a pupil's family in experiments, yet these factors contribute to variation in pupil school achievement. Concern about this problem is widespread, and some sociologists of positivistic bent argue that causal conclusions about nonmanipulatable variables are justified when theory generates models involving such variables and those models are, in turn, supported with evidence using statistical controls (see Heiss, 1975; or James, Mulaik, and Brett, 1982 — also see Biddle, Slavings, and Anderson, 1985; and Marini and Singer, 1988 for recent reviews of causality issues).

Kerlinger also makes the point that social research leads to *theoretical* knowledge, and even though its theoretical insights are never ultimately 'proven', the basic purpose for conducting research is to gain those insights. Like most positivists, Kerlinger also argues that social research 'tests' but does not 'generate' theory, thus stressing deductive rather than inductive reasoning. These arguments may be traced to the influence of key figures in the history of philosophy, notably the Logical Positivists and Karl Popper, but they leave open questions about where theories come from and they are discovered (which does not mean that quantitative research on scientific discovery is impossible to conduct, see Langley, Simon, Bradshaw, and Zytkow, 1987).

In addition, Kerlinger argues for a distinction that is now widely used among social researchers — that between *basic* and *applied* research. In general, basic research is thought to be driven by theory, to reflect the questions of researchers, and to generate 'conclusions', whereas applied research starts with practical concerns, reflects the needs of knowledge users, and generates 'decisions'. We have some reservations about the depth of this distinction (see Anderson, 1987), but it has been around for at least 50 years [see Chapter 1] and also appears in the natural sciences where basic and applied research are often regarded as being fundamentally different. Moreover, funding procedures for basic and applied research are often assigned to different governmental agencies, with preference going to the latter because early pay-off seems more likely.

Given this distinction, it is reasonable to examine both basic and applied research as models for the generation of useful knowledge. The case for basic research is made by J.W. Getzels [Chapter 9] who argues that practical knowledge ultimately devolves from theoretical insights which are best generated by basic investigations. Getzels also provides examples of basic research impact in education and suggests that such impact stems not only from the generation of empirical information through research but also from the concepts, explanations, or ways of thinking ('paradigms') about social events which basic social research evolves. Indeed, if we take Getzels seriously, basic research probably has *more* potential for influencing education than applied research — although it may not be focused on specific questions that governments or educators want answered in the near future.

In contrast, the case for applied research is made by James S. Coleman [Chapter 10] who argues that, whereas basic studies are largely designed to generate journal publications for the researcher, applied studies are more often focused on issues relevant to potential users. Coleman also describes applied studies which have affected education although he observes that those effects were not always the ones intended by the researchers and those who funded the research. In fact, Coleman wonders why so much applied research is "not used by those in positions of policy, but [is] left to gather dust on a shelf." This complaint about the actual effects of applied research is taken up in greater detail by David K. Cohen and Michael S. Garet [Chapter 11] who discuss both the shifting social contexts of policy making and some of the inherent problems of applied research. Their argument suggests that governments fund applied studies assuming that such studies will generate 'definitive' knowledge needed for making specific decisions, but that such assumptions are unrealistic. Instead, Cohen and Garet urge that applied research be considered a form of 'social discourse' in which policy makers and researchers interact to generate potentially useful knowledge.

Cohen and Garet raise questions about the image of applied research, but other authors have challenged the basic tenets of the positivist model. As we learned from Cook [Chapter 4], various questions have been raised by social researchers themselves about the traditional image of their craft. Some of these questions concern problems inherent in the study of social events. For example, Blalock [in Chapter 5] suggests that, unlike much research in the natural sciences, social research is plagued by serious measurement problems, social events are often affected by many variables and tend to change rapidly, determinants of social behaviour may differ when one goes from context to context, the boundaries of social events are often fuzzy and imprecise, and the collection of social data is often expensive which means that researchers are dependent on governments or other powerful agents for funds or are forced into doing trivial research.

These problems challenge positivist social research. If, for example, the determinants of social behaviour often differ from context to context, then one cannot be sure that the results from one survey or experiment will generalize to another context not yet studied. (Techniques found to improve pupil achievement in a public school, for example, may or may not 'work' in a parochial school.) This does not mean that all social effects are context-bound. Some may be sharply bound while others may generalize widely, but we will not know which effects will and will not generalize until we have studied them in various contexts. In fairness, thoughtful positivists, such as Kerlinger, are concerned about this challenge. But too often social researchers and policy advisors write as if they believe that the results of a single study will generalize indefinitely, across space and time.

The challenges posed by Blalock are serious, but there are worse. As Cook suggests [Chapter 4], some positivists appear to assume that the findings of social research speak for themselves, but this is nonsense. Empirical findings never stand alone but are always embedded within an interpretive context (or 'paradigm') which makes assumptions about concepts, operations, and analytic tools. This issue is also contentious for the physical sciences (see Kuhn, 1962) but is writ large in social research where value commitments seem inevitably to intrude in the decisions of the researcher or patron who funds the research. The wise social researcher acknowledges these commitments and plans activities to minimize their effects. But unfortunately, as Selleck reminds us [in Chapter

25], a lot of well-intentioned social research reflects value commitments that seem not to be recognized by the researcher.

Other critics point out that when social research involves collecting data from sentient beings, the research act becomes a form of social interaction. To the extent that this occurs, the researcher cannot be the 'objective' scientist portrayed in positivist models. Others have suggested that social processes involve interacting and evolving parts, and for such processes the simple concept of A causing B is inappropriate. Again, the tendency of positivists to study variables in isolation from one another leads some critics to observe that the researcher misses important events or fails to perceive the outline of the forest. And the strong insistence on deductive logic in positivist writings is anathema to some critics who view the proper task of social research to be the discovery of inductive insight.

Then there is the problem posed by the fact that the objects of study in the social sciences are self-aware human beings who, despite all constraints, continue to make their own choices. Kenneth J. Gergen [Chapter 12] argues that when knowledge about social events is promulgated, awareness of that knowledge may change those events in the future. (To illustrate, the mere act of alerting teachers to their observable classroom behaviours may cause those behaviours to change — see Good and Brophy, 1974.) Gergen also discusses the fact that many social effects are laid in a temporal context and that those effects tend to change unpredictably over time. He proposes an alternative model which conceives social research as an activity that generates only insights about contemporary social history. This does not mean that social research is useless, of course. A snapshot, diary, or analysis of current affairs is clearly preferable to total ignorance, but these mechanisms lack the panache that we normally associate with research.

Gergen's vision of social research as an activity bound by history is not the only alternative to positivist models. Others are summarized in a model offered by Egon G. Guba and Yvonna S. Lincoln [Chapter 13]. The Guba-Lincoln model, called "Constructivist Inquiry", stresses the problematic character of social research, the need for close contact between researchers and their subjects, the interdependence of social evidence and values, qualitative procedures which do not depend on formal measurement and statistical manipulations, and the inductive discovery of insights which may or may not generalize to contexts not studied. Such a model may be used for portraying the techniques of ethnographic research such as participant observation and exploratory interviewing [see Chapter 15], case-studies [Chapter 19], and some types of evaluation research [Chapter 23].

Those who advance alternative models for social research (particularly advocates of qualitative methods) sometimes feel that they are an embattled minority and, not unlike minorities throughout the ages, can be pretty aggressive in defending their position. At the same time supporters of positivism can be quite insensitive to the problems inherent in their models and oblivious of the advantages of alternative models. We do not choose to take sides in this debate. Instead, we suggest that there are legitimate cases to be made for various and diverse strategies for social research which will depend on one's purposes. Alternative methods shine when they generate insights about the dynamics of social contexts with which we were not familiar. Positivistic research sparkles when it tests crisp theories with persuasive empirical evidence. No one approach has an exclusive mandate for generating knowledge that either satisfies human curiosity or is useful for those whose job is to get things done as effectively as possible.

How then is one to conceive the knowledge types that social research generates? Answers to this question should reflect several ideas from the above paragraphs. For one, research-generated knowledge consists of insights that are communicated with symbols and are always laid within an interpretive context. This does not mean that such insights are spun out of thin air. On the contrary, good social research also provides evidence for its insights, but its findings only have meaning when they are interpreted within a theoretical paradigm with which we are familiar. For another, various forms of social research generate different types of knowledge, and one should recognize these various types and their potential contributions. And for a third, one should also recognize that the insights generated through social research are fragmentary images, seen through a glass darkly, of an indefinitely complex reality.

Such observations suggest that social research can generate several types of knowledge elements. Among others, these include: *technical concepts* denoting social events; *propositions* about events and their relations; and *explanations* for social processes. To illustrate, recent research on teaching and its effects has generated:

Technical concepts for describing classroom teaching — such as Kounin's (1970) concepts of "Momentum", "Withitness", "Group Alerting", and others denoting aspects of classroom management.

Propositions about relations between teaching strategies and pupil outcomes — such as those summarized by Slavin (1987) for the effects of ability grouping in American public, primary schools. In brief: self-contained classes grouped by overall ability have few effects; but ability groups for specific subjects (particularly groups that cross grade levels) can increase pupils' achievements.

Explanations for observable effects in classrooms — such as those of Brophy and Good (1974) for "The Pygmalion Effect" which denotes inadvertent tendencies among some teachers to treat pupils differently depending on whether they think those pupils are 'bright' or 'dull' [see Chapter 23]. As Brophy and Good note, this effect is a product of unawareness on the part of teachers and can be countered by promoting analytic understanding and a proactive teaching style.

Since concepts, propositions, and explanations are the building blocks of theory, it would also be correct to say (with Kerlinger) that social research generates *theory*. Moreover, it is useful to state that research generates *theory* because this term reminds us of the tentative nature of social research knowledge, helps us to avoid the 'fact' assumption of the simple impact model, and suggests that most research impact comes about because users become aware of theories generated through social research.

But, with all respect to Kerlinger, social research also generates other knowledge elements in addition to theory. These include the *designs and strategies* through which social research is conducted, the *tools* with which social events are measured, and the *evidence* generated about social events and their relations. These latter elements are normally used to support theoretical claims in reports of social research. (Thus, those who report ethnographic research usually provide details about their research contexts, procedures, and evidence for the discoveries they have made, and those who write about experiments explain the design of their studies, the measuring instruments they used, and the statistical significance of their results.) But occasionally these latter knowledge elements are stripped away from the theories with which they were originally associated and can have an impact of their own. To illustrate, IQ tests — a research tool — were originally developed by Alfred Binet for a limited purpose but have since been used for other tasks that would probably have surprised and dismayed their inventor [see Chapter 22].

Various forms of research are associated with the production of different types of knowledge elements. Ethnographic research can generate new concepts about teacher behaviours in classrooms; surveys can generate propositions about events with which teacher behaviours are associated; experiments can test the validity of explanations for effects of teaching. Moreover, each type of knowledge element can potentially affect users. New concepts about teaching can enable an educator, for example, to think about potential problems; new propositions about teaching can suggest ways to solve problems; new explanations for the effects of teaching can suggest why one solution is more likely to work than another.

The research picture, then, is painted from a many-coloured palette. Social research should be thought of as an enterprise which produces numerous types of knowledge. Moreover, these knowledge types may have many uses for educators, depending on their purposes.

Knowledge Generation and Knowledge Impact

The fact that research knowledge can influence practice does not mean that it has simple effects. Many authors have been intrigued by the complex nature of social research impact, and we turn next to this literature.

A convenient starting point is the 'simple' impact model discussed earlier. As was noted, enthusiasm for the 'simple' model seems to be endemic, and examples which portray research impact within education in 'simple' terms appear in Chapters 17 and 23. In effect, the 'simple' model assumes that the user is given timely access to research knowledge which may be applied independently of the context in which knowledge should be interpreted. Moreover, it assumes that the user is an isolated actor, able to reach a decision based only on implications of research knowledge, and implies that the decision made will advantage everyone concerned.

Fortunately, alternative models for conceiving the impact of social research have appeared, and some of these may be found in an essay by Carol Weiss [Chapter 14]. After describing two versions of the 'simple' model, Weiss suggests five other ways for conceiving social research impact: in *interactive* terms, as *political* activity, in *tactical* terms, as a form of *enlightenment*, and as part of the *intellectual enterprise* of the society. Other useful discussions and alternative models may be found in Bulmer (1982), Heller (1986), Husén (1988), Lindblom and Cohen (1979), and Shavelson (1988).

Useful studies of research knowledge impact have also appeared, and we have included reports from two of these in the present volume. In the first, Carol Weiss [Chapter 15] discusses findings from her study of research knowledge use among mental health administrators in the United States. The selection discusses those administrators' answers to questions about whether they had used social research knowledge and whether they sought out that knowledge when making decisions. Responses indicated that impact resulted more often from "accretion" than from a single telling study. Respondents were frequently found to be familiar with aspects of social research knowledge but had difficulty associating that knowledge with any particular studies. And research knowledge was found to have many types of effects on respondents' decisions.

In the second report, Nathan Caplan [Chapter 16] discusses his research with high-level federal bureaucrats in Washington. These federal officials were asked to volunteer instances in which they had used social research knowledge for making decisions. Caplan found that many respondents reported familiarity with social research knowledge, but whether that knowledge was or was not used depended on personal characteristics of respondents, the contexts of decision making, and mechanisms through which respondents were linked to research knowledge. These two studies suggest that only rarely will the findings of a particular study lead to crisp, unambiguous policy decisions.

The reports of Weiss and Caplan were not about education particularly, and systematic studies of research impact in education are hard to find. But lack of evidence has not inhibited discussion of this topic, and several strategies have been proposed for improving research usage. Most assume that researchers and users inhabit different cultures [again see Chapter 6] and the idea is to improve linkage between the two domains. Perhaps the simplest strategy is to promote contact between the researcher and the user. Advantages of this form of connection are discussed [in Chapter 17] by T. Neville Postlethwaite. As Postlethwaite points out, when the researcher and user are associated, each is more able to respond to the other's concerns — the researcher to questions that are of relevance to the user; the user to knowledge produced by the researcher.

Postlethwaite also assumes that the user is a central administrator who is given responsibility for making educational policy and that, once taken, policy decisions will generate consonant action in the schools. This may work in a country where control over education is centralized and administrators are in close contact with those who work in schools. It is less realistic in larger countries where control over education is diffuse and administrators have little contact with school personnel. Moreover, the Postlethwaite model overlooks the possibility of conflicts of interest among the various parties who are concerned with education and that all parties, not just powerful administrators, might wish to respond to research knowledge. Such possibilities were discussed, however, by Coleman [in Chapter 10] who called for widespread dissemination of research knowledge in the mass media.

This latter suggestion is also attractive, but it is not without problems. Among others, some researchers have greater access to the media than do other researchers, and media coverage may unduly emphasize the interests and political commitments of reporters, their employers, and other powerful interests. In addition, media reports almost inevitably strip away the qualifications, theory, and contextual details associated with social research, so research knowledge is debased. Nevertheless, the mass media are one of the most frequent means through which research knowledge is transmitted to users (see Anderson, 1984). A major study of the media reportage of social research was conducted by Weiss and Singer (1988), and an example of media use by social researchers appears in Chapter 24.

How else does research get to potential users? Some of it percolates through by word of mouth and informal networks. Studies of such informal processes were at one time quite popular within agriculture (see, for example, Oeser and Emery, 1958; Rogers, 1983). Educators, too, have their networks. Some meet regularly at the club, or in conventions and workshops, and share ideas which may contain knowledge elements from research. Moreover, professional meetings offer opportunities for vendors to display equipment and materials, and the latter are also sometimes promoted with knowledge elements that were once associated with research.

Which raises an interesting point. Research knowledge often reaches the user in debased forms. Sometimes the user may know that a concept or proposition was generated through research but may not understand the theoretical context or limited empirical support associated with that element. On other occasions, the user may learn about a 'good idea' but not know that the idea was generated through research. And sometimes the user may assume that an innovative notion was research-generated, but no associated research has yet been reported or, worse, available research knowledge tends to contradict the usefulness of that innovation. All of which says that informal dispersal of social research knowledge is dicey.

The disadvantages of informal knowledge dispersal are widely understood, and many support agencies now take formal actions to disseminate the social research knowledge they have funded. Sometimes those actions involve media 'events', sometimes they involve publishing and distributing reports of research, sometimes they involve presentations of research results in seminars, workshops, and training sessions for potential users. Dissemination is big business, and many support agencies spend large portions of their budgets on dissemination (rather than in funding social research). Underlying these efforts seems to be the thesis that users will benefit if only they are provided the 'good news' that research has generated. Moreover, this thesis had a venerable heritage in the Enlightenment. (James Madison argued that "knowledge will forever govern ignorance, and a people who mean to be their own governors must arm themselves with the power which knowledge gives.") Unfortunately, the thesis, at least in its simple version, is questionable — how are users to resolve conflicting messages flooding in from competing dissemination efforts? Jack Knott and Aaron Wildavsky [Chapter 18] explore the conditions when dissemination probably does and does not work and suggest conditions that affect dissemination and its impact.

How else might one promote the indirect linking of researchers and users in education? We know of several techniques that address this need. One appears in the form of *SET*, the semi-annual packet of selected research results and reviews that are written specifically for educators and policy makers by officials of the Australian Council for Educational Research and the New Zealand Council for Educational Research. SET has a large subscription list in the two countries where it is prepared and forms a major vehicle through which potential users are alerted to significant social research knowledge.

A second technique is the employment of persons to review and summarize research pertinent to specific decisions of interest to policy makers. The concept of a 'knowledge broker' or policy analyst is new in Western societies, but already sufficient demand exists for such persons that training programs have appeared. A useful discussion of this role may be found in Trow (1984).

In addition, researchers themselves can assume active roles which lead to improving links between themselves and users. Four such roles are discussed by Patricia Thomas [in Chapter 19]: the *limestone* role which relies on cumulative or indirect impact, the *gadfly* role, the *insider* role, and the employment of *pressure groups*. In addition, certain researchers seem to be adept at promoting media attention for their research, and such attention also tends to improve links with users [see, for example, Chapters 10 and 24]. Moreover, many researchers disburse knowledge through university lectures and the authorship of textbooks. Of course, this latter mechanism means that research impact is delayed until today's students become tomorrow's professional practitioners.

Research Knowledge and Educational Change

The fact that research knowledge is made available to users does not mean that it will necessarily be used. Teachers, administrators, and other users have needs which are embedded in a culture that is often refractory to ideas from the research domain, especially if those ideas imply changing practices with which practitioners are comfortable. But if dissatisfaction with the status quo exists, new ideas may then get a more favourable hearing. An example of this principle may be found in the famous decision by the Supreme Court outlawing segregation in US public schools, *Brown vs. Board of Education* [see Chapter 20 by Irving Louis Horowitz and James Everett Katz]. This decision was based, in part, on social research knowledge which tended to reinforce dissatisfaction with segregationist practices then in place in US public schools.

Change also seems more likely when an alternative policy has been suggested and legitimated by a respectable authority. A number of mechanisms have been used to alert legislators and citizens to policy alternatives, of which a potent example is the appointment of a 'special commission', 'blue ribbon committee', or expert enquiry which is asked to review relevant materials, including research knowledge, and to prepare recommendations for legislative action. This mechanism has been popular in the United States, Commonwealth countries, and Scandinavia, and it has sometimes produced significant changes in educational policy in those countries. In some instances such commissions may ask for specific research reports or their memberships may include professional researchers. A good review of this and other mechanisms open to governments was prepared by Maurice Kogan and J. Myron Atkin [Chapter 21].

In thinking about the potential effects of research knowledge, one should recognize that several patterns of linkage are possible. In the *traditional model*, research comes first, and the knowledge it generates is then made available for stimulating social change. In *evaluation research*, social action comes first, and the knowledge generated through research is then available for subsequent decisions. In *action research*, social change and social research interact regularly. And in the *John Dewey vision of progressive education*, social research becomes an integral part of user activity. These patterns suggest somewhat different role relationships between researchers and users, and these latter may also affect linkage. To illustrate, the traditional model suggests an authoritative role for the researcher who is thought to bring 'expert' knowledge to the user, but some users may reject the idea that 'expert' advice should be followed when it comes to social affairs about which they have personal and detailed knowledge. In contrast, action research involves an alliance between researchers and users, which, critics argue, compromises the independence conditions necessary for generating objective knowledge.

In addtion, one should also recognize that knowledge can influence education not only by promoting useful change but also by supporting the status quo or facilitating actions that are questionable. Moreover, these latter outcomes are also a product of the political climate in which that research knowledge is interpreted. To illustrate, the history of IQ testing is one in which research knowledge has been used for purposes of social control. Although originally designed for diagnostic purposes, IQ tests have subsequently been used for eugenic screening, the support of racial bigotry, and the enforced 'tracking' of countless pupils, particularly in American and British schools. As suggested by Leon Kamin [Chapter 22], these outcomes seem to have reflected both dubious beliefs about innate intelligence and predispositions to prejudice against minorities and those who were poor.

So far we have examined mainly research impact at the system or national levels. Research knowledge may also influence teachers, schools, and local schools directly. In fact much evaluation research is pitched at practitioners, and examples may be found in an essay by Marvin C. Alkin, Richard Daillak, and Peter White [Chapter 23]. As these authors point out, although evaluation research has been criticized for being 'ineffective', examples may be found for both its 'mainstream' (i.e., 'simple') effects and its broader impact in schools and school systems. This observation leads Alkin *et al.* to ponder potential meanings for the concept of research 'utilization' and to offer their own inclusive definition for this concept. They conclude that numerous interest groups in education may use research knowledge, that research knowledge can be used in various ways, and that educational decisions reflect ideological and political pressures as well as knowledge from research and other sources.

Finally, we should also recognize that social research, itself, is not immune to political and ideological influences on its methods and interpretations. Two examples appear in the selections. In the first, Samuel Wineburg discusses research by Robert Rosenthal and others on "The Pygmalion Effect" [Chapter 24]. This research concluded that (some) teachers inadvertently encourage levels of pupil achievement which confirm their preconceptions about pupil intelligence. This study had a massive impact on educational research, on teacher education, and on court decisions concerning education. As Wineburg points out, the impact was great because the research conclusions fitted so neatly into the prevailing beliefs of the time.

In the second, R.J.W. Selleck reviews the founding, in the early 1830s, of the Manchester Statistical Society which began its efforts with educational research [Chapter 25]. As Selleck points out, one can learn a lot from these early efforts. Not only did the Mancunians pioneer a number of research techniques that are used to this day, but their work (like ours) was designed within a political context and produced recommendations for alleviating the lot of the poor through education but left untouched the conditions which produced poverty and also ended up by serving, in part, the needs of entrenched interests.

Summing Up

We began this essay by asking several questions. Does social research have an impact? And if it does, why does that impact appear? What is the nature of the knowledge created by social research, how does that knowledge affect education, and why has social research received such a bad press?

We are now able to answer some of these questions. Regarding the first, we conclude that (despite bad press) not only can social research have an impact on education but its effects have been striking. This does not mean that all social research has an impact. Indeed, some research seems to have little impact, and in other cases social research seems to have supported the status quo in education or to have had effects that were not anticipated by researchers or their supporters. Moreover, research impact can probably be improved. But — despite all aridity — it is clear that social research has had substantial effects on education.

Why then is social research so often criticized? In part, the criticism of social research seems to result from belief in a 'simple' model for knowledge generation and impact which has it that social research can generate *facts* and that those facts can lead users to make unfettered decisions that will improve social life. This 'simple' model seems to be accepted by many persons and to underlie a good deal of social research funding — particularly funding for applied studies. However, the 'simple' model is both narrow and unrealistic, and when social research fails to deliver the crisp *facts* expected of it, and its knowledge does not have hoped for effects within education and elsewhere, believers in the 'simple' model get discouraged.

We have suggested that a more realistic model should begin with the realization that social research can generate various types of knowledge: elements of theory (such as technical concepts, propositions, and explanations); and empirical elements (designs for research, research tools, evidence). These knowledge elements have meaning because they are embedded within systems of thought and investigation ('paradigms'), and each type of knowledge has its own potential for affecting the decisions of those in positions of influence. Thus, social research should be conceived to have various potentials for affecting users.

This does not mean that all social research knowledge is known to users or that it has straightforward effects. Educational impact seems to be more likely when mechanisms are in place which make research knowledge available to users, but few studies have yet appeared concerning the effects of various mechanisms. And even when educational users have research knowledge, the decisions they make seem to reflect the needs of various interest groups, as well as ideologies and political pressures, but the latter issues have also attracted little research to date. A lot remains to be learned about research impact in education — which points out the need for additional research on the contexts and effects of social research.

References

AMERICAN SOCIOLOGICAL ASSOCIATION (1978). NIE plans new programs; plus expansion for others. *Footnotes*, 6, 1–3.

ANDERSON, D.S. (1984). The use of social science knowledge in the formulation of policy advice. *Youth Studies Bulletin*, 3(3), 110–132.

ANDERSON, D.S. (1987). Where do the questions come from, for whom are the answers intended? An exploration of research and policy. *Australian Educational Researcher*, 13(1), 1–25.

BIDDLE, B.J. (1987). Social research and social policy: The theoretical connection. *The American Sociologist*, 18(2:Summer), 158–166.

BIDDLE, B.J., SLAVINGS, R.L., and ANDERSON, D.S. (1985). Panel studies and causal inference. *The Journal of Applied Behavioral Science*, 21(1), 79–93.

BROPHY, J.E. and GOOD, T.L. (1974). *Teacher-student relationships: Causes and consequences*. New York: Holt, Rinehart, and Winston.

BULMER, M. (1982). *The uses of social research: Social investigation in public policy making*. London: George Allen and Unwin.

CUBAN, L. (1990). Reforming again, again, and again. *Educational Researcher*, 19(1), 3–13.

ELMORE, R.F. and MCLAUGHLIN, M.W. (1988). *Steady work: Policy, practice, and the reform of American education*. Santa Monica, CA: The Rand Corporation.

GLASS, G.V. (1979). Policy for the unpredictable (uncertainty research and policy). *Educational Researcher*, 8(9), 12–14.

GOOD, T.L. and BROPHY, J.E. (1974). Changing teacher and student behavior: An empirical investigation. *Journal of Educational Psychology*, 66, 390–405.

HEISS, D.R. (1975). *Causal analysis*. New York: Wiley.

HELLER, F. (Ed.). (1986). *The use and abuse of social science*. Beverly Hills, CA: Sage.

HUSÉN, T. (1988). *Educational research, methodology, and measurement* (pp. 173–178). New York: Pergamon.

JAMES, L.R., MULAIK, S.A. and BRETT, J.M. (1982). *Causal analysis: Assumptions, models, and data.* Beverly Hills: Sage.

KOUNIN, J.S. (1970). *Discipline and group management in classrooms.* New York: Holt, Rinehart, and Winston.

KUHN, T.S. (1962). *The structure of scientific revolutions.* Chicago: University of Chicago Press.

LANGLEY, P., SIMON, H.A., BRADSHAW, G.L. and ZYTKOW, J.M. (1987). *Scientific discovery: Computational explorations of the creative process.* Cambridge, MA: MIT Press.

LINDBLOM, C.E. and COHEN, D.K. (1979). *Usable knowledge: Social science and social problem solving.* New Haven, CT: Yale University Press.

MARINI, M.M. and SINGER, B. (1988). Causality in the social sciences. In C.C. CLOGG (Ed.), *Sociological methodology.* Washington, DC: American Sociological Association.

OESER, O.A. and EMERY, F.E. (1958). *Information, decision and action.* Melbourne: Melbourne University Press.

PILE, W. (1976). (Quoted in Nisbet, J., and Broadfoot, P. *The impact of research on policy and practice in education.* Aberdeen: The University Press, pp. 1–2.)

POPKEWITZ, T.S., TABACHNICK, B.R., and WEHLAGE, G. (1982). *The myth of educational reform.* Madison, WI: University of Wisconsin Press.

ROGERS, E.M. (1983). *Diffusion of innovations* (3rd ed.). New York: Free Press.

SHAVELSON, R.J. (1988). Contributions of educational research to policy and practice: Constructing, challenging, changing cognition. *Educational Researcher, 17*(7), 4–22.

SLAVIN, R.E. (1987). Ability grouping and student achievement in elementary schools: A best-evidence synthesis. *Review of Educational Research, 57,* 293–336.

TRAVERS, R.M.W. (1983). *How research has changed American schools: A history from 1840 to the present.* Kalamazoo, MI: Mythos Press.

TROW, M. (1984). Researchers, policy analysts and policy intellectuals. In T. HUSÉN & M. KOGAN (Eds), *Educational research & policy: How do they relate?* (pp. 261–282). Oxford: Pergamon Press.

WEISS, C.H., and SINGER, E. with ENDRENY, P. (1988). *Reporting of social science in the national media.* New York: Sage.

Part 1
Can Social Research Have an Effect?

Chapter 1

Basic and Applied Social Psychology*

Dorwin Cartwright

In the acute social crisis of our time many people are turning to social science for the solution of our social problems. Society seems to be saying, in effect, "Scientific methodology in the natural sciences and their accompanying technologies has brought us to the brink of extinction; let it save us through the social sciences and their technologies." The great foundations, governmental agencies, business organizations, and the universities are responding to this demand by directing increasing amounts of money and personnel to activities dealing with human relations, intergroup relations, and social 'problems' generally.

Those social scientists responsible for the utilization of these funds are deeply impressed by the social responsibility placed upon them. They are suddenly confronted by issues made acute by the requirement that policies be set and action taken immediately. One such issue is especially bothersome. It may be stated in the form of a question: What is the proper relation between applied and basic research at this point in the development of social science? On the one hand, society is calling for speedy answers to its problems lest the answers come too late. On the other hand, sound recommendations for action can only be based upon a thorough knowledge of the causal systems and the interrelations of the variables determining the workings of society. Can social science safely devote its limited resources to the solution of immediate social problems? Can it safely work only on the basic scientific problems?

This paper will not pretend to provide final answers to these difficult questions. Merton's keen analysis of the situation with his proposal for investigation of the issues (1949) offers a method of approach, however, which should be taken seriously. Only by examining in detail the known effects of concentrating efforts in one direction or the other can we reach sound decisions. Abstract theorizing about the nature of basic and applied

---

* Abridged from 'Basic and Applied Social Psychology' by D. Cartwright, 1949, *Philosophy of Science*, *16*, pp. 198–208.

research can too easily mislead us. Plausible logical relations between the two are easy to elaborate, but there is a justified skepticism concerning the results of such exercises up to the present. In order to be as realistic as possible, I shall confine my remarks here to the field of work that I know best: social psychology.

It may help us understand our central problems if we examine in some detail the effects upon basic social psychology produced by the greatly expanded activities that have taken place during the past decade in applied fields. During this brief span of years applied social psychology has captured an unprecedented proportion of the time and energy of social psychologists. As a result of this concentration on applied problems, what have been the gains or losses for basic social psychology?

Because there has been no adequately quantitative or controlled research upon this question, only opinions can be expressed in answer to it. The question is of such vital importance to the development of social science, however, that in the absence of conclusive evidence 'informed opinions' should be sought and the experience of those working in the field placed upon the table for examination and comparison. The following observations derive from a study of the recent history of social psychology (Cartwright, 1948) and are presented in the hope that they may contribute to this end.

The Prestige of Social Psychology

That the prestige of social psychology has risen markedly during the past decade should be readily admitted by all who know the facts. The reasons for this rise, however, are more open to dispute. The trends of the times, the atomic crisis, have set people about looking for new solutions, and social psychology has for this reason been scrutinized as a possible panacea. Yet it is unlikely that people would have bothered to investigate the possibilities of social psychology 10 years ago even if the atomic physicists had been more rapid in their discoveries. The more likely hypothesis is that social psychologists have come during the past decade to be viewed somewhat more as practical men who know something useful about the social problems of the day and that their many activities in the realm of applied social psychology during the period have contributed to this change of perception.

It appears that in contemporary American culture the social standing of a professional field depends to a high degree upon the practical consequences that flow in a rather direct way from its activities. Despite the highly publicized failure of the recent election polls with all the concomitant aggressions against the impudent pundits who would dare to measure the human mind, the net result of social psychology's excursion into the world of practical affairs has been, on the whole, to heighten the prestige of the entire field.

Access of the Proper Phenomena for Social Psychological Investigation

The prestige attributed to a professional field does not follow automatically the potential practical value possessed by that field. As Merton has properly stressed, applied social scientists always work in a social context, and the immediate evaluation of their contributions is often determined more by their skills of interpersonal relations and the institutional setting in which they work than by the intrinsic nature of their work. Ten years ago it was the rare social psychologist who felt at home in the business world, in governmental agencies, in a union hall, or even among social workers. Furthermore, there existed very few institutional arrangements providing a basis for cooperative work. It is no accident that the men who made the earliest advances in the application of social psychology, who worked out a *modus vivendi* in relation to practical men, were often regarded by their 'pure' colleagues as unusually smooth and polished 'operators'. Nor is it surprising that frequently they displayed social values closely similar to those held by their clients. Today the number of social psychologists working on 'even terms' with men of practical affairs has greatly increased, and those who are particularly skillful in developing good working relations are no longer viewed as peculiar deviates. Much attention is now given to the role of the social science consultant (Jaques, 1947; McGregor, 1948) by members of the profession both for their own improvement and for the instruction of their students. This is not to say that working relations are now generally ideal nor that the optimal institutional setting for applied research is yet known. It is important, however, to record that great advances have been made in this direction in very recent years.

The growing prestige of social psychology together with the development of better skills of interpersonal and interorganizational relations have begun to have profound effects upon the nature of social psychology as a science. If social psychology is defined as the study of human behavior as it influences and is influenced by the behavior of other individuals, then it is clear that the social psychologist puts himself in a better position to study the proper phenomena of his science if he works out arrangements whereby he can study human behavior in business organizations, labor unions, governmental agencies, housing projects, and the like. The question remains to be answered whether he has yet worked out the kinds of relations that permit the application of sound methods of research to these phenomena, but there can be no doubt that he has greater access to social phenomena as a result of the services he promises to render to action organizations.

25

Manipulation of Variables

In a similar way the applied social psychologist creates for himself the opportunity of manipulating variables affecting social behavior. Depending on the circumstances, this opportunity arises in a variety of ways. The assignment given to the social psychologist is often that of discovering ways of producing a desired effect (how to heighten employee morale, how to develop loyalty to a union, how to reduce intergroup hostilities, etc.). In other words, the assignment is to discover those variables causally related to the one in terms of which change is desired. In the course of fulfilling this assignment the social psychologist is frequently given permission to set up experimental groups, conditions, or programs; that is, he is allowed to manipulate variables affecting social behavior. Even when he is not given the opportunity to do experiments in the course of arriving at his conclusions for action, the social psychologist often has the chance to do a 'before and after' experiment by describing the state of affairs before his recommendations are put into effect (if they are) and comparing them with conditions after the new policy has been inaugurated.

It should be noted in this connection that knowledge useful to a science can be obtained through manipulations of the sort here described only to the extent that accurate, penetrating, and quantitative observations of the relevant variables are made either on experimental and control situations or on before and after conditions. There has been no dearth of social experimentation in the world, but it has made little contribution to our accumulated knowledge largely because no adequate measurement of the effects has been carried out. To the extent that such 'experiments' are influenced by social psychologists they may produce more desirable practical results, but unless they are accompanied by the full array of scientific methodology they will contribute just as little to our scientific knowledge as if they were designed without benefit of such advice. . . .

Development of Conceptual Systems

Conant's advice (1947) that any scientific undertaking should be evaluated in terms of the extent of its valid application of a conceptual scheme to empirical data is most pertinent for our thinking about social psychology. In attempting to form a judgment about the effects upon basic social psychology of the heavy emphasis upon practical problems in recent years, one may inquire whether the applied research has generated any new concepts or demonstrated the valid application of old concepts to new ranges of phenomena.

In regard to the generation of new concepts the answer must be disappointing. If one goes through the work of the war-related research organizations and searches for new concepts that can be fitted into a coherent system, virtually nothing is discovered. There have been several attempts (Bruner, 1944; Doob, 1948; Lewin, 1943) to give a theoretical interpretation to data gathered by these agencies, but with a few notable exceptions, the conceptual schemes employed were developed entirely apart from the research being reported.

Somewhat more encouraging is the evidence concerning the application of concepts to new realms of phenomena. The wartime excursion of social psychologists into the domain of economics during the government's combat against inflation (Hilgard, 1946; Katona, 1945, 1947) is a good example. Concepts developed to account for human behavior in areas far removed from economics were shown to account for significant segments of economic behavior. The work on rumor during the war provides another example (Allport and Postman, 1947; Knapp, 1944). Here, concepts developed in the experimental studies of perception and memory were shown to apply to the origin and spread of rumors. Other examples could be brought forth, but the general conclusion is inescapable that the great bulk of the practical research conducted during the war has not and will not contribute directly to the extension of any empirically testable conceptual scheme.

Although the evidence is clear that applied research activities of recent years have contributed little to the development of empirically oriented theory, it does not necessarily follow that emphasis upon applied research has retarded theoretical development. To reach this conclusion would require some judgment about the rate of progress that would have been made under other conditions, and it is virtually impossible to make such a judgment. The considerations enumerated in the preceding sections of this paper suggest, however, that by increasing the financial resources for social psychology, by making more accessible the proper phenomena for investigation, and by improving the opportunity to manipulate important variables, the opportunities for good concept building have been greatly increased. Two further factors will greatly influence whether or not these opportunities are to be realized. Empirically relevant and quantitatively precise conceptual systems cannot be developed without the existence of good research instruments. Nor can they be created unless well trained and competent minds are attracted to the field. The following sections of this paper will examine the effects of recent applied research activities upon the development of research instruments and upon the attraction of competent personnel to social psychology.

Development of Research Instruments

In social psychology the development of a research instrument is rarely accomplished by a single individual or research organization. The sample survey, which is the most highly developed tool capable of dealing with major social variables, has been significantly influenced in its development by the work of scores of people. In this cooperative undertaking contributions have come from social scientists with both theoretical and applied interests. It is clear, however, that the sample survey would not now have its present research power had it not been the major tool of organizations primarily devoted to applied research. The perfecting of sampling procedures, of ways to recruit, train and supervise a field staff, of techniques for the quantitative analysis of large quantities of narrative interview material, and of the other processes involved in the sample survey has been expensive and has required the existence of large research organizations. Until very recently the opportunity to work on these techniques has been available only to those social scientists who were willing to devote their major energies to the solution of practical problems.

It is difficult to know how far one may safely generalize from this experience. Certainly, the pressure to solve practical problems may result in the invention of new research techniques. It is interesting to note, however, that most of the major advances made by applied research groups (like the Bureau of the Census, the Division of Program Surveys, etc.) have been accomplished with the close cooperation of university research centers or by men drawn from basic research for a temporary period of time. Furthermore, a study of the invention of techniques for the quantitative observation of small group processes (committees, conferences, classes, etc.) suggests that the major advances here have come from those working on basic problems. A detailed analysis of the exact way in which a whole variety of social psychological research instruments have actually been developed will be required before any safe generalizations can be made about the relative contributions of basic and applied research activities to the improvement of research methodology. As a tentative conclusion it may be proposed that the net effect of the recent emphasis upon applied research has been to stimulate the invention and refinement of research instruments capable of dealing quantitatively with major social variables. It must be added, though, that this state of affairs was undoubtedly influenced by the historic fact that large sums of money were first made available to social psychologists working on applied problems. If, in the next few years, comparable sums of money were to divert energies back to basic research there is no reason to conclude from past experience that methodological improvements would be retarded.

Personnel Attracted to Social Psychology

One implication of the analysis up to this point would seem to be that the kind of people needed to engage in basic social psychology should possess not only an interest and skill in theorizing and in the development of empirically relevant conceptual systems but also an interest and skill in dealing with the content of the problems, namely, social processes. The war drew into the governmental research agencies many men who have been primarily interested in theoretical problems before the war. Their experiences gave them a much greater insight into the operation of social processes than they had had before and consequently made them better fitted to meet the dual requirements for sound basic social research. With the end of the war most (though by no means all) of these men have returned to universities. The rapid development following the war of research centers on campuses across the country which are devoted both to basic and applied research reflects, in large part, this experience. It is yet too soon to estimate how vigorously these centers will advance the development of research aimed at building basic theory. At present they appear to hold great promise because they do combine theoretical interests with developed research instruments in a setting giving considerable access to social phenomena. Whether or not they will succeed in overcoming pressures to concentrate their resources too much on immediate, practical problems and to turn out the kind of research most easily understood by laymen remains to be seen.

The experience of the strictly applied research organizations shows that these pressures can be great and that they can seriously influence the kinds of personnel drawn into social psychological research. The standards commonly invoked to evaluate applied research by those 'buying' the research are different from those employed by basic scientists. A given applied research project is likely to be termed successful if it is completed quickly, apparently conducted without a waste of money, and terminated by the delivery to the client of data that are clear and understandable to him. These criteria have placed a premium upon people who are skilled in the related techniques of collecting the kind of data whose surface appearance to the layman is one of neatness, simplicity, and direct bearing upon the immediate issue. Experience suggests that training in journalism, accounting, public relations, business administration, graphical presentation, or public speaking may be better for these purposes than a background in academic social psychology and experimental method. People who want to complicate the research report with complex statistical analyses, with data whose relation to a conceptual system may be clear but which have no superficial relation to the problem, or with any other attempt to penetrate beneath the surface have found it hard to work in many research organizations devoted exclusively to applied research. This trend appears especially pronounced when the organization is run as a commercial enterprise. One would search in vain for persons adequately trained in social science among the personnel of some very large and financially successful organizations devoted to applied social psychological research. . . .

Summary and Conclusions

This brief examination of the recent history of social psychology reveals influences both beneficial and detrimental to the development of basic social psychology. A possible way of summarizing these trends would be to state that during the past decade social psychology, by means of an extensive excursion into applied fields, has put itself in a better position to do significant basic research. It has heightened its prestige, making available more funds, greater access to its proper phenomena for investigation, and the opportunity to manipulate its significant variables. It has developed new and powerful research instruments. Out of this concentration on applied research it has not, however, modified its body of concepts and theories to any great extent. And it has succumbed rather often to pressures that would reward on the basis of the superficial appearances of the research rather than on its scientific merit.

That social psychology has improved its ability to help solve immediate, practical social problems there can be no doubt. But it is equally clear that it possesses no ready answers for the major social problems of the day; it does not know how to prevent atomic war, eliminate racial prejudices, or establish labor-management peace. It can, perhaps, move toward solutions of these problems by conducting research on the immediate problems faced day-to-day by administrators and practitioners. But serious doubts may be raised as to whether the fundamental social problems of the modern world can be solved without a major emphasis upon research designed essentially to refine concepts and to test the relationships among theoretical constructs.

Because of the unique problems of gaining access to social variables and of manipulating them, the laboratory of the social psychologist must be located in the social world (although research on fabricated groups is an important part of the social psychologist's work). In order to be permitted to do basic experiments upon major social variables, it appears that social psychologists will have to be prepared to provide services in return for the privileges they request. In actual practice, therefore, a blending of basic and applied research is required. The fundamental problem to be solved by research administrators in the coming years is how to accomplish this fusion without detriment to either research objective. Recent experience suggests that particular effort will be required to protect research resources from too great demands for the solution of the pressing day-to-day problems of society.

References

ALLPORT, G.W. and POSTMAN, L. (1947). *The psychology of rumor*. New York: Holt.

BRUNER, J.S. (1944). *Mandate from the people*. New York: Duell, Sloane and Pearce.

CARTWRIGHT, D. (1948). Social psychology in the United States during the *Second World War*. *Human Relations, 1*, 333–352.

CONANT, J.B. (1947). *On understanding science*. New Haven: Yale University Press.

DOOB, L. (1948). *Public opinion and propaganda*. New York: Holt.

HILGARD, E.R. (1946). Psychological factors in the restoration of the civilian economy. *Journal of Consulting Psychology, 10*, 15–22.

JAQUES, E. (Ed.). (1947). Social therapy. *Journal of Social Issues, 3*(2).

KATONA, G. (1945). *Price control and business*. Bloomington: Principia Press.

KATONA, G. (1947). Contribution of psychological data to economic analysis. *Journal of the American Statistical Association, 42*, 449–459.

KNAPP, R. (1944). A psychology of rumor. *Public Opinion Quarterly, 9*, 22–37.

LEWIN, K. (1943). Forces behind food habits and methods of change. *Bulletin of the National Research Council, 108*, 35–65.

McGREGOR, D. (Ed.). (1948). The consultant role and organizational leadership: Improving human relations in industry. *Journal of Social Issues, 4*(3).

MERTON, R.K. (1949). The role of applied social science in the formation of policy: A research memorandum. *Philosophy of Science, 16* (July), 161–181.

Chapter 2

The National Interest in the Support of Basic Research*

Committee on Basic Research in the Behavioral and Social Sciences (Edited by Robert McCormick Adams, Neil J. Smelser and Donald J. Treiman)

Conclusions

In the committee's judgment, the evidence [we have] surveyed ... on research advances in the behavioral and social sciences and the range of uses to which such advances have been put leads to a single, fundamental conclusion: Basic research in the behavioral and social sciences is a national resource that should be sustained and encouraged through public support. Federal investment in basic research in the behavioral and social sciences, like investment in other branches of science, is an investment in the future welfare of the nation. Supporting this conclusion are a number of considerations.

1. Basic research in the behavioral and social sciences has yielded an impressive array of accomplishments, and there is every reason to expect the yield from future research to be at least as great. At an accelerating rate during recent decades, such research has been responsible for (a) greatly increased substantive knowledge of individual behavior, social institutions, and cultural patterns under a wide variety of changing as well as stable conditions; (b) markedly improved methods of data collection and analysis which have not only led to new discoveries and the resolution of old debates but also have provided the foundation for information technologies (e.g., sample surveys, standardized tests, economic indicators) now regarded as indispensable in the public and private sectors; and (c)

* Abridged from *Behavioral and Social Science Research: A National Resource* (pp. 93–102) by the Committee on Basic Research in the Behavioral and Social Sciences, 1982, Washington, DC: Commission on Behavioral and Social Sciences, National Research Council.

continuing development of pedagogical and therapeutic procedures, of devices and arrangements for improving human performance and the human environment, and of procedures for evaluating public policies and proposed programs. Some of these developments [were] reviewed in the ... report [and supporting papers which generated these conclusions]; many others could be cited as well. On the basis of these kinds of contributions, the behavioral and social sciences merit support.

2. The benefits of basic research are seldom if ever predictable in advance; they are often unanticipated and still more often the outcome of complex, discontinuous sequences of discovery, insight, and invention. Investment in basic research must be regarded as investment in a process that is expected to yield substantial contributions to individual and social well-being, but it cannot be regarded as a direct purchase of those contributions. There are several reasons for this.

First, it is generally not clear in advance where or when major scientific discoveries or breakthroughs will occur. The history of research in all fields is one of unforeseen interpretations of findings, insights, and methodological advances, false starts, miscues, and provisional answers later superseded by superior formulations. Sequences of steps that, with hindsight, seem to constitute a consistent advance toward a particular goal often were experienced by those responsible for them as confused, accidental, and haphazard. Similarly, rates of progress are seldom predictable to those immediately involved. Although cumulative over the long run, the orderliness of scientific research generally emerges only in retrospect. Hence it generally is not possible to identify specific areas or topics as targets for special attention or intensive support with any confidence that they and not some other area will yield major new insights or discoveries.

Second, specific research findings rarely translate automatically or directly to any particular use or application. Once it is published, scientific knowledge becomes available for any and all possible applications. A common — and indeed highly desirable — fate is that a particular finding will be utilized in ways never even imagined by its discoverers. And, conversely, a given application typically will exploit findings, methods, and procedures from a wide variety of disciplines and research areas, often in a long and complex chain of development.

An attempt to trace the research and development underlying 10 major clinical advances in medicine and surgery (between 1945 and 1975) confirms this view. On the basis of a thorough review of the research literature, Comroe and Dripps (1977) identified 663 articles that they regarded as essential for one or more of the advances. Four points are of special interest. First, more than 40% of the articles "reported research done by scientists whose goal at that time was *unrelated* to the later clinical advance.... Such unrelated research was often unexpected, unpredictable, and usually greatly accelerated advance in many fields (Comroe and Dripps, 1977, p. 2). Second, each of the clinical advances depended on the cumulation of dozens of studies conducted by hundreds of investigators; no advance could be attributed to the work of a single researcher or a single research group. Third, the lag between an initial discovery and its effective clinical application was usually substantial: Of 111 discoveries investigated, 57% had been applied more than 20 years after publication. Finally, the 663 articles identified as essential contributions were culled from a review of more than 6,000 published articles. It is highly improbable that "essential contributions" could have been identified in advance, especially given the typical long lag before application.

These findings provide firm support for the conclusion that basic research must be encouraged without regard for its immediate applicability. While we do not know from the study just described what fraction of basic research eventually comes to be applied, we do know that, in the biomedical field at least, clinical (that is, applied) advances depend heavily on basic research efforts, that it takes a great deal of research to produce each "essential contribution", and that it is impossible to predict in advance which contributions will prove essential. Moreover, applications are often very slow in coming; hence a demand for short-run payoff would be shortsighted indeed.

While parallel research in the behavioral and social sciences has not yet been conducted, the process described by Comroe and Dripps for the biomedical sciences is probably applicable to them as well. . . . Certainly, most of the applications [we have studied] have drawn on basic research developments in a variety of disciplines, as have many of the[ir] applications. . . .

3. *The coupling between basic research in the behavioral and social sciences and its applications to public policy is significant and growing, but it is also inherently loose, uncertain, incomplete, and often slow.* Policies are properly constrained by political, social, and cultural considerations that may change in importance. To apply similar constraints to basic research would limit its effectiveness as a long-term source of new insights and approaches needed to meet unanticipated conditions. The health and vitality of scientific investigations require that at times they probe into areas of deeply held beliefs about human nature and the world. Research on the origins of the universe, on the evolution of life, on recombinant DNA, and on the heritability of traits can have this quality. In the behavioral and social sciences, that quality sometimes can apply to human evolution, to the mutually supporting or opposing influences of families, communities, and government agencies on individual development and economic well-being, and to many areas of deviance and unconventional or asocial behavior. Hence any direct transmission of findings is

hindered by the differences between contexts in which scientific knowledge is generated and consumed. If the primary purpose of basic research were to effect social change or reform, it would be a frustratingly unpredictable and at best marginally effective way to achieve that end. But what identifies research as basic is for the most part a fundamentally different motivation — the concern to understand and explain human behavior and the consequences of social arrangements.

Moreover, public policy decisions in all areas, including those involving scientific and technical considerations, are made and implemented through a political process rather than by means of strictly technical judgments. Decisions involve considerations that are not resolvable on technical grounds, such as individual and group values, ideological stances, and tolerance for risk and uncertainty. While expert advice and technical judgments may make an important contribution, public choices depend primarily on a balancing of short-run and long-run considerations as to the deployment of scarce resources that are worked out in compromise among cooperating, competing, and conflicting interests. This is true of policies affecting the location of dams and nuclear power plants, the provision of artificial kidney machines, and the choice of weapons systems as well as decisions regarding fiscal policy, crime control, school desegregation, and remedial reading. The persistence of disturbingly high (although possibly declining) inflation rates should not be regarded as a failure of economics, nor crime in the streets as a failure of sociology, nor venereal disease as a failure of medicine, nor the medfly invasion of California as a failure of entomology, nor the nuclear arms race as a failure of physics. Each case mentioned is the consequence of a myriad of factors, only some of which are amenable to scientific or technical resolution.

Especially great difficulties in applying empirical knowledge to purposive action can arise when there is lack of consensus on what constitutes a problem or what solutions are acceptable. In many areas connected with health, there is widespread acceptance of the social values in question. One of the reasons that applications such as the Salk vaccine program are relatively uncontroversial is that there is a basic consensus supporting innovations to improve health; the only issues involved are technical ones regarding the efficacy and safety of alternative vaccines. But that is not always the case. When such consensus breaks down, as it has with respect to abortion, technical knowledge is no longer a sufficient basis for action. Issues regarding what kinds of knowledge from the social and behavioral sciences are felt to be pertinent often entail a similar lack of consensus. The case of poverty [may be cited in this connection]. Is it strictly an economic condition resulting from major social malfunctions, so that those caught up in it deserve every assistance as they strive to escape? Or is it also a set of self-reinforcing attitudes and behaviors with negative moral overtones that society should seek ways to modify? Both the definition of the problem itself and appropriate solutions depend on one's value position along a wide spectrum of possibilities between these polar positions.

Finally, many social policies have multiple, sometimes unanticipated consequences, so that the effort to solve one problem may simply exacerbate others. For example, efforts to improve the educational opportunities of minority children through school desegregation may have resulted in some instances in increased residential segregation as a result of 'white flight' beyond the boundaries of school districts. In a complex society in which people are free to act in their own interests, as best they perceive them, the translation of knowledge from the social sciences into the solution of social problems is likely to be particularly difficult.

Despite this, there is evidence that basic research in the social and behavioral sciences does have an important impact on public policy. As with other sorts of applications, the impact is long term and relatively indirect (Weiss, 1977, pp. 534–535, emphasis added):

> Evidence suggests that government officials use research less to arrive at solutions than to orient themselves to problems. They use research to help them think about issues and define the problematics of a situation, to gain new ideas and new perspectives. They use research to help formulate problems and to set the agenda for future policy actions. *And much of this use is not deliberate, direct, and targeted, but a result of long-term percolation of social science concepts, theories, and findings into the climate of informed opinion....*

This kind of diffuse, undirected seepage of social research into the policy sphere can gradually change the whole focus of debate over policy issues. The process is difficult to document, but it appears likely that social research has helped shift the agenda and change the formulation of issues in a wide array of fields: compensatory education, punishment for alcohol and drug offenses, large-scale public housing, institutionalization of the mentally retarded, welfare reform, prepaid health care, child abuse, job training, court reform, and legislative reapportionment.... It is worth noting that the "long-term percolation of ... concepts, theories, and findings into the climate of informed opinion" is a major benefit of basic research in all fields, entirely apart from direct practical applications. We should not lose sight of the social value of a continuing, cumulative growth of knowledge and understanding. Without regard for the practical payoffs that may follow, our lives are enriched by new and basic discoveries of unforeseen regularity or patterning.

4. The federal government is an indispensable and appropriate source of support for basic research. Basic research is, in the parlance of economists, a public good. Since free exchange and wide dissemination are conditions of its growth, its benefits must be freely available to all and cannot be controlled by those who conduct or have financed the research. Given this and especially given the necessary time lags and unpredictability of research outcomes, there is no reason to expect that either the private sector or federal agencies charged with other missions will serve as adequate sources of support for basic research. The efficient allocation of resources for public goods in general and for basic research in particular is through public funding.

While there is no doubt that important research will continue to be done by researchers operating without funds or with the limited funds they can obtain from their own institutions and from nonfederal sources, a large fraction, perhaps the bulk, of basic research in the behavioral and social sciences would no longer be possible without financial support at levels beyond what these sources — most of them already under heavy pressure — can make available. Adequate funding for basic research in the behavioral and social sciences cannot be provided by dispersed institutional or market forces. Instead, it must continue to be primarily entrusted, as at present, to government agencies whose specific mission is the implementation of a long-term investment strategy with regard to the maintenance and promotion of basic research as a national resource.

The rationale for funding basic research is quite different from prevailing rationales for funding mission-oriented research. Most of the latter, the committee assumes, will continue to be carried on even in the face of severely restricted budgetary conditions. Since mission-oriented research is designed to meet specific needs or problems, largely on an *ad hoc* basis, funding for it is provided by numerous government agencies, institutions, and private firms as a necessary adjunct to their own ongoing programs. Such a funding pattern by itself, however, makes no provision for continuing replenishment of the stock of insights, ideas, and conceptual as well as analytic tools that grow from the findings of basic research.

Implicit in the foregoing remarks is the assumption that basic research in the behavioral and social sciences must be understood as part of a broader continuum of research activities. Diverse in themselves, the behavioral and social sciences include some disciplines that at their margins merge almost imperceptibly with some of the physical and biological sciences, and others that similarly approach the humanities. Supplementing these continuities in subject matter that cross formal, disciplinary frontiers are similarities in method and outlook that extend across all fields of science. The special complexities, uncertainties, and entanglements of the human subject matter notwithstanding, the behavioral and social sciences are sciences like all others. Hence the same arguments that lead to a judgment to invest public funds in scientific research in general are equally valid for the behavioral and social sciences. . . .

Robert McCormick Adams, Neil J. Smelser, and Donald J. Treiman

Summary

The essential themes developed in this report can be briefly summarized. Basic research is carried on in order to create and husband a stock of knowledge, with the confidence that such a stock will be drawn on — for further advances in knowledge as well as for diverse and important practical ends — in ways that seldom can be accurately foreseen. Familiarization with and participation in basic social and behavioral research also play a vital part in graduate professional training. Such training is needed to assess the relevance of available or prospective findings for the design, implementation, and evaluation of social programs. Hence even mission-oriented researchers need to be thoroughly acquainted with the methods and the results of basic research. Neither the creation of new knowledge nor the training of practitioners is an objective that can be most profitably pursued in irregular spurts and pauses or only in relation to narrowly targeted applications. The power of basic research to improve and enrich our lives grows out of the mutual reinforcement and synergism of many interlocking ideas, findings, and practical outcomes. It cannot be understood and properly utilized if we concentrate instead on isolated, product-centered outcomes.

These observations do not provide a prescription for what the sources and level of support of basic research in the behavioral and social sciences should be. But they do suggest that a disinterested, long-term program of support, carried out as a broad, farsighted investment policy rather than to meet the immediate policy objectives of particular agencies, is in the national interest.

References

COMROE, J.H., Jr. and DRIPPS, R.D. (1977). *The top ten clinical advances in cardiovascular-pulmonary medicine and surgery, 1945–1975.* (DHEW [NIH] Publication No. 78–1521). Washington, DC: U.S. Government Printing Office.

WEISS, C.H. (1977). Research for policy's sake: The enlightenment function of social science research. *Policy Analysis*, 3, 531–545.

Chapter 3

What Ails Education Research*

Chester E. Finn, Jr.

My purpose is to reflect on the state of education research and on what ails it. Part of what ails it, of course, is that the public regards much of our work with more than a trace of skepticism. Education research rarely gets credit for such headway as is being made in American education. Rather, it tends to be associated with educational faddism on the one hand and pointy-headed intellectualism on the other.

To put it simply, our labors haven't produced enough findings that Americans can use or even see the use of. Over the past two decades, there has been a goodly amount of systematic inquiry and a flood of studies, reports, and recommendations, yet our education system has by many measures worsened. I do not say that research has caused the decline, only that it has failed to counteract it. Education research has not fulfilled its role in the effort to improve our schools, perhaps because it runs into much skepticism from practitioners and policy makers. Hence, its effects are limited, and this in turn fosters skepticism as to its potential — a wicked cycle.

We all wish that education research enjoyed the attention and respect given the hard sciences. We suffer from status envy. But hard sciences are assumed to make a perceptible difference in people's lives. There is an intensity, an urgency about biotechnology and medicine and nuclear physics — a sense that tomorrow's answers may be too late, and that today's are already useful. Witness the world's top physicists assembling urgently in recent months to make the most of abrupt breakthroughs in superconductivity. Consider AIDS — doctors and medical researchers working around the clock to fight the virus and epidemic. There's no fooling around here: When they find a cure (does anyone doubt that one day they will?), we'll all breathe a sigh of relief.

* Abridged from 'What Ails Education Research' by C.E. Finn, Jr., 1988, *Educational Researcher*, *17*(1), pp. 5–8.

Unlike AIDS, ignorance is no emergency. It's more like a chronic affliction, a wasting disease. It's been around for some time now, and isn't likely to go away soon. Yet the impulse to eradicate it has quickened. People want reliable and effective methods of instruction for their children. They want sound approaches that produce results. . . .

The next few years offer an authentic opportunity. Not since Sputnik has the hunger for education reform been so urgent or the need for our efforts so great. A day doesn't go by without headlines on 'competitiveness', and under them a paragraph on the importance of education to America's economic and social vitality. The two are inextricably linked, most Americans realize. But what many overlook is the useful role that research can play in efforts to improve our schools and colleges. Education research is like a compass pointing toward improvements and providing means of measuring them, of keeping them on course.

Our mission in the Office of Educational Research and Improvement (OERI)[1] is to support significant, useful, high quality research and to put its findings into the hands of Americans who can use them. Of course, only a fraction of such research is conceived in Washington. We in OERI therefore strive to identify important and innovative research ideas from elsewhere — some of which we support through the Field-Initiated Studies Program (FIS), formerly known as the Unsolicited Proposals Program.

For a time, this program was dormant. Indeed, the 1986 FIS competition marked the first time in three years that OERI (or its predecessor, the National Institute for Education) 'opened the transom' to attract diverse unsolicited proposals for research. We accepted them from January through July of 1986. During that half year, 342 applications poured in, a whopping total by anyone's standards, especially as the FIS program had only $500,000 to award. At the end of the fiscal year, we scraped together all our loose change and were able to up the total to $725,000, which enabled us to fund 10 proposals. But this was still less than 3% of those we received.

To determine which proposals to fund, we used a two-tiered peer review process. It worked like this. At the first tier, 18 scholars judged the technical soundness and adequacy of the research design of each submission. These 18 experts 'reviewed' — that is, they read, scored, and critiqued — applications proposing to conduct research in their areas of specialization. (At this stage, each proposal was evaluated by three of the

---

[1] [The OERI, formerly called the National Institute of Education (NIE), is the federal agency charged with supporting educational research through federal funds in the United States. It was set up in 1973 but has been subject to dispute and is now funded with less than 25% of its original resources, adjusting for inflation. It presently awards about 1% of its resources for the support of field-initiated studies.]

reviewers.) Reviews were based on seven familiar criteria listed in the 'Code of Federal Regulations': plan of operation, budget, quality of personnel, evaluation plan, adequacy of resources, significance, and technical soundness. Reviewers selected 47 proposals to advance to the second tier, where eight fresh reviewers rated each proposal, mainly in terms of significance. (Technical merit was no longer at issue, but we still had more proposals than resources.) Choices were required. But how to judge the competitors, most of which proposed to do wholly different things? We had a classic 'apples and oranges' problem. The second panel helped us decide which fruit to serve.

Let me say a bit more about what came through the transom in the first place. Two-thirds (225) of the proposals originated in colleges and universities; the other third came from private and nonprofit organizations (56), individuals (24), schools and school systems (22), and state and local governments (9). Those from institutions of higher education were split almost equally between education departments and other departments, including English, business, psychology, history, math, and science.

A third of the submissions that were 'eligible' to be judged (more about that presently) proposed to conduct fairly basic research. Another quarter aimed to conduct development activities of some sort. In other words, about three-fifths of the eligible submissions proposed to engage in actual research and development. Six broad areas of inquiry attracted more than 20 proposals each: language curriculum (reading, writing, and others), higher education, school administration, adult literacy and dropouts, science, and early education and parent involvement.

Specific topics were, as one might expect, a mixed bag. Here's a partial sampling: education research in agriculture, remediation of a foreign accent, photo-documentation of 19th century commercial buildings, campfire teen leadership, word weaving, children's perceptions of subculture clothing, math anxiety, the relationship between metacognitive processes and eye movement coordination among literate and illiterate adults, psychological language theories behind *Sesame Street*, and the war of wills between parents and children.

My purpose is not to mock. There are few topics that couldn't yield something worth knowing, assuming the works were well conceived and executed. But when resources are scarce (when aren't they?) we have to make choices. And some of what was offered for our consideration was pretty marginal.

As I indicated, not all of the 336 submissions were eligible to go through the review process. Forty-eight were disqualified before the competition even began. They lacked basic information. Hence, one out of seven proposals couldn't even be judged because it was in some important sense incomplete.

Incompleteness was not limited to the 48 that were disqualified, I discovered after plucking out and reading through a semi-random sample

— every 10th one, 34 proposals in all — from the 336 submissions. I wanted to gain a clearer sense of the kinds of proposals the FIS competition had attracted. The sample turned out to be fairly representative: one of them was funded, four others made the finals, while three had been bumped from the competition as ineligible. Reviewer scores on the 31 eligible proposals I examined ranged from 26 (out of 100) to 88. The average was 53.

I've skimmed them all. I've also read the reviewers' comments. And I must report that too many of these proposals are an embarrassment to the education research community. They're burdened with skimpy plans, fat budgets, dubious experiments, worn-out hypotheses, disorganized writing, missing information, and ungeneralizable results. But the most lamentable shortcoming I encountered was that so many dealt with matters so esoteric or minuscule that they would benefit only a handful of people, assuming of course that they succeeded in doing what they proposed.... If resources were limitless, [such] projects might eventually have yielded something useful to someone. But times are lean. We can fund only those proposals likely to deliver significant, generalizable, useful results....

Earlier, I mentioned superconductivity. I'd like to think that a breakthrough in education research could stir a level of activity similar to that among ceramists, chemists, and others who are meeting and experimenting and working practically nonstop to develop applications for the new ceramic superconductors....

The imperative to compete is no less urgent in education than in electronics. Never has tomorrow so depended on what students are doing today. And never have Americans been more ready to consider our findings — assuming they are worth considering!

Chapter 4

Postpositivist Criticisms, Reform Associations, and Uncertainties about Social Research*

Thomas D. Cook

This [selection] is concerned with what I think is the most pressing methodological problem of our day: How can scientific practice be justified in light of the cogent criticisms of its most basic premises by philosophers, historians, and sociologists of science? This difficulty is felt more acutely within the social than the natural sciences, and perhaps most acutely by those who have worked at the interface between social science and social policy. This is because social science theory and method were used in the 1960s and 1970s to help design and evaluate social programs aimed at ameliorating social problems, but the results from these programs were disappointing. Was this because social science is an inappropriate source of input into social policy and cannot produce effective programs or clear-cut evaluations? If so, the reasoning goes, might social policy benefit no more from social *science* knowledge than from other forms of knowledge about society and human nature?...

In a world where one way of conducting research was universally considered to be 'correct', scientific practice would be easy. Researchers would simply do what is correct.... The current uncertainty [about correct practice] arises, I think, from two principal sources. The first is the systematic attack on the theory of knowledge that was dominant until 20 years ago in most philosophy of science; the second is the move social scientists made toward causal research in field settings. This meant a move away from the laboratory and the traditions of causal research it represents based on control over stimulus materials and external events, and also a move away from the descriptive theory and cross-sectional research methods then prevalent among sociologists and political scientists. Given these moves, lessons had to be learned from experience about what

---

* Abridged from *Social Science and Social Policy* (pp. 21–62) edited by R.L. Shotland and M.M. Mark, 1985, Beverly Hills, CA: Sage.

happens when control is reduced while the ambition to infer is simultaneously increased — the state of affairs during the Great Society years.

The Attack on Positivism

An amusing incident took place in 1961 in Tübingen during a special symposium held on epistemological issues in the social sciences. [Karl] Popper was the first speaker, and [Theodor] Adorno was the second. It was widely expected that Popper would defend epistemological positions believed to be 'positivist' and that Adorno would challenge these positions. However, because Popper unequivocably denounced positivism, the anticipated confrontation did not materialize. It was then left to [Ralf] Dahrendorf, the rapporteur, to reveal why. He noted that Popper defined positivism in terms of the 'empty bucket' theory of induction. This assumes that some associations repeatedly occur in nature that can be validly observed by senses that bring no prior knowledge to bear, and from these observations general laws can be induced. This conception of positivism is quite different from the more hypothetico-deductive version that Adorno attacked. The latter assumes that totally explicit theories are possible from which hypotheses can be deduced that can subsequently be confronted with empirical data that will confirm or reject the theory from which the hypotheses were derived.

The difficulties Popper and Adorno had in agreeing on a definition of positivism incline me not to offer my own. Because many varieties of positivism can be constructed, I will outline the ontological, epistemological, and methodological assumptions that characterize the scientific beliefs and practices that are today more likely to be labeled 'positivist', irrespective of their links to past theories of positivism. I do not want to suggest that any social (or natural) scientist has ever subscribed to all these assumptions, or that they adequately describe scientific practice as it occurs, or that practice has evolved only from positivism or from any other single philosophy of science for that matter. Scientific practice has multiple origins that include the trial-and-error behavior of practitioners, selective adaptations from prior philosophies, and research on research. Nonetheless, the assumptions I call positivist were widely disseminated after 1930 and were used to justify a particular set of scientific practices. These assumptions were partly based on logic and partly on how philosophers thought physicists went about the business of doing research and constructing theories.

Ontological Assumptions

Positivists are realists and assume the existence of the world outside of the mind. They further assume that this world is lawfully ordered and that the major task of science is to describe this order. The order is assumed to be deterministic in its manifestations (rather than probabilistic) so that once the laws of nature are known, perfect prediction will result. Indeed, only when perfect prediction has been achieved do positivists want to speak of having discovered a law. Laws are preferred if they are general and apply to many phenomena, if they are functional in form and specify how observable forces are related to each other, and if they are parsimonious because few forces need to be invoked. Einstein's $e = mc^2$ meets these criteria. It applies to all motion and subsumes all prior theories of motion; it specifies the form of a relationship; and because one parameter is a constant only one other needs to be estimated. Most positivists further assume that the terms in their laws will be ahistorical, based on forces that are permanent fixtures of the external world, and nonmentalistic, devoid of conceptions based on intentions and wishes.

All these ontological assumptions have come under attack. Some are probably false. For instance, to assume determinism flies in the face of discoveries from particle physics and molecular biology suggests that the most basic elements of the universe are related probabilistically. The assumptions have come under attack in the social sciences because of their dubious relevance to human nature, social organization, and the current status of social theory. Practicing social scientists know that perfect prediction (i.e., $R^2 = 1$) is impossible with current theories. They also realize that to increase prediction nearly always entails adding more constructs to a theoretical system. But this jeopardizes parsimony. They also believe that most research areas are circumscribed in coverage (i.e., they apply only to, say, attitude change or intergroup cooperation) and that making them more general would probably lead to highly abstract verbal theories with little predictive power for particular instances. To take perfect prediction as a criterion for inferring laws and generalities seems inordinately unrealistic to many of those who criticize the relevance of physics to the social sciences.

Positivists gravitate to prediction because it depends on observing the correlation between variables; they want to avoid constructs like 'causation' that cannot be directly observed. But prediction does not necessarily lead to causal or explanatory knowledge (Bhaskar, 1979; Scriven, 1971) and does not guarantee control over events (Collingwood, 1940). For instance, we can almost perfectly predict the length of any day from the length of prior days and the length of the same day one year ago. But that hardly helps either to explain the length of a day or to modify its length. Because prediction, whether in a deterministic or probabilistic mode, does not necessarily entail explanation or manipulation, some critics of positivism reject it as the sole, or even major, criterion for judging the adequacy of theories. Most want to replace it with causal explanation.

But in the social sciences such explanation is not likely to take the simple form of the laws of physics. Most social phenomena are multiply determined; each unique cause may be related to other causes in complex ways; and each cause may itself be complexly and multiply determined by other forces that are not themselves direct causes of what is being explained. To practicing social scientists, causal explanation is not likely — in the near term, at least — to involve simple relationships that look like parsimonious laws. Instead, multiple causal determinants, multiple causal paths, and multiple causal contingencies have to be assumed, making human nature and social relationships seem more like pretzels than single-headed arrows from A to B or simple functional equations — more like convoluted multivariate statistical interactions than simple main effects (e.g., Cronbach and Snow, 1976; House, 1980; McGuire, 1984).

It is difficult to assume that the circumscribed level of prediction that social scientists now attain will remain stable over settings and times. To exemplify this, replace the analogy of physics with that of macrobiology. Unlike the case with physical objects, animals (including man) seek to control their environments, and the knowledge they achieve is often stored as genetic mutations or as the teachings of priests, grandmothers, law books, and even methodology texts. The past lives on in the behavioral and cognitive present, influencing how we define problems, select possible solutions, and envisage future opportunities. Because it is rare that only one response will be adequate for meeting individual or species' 'needs', a macrobiological perspective suggests that the same set of external contingencies can result in a wide variety of apparently adaptive responses, with the form of the response depending on what unfolds from within, what has transpired in the past, and what is available in the present, including chance and present plans for the future. The argument is, then, that laws about human nature and social life cannot be inferred using the physicists' assumptions of ahistoricity and nonmentalism.

The preceding arguments are about how human nature and social relationships are organized in the real world. They are not about whether there is an external world. However, even this fundamental assumption has come under attack from scholars who contend that humans have a compulsion to understand their world, and, in so doing, construct meanings in their minds. Because people respond to such constructions rather than to the external world itself, critics like Habermas (1972) or Harré and Secord (1972) contend that it is mind that determines behavior and not the world outside of the mind, if there is one. Note that this denial of realism is not based on a direct refutation. Rather, it postulates that we do not need to assume an external world if we can never prove that one exists and if we believe that humans react anyway to mental constructions of the world rather than to the world itself.

Epistemological Assumptions

Crucial to positivism is the assumption that 'objective' knowledge is possible — that theory-neutral observations can be made that tap directly into nature and are not affected by the wishes, hopes, expectations, category systems, etc. of observers. So pervasive is the role of observation that positivists espouse a definitional operationalism that makes an entity no more or less than its measure. From this belief follows the dictum that 'IQ is what IQ tests measure'; IQ is not seen to be a hypothetical entity defining the cognitive skills that are considered most useful for manipulating abstract knowledge.

Attacks on the neutrality or objectivity of observation have come from many quarters, largely on the grounds that science is conducted by people, and people cannot divorce themselves from their prior knowledge and expectations. The subjective components in observation may come from many sources — the social class biases stressed by Marxists, the paradigmatic biases emphasized by Kuhn (1962), or the investigator expectancies stressed by Merton (1957) and Rosenthal (Rosenthal and Jacobson, 1968). To those who crave certain knowledge from the senses no consolation is offered from modern developments in epistemology, metascience, or human perception (Campbell, 1974). And to those who believe that individuals may be biased but multiple observers may not be in the aggregate, it must be pointed out that Kuhn's work (1962) became so salient because his thesis was that *all* scientists in a particular field at a particular time may share the same set of fallacious and unacknowledged assumptions that enter into all observations of nature.

Critics have also taken issue with according a special status to observables. Science has often progressed because bold thinkers were willing to postulate the unobservable, and, in some cases, were eventually proven correct. We still today cannot see the core of the earth, and yet geologists and mineralogists do research on how it might be composed. Moreover, some theories have only improved explanatory power by invoking constructs that cannot be directly observed, as with recent shifts by behaviorists to incorporate cognitive and affective phenomena (e.g., Bandura, 1977; Bower, 1981). The pragmatic case, then, is that neither prediction nor explanation is enhanced by restricting oneself to observables.

The epistemological basis of positivism goes beyond postulating the possibility of observation that is both theory-neutral and comprehensive. Logic is also involved. Inductivist versions of positivism rely on abstracting general statements from observed regularities. To achieve this requires a defensible theory of induction, but none is yet available (Popper, 1959). Although attempts have been made to construct defenses of induction, it is not clear that they can deal with the logical problem inherent in inferring from past regularities that the same regularity will continue into the future. Among social scientists, a hypothetico-deductive version of positivism has had more adherents than a pure inductivist version. Accepting this critique of induction, hypothetico-deductivists recommend that scientists should strive to deduce unique observable hypotheses from a theory and they should then confront these hypotheses with observational data that will definitively confirm or disconfirm the hypotheses and their parent theory.

One of the many assumptions behind the hypothetico-deductive approach is that the theory being scrutinized is totally explicit in the constructs and patterns of relationship it specifies and in the ways it specifies how each construct should be measured. If a theory is not specific on these matters, disconfirming observations can be used, not to reject the theory — as is required in positivism — but rather to add novel theoretical contingencies that encompass the disconfirmations by specifying when a particular relationship should and should not be found or how a construct should and should not be measured. Unfortunately, nearly all of the social science theories of today are so 'squishy' or 'incommensurable' that little ingenuity is required to accommodate disconfirming results. Moreover, the passion that leads individuals to develop theories may often incline them to reject deviant findings in preference to accepting them as the new 'truth'. And when many of the major scholars in a field are proponents of a particular theory, disconfirmations will have an even more difficult battle because they then need to prevail against a powerful 'invisible college' of scientific opinion-makers.

Methodological Assumptions

The primacy of identifying functional relationships between observables means that observation and quantitative measurement play large roles in positivism. Without such data one cannot sensitively test the specific equations that predict an outcome. From the importance of quantified observation follow several important methodological consequences. The first is a stress on developing better techniques of measurement, e.g., more powerful telescopes, microscopes, X-rays, attitude scales, physiological measures, etc. The second is a move toward experimentation and laboratory sciences. Measurement is easier when the objects of study do not change in unknown ways, as occurs in much physics in which inert objects are studied and all the external sources of change in these objects have been earlier identified and can either be kept out of the explanatory system by such means as lead-lined walls or can be directly measured in credible ways.

However, the objects of study are not inert in the human sciences. They mature. They react to historical events. Moreover, we do not know all of the factors to which people react, and many of those we do know about are not measurable. From this arises the rationale for laboratory research, with its goal of isolation and control over extraneous variables. However, humans are adaptable and can construct beliefs and behaviors that help them adapt to the unique ecology of the laboratory. For instance, we know that humans often react to the suspicion they are being observed. But sometimes they react negatively, sometimes with resignation, and sometimes even with a misguided sense of helpfulness (Weber and Cook, 1972). Unfortunately, we do not know when they react each way; and even if we did we could not easily quantify how much the knowledge of being observed influenced particular responses. Because these theoretical irrelevancies cannot be totally specified, some scholars believe that it is preferable to prevent them from occurring at all. This means leaving the lab and conducting field research with unobtrusive measurement.

The concern with perfect prediction leads positivists to methods based on analytic reductionism — breaking an observed relationship down into the components that are necessary and sufficient for a relationship to occur. Positivists would not be satisfied with establishing that X is sometimes related to Y. They would like to discover what it is about X that is invariably related to some particular aspect of Y. To do this they decompose X and Y into their constituent elements, each of which will eventually be studied in its own right. But decomposing X into its causally efficacious components (say X') and Y into its causally impacted elements (say Y') may still not be enough. Perfect prediction may further depend on relating X' and Y' to 'third variables' that codetermine their relationship, especially the more microscopically specified variables that occur after X' has changed and before Y' has been influenced. The upshot of the urge to improve prediction through decomposition and the discovery of substantively relevant mediating variables is a science that slowly gravitates to a more reductionist level of analysis, relatively closed systems as testing sites (e.g., the laboratory), and a form of research in which the control afforded by experimentation is valued more than the holism facilitated by naturalism.

Positivism is also associated with the belief that a single 'crucial experiment' can definitively test a theory (or the difference in viability between one or more theories). Brute empiricism of the kind, 'What will happen if I do X?' is not prized; nor is descriptive research that is devoid of hypothesis testing or willful intrusions into nature. The emphasis on the crucial experiment also leaves out of science phenomena that cannot be easily quantified or controlled, thereby running the risk that substantive importance may play less of a role in selecting research topics than the degree to which quantification, control, prediction, experimentation, and theory testing are possible. We can see in the attack on positivist methods a rejection of the primacy of observation over introspection, quantification over understanding, micro-level over macro-level analysis, control over naturalism, theory testing over discovery, and crucial experiments conducted on select parts of nature over more tentative probing of all of nature.

The Consequences of Such Attacks

When scientists share a common set of assumptions it is presumably easier to decide how to proceed with the practice of science. One simply selects the kinds of problems and methods commensurate with the guiding assumptions. But when — as today — foundations are under attack, question and method choice become more problematic. It is now not easy to assume one is trying to describe a social world that is lawfully fixed, deterministically ordered, and can be perfectly described with elegant and simple functional relationships; it is not now easy to assume that everything of importance can be measured, that value-free measurement is possible, and that our theories are perfectly specified. It is not now easy to assume that closed-system methods generalize to open-system contexts, that crucial experiments are possible that provide definitive tests of theories, and that little value should be accorded to methods of discovery as opposed to methods of testing. . . .

Social Reform in the 1960s and 1970s

The Kennedy, Johnson, and Nixon presidencies [in the United States] were associated with social reforms in many sectors of the social welfare system. By and large, these proved to be disappointing in their effects. The major reasons for this were probably (a) inadequacies in the knowledge of society undergirding the design and implementation of social programs; (b) inadequacies of the social science methods used to evaluate these programs; and (c) limitations in the range of values and interests incorporated into both the definition of social problems and the selection of approaches designed to ameliorate these problems. Because these diagnoses overlap with the critique of positivism, and disappointment with the gains of the Great Society and its offshoots occurred at about the same time positivism came under attack, it is difficult — if not impossible — to distinguish . . . the attack on positivism . . . from the intellectual inquests on the Great Society.

We turn now to a discussion of *how* disappointment with social reform attempts influenced practice among social scientists. We argue that uncertainty was created about the degree of authority warranted by substantive social theory, by the research techniques then most widely accepted, and by the use of formal decision makers as the sole source for generating policy-relevant research questions.

The Decrease in Authority Experienced by Substantive Theory

Every social program is implicitly or explicitly undergirded by theoretical postulates about factors that will ameliorate a social problem, whether it is poor academic achievement, underemployment, or prison recidivism. Not surprisingly, social planners and program developers looked to social scientists for some of the knowledge they needed to design into specific practices that might ameliorate these problems. In retrospect, we can see that such expectations were inappropriate.

One difficulty that quickly became obvious was that most of the hypotheses used were internally inadequate. That is, doubts quickly became clear about the validity of such hypotheses as better food promotes learning in poor children; more police visibility reduces crime; rehabilitation lowers prison recidivism, largely because the relevant theories failed to specify the types of conditions under which a given relationship did and did not hold. The contact hypothesis in race relations is an instructive example in this regard because some contingencies were specified from its earliest days in the 1930s (Allport, 1935), but these were inadequate and new contingencies were added (Amir, 1969). But these, in their turn, did not turn out to be comprehensive enough, and we still cannot structure interracial contact that reliably decreases prejudice except in certain very controlled settings in schools.

A second problem with the substantive theories was that they were not comprehensive enough to use as action blueprints. In order to tell service deliverers about the specific acts they should perform under various sets of circumstances much improvisation had to take place on the part of program developers and local personnel. They were forced to build some forms of knowledge into program designs that were not contained in the substantive theories of social scientists. Instead, they came from practitioner knowledge or from trial and error learning.

Finally, a new awareness emerged of how problematic it was to implement well in practice those relatively few activities about which substantive theories were indeed explicit. Pressman and Wildavsky (1979) stressed the implementation problems stemming from chaotic events that occur at the site of service delivery where the activities of multiple actors have to be coordinated; Williams (1980) stressed the problems of communication, commitment, and capacity that occur in trying to implement changes in multilevel organizational hierarchies; Fullan (1982) stressed practitioners' reluctance to accede to changes that were asked of them by superiors or outsiders who did not seem to understand or appreciate the pressures on service deliverers; and, finally, Berman (1980) and Bardach (1977) stressed how much implementation depends on system-level considerations of power, language, and history that bind or separate different groups in organizational contexts.

By the middle of the 1970s the authority of substantive social science theory for girding program design was under heavy attack, and alternatives and supplements were sought. Thus, the decrement in authority attributed to theory was accompanied by a corresponding increase in the authority attributed to other forms of knowledge, particularly practitioner wisdom. The claims on its behalf went beyond stressing how it was needed to fill in the gaps in social science knowledge. Claims were also heard that the practices advocated by social service professionals might be just as legitimate as scientific knowledge. The rationale offered was that in a vast nation like the United States, practice is likely to invent many variants, most of which never enter into the 'permanent' stock of professional wisdom because they do not seem to be effective or only seem effective in restricted contexts. This suggests that the practices remaining in the permanent stock should include many that have repeatedly withstood unsystematic tests of their adequacy. The implication is that practice should be treated more like a legitimate, alternative form of relevant knowledge than as an ugly stepsister to science.

During the same period, a new value was accorded to observing closely what goes on in programs as they are first implemented. The expectation was that such observational studies would help improve the internal operations of programs and would also lay down a body of general knowledge from which principles about the design, implementation, and revision of social programs could be induced. Implicit in the advocacy of grounded observation was the critique that substantive social theory is often too abstract, too little tested in multiple action contexts, and too rarely formulated with implementation in mind. Consequently it fails to reflect, or be responsive to, the contextual density in which clients and practitioners actually operate and on which the effectiveness of programs depends. The growing pessimism about substantive theory was leavened, then, by growing optimism about the validity and utility of practitioner wisdom and about the roles that grounded observation can play when it is not guided by preordained theoretical concepts.

The Decrease in Authority Experienced by Particular Social Science Methods

In positivist science decision rules were clear and justified 'authoritative' statements about scientific practice. As applied to the social sciences, most of the rules were about which methods to use in pursuing particular types of questions; thus, to probe causal questions, randomized experiments were advocated; to probe descriptive questions about populations, sample surveys were proposed; and to probe descriptive issues about system relationships, participant observation was proposed. Rules were further formulated about how to do experiments, surveys, and observational studies and about the types of invalid inference that would result if inappropriate methods were chosen. In the 1950s and 1960s it was not difficult to know what were the proper things to do in the social sciences. But experience in the evaluation of social programs led to a weakening of the old links between research functions and methods. Previously advocated methods came to be seen as less deserving of hegemony for the tasks for which they were originally designed; other methods came to be seen as deserving more merit than had previously been allotted to them.

Perhaps the most famous example of this concerns methods for probing the causal effects of programs. Pessimism arose about the efficacy of randomized experiments for this purpose because so many experiments proved to be difficult to mount or to maintain in the desired form over time, especially because of the frequency of treatment-correlated attrition from the study. Moreover, the findings of most experiments were greeted, not with universal approval, but with cacophonous discord about what had really been discovered (Lindblom and Cohen, 1979). Although some of the criticisms were not relevant to random assignment *per se*, others were. One criticism stressed how random assignment exacerbated invidious comparisons between groups receiving treatments of different value; another stressed the differential attrition that can arise when treatments differ in desirability; and yet another mentioned how random assignment often led to undesirable restrictions to the external validity of studies. Thus, the crucible of experience forced out many of the problems inherent in conducting randomized experiments in open-system contexts. The same identification of weaknesses through experience happened with other forms of experimentation. The authority of many quasi-experimental designs came to suffer from an enhanced realization of the difficulty of specifying all the relevant ways in which treatment groups were nonequivalent and perfectly measuring all the constructs specified in models of such initial nonequivalence.

As might be expected, the identification of problems with particular methods also led to attempts to improve them. Thus arose the advocacy of randomized experiments in which all irrelevant sources of desirability between treatments were reduced; in which the units receiving one treatment could not communicate with those receiving another; and in which the implementation of the experimental design was monitored so as to detect differential attrition early in order to deal with it before it became too late (Cook and Campbell, 1979). (It was also hoped that such monitoring would improve the chances of detecting side effects and of specifying the different populations and settings in which a treatment might have an impact.) In the quasi-experimental domain, the identification of problems led to more self-consciousness about the need for explicit and defensible selection models and to attempts to circumvent the nonequivalence problem in other ways than through measurement and subsequent statistical manipulation; e.g., by means of dry-run experiments in which pretest measurement occurs on two separate occasions; by means of switching replication experiments in which treatments are eventually given to controls; or by means of nonequivalent dependent variables, only one of which is supposed to be affected by a treatment but each of which should be affected by the most plausible alternative interpretations of a treatment effect (Cook and Campbell, 1979). But although experimental methods were improved because of the knowledge generated from the problems identified during the course of social reform attempts, perfection did not result. Experimental methods were still stigmatized.

Some critics of the experiment argued that it was not enough to 'band-aid' marginal improvements onto methods that, in their opinion, were fundamentally flawed. The most radical critics of the experiment wanted to search for truly novel methods of causal inference. In particular, a variety of qualitative alternatives were espoused. They were espoused not only on grounds that they facilitated inferences about simple causal relationships, but it was also stressed that they made it easier to assess the quality of treatment implementation, to detect unanticipated side effects, and to provide contextual understanding (Patton, 1978). Supporting this advocacy were theories that explicitly set out to create a logical basis for inference based on qualitative data (e.g., Scriven's 1976 *modus operandi* approach and Campbell's apparent renunciation of the monolithic supremacy of experiments in Cook and Reichardt, 1979). With qualitative techniques added to the list of possible causal methods and with doubts being so public about the efficacy of randomized experiments, the authority of experiments shrank and method choice became all the more difficult for those who wanted to answer causal questions.

It would be wrong to believe that a decrement in authority was only experienced with experimental methods. As a means for describing populations, survey research methods have been much advocated and are regularly employed. However, recent critiques have stressed the practical difficulties that sometimes occur when trying to implement them; e.g., when resources permit mounting a demonstration project at only a few sites but generalization to the nation at large is desired (Cook, Leviton, and Shadish, 1985). Also, ethical and political pressures demand that social research be increasingly conducted with groups and organizations that are fully informed about the research and can opt not to participate. Volunteer biases arise, and need adding to those associated with telephone ownership, being away from the home by day, etc.

As with experiments, the absolute decrement in authority attributed to survey methods was accompanied by an increase in the authority attributed to alternative means of generalization. Cook and Campbell (1979) proposed basing inferences about generalizability in terms of the degree to which relationships were dependably replicated across purposive but heterogeneous samples of respondents and settings, or on the degree to which the samples studied were impressionistically modal of a desired target population (see also St. Pierre and Cook, 1984). The popularity of meta-analysis seems also to have added credibility to the idea that generalized statements are often warranted when findings have been multiply replicated across heterogeneous samples of respondents, settings, and times, none of which were chosen with known probability from a designated population. Although inferences based on continuities across heterogeneous instances do not have the same logical warrant as inferences based on samples in which the probability of selection is known, they are nonetheless not completely without worth. This being so, we can see that the authority of the sample survey was squeezed from two ends: Increased doubts arose about its absolute adequacy, and an enhanced justification was offered for some alternatives that are more easily implemented. This double squeeze is exactly what occurred with experiments.

The experiences gained in designing and evaluating social reforms in the 1960s and 1970s led to another important insight about method choice. Such choice is made all the more difficult, not only because many methods exist for fulfilling any one research function, but also because multiple functions have to be met in most individual research studies. To be more specific, in the 1960s and 1970s applied social scientists with backgrounds in psychology became increasingly aware that experimental design was only a part of research design, and that the latter involved choices about sampling, measurement, data collection, data analysis, and strategies for disseminating results. Correspondingly, researchers with backgrounds in sociology and economics became more aware of causal concerns and experimental design.

More important than the realization of more decision points and more alternatives at each point was the realization that the methods chosen for one research function might constrain the range of methods available for fulfilling another function. Thus, when a particular experimental design was chosen, this constrained sampling options, and vice versa. Likewise, if a particular data collection procedure was chosen, the choice of data analysis was constrained, and vice versa. Research design came to be seen more as the art of reconciling conflicting demands imposed by the constraints that followed once a particular method was chosen for fulfilling a particular research function. Scholars even came to realize that one may sometimes choose a generally inferior method on the dual grounds that it provides valid 'enough' results about, say, causal connections *and* also makes it easier to select a different method for fulfilling a different research function; say, generalization. Methods have to be selected not only for their logical adequacy, but also for their fit to the rest of an overall research design and to the priorities built into that design. Because of this realization method choice became even more difficult.

Thomas D. Cook

The Decrease in Authority Experienced by Formal Decision Makers

Most social scientists in the 1960s seem to have been willing to work within a system for defining and solving social problems that was set by formal decision makers from the executive and legislative branches of government. Social scientists were widely seen to be the servants of such persons, helping them to plan policy and programs and test how efficacious they were. So long as this source of policy-relevant questions remained unproblematic, it was not especially difficult for researchers interested in social policy to formulate the issues and questions they sought to investigate.

But experience in the 1960s and 1970s made it clear that in the world of social policy it is rare to find clear definitions of problems, potential solutions, and research questions, for a lack of specificity helps create the political consensus required for obtaining agreements about action from a group of heterogeneous and powerful interests. Moreover, decision makers do not operate in a void. They are open to multiple sources of influence and to many conflicting values. In deciding what to support, decision makers consider many points of view — national ideology, personal preference, political survival, and personal advantage. They also sometimes consider social science evidence. But this is only one of many inputs into decision making and will rarely be of sufficient centrality to determine decisions (Weiss and Weiss, 1981). The political system is a world where many statements are deliberately unclear and do not reflect what is intended, many conflicting forces operate, many different forms of knowledge are respected, and action is multiply determined. But although the political system is open and includes many actors representing many points of view, formal decision makers may themselves be relatively homogeneous in some respects. They may be especially inclined, for instance, to blame social groups and individuals in need for their plight, to propose solutions that are marginally ameliorist and not radical, to favor solutions that directly or indirectly favor the interests of business, and to press for actions that promise seemingly dramatic results in a short period. Given the growing evidence about how the political system operates, it is not surprising that a decrement occurred among some social scientists in the authority they were prepared to attribute to formal decision makers as the sole, or even the major, source of problem definitions, potential solutions, and information needs.

As with theories and methods, the decline of formal decision makers as the major source of priorities and values was associated with the rise of other alternatives. Foremost among these was a pluralist conception based on conducting policy research whose assumptions and questions reflect the values and information needs of multiple stakeholders. Researchers were no longer encouraged to see themselves as servants of powerful, formal decision makers. Instead, they were urged to consider and consult with all interested parties. In the health system, this meant not only federal agencies and congressional committees and their staffs, but also hospital administrators and the professional associations representing them; physicians and nurses and the associations representing them; insurance companies; hospital patients; and health policy researchers. These groups have different interests concerning health matters and different information needs about particular health programs. Formal decision makers can only imperfectly represent these multiple interests, each of which could probably represent itself much better. Consequently, pluralists emphasize that researchers should avoid building the restricted set of assumptions of the powerful into their research; they want researchers to consult with all the relevant stakeholder groups in the sector under study.

Some theorists advocate pluralism in the formulation of policy questions, not only because this reflects the form of democracy in which they believe, but also because they believe that consulting with multiple stakeholders is more likely to lead to research results being used in policy debates. This is because the results should be relevant to more groups, and more groups should then know of them (Leviton and Hughes, 1981). Other theorists see pluralism as a means of raising the researcher's consciousness about the social values latent in how formal decision makers interpret problems and questions. However, stakeholder analysis is not the only means of forcing out hidden assumptions and values. Other means to this end include procedures such as the Science Court and substantive standing committees in the manner of the National Research Council (briefly reviewed in Hennigan, Flay and Cook, 1980), as well as textual analysis in the manner of hermeneutics and the Delphi technique. However, the major point is not that techniques exist to make assumptions explicit; rather, it is that in the last 20 years a decline in the authority of formal decision makers has taken place that required the development or use of such techniques. It is not now easy to see formal decision makers as the major, legitimate source of research priorities and of the values built into the design of research or the interpretations of findings. Related to this decline is an increase in the authority of alternative sources of questions and values, particularly pluralist sources or sources based on some form of critical analysis.

Declines are not Disappearances

With theory, methods, and values I have described a decrease in the authority of established choice alternatives and a growth in the authority of other alternatives, some of them previously discredited. It is important in this respect to note that the decreases in authority were not to a level that made the dominant alternatives lose all their authority. Substantive theory is still useful for program design; certain methods are still useful for generating particular forms of knowledge; and formal decision makers are still useful for producing research that gets used. Indeed, in all three cases it is probably still possible to argue that, of all the possible alternatives, the old one is the best, [but] in the last 20 years we have witnessed the overthrow of the hegemony previously attributed to particular choices and a consequent increase in the difficulties of choice for practising social scientists.

References

ALLPORT, G.W. (1935). Attitudes. In C.M. MURCHISON (Ed.), *Handbook of social psychology*. Worcester, MA: Clark University Press.

AMIR, Y. (1969). Contact hypothesis in ethnic relations. *Psychological Bulletin, 71*, 319–342.

BANDURA, A. (1977). Toward a unifying theory of behavioral change. *Psychological Review, 84*, 191–215.

BARDACH, E. (1977). *The implementation game*. Cambridge, MA: MIT Press.

BERMAN, P. (1980). Thinking about programmed and adaptive implementation: Matching strategies to situations. In H.M. INGRAM and D.E. MANN (Eds), *Why policies succeed or fail* (pp. 205–227). Beverly Hills, CA: Sage.

BHASKAR, R. (1979). *The possibility of naturalism*. Sussex: Harvester.

BOWER, G.H. (1981). Emotional mood and memory. *American Psychologist, 36*, 129–148.

CAMPBELL, D.T. (1974). Evolutionary epistemology. In P.A. SCHLIPP (Ed.), *The philosophy of Karl Popper. The library of living philosophers* (Vol. 14, 1). LaSalle, IL: Open Court Publishing.

COLLINGWOOD, R.G. (1940). *An essay on metaphysics*. Oxford, England: Clarendon Press.

COOK, T.D. and CAMPBELL, D.T. (1979). *Quasi-experimentation: Design and analysis issues for social research in field settings*. Boston: Houghton Mifflin.

COOK, T.D., LEVITON, L.C. and SHADISH, W. (1985). Program evaluation. In G. LINDSEY and E. ARONSON (Eds), *Handbook of social psychology* (3rd ed., pp. 699–777). Boston: Addison-Wesley.

COOK, T.D. and REICHARDT, C.S. (Eds). (1979). *Qualitative and quantitative methods in evaluation*. Beverly Hills, CA: Sage.

CRONBACH, L.J. and SNOW, R.E. (1976). *Aptitudes and instructional methods*. New York: Irvington.

FULLAN, M. (1982). *The meaning of educational change*. New York: Teachers College Press.

HABERMAS, J. (1972). *Knowledge and human interests*. London: Heinemann.

HARRÉ, R. and SECORD, P. (1972). *The explanation of social behaviour*. Oxford: Basil Blackwell.

HENNIGAN, K.M., FLAY, B.R., and COOK, T.D. (1980). 'Give me the facts!': The use of social science evidence in formulating national policy. In R.F. KIDD and M.J. SAKS (Eds), *Advances in applied social psychology* (Vol. 1, pp. 113–148). Hillsdale, NJ: Erlbaum.

HOUSE, E.R. (1980). *Evaluating with validity.* Beverly Hills, CA: Sage.

KUHN, T.S. (1962). *The structure of scientific revolutions.* Chicago: University of Chicago Press.

LEVITON, L.C. and HUGHES, E.F. (1981). Research in the utilization of evaluations: Review and syntheses. *Evaluation Review, 5,* 525–548.

LINDBLOM, C.E. and COHEN, D.K. (1979). *Usable knowledge.* New Haven, CT: Yale University Press.

McGUIRE, W.J. (1984). Contextualism. In L. BERKOWITZ (Ed.), *Advances in experimental social psychology.* New York: Academic Press.

MERTON, R.K. (1957). Bureaucratic structure and personality. In *Social theory and social structure.* New York: Free Press.

PATTON, M.Q. (1978). *Utilization-focused evaluation.* Beverly Hills, CA: Sage.

POPPER, K.R. (1959). *The logic of scientific discovery.* New York: Basic Books.

PRESSMAN, J. and WILDAVSKY, A. (1979). *Implementation: How great expectations in Washington are dashed in Oakland* (2nd ed.). Berkeley: University of California Press.

ROSENTHAL, R. and JACOBSON, L. (1968). *Pygmalion in the classroom.* New York: Holt, Rinehart & Winston.

SCRIVEN, M. (1971). The logic of cause. *Theory and Decision, 2,* 3–16.

SCRIVEN, M. (1976). Maximizing the power of causal investigation: The modus operandi method. In G.V. GLASS (Ed.), *Evaluation studies review annual* (Vol. 1). Beverly Hills, CA: Sage.

ST. PIERRE, R. and COOK, T.D. (1984). Sampling strategies in program evaluation. In R. CONNER (Ed.), *Evaluation studies review annual* (Vol. 9). Beverly Hills, CA: Sage.

WEBER, S.J. and COOK, T.D. (1972). Subject effects in laboratory research: An examination of subject roles, demand characteristics, and valid inferences. *Psychological Bulletin, 77,* 273–295.

WEISS, J.A. and WEISS, C.H. (1981). Social scientists and decision makers look at the usefulness of mental health research. *American Psychologist, 36,* 837–847.

WILLIAMS, W. (1980). *The implementation perspective.* Berkeley: University of California Press.

Chapter 5

Dilemmas in Social Research*

Hubert M. Blalock, Jr.

It does not require a fine-tuned measuring instrument to show that many social scientists are not happy with the way things are going. We see declining student enrolments and an economic retrenchment that threatens many of our members with unemployment or reduced opportunities for productive research and teaching. We want to have an impact on policy making. Yet the opportunities have not been forthcoming except on a very limited and selective basis. Why won't anyone listen to us? And what is happening to our individual disciplines? Are we becoming a polyglot category of scholars held together primarily by the negative fact that most of us have been clumped together into specific social science departments? . . .

The thesis of the present work is that many of our problems are created by two types of ingredients. On the one hand are a number of very tough intellectual challenges stemming from the complexity of the social world we are attempting to study. On the other there are our own diverse intellectual backgrounds, interests, and behaviors. If we are to understand our present difficulties, we must examine the interplay between these two kinds of factors: ourselves and the limitations imposed on us by the nature of our subject matter. Who are we? What are our expectations and intellectual orientations? What do we want to explain and why? How do we organize ourselves to do so? Just what are the features of social reality that create problems for us in terms of complexities and ambiguities that are difficult to resolve? What are the kinds of social issues that seem to require immediate answers and that produce tensions between the desire to understand phenomena as thoroughly as we can and the practical necessity of acting on the basis of ambiguous empirical evidence?

---

* Abridged from *Basic Dilemmas in the Social Sciences* (pp. 13–36) by H.M. Blalock, Jr., 1984, Beverly Hills, CA: Sage.

[Diverse Backgrounds in the Social Sciences]

We have been attracted to our disciplines for a variety of reasons, but it is essential in this connection to realize that most of us are something of a cross between scientists and humanists. Many of those who take a 'hard science' orientation were initially drawn to the social sciences because they were deeply disturbed about some aspect of society they wanted to see corrected. I selected sociology because I was concerned about the treatment of black and other minorities in American society. Some persons are attracted to demography because they believe that worldwide population problems must be solved if human beings are ever to achieve a reasonably satisfactory life on this planet. Others are concerned about the stability of families or the prevention of delinquency.

Other social scientists have a much more hostile orientation toward the sciences or else believe that the primary role of social scientists is to act as social critics. We should serve as analysts whose principal task is to appraise existing social institutions: to point out their functions, shortcomings, and sources of support, with a view to modifying them in one or another direction. Or we should seek an understanding of human behaviors that is more akin to that of the poet or artist rather than that of the scientist. It is argued that science merely serves the interests of those who sponsor the research and thus is fundamentally a conservative force that should be attacked rather than emulated. Not surprisingly, there have been numerous debates concerning the legitimacy of the social science enterprise itself. For instance, the 1960s was a traumatic decade for several of the social sciences — particularly sociology, cultural anthropology, and political science — because the credibility of the sciences was under attack by a substantial proportion of our members.

Thus social scientists are far from homogeneous in terms of intellectual orientations. Indeed, we are just about as heterogeneous a grouping of scholars as one would ever expect to encounter. In some instances differences within a given discipline are far greater than those between fields, making it easier, for example, for many sociologists and political scientists to communicate with one another than to do so with their own colleagues. This extreme heterogeneity has some positive consequences but also a number of not-so-happy outcomes. Put together an extremely heterogeneous group of scholars and an elusive social reality we are attempting to study, and you have the ingredients of a very confusing intellectual atmosphere.

A Combination of Complexities

It may be relatively easy to deal with complexities as long as they occur one at a time. Generally, complexities produce situations in which there are too many unknowns relative to the available pieces of empirical information. By making simplifying assumptions of one kind or another one may reduce this set of unknowns to manageable proportions. If their numbers are not too large, it may also be possible to collect additional data to provide consistency checks, so that the reasonableness of the assumptions may be assessed indirectly. When two or more complexities are introduced *simultaneously*, however, the situation may get out of hand and become intractable without some rather strong a priori assumptions that may have the effect of doing away with the problem altogether. For instance, when one allows for unknown lag periods and measurement errors in dynamic analyses, there may be too many unknowns unless one assumes, a priori, that either the measurement errors are absent or that the lag periods are known.

Perhaps the most fundamental reason why we experience so many ambiguities in interpreting the results of social research and in testing theories with real data is that we are usually confronted by such simultaneous complications.... [Such complications create formidable problems which] have important implications in terms of the debates that emerge, the ways in which we organize to collect our data, the general research and theory-building strategies we endorse, and, of course, the rate at which our knowledge base accumulates or fails to accumulate. Our morale, expectations, and professional norms are also affected indirectly. It cannot be overemphasized, then, that these 'real-world' complexities, if taken as givens, have a truly major impact on the entire social science enterprise. What are some of them?

First, virtually all social processes are far more complex than we often realize. Our explanatory laws must therefore be both multivariate and probabilistic; furthermore, the variables we usually select as 'independent' are, themselves, often highly intercorrelated and influenced by the variables we are attempting to explain. It appears as though the simultaneous equations that would be needed to account for most reasonably complex social phenomena will need to contain upwards of 20 variables and, realistically, as many as 50 to 100. And even were we able to specify models of this degree of complexity, there would still be error terms needed to account for the remaining indeterminacy in the system.

Second, measurement problems in the social sciences are formidable. Physical scientists are, of course, used to the indirect measurement of postulated properties such as mass, heat energy, or electrical charge. But the assumptions needed to link operational measures to these physical properties are much more precise and justifiable than is possible, say, when a social scientist wishes to infer the 'power' of a corporate executive on the basis of the responses of other parties. A very complex auxiliary measurement theory is often needed in the social sciences to understand this linkage problem. Our present knowledge as to how to construct and analyze data with such measurement models is developing, but it is not yet sufficient to provide really definitive guidelines for measurement. In effect, measurement problems produce a host of unknowns that must be added to those involved in one's substantive theory. Sometimes the number of such unknowns, relative to the amount of empirical information, creates a hopeless situation that cannot be resolved without a combination of additional information and untested a priori assumptions.

Third, as is also common with the physical sciences, rates of change in social phenomena are sometimes far too rapid to be studied with present resources, sometimes they are far too slow. Many important data are simply lost in history and can never be obtained at any cost. Ideally we might like to have detailed information about individuals over their lifetimes, but ethical and practical obstacles to the collection of such data are overwhelming. Furthermore, many social phenomena are changing all at once and continuously, making it difficult to infer temporal sequences or to pin down dates of their onset or termination. True, there are discrete 'events', but often these readily identifiable phenomena are of interest only as indicators of the variables of greatest interest to us. When there is multiple causation, feedbacks of varying and unknown durations, and continuous changes in a large proportion of one's variables, and when measurement errors of unknown magnitudes also exist, one can begin to imagine the magnitude of the difficulties one faces in attempting to disentangle causes and effects.

Fourth, there is a tremendous variety of behaviors and other phenomena we wish to explain. Are there any systematic ways in which we can reduce the complexity of the situation by identifying a much smaller number of more inclusive variables or social processes, taking concrete events as special instances? Certainly we may come up with rather general labels for these variables and processes, but problems of measurement comparability loom large when we do so. How, for instance, can one compare aggressive behaviors, political participation, or worker alienation across a variety of contexts? Must our measurement operations change if we move from a very simple laboratory situation to a more complex one — and if so, then how do we distinguish measurement noncomparability from substantive differences across these settings? What strategies can we use to define manifestly different behaviors, all of which are presumed to have similar consequences, when these very consequences are influenced by other factors besides the behaviors we are attempting to measure? It is perhaps a truism that all analyses require simplifications and abstractions, but of what kinds and according to what rationales? If we do not attempt such simplifications, what are we left with, apart from descriptive materials? *Someone* must eventually try to add up such descriptions to provide more general principles. But it is far from obvious how to proceed.

Fifth, the reality we must deal with is often fuzzy or imprecise. Even when we wish to obtain precise measures we may therefore be unable to do so without making arbitrary decisions, each of which may yield somewhat different conclusions. For instance, the boundaries of an urban area or informal clique may be indeterminate. If we select arbitrary boundaries — say those coinciding with political lines — we may obtain a precise measurement of residential segregation, but different boundaries would undoubtedly yield somewhat different results. There is therefore a kind of social science analogue of Heisenberg's Uncertainty Principle in operation, placing limits on the degree of precision of our measuring instruments and therefore the accuracy and adequacy of our scientific predictions. If we simply make measurement decision by fiat, asserting that we must use only the available data, problems of measurement comparability will loom very large.

Finally, there is no obvious way to divide up the labor, either among the separate social science disciplines or within any one of them. To be sure, there are some arbitrary disciplinary boundaries that have been arrived at through historical accident. The problem is that multiple explanatory variables spill across the currently defined domains of each of the social sciences. One cannot arbitrarily omit any large fraction of these variables without doing injustice to social reality. If one social scientist uses a set of, say, 10 explanatory variables and a second investigator a partially overlapping set of 6, one can rarely fit the two studies together because of the missing information in each study. If each investigator also has used somewhat different measures on different populations at different points in time, the number of implicit or explicit assumptions needed to lace the studies together begins to mount exponentially. Imagine, then, the difficulty in adding up the findings of disparate studies, each with a somewhat different focus and employing different methodologies in widely differing contexts. Given the rather high intercorrelations that often exist among potential explanatory variables, the setup is wide open for ideological and disciplinary biases to influence the interpretation.

The situation is disturbing enough, but we must add another set of ingredients. Most social research — particularly *data collection* — is very expensive and time consuming. Often our data are collected by someone else, such as a government agency. Sometimes we are fortunate enough to have roughly comparable time-series data over a rather long period, perhaps several decades. But the more usual situation involves single investigators or very small research teams collecting their own data with modest and short-term funding. Nor is this funding equally available in all fields or for all purposes, with the result that gaps in our knowledge are distributed unevenly. Let me note a few specific difficulties in this respect.

From many standpoints experimental designs represent an ideal way to proceed. Social scientists can only experiment on certain kinds of individuals under restricted conditions, however. Experiments are typically conducted on powerless people — schoolchildren, introductory psychology students, or hospital patients. We do not experiment on the

Washington State Legislature or the board of directors of Boeing, as much as we might enjoy doing so if this were feasible. Nor can experiments be carried out over more than a few days or involve risky or noxious stimuli. Therefore, experimental manipulations usually involve very minor and short-run changes that are difficult to measure or assess over some prolonged period. Nor are there any scientifically sound bases for generalizing from such powerless or cooperative subjects to bank executives, professional criminals, or political elites. The number of true experiments that can be conducted is thus very small, constituting a narrow band among the topics in which social scientists are interested.

Social surveys are extremely expensive and beyond the means of virtually all individual investigators. They must therefore be financed by someone, and of course these outside parties may 'call the shots' in terms of what is and is not investigated. One of the outcries on the part of radical and minority social scientists during the 1960s was that elites are seldom studied in this way. More often a so-called problem is defined to exist in terms of some undesired *minority* behavior, such as poor school performance, above-average illegitimacy levels, or high crime and delinquency rates. The problem is thus defined to be one of changing the *minority* rather than elites or social institutions. These objections of radical and minority social scientists were sometimes overstated, in an obvious attack on science-oriented quantitative research. But there was considerable truth to them, and the arguments remain valid today. If research is expensive, we can fully expect that financing will be selective and that many important questions will not be studied. Some subareas will be financially starved whereas others will be overfed, and this will have little or nothing to do with their social importance or their relevance for the advancement of social science knowledge.

Practically all funding in the social sciences is short-term in nature, so that replications or prolonged time-series analyses are only rarely accomplished except in a few well-financed, popular areas where an obvious payoff may be expected. If one adds to this the fact that most social research is conducted by individual investigators who must make tenure at their universities or apply each year for new grants, and who can hardly afford to collect data over a 20-year period, it becomes obvious that many kinds of important analyses simply will not be made. It is not as though one could carefully collect data over a long period but with a relatively high degree of assurance of a later payoff. Most social research is risky and unlikely to yield dramatic results; therefore a premium is placed on relatively quick projects. Someone who invests 5 years or so on a major survey usually will have learned a lesson — namely, not to do it again without a considerable recuperation period.

Other kinds of data-collection methods are far more exploratory in nature and much more suitable for small-scale, individual efforts. But here there is a tendency to select research topics for idiosyncratic reasons and to use research strategies that are difficult to replicate. The result is usually a series of disjointed efforts — some of which may be highly insightful — that do not flow naturally into larger-scale, more systematic research despite general agreement that this would be desirable. One reason is that social scientists are not organized to do team research, except on an *ad hoc* or short-term basis.

The Anti-science Attack

The social sciences, lodged as they are between the natural sciences and humanities, have almost inevitably become a battleground over the suitability of natural science models and approaches to the study of human behaviors and social processes. The intensity of the debates waxes and wanes, sometimes owing to changes in our environment — as for an example, the Vietnam and Civil Rights periods of the late 1960s and early 1970s — and sometimes simply because each new generation of social scientists raises the issues anew and then becomes tired of the ensuing arguments. Yet the issues are admittedly important ones. On some occasions positions are stated so dogmatically that motives are transparent, as for example the effort to discredit the use of any data that might effectively challenge a particular viewpoint. But there also may be occasions when the debate becomes more productive by bringing to light issues that have been neglected or set aside because earlier answers had proved ineffective.

Those of us who believe in a science-oriented approach, suitably modified to the special problems faced by the social sciences, must continually examine some of the most telling points made by humanists and others who remain skeptical of natural science approaches. . . .

Toward a Constructive Resolution

It is all well and good to admit problems and shortcomings and even to commit oneself to stating possible biases for readers to evaluate. But it is quite another matter to find reasonably *systematic* ways in which potential biases or misspecifications can be evaluated and even measured quantitatively to assess their seriousness. We must first admit that there can never be ironclad guarantees against unknown biases precisely because they *are* unknown. But through a combination of collective efforts by means of which one person's biases or omissions are corrected by another's insights, plus some rather rigorous guidelines for data analysis and theory construction, we can improve the situation considerably. I believe that a good starting point in this process is exposure to well-known principles of multivariate analysis and scaling and measurement theory.

When we introduce the ideas of multiple regression to students, we may also instill in them a strong sense of the necessity for intellectual integrity. When we express some dependent variable Y as a function of an arbitrary number of independent variables, we do not impose restrictions on what these variables may be or on how many to include. When we talk about how much of the total variance is explained by any one variable, controlling for the others, again we are stressing that each variable — no matter what it is — has an equal opportunity to account for this unexplained variance.

We then may go on to spell out a whole series of complications and how to handle them. For instance, we know that high intercorrelations among independent variables will create difficulties in interpretation, as well as large sampling errors. We may then alert researchers that in such instances it may be highly misleading to attempt to separate out the effects of each variable. We may also discuss the implications of measurement errors of various types, presenting techniques for assessing such errors and making corrections for them. We may also explain how nonlinearities may be examined and tested and how nonadditive joint effects may be investigated systematically rather than on an *ad hoc* basis. And we may stress that this can and should be done regardless of which variables have been inserted into the model.

We may also explain why assumptions about omitted variables are so crucial and what kinds of distortions are produced if these assumptions are incorrect. This then sensitizes one to the need to theorize about omitted variables or variables that have been measured poorly. With explicit equations in front of them, one's readers may then include such variables in their own studies and assess whether or not their results are sufficiently close to those previously found. Readers may also be alerted to biases produced when ordinary least-squares procedures are used with simultaneous-equation data, as well as complications produced by autocorrelated error terms or other sources of misspecifications.

Social scientists properly exposed to these and other technical issues cannot avoid coming out of the experience without some sense of concern that as many complications as feasible be examined and the results interpreted to the reader. The essential communality of all these analytic techniques, when properly employed, is that assumptions are brought into the open and stated explicitly so that they may be readily challenged. Furthermore, one is told how additional complications may be handled and variables brought into the explanatory system in an evenhanded way. One may also eliminate variables that do not work, again on objective rather than arbitrary bases.

Readers also have to be warned about pitfalls, but again this can be done without regard to the particular explanatory variables under consideration. They can be sensitized to the obvious fact that variables that are virtually constant cannot be expected to explain much variance and the implications for design noted. For example, if I select a population that is homogeneous with respect to variable X_1 but heterogeneous with respect to X_2 whereas someone else's design reverses this pattern, we may fully expect that X_2 will work relatively better in my study and X_1 in the second study. Similarly, if the random measurement error variance in X_1 (relative to the true variance) is much greater than that in X_2 (relative to its true variance), I may expect an underestimate of X_1's effects, relative to those of X_2. Readers are thus alerted to certain kinds of artifacts of measurement or research design, so that they will be sensitized to possible differences among study results.

None of this guarantees that an individual investigator's biases will not result in the selective or poor measurement of important variables. Since others will be in a position to add some variables of their own, this particular kind of problem does not appear too serious. Much more problematic, however, are disciplinary biases that result in the neglect of whole sets of factors as being outside the province of study or presumed to have negligible impacts. Here a more catholic or eclectic orientation may be encouraged so as to introduce a much wider range of explanatory variables that may have gone unnoticed even by individual investigators of differing ideological persuasions. Also, particular data collection techniques — such as survey research — may lead to the omission of certain kinds of variables, as for example early socialization experiences or contextual factors. In these instances as well readers can be sensitized to the need to use increasingly inclusive explanatory systems.

Another interpretive bias may exist whenever explanatory variables are moderately intercorrelated. The kind of intellectual dispute that may then take place is often of this form: 'My variables are better than yours! Yours are mere correlates or symptoms of the "true" explanatory variables.' If there are high intercorrelations among the two sets, it may be impossible to resolve such disputes empirically without much better data and larger samples. Readers may, however, be alerted to this multicollinearity problem so that they are not misled by such disputes.

Confusion may also be created by vaguely defined theoretical constructs that shift their meanings according to the circumstances. Once more, if social scientists are alerted to this type of problem and have become sensitized to the scaling and measurement error literatures, such ambiguities can often be resolved or at least brought out into the open. Constructs that appear to have a simple meaning often tend to be multidimensional in nature, a fact that may be uncovered by any number of scaling or factor analysis techniques. This is not to say that such conceptualization-measurement problems are straightforward, but at least there are relatively systematic approaches that can be used to help clarify them in a reasonably objective manner. I would argue that this is the way we must proceed if we are to answer, one by one, any reasonably specific objections to the thesis that the ideal of value-free science may be approximated within the social sciences. Complete objectivity cannot be achieved in any single study, but successive approximations can be obtained provided that assumptions are brought into the open and the rules of the game carefully analyzed and then made familiar to social science practitioners.

Chapter 6

Why Isn't Educational Research More Useful?*

Henry M. Levin

That our educational systems are beset with enormous challenges is surely an understatement. The problems of creating prodigious educational expansion of the 1960s have continued in the Third World and have been joined by the problems of educational inequality and surplus of educated persons in the industrialized societies. Questions have been raised about the methods of educational finance, the structure and organization of education, curriculum and teacher preparation, and in recent years there have even been challenges to the view that the schools can be used as an instrument of social change and equality.

In response to these dilemmas, many nations have initiated ambitious programmes of educational research and evaluation to assist in formulating educational policy. These programmes have focused on practical matters of curriculum construction, educational reform, teacher training, and use of educational technologies as well as the more general issues of ascertaining how youngsters learn, the effects of education on income and occupational status, the determinants of educational achievement and so on. National institutes have been created to coordinate and finance educational research and evaluation, and there has been an explicit expectation that a systematic and competent set of investigations can provide useful insights for addressing educational needs and problems.

To support this explosion of interest in educational research and evaluation, virtually all of the societies of both the developed and developing world have also instituted programmes for training educational researchers. The traditional study of pedagogy has yielded to increasing input from such disciplines as psychology, sociology, anthropology, economics, political science and statistics in the search for methodologies that will be useful for educational inquiry. A strong role in promoting these

* Abridged from 'Why Isn't Educational Research More Useful?' by H.M. Levin, 1978, *Prospects*, 8(2), pp. 157–166.

activities has been played by such international agencies as Unesco, the Organization for Economic Cooperation and Development (OECD), the International Institute of Educational Planning (IIEP), the Council of Europe, the International Bank for Reconstruction and Development or World Bank (IBRD), the Organization of American States (OAS), and many private foundations. These agencies have sponsored research and training projects for preparing research personnel and carrying out investigations, and they have sponsored conferences and publications for discussion and dissemination of research ideas and findings.

In addition, a number of large international research projects have been initiated by these agencies in order to compare results among countries. These projects have addressed such policy issues as postsecondary education, the comprehensive secondary school, educational finance, and lifelong or recurrent education. Perhaps the most ambitious of these activities has been the international evaluation of educational achievement carried out by the International Education Association (IEA) under the leadership of the Swedish psychologist, Torsten Husén. This particular set of studies examined the determinants of achievement in mathematics, science, foreign languages, reading, literature, and civic education among some 21 countries. To indicate the magnitude of this undertaking, the more recent phases obtained data from 19 countries using 14 different languages for 9,700 schools, 50,000 teachers, and 258,000 students. Nine major volumes of research findings were produced from the analyses of these data on such matters as the relative importance of family background and school factors on academic achievement for the countries that were surveyed.

Yet, with all of these developments and some notable triumphs, the initial optimism accompanying the expansion and improvement of educational research is beginning to be accompanied by a rising scepticism on the part of policy makers. Indications of this scepticism are reflected in such factors as the 'push' to make educational research more practical, on the basis that it does not address the most important policy question as well as the demands for more prescriptive answers from the researchers on major educational dilemmas. Perhaps even more to the point, educational research is having an increasingly difficult time in obtaining government and foundation funds in competition with other government services. In the United States, the National Institute of Education has been unable to obtain increases in funding appropriations from the Congress that would compensate even for rising price levels.

It appears, then, that educational research may be entering a phase in which it may be confronted with demands for justifying its existence. At least one question that is likely to arise is: Why isn't educational research more useful in solving policy issues? The casual response to that question might be that educational research will become more useful as its volume and quality rise. Improvements in the quality and volume of educational research are linked, in turn, to the expansion of funding, training of researchers, and research activity. But, in this article I will assert that the problem of 'usefulness' of educational research will be a continuing one no matter what the quality or level of research endeavour. Rather, the problem of usefulness is one that derives from differences in the contexts and methods that characterize the research and policy functions. Some of these differences will be described, and their consequences will be analyzed.

Educational Policy

By educational policy I refer to the formation of the direction of the educational system as well as the implementation of the decisions that are made in the policy process. Depending on the organization of education in any particular society, this process can take place at highly centralized levels such as the nation or region or at lower levels such as school districts, school plants, and even individual classrooms. At each level decisions must be made about the nature and scope of the educational system, personnel requirements, curriculum, funding needs, and other factors which affect the operation and the results of the educational endeavour. In this brief article I will focus primarily on educational policy at the national or regional level, but it is important to note that a similar analysis could be drawn for the lower levels.

Decisions at these higher levels are normally made by persons who are political appointees as well as by members of their staffs. That is, the crucial decision makers have obtained their positions as members of a particular government party, and their policies must be consistent with those of the present government. Second, such decision makers are likely to be found in one or two ministries that are charged with responsibility for education. That is, they have little or no control over such other areas as health, housing, economic development, taxation, or labour policies. Typically, these persons are not trained in education research, and the time horizon over which they must make decisions is limited to a particular period of relatively short duration. That is, they cannot wait long for an answer, particularly if the problem is pressing or if elections or other imminent political changes are near.

If this sketch of the role of the educational policy makers is appropriate, we might ask how educational research might be useful to the policy function. Perhaps the following aspects are important. First, it must address the particular questions that are being faced by the policy maker. Second, it must be timely in providing appropriate research findings in time for making the correct decision. Third, it should be written in such a way as to be understandable to a person who is not an expert on educational research. And, fourth, it should not violate the particular political constraints which are placed upon the policy maker.

The first criterion suggests that even excellent research that does not focus on areas of decision is irrelevant to the policy maker. In contrast, the most useful research will be that which contributes to the solution of problems on the policy-maker's agenda. Timeliness is also very important. If the decision horizon is a matter of weeks, then the promise of research results in several months or years is not very helpful. Accordingly, the ability to initiate and complete research in a short time is a useful dimension. Third, the fact that the policy maker will not normally possess proficiencies in research means that he will have difficulty in understanding the highly specialized language and techniques of educational investigation. Therefore, he needs to have research studies that are presented in such a way that they are understandable to the non-expert.

Finally, useful research will provide findings and implications that suggest actions within the political constraints faced by the policy maker. Research that points to the need to restructure major political and social institutions or that implicates exploitative labour policies of employers as the root of the condition of the poor and their educational condition will hardly seem appealing to a Minister of Education who represents the dominant political party and ideology. Moreover, even if he were convinced that the research was correct in this indictment, the ability to restructure society is quite beyond his grasp. In fact, useful research findings will tend to be those which reinforce the directions of the existing government and enable it to solve its problems with small and marginal reforms.

Educational Research

But how do these characteristics of usefulness to the educational policy maker compare with the nature of educational research? Educational research might be thought of as a systematic attempt to ascertain the impact of different influences and organizational arrangements on educational outcomes and their individual and social impact. Thus, educational investigations may entail the examination of the determinants of such results as academic achievement, attitudes, personality traits, and civic responsibility as well as the relationships between these characteristics and adult attainments such as income, work productivity, political participation, artistic accomplishment, and other aspects of adult life. It might also examine the relationship between educational and training investments and economic growth as well as changes in the distribution of educational opportunities and the distribution of income. In a broad sense, educational research focuses on the process of education as both a cause and a consequence of the characteristics of individuals, the organization and practices of the educational sector, and the institutions of the sponsoring society.

Educational research may examine the effects of particular types of teachers or curriculum on student achievement or the effect of ethnic integration of classrooms on cultural attitudes. It may focus on the appropriate ways to measure academic progress through the design of testing instruments for measuring personality traits or achievement. It may seek to determine why some schools indicate higher academic achievement than others or what type of system of educational finance will maximize opportunities. Alternatively, the research may attempt to determine how investments in education affect the growth of national income and changes in its distribution.

How are these activities to be accomplished? In general, there are four approaches, and each is utilized according to the nature of the problem. The experimental approach is used whenever it is possible to satisfy its requirements of allocating students randomly to different instructional treatments in order to ascertain whether the effects of the treatments will differ on the criterion of interest, for example reading proficiencies. Such an approach requires that it is possible to set out a study in which distinct treatments can be applied for reasonable periods of time to different groups while other factors do not change. Moreover, they assume that students can be assigned randomly to groups.

But, often it is not possible to satisfy these conditions. For example, it is rarely possible to assign students randomly to longer-term experiences and to alter systematically these experiences or treatments. Rather, it is advisable to attempt to ascertain the effects of existing educational experiences on students in the natural educational environment. In this case, a quasi-experimental approach is used in which statistical and other methodologies are used to attempt to isolate the unique effects of particular influences on educational results. This was the method used in the 'studies of international achievement' where an effort was made to ascertain the separate effects of home and school influences on achievement in different subjects. Such an approach is also useful for trying to determine the effects of education on results that take place much after the educational experience is completed. For example, many attempts have been made to explore the effects of educational attainments on earnings and occupational status by relating a large number of influences such as family background, educational accomplishments, and other relevant factors to the adult earnings and occupations of individuals. Obviously, it would be impossible to create an experiment in which we randomly assigned children to different amounts and types of education to determine what their adult accomplishments would be some 20 years later. By using a quasi-experimental approach where relevant influences are controlled statistically it is possible to approximate an answer to the question.

A third area of educational inquiry refers to analytical studies of a philosophical nature. This activity attempts to answer questions by setting out a logical framework that will enable one to see the implications of different premises, and it can ultimately be combined with one of the empirical approaches that was described above. For example, one might wish to ascertain an appropriate approach to moral education in a particular society. The analytical approach would begin with a specification of the premises of appropriate moral behaviour, and then it would attempt to connect these behaviours to specific educational experiences that are logically relevant. A fourth approach to educational research is the historical inquiry that attempts to link historical movements and events to the formation and modification of the educational system as well as the effects of education on social change. These studies seek to understand the process of educational and related social change through an understanding of the historical influences that surround them.

Educational researchers using these techniques are likely to be found in major universities and in specialized government agencies such as national research institutes. By virtue of the high level of skills required for carrying out research, such persons are likely to be highly educated with doctorates or at least some training beyond the first degree. Moreover, they are often engaged as instructors in training other educational researchers. Status in the field is conferred largely by both national and international recognition of the quality of published work, and a specific indicator of such status is the frequency with which one's research articles or monographs are cited by other researchers.

Although researchers may have strong political affiliations and may operate under stringent political constraints in certain societies, these are almost invariably less inhibiting than those which face the policy maker. To a large degree the quality of the research will be judged by a national or international community of researchers and scholars. And the acceptance of research results by other researchers will be the major professional criterion for ascertaining the quality of research.

But the nature of the research exercise and the training and context which characterize the educational researcher suggest some strong divergences from the needs of the policy maker. Recall that the policy maker would find educational research more useful if it were topical with respect to his agenda, timely with respect to when the decision must be made, understandable in its presentation, and consistent with the political constraints on policy actions. In contrast, educational researchers will tend to choose topics of research based largely on the longer run concerns of the research profession in conjunction with what appear to be important issues in education. But the choice of a research topic is likely to be both broader and narrower than the types of decisions that face the policy maker. For example, studies of the role of educational expansion on labour markets and inequality will tend to be broader than any particular decision that must be faced by the policy maker, while that on the effect of bilingual studies on the achievement of ethnic minorities might be narrower, even though both topics appear to have policy relevance.

Compounding the fact that even policy-related research will not be tailored normally to the precise questions faced by the policy maker, the timing of educational research is also in conflict with his needs. Typically, it takes a number of years between the initiation of a research project and its completion. The time requirement is necessary for permitting the appropriate literature survey and formulation of the problem in terms of a research design; the collection of data which often require extensive testing programmes or surveys; the analysis of the data using sophisticated statistical approaches; and the interpretation of the results. Only at this point can the study be drafted in a written form for the scrutiny of other researchers and interested readers.

Even after this lengthy period, the study is still not normally available to policy makers as it is submitted to other researchers to check for weaknesses or biases. If the results are particularly important, there will be attempts to replicate them by other researchers using other data. Only after a substantial period of time beyond the completion of the original study will the results be considered reliable enough to suggest for policy purposes. This heavy time requirement means that good research cannot be chartered by policy makers within the normal time horizon over which decisions must be made. Indeed, only by chance will the findings of a relevant study be available for utilization.

The complexity of educational research and the specialized terminology that is used to communicate procedures and results to other researchers means that studies will normally be written in ways that are not easily understandable by the non-specialist. Moreover, the fact that the researcher will be writing primarily for other researchers provides little incentive to draft studies for the use of persons without research training. Given the filtering process by which research results are reviewed first by other researchers, it is not surprising that the reports are written for a research audience rather than a policy one. But this fact will surely reduce the comprehensibility for research and research results for the policy maker.

Finally, the political and administrative constraints on the policy maker are not reflected in similar constraints on the researcher. It is true that researchers may be politically sensitive in their choices of topics and in the manner in which they state their conclusions if their own positions and funding are determined by the State. And in countries that permit intellectual discourse that fits only a given ideology, there will also be very stringent constraints. But to a very large degree the researcher will have fewer political constraints on his choice of subject, method and conclusions than will the policy maker. To the degree that the research demonstrates that educational problems are found to reflect the deeper malaise of poverty or repression in other spheres of society as many recent studies have shown, there will be little that an educational minister or bureaucrat can do. Further, the research may actually even undermine his position if it seems to demonstrate that present policies will not provide answers to pressing educational problems.

Conflicting Needs of Research and Policy

From the foregoing, I think that it can be demonstrated that there are some natural differences between the educational policy process and the educational research process that may lead to conflicts between the apparent needs of the former and the contributions of the latter. I have also argued that these differences are intrinsic to the processes rather than being idiosyncratic. Of course, the efficient policy maker might respond by saying that these differences are not intrinsic and that educational research can be made more responsive to the demands of policy by tightening the linkages. For example, to the degree that the State provides most of the funding for educational research, policy makers could set out a number of restrictions. Researchers could be required to address a specific list of problems. They could be given rigid deadlines for providing results. They could be requested to write their research reports for the non-specialist, and they could be coerced into presenting only those findings that are politically acceptable.

Certainly, there are elements of this type of coercion in many societies, and there will be some perceived restrictions on any research which is funded by the State even if the restrictions are not explicit. But to adopt the policies that were set out above would so corrupt the research process that it would no longer be useful for making decisions. Rather, all of these restrictions would prevent an honest inquiry of high quality from taking place, and in the long run the research function would become a recognized propaganda activity of the State with no credibility beyond that.

In short, I am arguing that there should be a tension between educational policy and research. They represent two different cultures with different requirements. The former is restrictive and decision oriented with an emphasis on the short run. The latter is much less restrictive and can provide the types of information needed for moulding the more visionary world of the future. Even though a Minister of Education is frustrated by a report that illiteracy and the failure of schooling for the poor is largely a derivative of poverty itself, it is important to increase the awareness of the government and of society about the basic relations between economic circumstances of the population and their educational welfare. That is, relatively independent educational research activity is more likely to provide a healthy challenge to prevailing and destructive dogmas than one which is completely controlled by the State and its ministerial apparatus.

One final point is especially important. To a very large degree it appears that educational research is expected to solve educational dilemmas because such problems are considered to be technical in nature. Thus problems of illiteracy, unequal educational attainments, educated unemployed and so on are treated as issues which are essentially amenable only to technical solutions. Given this presumption, educational research represents the investigatory approach that can provide appropriate technically valid answers. Many of these problems are not technical at all, but political. For example, Cuba was able to make a transition from one of the lowest literacy rates in Latin America to one of the highest ones in a period of less than a decade by virtue of a radical change in political ideology after 1959. Likewise, large numbers of educated unemployed persons will continue to exist as long as there are needs for large reserve armies of labour to keep labour discipline high for fear of unemployment and to keep wages low for the benefit of national and multinational investors. In this respect, educational research cannot provide answers to such problems, for they are political in nature rather than educational.

Chapter 7

Erosion of the Education Research Infrastructure: A Reply to Finn*

Richard J. Shavelson and David C. Berliner

Assistant Secretary of Education Finn claims that the public regards much of educational research with skepticism, associating it with either educational faddism or "pointy-headed intellectualism." The public holds these perceptions because, according to Dr. Finn, education research hasn't "produced enough findings that Americans can use or even see the use of", "has not fulfilled its role in the effort to improve our schools" and, he implies, has not provided people with "reliable and effective methods of instruction for their children". By reporting and not refuting public perceptions, is the Assistant Secretary agreeing with them? We think so.

The Assistant Secretary surmises, from the field's response to the Office of Educational Research and Improvement's (OERI) first field-initiated research program in three years, that education research is unlikely to change the public's and policy-makers' perceptions. Many proposals were "an embarrassment to the education research community . . . burdened with skimpy plans, fat budgets, dubious experiments, worn-out hypotheses, disorganized writing, missing information, and ungeneralizable results."

Erosion of Education Research Infrastructure

We disagree. What ails education research first and foremost is the federal government's failure, particularly the U.S. Department of Education's failure under the current administration, to provide political leadership and financial support for education research. The frail infrastructure for education research and scholarship — the people, institutions, and

* Abridged from 'Erosion of the Education Research Infrastructure: A Reply to Finn' by R.J. Shavelson and D.C. Berliner, 1988, *Educational Researcher*, *17*(1), pp. 9–12.

resources — that was built in the late 1960s and early 1970s has been severely eroded by this lack of support.

Dr. Finn's paper provides a concrete instance, even a declaration, of U.S. Department of Education's lack of political and financial support. In what follows, we contend that public and congressional support for education research is undermined by the Assistant Secretary of Education. This happens because he: (a) misrepresents education research's contributions to educational improvement, (b) misunderstands the nature of education research and its contributions to educational improvement, [and] (c) maligns the education research enterprise.... Moreover, his comparison of education research with "hard science" and medical research invites comparisons of financial support that reveal remarkable undernourishment of the education research enterprise.

Lack of Political Support

Misrepresents Education Research's Contributions

The Assistant Secretary claims that, "[t]o put it simply, our labors haven't produced enough findings that Americans can use or even see the use of." This statement is false. Research has made significant substantive and methodological contributions to education. Indeed, given OERI's meager investment in education research, the yield is substantial. Substantively, for example, the effective schools research has had a profound influence on school systems across the country. The eight concepts underlying effective schools — clear school mission; effective instructional leadership and practices; high expectations; safe, orderly, and positive school environment; ongoing curriculum improvement; maximum use of instructional time; frequent monitoring of student progress; and positive home-school-community relations — have given school systems a set of goals to work toward; a sense of mission. Other substantive contributions abound. The research, development, and validation of cooperative learning have benefited thousands of youngsters. Indeed, a government agency seeking 'good press' might also point to the American Federation of Teachers (AFT) program for research dissemination and its contribution to a reduction of discipline problems in classrooms throughout America. Moreover, educational researchers have provided methodological leadership in several social science areas. In psychometrics, for example, generalizability theory and item response theory have significantly influenced testing; the former especially in performance measurement, the latter in national, state, and local aptitude and achievement testing.

Perhaps Dr. Finn would have been more accurate had he pointed out that the education research community has not done a good job in selling its contributions: The contributions of educational research often go un-noticed. The Assistant Secretary doesn't do a good selling job either, but, unfortunately, his comments don't go unnoticed.

Misunderstands Nature of Education Research and Its Contributions to Improvement

Apparently Dr. Finn conceives that education research should engineer or cause improvements in education. Just as people want cures, not excuses, for AIDS, so too do they want "reliable and effective methods of instruc-tion for their children." But educational research cannot (and perhaps should not) be expected to produce anything like a pill or injection that will do the job; not in our lifetime, if ever. In fact, two programs of educational research provide findings that convince us that simple mechanistic concepts from engineering and medicine are incorrectly ap-plied to the field of education. Vygotsky, for example, reminded us that learning is a social event, and contemporary scholars of cognition inform us that learning is a constructive activity. With learning both socially mediated and individually constructed, we believe that prescriptions for education policy or practice are impossible; reliability of the kind Dr. Finn believes possible is an inappropriate criterion to hold education research up to.

We see this causal, engineering concept of education research in other places as well. For example, the Assistant Secretary points out that "over the past two decades, there has been a goodly amount of systematic inquiry and a flood of studies, reports, and recommendations, yet our education system has by many measures worsened." Despite his weak protestations about causality, Dr. Finn then reveals he believes causal relations are at work by his canard that the educational research commu-nity is responsible for not counteracting the decline of the educational system. Similar logic would lead us to conclude that the expenditure of enormous sums of money for studies, reports, and recommendations to combat heart disease has been worthless since the rate of heart attacks among women has been on the increase for years. In fact, the increase in the amount of money spent and the number of persons involved in that research endeavor is paralleled quite closely by the magnitude of the increase in heart disease among women. This leads quite naturally to the conclusion that it is federal and foundational support of research that is causing the increased incidence of heart disease among women. If this sounds logical then so does the Assistant Secretary. What we believe is that such arguments are specious and harmful.

Dr. Finn also appears to hold a somewhat narrow view of what counts as good educational research. Moreover, he may not have a deep under-standing of research outside of what counts for him. What counts for him, according to his article..., is applied research that deals with school level variables he perceives as having policy implications, such as research on the "dynamics of communities and governance of schools", "education productivity", and "organizational structure and building-level autonomy". This narrow conception may explain, in part, why he found so many of the proposals submitted to the field-initiated competition "so esoteric or minuscule that they would benefit only a handful of people..."

Maligns Education Research Enterprise

According to Dr. Finn, "We all wish that education research enjoyed the attention and respect given the hard sciences.... [H]ard sciences are assumed to make a perceptible difference in people's lives."...

The Assistant Secretary claims, by analogy, that the intensity he sees in hard science research is missing from education research. "Witness the world's top physicists assembling urgently in recent months to make the most of abrupt breakthroughs in superconductivity." Dr. Finn is perhaps inexperienced in the ways of education research because he assumes that only AIDS researchers (respectable "doctors" and "medical researchers") or physicists and engineers ("real scientists") work around the clock. How does he think education researchers work when in the library, laboratory, or field caught up in an intellectual or practical problem? Any implication of a lack of commitment by educational researchers is simply unfair. Dr. Finn, however, is probably correct when he says that we aren't "assembling urgently" on critical education problems. This is not from lack of commitment, but from a lack of financial support. Indeed, his own staff, entrusted with the monitoring of the nation's education research and charged with keeping abreast of the field, has been prevented from attending major assemblies of educational researchers, most notably some of our annual meetings.

We also find it unfortunate that the Assistant Secretary maligns us with his claim that we engage in educational faddism. What would one call it when a few hundred university professors drop everything that they were doing and convert their laboratories to study superconductivity? And what should we call it when immunologists, oncologists, internists, and others in the medical profession drop their current work and gear up to study AIDS? When a few dozen researchers turn their attention to studies of effective schools, follow contemporary breakthroughs in cognitive psychology, explore training in metacognition, study gender differences in school learning, or try to unravel the complexities of international comparisons, they are accused of faddism. Not fair. Scholars in every field follow both where the discipline leads and where the federal dollars are....

Lack of Financial Support

We are pleased that Dr. Finn is trying to garner more money for the Field Initiated Studies (FIS) program. Unfortunately the amounts being discussed are totally inadequate for the task at hand, even at double or quadruple the present allocation. Let us turn the Assistant Secretary's AIDS and super conductivity research analogies on their heads and compare his attempt to garner additional funds for field-initiated research with funding in the medical and physical sciences. As the nation began to worry about an AIDS epidemic, $252 million was allocated for research. In fact, we see 6.2 billion federal dollars spent for medical research in general. When a national need was sensed recently, the government quickly responded by investing $8 million for superconductivity research. Yet when this administration discovered a national crisis in education based on dozens of reports that documented serious problems with the nation's schools, the funding for educational research decreased! While 15% of the federal dollars that go to defense are used to support research, only 0.1% of the federal dollars spent on educational programs are used to support research.

The public statements about educational research that we think characterize this administration's leadership will continue to interfere with the wise use of public funds. Consider, realistically, what it takes to support quality research. The annual cost of a senior scholar and his or her research team of two half-time research assistants and a half-time secretary, including benefits and overhead, is in the neighborhood of $150,000. Because intellectual or practical problems of any significance cannot be solved in just one year, scholars look for projects with duration of, say, three years. Thus, the entire budget for the FIS program last year, all of $500,000, only covers what is needed to fund one senior scholar for three years!

Not only has the Department of Education not provided resources for senior scholars, in recent years it has not supported outstanding graduate students and programs of young scholars through fellowships, research grants, professional training grants, or the like. The absence of such support erodes the research infrastructure. This policy stands in stark contrast to that of the National Science Foundation. The foundation provides strong support for graduate students and young scholars, fully recognizing a commitment to nurture the science and engineering infrastructure.

Concluding Remarks

The education research infrastructure is people, like us, doing our damnedest to produce new knowledge and test educational innovations with the long-term goal of understanding better and improving education. As we accrue experience in conducting educational research, we get a better sense of the important questions to ask, learn how to do the research better, and teach what we have learned to each other and to our students. This infrastructure is built upon individual commitment and support, both political and fiscal, primarily from federal agencies.

This infrastructure has been gravely eroded by a lack of support for educational research. Very talented individuals and research organizations have left education research and probably will not return unless conditions change. The nation's schools lose when talented researchers abandon educational problems. These scholars prefer to enter other areas of inquiry (e.g., military and medical research), where their expertise is met with appreciation, not mockery; where their research findings are proudly hailed by the agency that funds them; and where there is some chance that their new knowledge might be used to guide social action.

A strong education research infrastructure might well have produced the number and quality of proposals the Assistant Secretary expected. The challenge for OERI, then, is to build a sound education research infrastructure out of the mess that currently exists. Perhaps what is needed is a Marshall Plan for education research. [The American Educational Research Association] is committed to maintaining the frail infrastructure that currently exists and stands ready and willing to help build and improve it.

Part 2
Models for Social Research

Chapter 8

Science and Behavioral Research*

Fred N. Kerlinger

How do we 'know' the world? How can we understand people and what they do? We can read about the world and people and learn a great deal. For example, knowledge of people and their motives and behavior can be gotten from poems, novels, and psychology texts. To probe deep into people's feelings and motives, we can read Freud and Dostoevsky. A second way to learn about the world is to have others tell us about it. Parents and teachers tell children what the world is like. Politicians, newsmen, and professors constantly tell us what they think we should know. Such knowledge is derived from authority; some source we accept as authoritative gives it to us.

Observation is another important road to knowledge. We observe the world and people all our lives. We use our senses to receive and interpret information from outside ourselves. I see a car bearing down on me at great speed. I jump out of the way. I have observed the car and its speed, inferred danger, and taken action. Observation is obviously a very important source of knowledge.

Unfortunately, authority and ordinary observation are not always reliable guides. Whole populations of people will read, hear, and believe what demagogues say. And it has long been known that most people can be poor observers of even the simplest phenomena. Let two people, for example, observe an individual make gestures, and then ask them what the individual did. If they agree in their observations, it will be remarkable. If they agree in their interpretation of what the individual did, it will be still more remarkable. One of the difficulties is that no events are really simple. Another is that observers interact with and affect what they observe. Thus observation is an active process that is rarely if ever simple.

Science developed partly because of the need for a method of knowing and understanding more reliable and trustworthy than the relatively

---

* Abridged from *Behavioral Research: A Conceptual Approach* (pp. 1–18, 279–305) by F.N. Kerlinger, 1979, New York: Holt.

uncontrolled methods of knowing generally used. An approach to knowledge capable of yielding reliable and valid information about complex
phenomena, including the complex phenomenon of man himself, had to
be invented. Absolutistic, metaphysical, and mythological explanations of
natural phenomena had to be supplanted — or at least supplemented —
by an approach that was to some extent outside man. The success of
science as an approach to knowledge and understanding of natural
phenomena has been remarkable. But understanding science and the
approach used by scientists has been considerably less than remarkable.
Indeed, it can be said that science is seriously misunderstood. . . .

The General Nature of Science

Science is an enterprise exclusively concerned with knowledge and understanding of natural phenomena. Scientists want to know and understand
things. They want to be able to say: If we do such-and-such, then
so-and-so will happen. If we frustrate children, then they will probably
aggress against other children, their parents, their teachers, even themselves. If we observe an organization with relatively rigid rules that
severely restrict the members of the organization, say the teachers of a
school, then we can expect to find considerable dissatisfaction among the
members of the organization.

Scientists, then, want to 'know' about phenomena. They want, among
other things, to know what produces aggressive behavior in children and
adults. They want to know whether frustration leads to aggression. They
want to know the effects on organization members of restrictive and
permissive ways of administering organizations. In short, they want to
'understand' how psychological, sociological, and educational phenomena
are related.

To give us something specific to work with, let us examine two
research studies. One is an experiment, the other is not an experiment.
[In general,] an experiment is a research study in which different things
are done to different groups of subjects — pigeons, rats, children, adults
— to see whether what is done to them produces different effects in
the different groups. For instance, an educational researcher may have
teachers write complimentary remarks on the completed tests of one
group of high school children and nothing on the tests of another group of
children (see Page, 1958). Then the researcher sees how this 'manipulation', as it is called, affects the performance of the two groups on
subsequent tests.

In a nonexperimental study, on the other hand, there is no 'manipulation', no deliberate controlled attempt to produce different effects by
different manipulations. The relations among phenomena are studied with

no experimental intervention. The characteristics of subjects, 'as they are', are observed, and the relations among the characteristics are assessed with no attempt to change anything. For example, when sociologists study the relation between social class and school achievement, they take social class and school achievement 'as they are'. They measure the two 'variables', as they are called, and then study the relation between them. They do not try to change one of the variables to study the effects of the change on another variable....

An Experiment: Massive Reward and Reading Achievement

A great deal of research has been devoted to how people and animals learn. One of the most well-documented findings is that reward enhances learning. If responses are rewarded in some way, the same or similar responses will tend to be repeated when the same or similar conditions occur again. If, for example, children are told they have done well when they spell correctly, the correct spelling will tend to be remembered and used subsequently. (The results are not so predictable if punishment is used.) The theory behind the research, called reinforcement theory, is now being applied to educational situations, sometimes with gratifying results.

Clark and Walberg (1968) wondered if massive rewards might help to produce better reading achievement of potential school dropouts. They devised a simple experiment to test this notion. They used black children, 10 to 13 years old, who were one to four years behind in their school work. Two groups were set up in such a manner [e.g., by assigning pupils to the two groups by chance] that it could be assumed that they were approximately equal in characteristics that might affect the outcome. Intelligence, for instance, is known to affect school work like reading and arithmetic. The researchers must therefore try to make the two groups equal in intelligence before the study begins. If they do not, the outcome of the experiment may be due not to what is done in the experiment but to one group's having an average level of intelligence higher than that of the other group. In the kind of research in which two groups are used and some special treatment is given to one of the groups, this group has often been called the 'experimental group'. The other, to which nothing special is done, has been called the 'control group'.

At the beginning of the experiment *all* the pupils were praised for their work. This was used to establish reward rates for the teachers of the children. (Teachers, of course, differ in the amounts of reward they customarily use.) After six sessions the reward rates were stabilized and the experiment itself began. The teachers of the experimental group children, the children to receive the special or experimental treatment, were told to double or triple the rewards they gave, while the teachers of the control group children were told "to keep up the good work". At the end of a 3-week period, the children were given a reading test.

Analysis of the test results showed that the experimental, or "massive reward", group children did better on the test than the control group children. This conclusion was inferred from a statistical test of the difference between the average reading scores of the two groups: the average of the experimental group was greater than the average of the control group.... [Thus,] it can be said that massive reward was effective in increasing the average score of the experimental group as compared to the average score of the control group. Whether one can say that massive rewards work with black underachieving children and should be used with them will depend on further research addressed to seeing whether the same results are obtained repeatedly — this is called replication — and testing reinforcement in general with different kinds of children. In other words, the results of one study are suggestive, certainly not conclusive. Maybe black underachieving children should be given massive reinforcement — but maybe not.

A Nonexperimental Study: Social Class and Types of Upbringing

We now examine a nonexperimental study. Recall that in such a study there is no experimental manipulation; there is no differential treatment of groups of subjects. We take people and groups 'the way they are' and study the presumed influences of variables on the other variables, the relations between variables.... [In general, a 'variable' is] some psychological or sociological concept on which people or things vary or differ, for example, sex, social class, verbal ability, achievement. A 'relation' in science always means a relation between variables. When we say that variables *A* and *B* are related, we mean that there is something common to both variables, some connection between them....

Psychologists and sociologists have done a great deal of research on social class and have found it to be important in explaining different kinds of behavior: recreation, voting, and child-rearing, for example, are phenomena associated with social class. Miller and Swanson (1960) predicted, among other things, a relation between the social-class membership of parents and the time they weaned their children. A sample of 103 middle-class and working-class mothers in a large midwestern city were asked how they were bringing up their children.... [Their results indicated] a tendency for middle-class mothers to wean early and working-class mothers to wean late. Whenever we can make an if-then statement, we have a relation. In this case, we can say, though cautiously: If middle-class mother, then early weaning, and if working-class mother, then late weaning. Naturally one cannot say that this trend is present among all middle-class and working-class mothers. This is only one sample, and the trend may or may not be present among all mothers. More research would be required to strengthen the statement and one's faith in its 'truth'.

These two studies have a number of features that are characteristic of behavioral research. First, one is an experimental study and the other nonexperimental. Second, they illustrate objectivity, a characteristic of scientific research that we will examine shortly. Third, their use of elementary quantitative analysis will help give us some insight into analysis and statistics.... In the Clark and Walberg study, averages were calculated and compared, and in the Miller and Swanson study, frequencies were tabulated and compared. These are two of the commonest modes of quantitative analysis. Fourth, the problems, relations, and methodology of both studies are simple and clear....

More pertinent to the main theme of this [paper] is what the studies tried to do, what their purposes were. One of the purposes of the Clark and Walberg study was to understand and explain achievement, or rather, a certain aspect of achievement, so-called underachievement. One of the purposes of the Miller and Swanson study was to explain weaning, which is, of course, an aspect of child-rearing practice. The words 'understand' and 'explain' have to be interpreted broadly. When we say we 'understand' a phenomenon, we mean that we know its characteristics — or at least some of them — what produces it and what its relations are with other phenomena. We mean that we try to 'explain' the phenomenon. We can tell what probably caused it, what influences it now, what will influence it, what it influences. It is important to note here that our understanding of a phenomenon is always incomplete, partial, and probabilistic. Indeed, much of our knowledge of the world and its phenomena, especially human and social phenomena, is partial, even shaky....

Objectivity and Scientific Research

We break off our discussion of scientific goals and purposes to discuss two highly important characteristics of science. The first [is] objectivity,... a methodological characteristic.... The second is the empirical nature of science....

While easy to define, objectivity is not easy to understand because of its subtlety and its complex implications. It is a most important methodological aspect of science ... because its implementation makes it possible for scientists to test their ideas apart from themselves. They set up their experiments 'out there'. The experiments take place, so to speak, apart from themselves and their influence and predilections. Instead of being in their heads, the ideas being tested are objectified, made objects 'out there', objects that have an existence, as it were, apart from their inventors. Anyone can observe an experiment and how it is done, it is quite public.

All knowledge of the world is affected, even distorted to some extent,

91

by predispositions of observers. And the more complex the observations, the farther away they are from physical reality and the greater the inferences that must be made, the greater the probability of distortion. When the physical scientist measures weights, for instance, there is a low probability of distortion: little opportunity exists for personal views, biases, and preconceptions to enter the process. But consider the distortion possibilities in the study and measurement of authoritarianism, dogmatism, intelligence, level of aspiration, achievement, social class, anxiety, and creativity.

Take just one of these variables, creativity. Even though you and I agree that we will study and measure creativity, we may have quite different ideas of what creativity is. And these different ideas, these different perceptions, can influence our observations of, say, creativity in children. A behavioral act that to you indicates creativity may not indicate creativity to me, and these differences in perception can affect our measurements. In other words, the actual observations of creative behavior can be quite different, depending on who does the observing, unless some method to make the observations is agreed upon — and rigidly adhered to.

Objectivity is agreement among 'expert' judges on what is observed or what is to be done or has been done in research. Suppose one scientist observes something and records his observation, in numerical form, say. Another scientist of equal competence independently observes the same thing and records his observation. If the procedure can be repeated with the same or similar results — that is, the scientists' observations agree — then objectivity has been achieved. In some areas of science, for example physics and chemistry, objectivity is not a severe problem because instruments of high precision, like electronic microscopes, are used to make observations. Such instruments increase the probability of agreement among judges because different judges, by using them, are more likely to obtain and report the same results. Moreover, a machine is less likely to influence the observations and to be influenced by the nature of what is observed....

Before leaving objectivity, we should try to clarify and correct an important misconception. Many people, even some behavioral scientists, think that objectivity refers to a quality or characteristic of persons. While it is probably true that individuals differ in degree of objectivity — considering objectivity to be a trait that individuals possess — this has little or nothing to do with objectivity in science. Objectivity in science is a procedure, a method, a way of going about one's scientific business. It does not mean that scientists are personally more objective than other people, though many of them may be.

This misconception unfortunately creates mischief. Certain critics of science aim their major criticisms at objectivity, saying, for example, that the remoteness and coldness of science destroy human values, and thus science is fundamentally harmful. This remoteness and coldness, it is said, leads to dehumanization of the scientist and the people affected by science — all of us. Scientists are even depicted as monsters, even more dangerous because they come wrapped in virtuous cloaks.

The argument is a fabric woven of nonsense. It is true — but not in the romantic way of the critics — that science is remote and perhaps cold. This follows from its goal of abstractness and from its criterion of objectivity. General laws, general statements of relations, are necessarily abstract because they must apply to many specific cases. The ideal scientific law is a mathematical equation not because scientists love mysterious and esoteric symbols and mathematics (some do, of course), but because a mathematical equation is highly abstract and general. If empirically valid, it can explain many different manifestations of the law or statement of relation. 'Frustration leads to aggression' is a broad general statement of a relation. It is valuable because it covers many, if not all, manifestations of frustration and aggression. It is also remote, maybe even a little cold compared to a teacher's or a therapist's description of a single aggressive boy or girl.

Abstractness, part of the power of science, is always remote from ordinary preoccupations and the warmth of human relations. This is by definition; it is part of the nature of science. Without such abstractness there is no science. So it is with objectivity. It, too, tends to make science appear remote and cold. It appears remote and cold because the testing of scientific propositions is done 'out there', as much as possible away from people and their emotions, wishes, values, and attitudes, including those of the scientist. But this is precisely what must be done. One must obey the canon of objectivity — or give up science.

The Empirical Character of Science

The empirical character of science is considerably easier to understand than objectivity, perhaps because it is associated with what has become almost a stereotype of the scientist: as a white-coated grubber after facts. It is true that most scientists are constantly concerned with 'facts', but we must try to replace stereotyped notions with understanding of the reasons for concern with factual evidence. By now the reader will know that the viewpoint of this [essay] is strongly influenced by concern and preoccupation with theory and explanation. Nonscientists can say that they too are concerned with theory and explanation. And that is so. Philosophers seek, for example, to explain how we know things. Historians want to explain the origins of historical movements and events, for instance, the causes and consequences of the Civil War or of the Russian Revolution. Political theorists seek explanations of political movement like the influence of conservative thinking on the actions of political parties and figures.

Explanation as explanation, then, is not the sole prerogative of science. Nor is scientific emphasis on evidence an exclusive possession. Historians and political theorists, among others, invoke evidence to bolster their explanations of historical and political phenomena. What, then, is the difference? Why is science unique?...

Most of modern behavioral science is characterized by a strong empirical attitude and approach. Unfortunately, the word 'empirical' has been used in two ways that are quite different in meaning. In one, 'empirical' means guided by practical experience and observation and not by science and theory. This is a pragmatic view which says that if it works it is right. Never mind the reasons; what counts is that it works. This is *not* the meaning of 'empirical' as used by scientists (though scientists are not unpragmatic). For the scientist 'empirical' means guided by evidence obtained in systematic and controlled scientific research....

[To illustrate,] scientific research has been directed toward determining whether it is possible for animals and people to learn to control responses of the autonomic nervous system. Can they, for example, lower their heartbeat or increase their urine secretion at will (Miller, 1971, chapters 55 and 56)? Both older and newer beliefs say that this is not possible. So, a generalization is: It is not possible for people to control responses governed by the autonomic nervous system. It so happens that the statement is probably not true: It has been found that animals (and perhaps people) can be trained to do such things as raise and lower their heartbeats, raise and lower their urine secretion, and even alter their blood pressure (Miller, 1971, part XI). An empirically oriented statement would be: Animals can, within certain limits, control responses of the autonomic nervous system, given appropriate 'instruction.' Animals can be taught, for instance, to raise or lower their heartbeats and raise and lower their urine secretion. It isn't easy but it has been done. These are empirical statements since they are based on scientific evidence.

Because a statement is empirical does not necessarily mean that it is true. Since it is based on scientific research and evidence, it is more likely to be true than a statement based wholly on beliefs. Nevertheless, it may still not be true. The above statement about learning to control the autonomic nervous system to some extent, although at present supported by scientific research evidence, may turn out in the long run not to be true. It may not be possible to obtain the same results next year or the year after, or in Australia as well as in America. It is possible that the research findings supporting the statement were the result of some temporary and unrecognized cause which was characteristic only of the particular situation in which the research was done. Still, the probability of a statement based on empirical evidence being true is greater than the probability of a nonempirical statement being true. Carefully obtained empirical evidence, as we will see, is a healthy and necessary corrective of man's beliefs and a salutary means of decreasing ignorance. Nonempirical evidence, on the other hand, can and often does help perpetuate ignorance, as old proverbs do. Empirical evidence, in short, checks our frequently unbridled addiction to making assertions about the world, assertions that may or may not be true.

The word 'empirical' is thus important because it indicates a way of regarding the world and people profoundly different from the traditional way which seeks explanations by appealing to authority, common sense, or reason. Is man basically selfish? We can provide quotations from the Bible, Shakespeare, or Freud; we can say that it is self-evident or obvious that man is basically selfish or not selfish; or we can carefully reason on the basis of authority and observation and conclude that man is basically selfish or not selfish. This is more or less the traditional way.

Scientists, however, are not satisfied with this way. If they think that the question is scientifically answerable — many questions cannot be answered scientifically — then they approach the problem differently. Although they may set up a theoretical explanation, in the back of their minds is always the nagging question: What will scientific evidence say? After first deciding how to define and measure selfishness, a scientist will set up a study or a series of studies to try to determine to what extent selfishness motivates human behavior and how it does so. He will then do the study under controlled conditions, and, after analyzing the results obtained, will state conclusions that seem to spring from the evidence. The evidence, then, is central to the whole process. Without it the conclusions are usually scientifically worthless.

Some readers may wonder about the importance of this distinction between empirical and nonempirical approaches. They may say that it is obvious, even self-evident, that one looks for evidence for the statements that one makes. Reasonable people will always do this. But this is just the point: they often, perhaps most often, don't. Our belief systems — religious, political, economic, educational — are indeed powerful, and *they* frequently guide our behavior, not evidence. Actually, to use empirical evidence as a practice seems to be very difficult. If it were not, many of the social problems that face us, assuming good will and adequate motivation, could be solved. To understand science and scientific research, therefore, requires a conscious and sustained effort that is not at all easy because the necessary empirical attitude requires at least temporary suspension of powerful belief systems. In other words, the first and final court of appeals in science is empirical evidence.

The Purpose of Science: Theory and Explanation

The purpose of science has already been stated. We must now restate this purpose formally and try to dispel certain mistaken notions about its goals. *The purpose of science is theory.* Let's look closely at this bald and rather

Figure 1 The 'small theory' explaining achievement in college

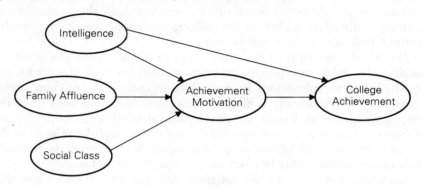

controversial statement. A theory is a systematic account of the relations among a set of variables. It is an explanation, usually of some particular though broad phenomenon. A psychologist may propose a theory of leadership of groups and organizations, or, like Freud, a theory of human motivation, or, like the influential European sociologist, Weber, a theory to account for modern capitalism, or, like the Swiss psychologist, Piaget, a theory of human knowing. Such theories are systematic attempts to 'explain' the various phenomena by postulating the relations among the phenomena to be explained and a number of 'explanatory variables', which are themselves related in systematic ways. The basic purpose of science is to achieve theory, to invent and find valid explanations of natural phenomena.

To try to take some of the mystery from the word, let us look at a fictitious example of a 'small theory' whose purpose is to explain achievement in college or the university. We relate four variables — intelligence, family affluence, social class, and achievement motivation — to college achievement in such a way that we 'explain' it satisfactorily. To do so, we use the ideas of direct and indirect influences. College students differ a great deal in their success in college, and we want to explain these differences. Why do some students do well and others not so well? We assume that we are able to measure all the variables satisfactorily. The 'small theory' is given diagrammatically in Figure 1.

In the theory, two variables, intelligence and achievement motivation, are direct influences; they are both assumed to influence college achievement without going through other variables. These direct influences are shown in Figure 1 by the arrows from intelligence and achievement motivation to college achievement. The other two variables, family affluence and social class, are believed to have indirect influence on college achievement: they 'go through' achievement motivation. For example, it is assumed that, in general, the more affluent a family, the greater the achievement motivation. Similarly, social class influences achievement motivation: Middle-class young men and women have greater motivation to achieve than working-class young men and women. Intelligence, in addition to its direct influence on college achievement — the greater the intelligence, the greater the achievement — has an indirect influence on college achievement through achievement motivation: the greater the intelligence, the greater the achievement motivation.

We have, then, a theory of college achievement, which may be a good theory or a poor theory depending on how well it explains college achievement. It is quite testable; all the variables are amenable to satisfactory measurement (though a theory does not necessarily have to have only variables that are measurable), and there are analytic techniques that can yield fairly clear tests of the relations specified in the theory.

Purposes of science other than theory or explanation have been proposed. We need not labor the more technical of these since they are usually deducible from theory as purpose. There is one alleged purpose of science, however, that gives much trouble and that has badly confused clear understanding of what science is about. This alleged purpose is contained in statements like the following, all of which are closely related: 'The purpose of science is to improve the lot of man'; 'The purpose of psychology and sociology is to help improve human society'; 'The purpose of educational research is to improve educational thinking and practice'. The sentiments behind such statements are indeed strong — and no wonder. It seems obvious that the purpose of science is to improve man's lot; it seems so self-evident.

The confusion has no doubt arisen because the *effects* of scientific advance have often enhanced human welfare — they have, of course, also hurt human welfare — mainly through improved technology made possible mostly by disinterested scientific research and discoveries. But this does not mean that the *purpose* of science is the enhancement of human welfare, just as its purpose is *not* to help in waging war. A more accurate interpretation is that the improvement of life can be a byproduct of science, a fortunate though not necessary outcome of scientific work and discovery. . . .

Much of the misunderstanding in many people's minds about research and its presumed ameliorative purpose has probably risen from confusing science with engineering and technology. We diverge briefly, therefore, to explain the difference.

Engineering is a set of applied disciplines that depend mostly on science but that are not themselves science. It is the job of the engineer to devise technical solutions to practical problems. In so doing, he uses technology, which likewise often arises from science but is not itself science. Technology comprises technical methods and materials devised to achieve practical objectives. The teaching expert . . . devises a method to teach concepts. Computer experts devise machines and machine languages, . . . to achieve solutions to analytic problems. The teaching expert and the computer expert are highly important members of the intellectual community. But they are not scientists; they are basically engineers, though, admittedly, it is sometimes hard to draw a clear line between engineering and science. The essential clue to understanding the difference is the basic purpose of each. The purpose of engineering and technology is to solve relatively specific practical problems. The purpose of science is to understand natural phenomena. It is right and proper to expect and ask for solutions to practical problems from engineers. It is not right and proper to expect and ask for solutions to practical problems from scientists. . . .

Basic and Applied Research

Again, ask the question: What is research for? [As we have said,] the purpose of science is theory, or systematic explanation of natural phenomena. Let us assume that this statement is correct. If so, then the work of scientists should be centered on the study of the relations among phenomena. In the behavioral sciences this would mean research into such phenomena as learning, memory, perception, motivation, attribution, occupation, religious preference, organizations, personality, social class, social movements, ideology, attitudes, values, and so on. Such research is called basic research.

Basic research has had many definitions, most of them unsatisfactory in one way or another. It has even authoritatively been said that an adequate or operational definition of basic research is not possible (Kidd, 1959). Nevertheless, scientists and thinkers and writers on science know, if often vaguely, what the term means, especially in contrast to applied research. In any case, *basic research* is research done to test theory, to study relations among phenomena in order to understand the phenomena, with little or no thought of applications of the results of the research to practical problems. Despite the possible inadequacies of this definition, it is adequate to help us talk about basic research. It says what has been said throughout this [paper]: that scientific research is disciplined inquiry into the relations among natural phenomena, and adds that it is not done to achieve practical goals.

Applied research is research directed toward the solution of specified practical problems in delineated areas and from which amelioration or improvement of some process or activity, or achievement of practical goals, is expected. So-called programmatic and direct research are applied research. Such research is directed toward particular goals that promise solutions of usually pressing problems. It is the kind of research often cited by newspapers when research is discussed, because it is easy to understand the rationale and motivation of applied researchers and their sources of finance. . . .

The people of modern industrial nations are strongly pragmatic. They like and admire what works, especially what works quickly and efficiently. This attitude, probably strongest in the United States, is a healthy one in the sense that things get done. If there is a problem to be solved, bring in experts for advice, explore past solutions of similar problems, but above all do something. If the something works, fine. If it doesn't work, try something else. But find something that works.

There is a kind of slapdash style about many American solutions to problems, but there is little doubt that solutions are tried, which is probably better than ignoring problems, or analyzing them to death, or hoping that they will go away. Unfortunately, a strong pragmatic outlook and attitude is both a friend and an enemy of science. It is a friend as long as people, particularly people with power, perceive science as helpful in problem solution. If, on the other hand, they perceive science as ineffective in solving problems or as remote from practical concerns, then the pragmatic attitude becomes an enemy of science and basic research. This seems to be what is happening in Western countries today.

In keeping with this pragmatic attitude, most people assume that research can and should solve practical problems and improve human and social conditions. The assumption is false. Research does not lead directly to improvement in practice or in human and social conditions. The solution of a research problem is on a different level of discourse than the solution of an action problem. The outcome of research is usually the establishment of a relation of some kind between two or more phenomena. This is even true of applied research problems. Take a relatively simple applied outcome like that of the Clark and Walberg experiment. Recall that massive reinforcement had a fairly substantial effect on the reading achievement of black children who were seriously behind in reading.

Can these results be applied directly to educational practice? On the surface, it would seem so. If a research study shows that massive reinforcement helps underachieving children read better, then encourage teachers teaching such children to use massive reinforcement. Unfortunately, things are not so simple. Does massive reinforcement work with children of other ages? What difference does massive reinforcement make when used by different kinds of teachers? More subtle, is it possible that the prolonged use of massive reinforcement might have a deleterious effect on some or even all children? Might it, for example, have the effect of ultimately crippling children's internal motivation and initiative?

So even a seemingly obvious and simple outcome of research that is more applied than basic turns out to have no certain implications for practice. If we take the results of many basic research studies that seem to have implications for educational practice, we find an even greater gap. In most such studies the gulf between study findings and practice is wide and deep.

Studying relations and taking action are on two different levels of discourse which one cannot easily bridge. Scientific research never has the purpose of solving human and social problems, making decisions, and taking action. The researcher is preoccupied with, and should be preoccupied with, variables and their relations. He should never be required to think about or to spell out the implications of what he is doing or has done. To require this is to require a leap from an abstract relational level of discourse to a much more concrete and specific level. This cannot be done directly; it is not possible to do a research study and then have practitioners immediately use the results.

The expectation that research should lead rather quickly to change in practice springs in good part, as mentioned earlier, from the pragmatic and practical orientation of people. They conceive the purpose of research as human, environmental, and technical improvement. Research, in this view, must pay off; there must be a return on the investment in research. Practical answers and problem solutions are demanded of science and scientists.

A strong pragmatic attitude, then, virtually forces focus upon outcomes and getting things done. What is good is what works! Why it works is less important; most important is that it works. This is, in science, a defeating attitude, because as Thomson (1960) has pointed out, "The best way to make advances in technology ... turns out to be to understand the principle" (p. 997). He has also pointed out that this idea is a recent discovery and has only recently become true.

Practitioners often have little patience with what they conceive to be 'impractical', 'ivory tower' research. They want research to be put to practical work. One of the unfortunate manifestations of this general orientation to research is an urgent desire and demand for research to pay off, to yield quick returns. To talk about research for the sake of understanding seems to many of us foolish, even pathetic. There must be payoff! This is a futile expectation. Scientific research does not pay off in any simple way because it is not and cannot be aimed at practical problems (Brain, 1965; Brooks, 1971; Dubos, 1961; Townes, 1968; Waterman, 1966).

How about applied research? Is the same argument pertinent? After all, applied research is by definition directed toward application. Shouldn't we therefore demand payoff from applied research? The answer seems to be a highly qualified Yes. One can *expect* payoff, but it is unrealistic to demand it. An example was given earlier. The direct application of the results of the Clark and Walberg massive reinforcement study findings, obtained from applied research of commendable quality, was shown to be questionable. A possible payoff of this study is its suggestion that massive reinforcement *might* help certain kinds of children. . . .

Applied research can, of course, be used to help solve problems, but this problem solving does not ordinarily lead to understanding the complex phenomena of behavioral research. [Such problem solving] frequently highlights research, theory, and methodological problems, but it is doubtful that direct applications are possible with the phenomena of interest in behavioral research. Its results, however, can *suggest* things to do. But as usual practitioners must do the things. The research results only provide possible support for the decisions.

Reading is a good example. Answers to reading problems lie not in many researchers aimed at telling teachers how to teach reading. They lie in research aimed at understanding the many aspects of human learning and teaching connected with reading. Such understanding is arrived at, if it is ever arrived at, by invoking psychological and other theories related to reading and doing research over long periods directed at understanding reading-related phenomena. Research on reading itself is almost invariably unproductive. We must study reading in the context of perception, motivation, attitudes, values, intelligence, and so on. In other words, the goal should not be the improvement of reading! It should be understanding of the relations among the many complex phenomena related to reading. To improve something as complex as reading requires understanding of reading and many related phenomena, a very difficult task indeed. And there is, of course, no guarantee of improvement in children's reading, even if basic research on phenomena related to reading is done.

The demand for payoff of research, then, is an impossible demand. It is based on misunderstanding of what scientific research is and is not. Its persistence testifies to its strength. Its influence, unfortunately, can be particularly disturbing to individuals who seek to understand science and scientific research, because it implants erroneous notions of the purpose of research and what research can accomplish.

References

Brain, W.R. (1965). Science and antiscience. *Science, 148,* 192–198.

Brooks, H. (1971). Can science survive in the modern age. *Science, 174,* 21–30.

Clark, C.A. and Walberg, H.J. (1968). The influence of massive rewards on reading achievement in potential urban school dropouts. *American Educational Research Journal, 5,* 305–310.

Dubos, R. (1961). Scientist and public. *Science, 133,* 1207–1211.

Kidd, C.V. (1959). Basic research — Description versus definition. *Science, 129,* 368–371.

Miller, D.R. and Swanson, G.E. (1960). *Inner conflict and defense.* New York: Holt, Rinehart & Winston.

Miller, N.E. (1971). *Neal E. Miller: Selected papers.* Chicago: Aldine.

PAGE, E.B. (1958). Teacher comments and student performance: A seventy-four classroom experiment in school motivation. *Journal of Educational Psychology, 49*, 173–181.

THOMSON, G. (1960). The two aspects of science. *Science, 132*, 996–1000.

TOWNES, C.H. (1968). Quantum electronics, and surprise in development of technology, *Science, 159*, 699–703.

WATERMAN, A.T. (1966). Federal support of science. *Science, 153*, 1359–1361.

Chapter 9

Paradigm and Practice: On the Impact of Basic Research in Education*

J.W. Getzels

The skepticism of educators about the bearing of research — and particularly of basic or theory-oriented research — on the operation of schools is quite extraordinary. Even more extraordinary is the skepticism of the researchers themselves about the bearing of what they are doing on the operation of schools. On grounds of assertions that research findings have little practical bearing on the actual operation of schools, support for research in education by foundation and government agencies has been sacrificed for other more 'applied' activities, which presumably have instant practical bearing. I shall argue that the substance of the assertions that research has little bearing on the operation of schools and the patterns of support for research that follows from them are in egregious error; both must be altered if advances are to be made not only in educational inquiry but also in educational practice.

My argument proceeds in four parts. First, basic or theory-oriented research can have powerful effects on the operation of schools; I would challenge those who favor support for applied activity at the sacrifice of such studies to match the effects of their work against the effects that have accrued from the studies I shall cite. Second, far from contributing 'only tiny "bits"' of fragmentary and irrelevant knowledge as is so often charged, basic or theory-oriented research contributes to the broad conceptions and fundamental paradigms of human behavior; thus it provides the crucial contexts and guides for the substance and method of education. Third, these conceptions and paradigms enter into the preparation of school personnel and, in fact, as the paradigms are altered, preparation is altered. Fourth, I shall show the crucial practical, and ultimately applied, function the university performs through its basic research in formulating

---

* Abridged from *Impact of Research on Education: Some Case Studies* (pp. 477–517) edited by P. Suppes, 1978, Washington, DC: National Academy of Education.

and pursuing apparently impractical problems: the definition of problems that might otherwise remain unpursued for being unformulated. It is this role that is being enfeebled by the unhappy confluence of financial stringency and the anti-intellectualism of funding agencies, which reflects their mistaken beliefs regarding the separation of basic research from practical application.

Effects on Specific Classroom Practices

Despite the belief that basic research has little effect on practice, the fact is that basic research can have powerful effects. Rather than argue the issue in abstract terms as has been done so often, I shall cite specific illustrative basic studies that have had manifest effects on our attitudes toward pupils, on leadership style, on classroom management, and on the nature of curriculum.

Effect on Attitudes Toward Giftedness and Programs for the Gifted

Consider, as a first instance, teachers' attitudes toward giftedness and gifted pupils (Getzels, 1968; Getzels and Dillon, 1973). Genius and insanity, it was [long] held, are related and "great wits are sure to madness near allied", according to the familiar verse. There was hardly a belief regarding intellectual precocity and superior attainment that was more firmly fixed than that it was either a pathological condition in itself or was promoted by a pathological condition. Moreover, it was believed that unless their intellectual precocity was in some way restrained, [gifted] children would come to a bad end since "early ripe, early rot".

[In contrast], Terman's basic research (Burks, Jensen, and Terman, 1930; Terman, 1925; Terman and Oden, 1947, 1959) [showed] that instead of being inferior, the gifted children were superior to other children not only intellectually but also physically, socially, emotionally, and morally. Moreover, their superior achievement in school applied so generally to the different school subjects that it refuted another traditional belief that gifted children are usually 'one-sided'. As for "early ripe, early rot", Terman's periodic follow-up of the original gifted children showed that they maintained and even increased their early superiority.

To be sure, others had held similar beliefs about [gifted] children. But Terman's basic research demonstrated what had previously been argued only as opinion. As Carroll (1963) pointed out some years ago, the attitudes we hold today toward giftedness and toward gifted pupils stem [largely] from Terman's basic research.

Effect on Leadership Style and Classroom Environment

Consider next the impact of the apparently simple little study by Lewin, Lippitt, and White (1939) on how children behave when faced with different kinds of leadership. The observations showed that behavior appeared to be a function of whether the leader was "autocratic", "democratic" or "laissez-faire". These are of course part of today's lore, and it is doubtful that those who use the terms give their source a second thought. Indeed, is there an educator who is not in some wise aware of them to this day?

None of this is to say that the vocabulary and point of view that were introduced by the study were necessarily as salutary as their adherents claimed. Nonetheless, I cannot help wondering whether dollar for dollar (if by no other criterion) many practical packages or prescriptions have had a greater impact on the schools than this little basic inquiry.

I cannot help wondering, too, whether many of the packages or prescriptions that had an impact were not indebted to the concepts and findings of basic research. Would, for example, the various programmed instruction and behavior modification packages have been possible if Skinner's basic research on learning and reinforcement (with pigeons yet) had not been available?

Effects on Curriculum

Consider now, as another instance, the effect upon curriculum of Thorndike and Woodworth's (1901a, 1901b, 1901c) research on the doctrine of formal discipline [in which] the training of the mind was seen as analogous to the training of the body. Just as muscular powers could be strengthened through arduous physical exercises like running, jumping, or lifting dumbbells, [according to the doctrine of formal discipline] the faculties of the mind could be strengthened through arduous educational exercises, exercises which need have no knowledge value in themselves.

In the now-classic set of experiments, Thorndike and Woodworth tested the influence of exercises in technique, devoid of content, on one's ability to handle other problems. The general conclusion was that while there was some improvement, it was not due to any "mysterious transfer of practice" or "to an unanalyzable property of mental functions", but rather to a functioning of identical elements in the practice series and in the final test series. The Thorndike and Woodworth experiments were [thereafter] widely cited by the curriculum makers and contributed to profound alterations in the course of studies of the schools. [In particular, they brought into question earlier arguments for studying Latin and Greek.] Good reasons for learning Latin and Greek remained, but their use as dumb-bells to strengthen the muscles of the mind was not among them. I would urge anyone who doubts the contribution of basic research to the practice of education to compare several curriculum texts or guides on the place of Latin and Greek as school subjects before and after the Thorndike-Woodworth studies.

Effects on Broad Educational Policy

I come to the second issue, the charge that even when it is productive, basic research provides only 'tiny "bits" of knowledge' and, as such, is irrelevant and without influence on the broad problems of education. Nothing, it seems to me, can be further from the case. It is precisely basic or theory-oriented study in its cumulative impact that alters the general conceptions, and ultimately what Kuhn (1962) calls the paradigms, of the human being and his condition, which in turn have an influence on the broadest educational problems.

Consider, as one example, the alterations in architecture of the classroom, symbolic of more profound but less visible educational policies, of our conceptions of the 'learner'. Almost within sight of my office are four school buildings. In one, dating from the turn of the century, the spaces called classrooms are rectangular, the pupils' chairs are bolted to the floor, and the teacher's desk is front and center. In the second building, dating from the 1930s, the classrooms are square, the pupils' chairs are movable, and the teacher's desk is out of the way in a corner. In the third building, dating from the 1950s, the classrooms are also square but the pupils' desks are trapezoidal in shape so that when placed next to each other they form a circle, and the teacher's desk has vanished. In the fourth building there is a classroom constructed in the 1970s that is four times the size of the ordinary classroom and has no teacher's or pupils' desks but is filled instead with all manner of odds and ends from finger paints to Cuisinaire rods. I shall refer to the spaces in the first building as the 'rectangular' classroom; in the second as the 'square' classroom; in the third as the 'circular' classroom; and in the fourth as the 'open' classroom.

Since architectural space or form presumably follows from the function for which it is intended, and since the function — teaching and learning — is presumably the same for all four classrooms, why are there then these obvious differences among them?

Empty Organism: Rectangular Classroom

At the turn of the century, the prevailing psychological conception of the learner was that he was more or less an ideationally empty organism associating stimuli and responses through the operation of rewards and punishments under the control of the teacher. In effect, learning was 'teacher oriented'. It was no accident, then, that the prevailing methods and materials and even the school buildings and classrooms were teacher-centered. Typically, the classroom was rectangular in form with the teacher up front — sometimes even on a dais or platform — and the pupils in chairs rigidly fastened to the floor in straight rows facing forward so that they could not turn away from the presumed source of their learning experience: the teacher.

How then did we evolve from this apparently sensible and practical rectangular classroom and all that this symbolizes in curriculum and instructional method to [other versions of the classroom]? Many factors contributed to the transformation, including changes in social and political thought. And the flow of influence was not only from the laboratory to the classroom; it was from the classroom to the laboratory as well. But an important factor was the modification in our conception of the human being as learner, a modification having its source not so much in applied research directed at specific practices as in theory-oriented inquiry.

Active Organism: Square Classroom

It became evident that the earlier conception did not account for all or even most of the behavior observed in the learning situation (Segal and Lockman, 1972). The individual did not seem to experience what he was to learn as discrete stimuli. Instead he saw apparently discrete stimuli as 'belonging together', as making a configuration or Gestalt. In the learning laboratory, three discrete dots placed in certain relation to each other were seen not as three separate dots but as a single triangle; two open brackets facing each other were perceived as one rectangle; even chimpanzees learned by perceiving Gestalten. And in the classroom it was recognized that two pieces of information given separately by the teacher were often brought together by the learner himself into a single idea not given by the teacher in the separate pieces. Experimenters in the learning laboratory were dealing with problems of 'perception' and 'pragnanz'; and teachers in the classroom, with problems of 'insight' and 'closure'.

Moreover, personality theory was postulating that the human being was not psychologically an empty organism. [And] in research studies, when individuals were asked to recognize equally ambiguous words, some of which were congruent and others incongruent with their values, they tended to recognize the former more rapidly and accurately than the latter (Postman, Bruner, and McGinnis, 1948); when individuals were required to learn material favorable and unfavorable to their persuasions, they later recalled what was favorable and forgot what was unfavorable (Edwards, 1941; Levine and Murphy, 1943).

The conception of the learner as an empty organism was transformed into the conception of the learner as an active organism. From this point of view the learner — not the teacher — was the center of the learning process. It was no accident, then, that the teacher-oriented classroom became the pupil-centered classroom. The teacher's desk was shifted from the front of the room and the pupils' rigid chairs were replaced by movable chairs that could be shifted at will in the new square-shaped classroom according to the needs of the pupils. To be sure, the teacher often lined up the chairs in straight rows, but the intent of the altered classroom was not to have *only* straight rows.

Social Organism: Circular Classroom

If the conception of the learner in the initial period was predominantly as an empty organism, and in the next as an active organism, in the period that followed it was as a social organism. As has already been pointed out, it is hard to overestimate the impact on the classroom of the leadership and group climate studies by Lewin and his associates beginning in the late 1930s. Experiments in the laboratory were concerned with such matters as "interpersonal cohesion" and "communication networks"; and teachers in the classroom were concerned with "sociometric structure" and "group processes". Learning became more "group-centered".

And if learning itself is a social or group process, then a circular or group-centered classroom where everyone faces everyone else is the most sensible and practical learning environment. Again, these alterations did not occur because of any particular study that contributed a bundle of prescriptions for immediate application but because of theory-oriented studies that contributed to a conceptual and strategic transformation of a more general order.

Stimulus-seeking Organism: Open Classroom

What about the present? How did we get from the straight-row classroom or even the circular classroom to the so-called open classroom? The preceding views of the learner had this underlying paradigm in common: They were founded in a combination of the homeostatic model of self-maintenance and the drive-or-tension-reduction theory of behavior (Getzels, 1964; Hunt, 1960; White, 1959).

There has been a growing discontent with this paradigm of behavior, at least as it is applied to learning and other forms of intellectual activity. One obvious feature of animal behavior, as Robert White (1959) points out, is the tendency to explore the environment, [but] discontent with the drive-reduction paradigm has not been restricted to animal behavior. Piaget (1952, 1954), Hunt (1960), Schachtel (1959), and White (1959) among others, point out that the central fact in the growth and development of children is not hunger satisfaction or thirst satisfaction or some other so-called primary drive satisfaction; it is the opportunity for effective interaction with the environment as manifested in the child's curiosity and exploratory activity. In short, recent research directed toward the *understanding* of behavior [suggests the presence of] neurogenic and psychic needs that are gratified by stimulation — needs for excitement, novelty, sensory variation, and perhaps above all the challenge of the problematic (Getzels, 1964).

From this point of view, the learner is not only a problem-solving and stimulus-reducing organism but also a *problem-finding* and *stimulus-seeking* organism, [and] the so-called open classroom is isomorphic with the stimulus-seeking paradigm of the learner and the inquiry-centered view of a desirable learning environment. Barth (1972), to cite a specific case in point, describes his attempt to institute such a classroom and gives as the first assumption underlying this type of learning environment: "Children are innately curious and will explore without adult intervention" (p. 18).

[Thus], conceptions of the learner — conceptions having had their source, at least in part, in basic research — do have an impact on what goes on in the classroom. Far from providing only bits of knowledge irrelevant to the operation of schools, basic or theory-oriented research affects our paradigms of human behavior and thus implicitly or explicitly influences the forms and practices of the classroom.

Effects on Professional Preparation in Education

Basic research and paradigms have an impact not only on practice but also on professional preparation of school personnel. In the case of educational administrators, as one instance, a comparison of the textbooks indicates the influence of research. Between the foreword to the first edition of perhaps the most widely used text in educational administration (Campbell, Corbally, and Ramseyer, 1958) and the foreword to the fourth edition a dozen years later there is a crucial change — from reliance only on the study of *experiences* of already practicing administrators to the study also of *concepts* of administration (Getzels, 1977).

During the first quarter of this century, emphasis was on "scientific management". Management consisted of "knowing exactly what you wanted men to do, and then seeing to it they do it in the best and cheapest way" (Taylor, 1911, p. 21). Numerous treatises and textbooks — those by Bobbitt, Cubberley, Strayer, and Reeder — applied the principles to educational administration.

What came to be called the 'human relations' view developed during the second quarter of the century. This view held that human relations were the essence of an organization and that everyone in it should "evoke each other's ideas ... and integrate their viewpoints in pursuit of the common goal" (Metcalf and Urwick, 1940, p. 14). Support for the human relations view came from studies by Elton Mayo and his colleagues, notably F.J. Roethlisberger and William J. Dickson (1939). Educational administration was further influenced by Lewin's inquiry into different styles of leadership. The primary responsibility of the educational administrator came to be seen as facilitating interaction in the faculty group so that "all individuals affected by any decision should have a share in determining its character and form" (Yauch, 1949, p. 16).

Although the principles of scientific management and those of human relations were often antithetical, they had in common the conception of administration as a vocation or trade, not as a field of study. About mid-century a different view arose that synthesized the two — the administrator not only must know what to do but also must understand why he is doing it. The central issue in administration became the synthesis of the personal or individual and the impersonal or organizational requirements in order to maximize the 'actualization' of both.

This conceptual shift moved the focus in the preparation of administrators from a *solution orientation*, in which experienced administrators gave prescriptive answers to how-to-do-it questions, to an *inquiry orientation*, in which theory-rooted problems were posed. There was a concomitant shift in the research and in the texts during this period. Most telling in this respect is to follow the introduction of new ideas from the research reports through successive editions of the same authors' texts for preparing school administrators. Virtually none of the texts before 1950 referred to systematic theory of administration; virtually none of those after 1960 did not refer to it.

Basic Research and the University

Asked of any other institution, what is it about? What does it do? The answer is relatively simple. The work of a factory, a store, a hospital, may be described as producing solutions to manifest problems — problems that have already been identified and formulated. The work of a university cannot be described so simply. The work of the university and its scholarship lies uniquely in making explicit that which is problematical, in exploring enigmas that lack formulation as problems, to say nothing of solutions. As Einstein put the issue, "The formulation of a problem is often more essential than its solution.... To raise new questions, new possibilities, to regard old questions from a new angle, requires imagination and marks real advance in science" (Einstein and Infeld, 1947, p. 95) and, it may be safe to say, in activity of any worth. This, then, may be the paradox: Research may have the greatest effects on education not so much when it attempts to alter an element of practice directly, as indirectly — when it raises new questions and contributes to transformations in the general paradigms of the human being.

Summary

My contention is not that basic research inevitably has practical uses, or that the practical uses of the basic research to which I referred have invariably been salutary. Nor am I contending that development of mission-oriented material and curricula is not needed, or that research deriving from immediate classroom problems — say, whether to use one procedure as against another in teaching a particular subject — is without effect. Such research and development are manifestly of value; they require no defense. But in light of the increasing number of assertions that basic or, as it is invidiously called, 'merely theoretical' research is of little value for education, coupled with the increasing sacrifice of support for basic research for presumably more practical activities, I contend it is necessary to consider in specific terms the view that even for the curriculum, structure, and administration of schools there may ultimately be, to paraphrase Dewey, nothing as practical as research that is "merely theoretical."

References

BARTH, R.S. (1972). *Open education and the American school.* New York: Agathon Press.

BURKS, B.S., JENSEN, D.W. and TERMAN, L.M. (1930). *Genetic studies of genius: The promise of youth* (Vol. 3). Stanford, CA: Stanford University Press.

CAMPBELL, R.F., CORBALLY, J.E. and RAMSEYER, J.A. (1958). *Introduction to educational administration.* Boston: Allyn & Bacon.

CARROLL, J.B. (1963). Educational psychology: Achievements and prospects. Paper presented at the meeting of the National Society of College Teachers of Education, Chicago, February 14.

EDWARDS, A.L. (1941). Political frames of reference as a factor influencing recognition. *Journal of Abnormal and Social Psychology, 36,* 34–50.

EINSTEIN, A. and INFELD, L. (1947). *The evolution of physics.* Cambridge, England: Cambridge University Press.

GETZELS, J.W. (1964). Creative thinking, problem-solving, and instruction. In E.R. HILGARD (Ed.), *Theories of learning and instruction* (Sixty-third Yearbook of the National Society for the Study of Education, Part I). Chicago: University of Chicago Press.

GETZELS, J.W. (1968). The nature and nurture of the gifted child. In R.E. COOKE and S. LEVIN (Eds), *The biologic basis of pediatric practice* (Vol. 2). New York: McGraw-Hill.

GETZELS, J.W. (1977). Educational administration twenty years later, 1954–1974.

In L.L. CUNNINGHAM, W.G. HACK and R.O. NYSTRAND (Eds), *Educational administration: The developing decades*. Berkeley, CA: McCuthan.

GETZELS, J.W. and DILLON, J.T. (1973). The nature of giftedness and the education of the gifted. In R.M.W. TRAVERS (Ed.), *Second handbook of research on teaching*. Chicago: Rand-McNally.

HUNT, J.M. (1960). Experience and development of motivation: Some reinterpretations. *Child Development, 31,* 489–504.

KUHN, T.S. (1962). *The structure of scientific revolutions*. Chicago: University of Chicago Press.

LEVINE, J.M. and MURPHY, G. (1943). The learning and forgetting of controversial material. *Journal of Abnormal and Social Psychology, 38,* 505–517.

LEWIN, K., LIPPITT, R. and WHITE, R.K. (1939). Patterns of aggressive behavior in experimentally created 'social climates.' *Journal of Social Psychology, 10,* 271–299.

METCALF, H.C. and URWICK, L. (1940). *The collected papers of Mary Parker Follett*. New York: Harper and Row.

PIAGET, J. (1952). *The origins of intelligence in children*. New York: International Universities Press.

PIAGET, J. (1954). *The construction of reality in the child*. New York: Ballantine.

POSTMAN, L., BRUNER, J.S. and McGINNIS, E. (1948). Personal values as selective factors in perception. *Journal of Abnormal and Social Psychology, 43,* 142–154.

ROETHLISBERGER, F.J. and DICKSON, W.J. (1939). *Management and the worker*. Cambridge, MA: Harvard University Press.

SCHACHTEL, E.G. (1959). *Metamorphosis*. New York: Basic Books.

SEGAL, E.M. and LOCKMAN, R. (1972). Complex behavior or higher mental processes: Is there a paradigm shift? *American Psychologist, 27,* 46–55.

TAYLOR, F.W. (1911). *Shop management*. New York: Harper and Row.

TERMAN, L.M. (1925). *Genetic studies of genius. Mental and physical traits of a thousand gifted children* (Vol. 1). Stanford, CA: Stanford University Press.

TERMAN, L.M. and ODEN, M.H. (1947). *Genetic studies of genius. The gifted child grows up: Twenty-five years' follow-up of a superior group* (Vol. 4). Stanford, CA: Stanford University Press.

TERMAN, L.M. and ODEN, M.H. (1959). *Genetic studies of genius. The gifted group at mid-life: Thirty-five years' follow-up of the superior child* (Vol. 5). Stanford, CA: Stanford University Press.

THORNDIKE, E.L. and WOODWORTH, R.S. (1901a). The influence of improvement in one mental function upon the efficiency of other functions (Part 1). *Psychological Review, 8,* 247–261.

THORNDIKE, E.L. and WOODWORTH, R.S. (1901b). The influence of improvement in one mental function upon the efficiency of other functions (Part 2). *Psychological Review, 8,* 384–395.

THORNDIKE, E.L. and WOODWORTH, R.S. (1901c). The influence of improvement in one mental function upon the efficiency of other functions (Part 3). *Psychological Review, 8,* 553–564.

WHITE, R.W. (1959). Motivation reconsidered: The concept of competence. *Psychological Review, 66,* 297–333.

YAUCH, W.A. (1949). *Improving human relations in school administration*. New York: Harper and Row.

Chapter 10

Social Policy Research and Societal Decision Making*

James S. Coleman

A common complaint of those who carry out social policy research is that it is not used by those in positions of policy, but left to gather dust on a shelf. At the same time, a common complaint of those in positions of policy is that social research designed to address questions of policy — whether it is research which evaluates a programme, social experimentation, or another kind of social policy research — is that the research as carried out is irrelevant to policy decisions. Thus both sides agree that social policy research is not used, though each places the blame on the other party.

At the same time, some social policy research does come to be widely used in ways that were not intended. In particular, it comes to be used in conditions where there is extensive conflict over policy and in which the debate over policy goes beyond the bounds of normal bureaucratic decision making. For example, the report, "Equality of Educational Opportunity" prepared by the U.S. Office of Education under the Civil Rights Act, was never used by Federal agencies in formulating civil rights policy in education, but was widely used in the local conflicts over school desegregation, both in the courts and in the school boards. It appears from these and other cases that social policy research is most widely used where there is extensive conflict over policy, and is most used by those without direct control over policy, who challenge the policies of those in positions of authority.

In the United States, most social policy research is initiated by requests for proposals (RFP) from Federal agencies. When the research is evaluation of a social programme that is the responsibility of the agency, the research is — in partial contradiction to the complaint about irrelevancy above — sometimes used by the agency to support its request for

* Abridged from *Educational Research and Policy: How Do They Relate?* (pp. 131–141) edited by T. Husén and M. Kogan, 1984, Oxford: Pergamon Press.

budget allocation before Congress. However, three serious questions arise in this pattern of initiation and use: (a) Does the RFP ask for research that will provide information relevant to *all* interests surrounding the given policy, even including that opposed to the agency's interest? (b) Is the contractor sufficiently independent to design and carry out research that — even assuming an RFP attentive to a broad range of interest — could provide information inimical to the agency's interests? (c) If the results of the research do not support the agency's interests (e.g., interests in budget expansion), will the agency use and make known these results as widely as it would if the results supported the agency's position? The answer to all these questions is sometimes toward narrowly defined RFPs, contracted for by captive or subservient research organisations which design, execute, and analyse their research in ways that will be most flattering to their clients, and resulting in reports that are buried if they would harm the agency's interests and used only if they aid that interest.

In the United States there have been other ways of initiating social policy research, most prominently one: The researcher submits an unsolicited proposal for research in an area which that researcher believes to be important. Most such proposals are submitted to agencies with a research responsibility but no responsibility for action programmes. The deficiencies inherent in this mode of initiation become apparent when one recognises that the principal motivation of many of the academic social scientists who submit these proposals is an interest in publication in academic journals.

The principal mode of initiation of social policy research is by the RFP prepared by an official of the agency. There appears to be no institutionalised separation between the bureaucratic interests of continuing or expanding a programme and the interests in finding out about its functioning or effects. Thus in a rather haphazard way conflict of interest may or may not be built into the design of the RFP.

In the United States, members of Congress are often suspicious of the result of evaluations of social programmes initiated by the agency of the Executive Branch which has responsibility for the programme, despite the fact that the evaluation has been mandated in the act of Congress which authorised the programme. This suspicion appears to arise principally from the potential conflicts of interests discussed ... above, which in turn result from the failure to have institutional separation between responsibility for implementing a programme and responsibility for obtaining information about the functioning of the programme.

Some research which evaluates social programmes is done for the purpose of providing ongoing feedback to those with direct responsibility for the programme; some is done to provide those higher in the organisational structures of a government agency with information relevant to major modifications in the programme or its very continuation; and some is done to provide information relevant to the broadest social decision about the fate of the programme, which is made in the open, outside a bureaucracy, often in Congress with extensive public input. In these three different kinds of evaluation, research interests are aligned in different ways; yet the finding of research of all three sorts is often done from a single point within the agency, which is not insulated from the bureaucratic interests in maintaining or expanding the programme.

If results of social policy research favour one side in a policy dispute, there is ordinarily no means by which the other side can challenge the research results before they become fully public and are announced in the mass media. When these challenges come after that time, the result is a public squabble exploited and expanded by the mass media to extend its news value, but with the result of destroying the credibility of social research for the public, as well as neutralising any impact that social policy research might have in this policy area. An example is a report for the National Center for Educational Statistics (NCES) which I prepared with two co-authors, comparing public and private schools in the United States (Coleman, Hoffer and Kilgore, 1982). The report was [originally] released at a large conference (of about 300–400 persons) convened in Washington in April, 1981 by the National Center for Educational Statistics.

At the same time, there was in Congress legislation pending for tuition tax credits for parents of children attending private school. Some social scientists were apparently concerned that the report's release would aid that legislation (since the results were generally favourable to private schools), and one organised a set of reviews of the report, some of which were critical, which he circulated in the hallway before, during, and after the conference. Although the report had been reviewed beginning in September, 1980, by persons inside NCES, by reviewers at the University of Chicago (where the research was done), and by outside reviews commissioned by NCES, the report went through no institutionalised process which was publicised and thus would have given all those with some expertise the chance to challenge the report before its release to the general public through the mass media. It is not clear what the appropriate institutional process would be, but in its absence the outcome is unsatisfactory.

A 'science court' has sometimes been proposed for resolving issues in dispute which have relevance for policy, not only in social science, but in natural science as well. Although such a science court has not been implemented or even fully designed, its design would constitute some mixture of the scientific tenet of objectivity and the legal tenet of interest representation. This involves both the recognition that the methods of science are designed to insure objectivity and replicability, and the recognition that research outcomes have different consequences for different parties according to their interests. Thus each party with legitimate interests should have the opportunity to use the methods of science to challenge and probe the results which go against those interests.

The simultaneous initiation of more than one research project on the same policy-relevant issue has been suggested by some to help insure the correctness of results before they generally enter the public debate. But again, as with the idea of a science court, no fully developed institutional design (for example, for resolution of differences between two research projects on the same policy related issue) exists.

The separation of social policy research into several stages, with different organisational structure for each stage, may be a useful way to introduce pluralism into social policy research without the duplication that would make such work prohibitively expensive. In the design of the research, and in the data analysis, it is valuable to have a range of interests represented, while for the data-collection itself (given design of instruments), standard field methods ordinarily make such insurance unnecessary. The Freedom of Information Act in the United States, which makes publicly-collected data publicly available, is a step toward pluralism at the analysis stage, but attention to enforcement and utilisation of that Act is necessary if its value is to be realised.

These [various] points show the absence of any well-considered institutional structure for the initiation and use of social policy research and show also some of the ill consequences of this absence for social decision making. In what follows, I will attempt some analysis of the[se] problems and some suggestions of how — in the United States context — institutions might be developed to address the problems.

The Separation of Policy Making from Policy Research

Social policy research that is currently carried out for the U.S. Government is initiated through RFPs from agencies that have policy responsibility, and paid for with funds from the budget of those same agencies. Separation of the social policy research that is carried out to aid Congressional decision making from the policy-making function of the agencies is necessary if the latter interests are not to contaminate the research, nor keep it hidden when it serves those interests to do so. The institutional focus for such research obviously should be an arm of Congress rather than within the agency. Two such arms already exist, the General Accounting Office and the Congressional Budget Office, and both have taken some steps in the direction of such research — although neither has the budget nor the responsibility to contract for such research from outside contractors. With institutional structures in which social policy research was carried out by one of these arms of Congress or a new arm created for the purpose, the use of social policy research by the policy-making agency itself to guide *its* decisions would still, of course, be necessary. This could generate in many cases two research projects designed to evaluate the same programme, an example of the two-project device mentioned above.

The Institutionalisation of Interested-Party Scientific Review Prior to Release of Research Results

Regulatory agencies in the United States have developed a practice of publishing proposed regulations some period of time in advance of the actual decision to impose the regulation. Hearings are scheduled in which interested parties are given a chance to present evidence relevant to the proposed regulation. This device has an obvious flaw, in that the regulatory agency is in the position of both judge and advocate (since the agency's own research is often challenged by the research results presented by the interested parties). However, apart from this flaw, the practice does provide an opportunity for challenge of research results by parties with diverse interests and other sources of data before any policy is established. An analogous procedure for social policy research that is merely being published or released is very likely a more complex procedure than is warranted by the potential impact of the research. However, some forum at which there was an opportunity for scientific re-examination of the issue before the research result entered into public debate through the mass media would seem to be useful. If this is done it is obviously necessary for the forum to be designed with full impartiality, and with rules which prevent its being 'packed' by one set of interests. I have participated in at least seven such forums, which have seemed to vary greatly in their success.

The general problem of institutionalising some form of scientific review which makes use of the special perspectives of interested parties prior to release of social policy research results that touch on sensitive issues remains an unsolved one. In most cases, research results will not engage the attention of the mass media until some time after results are released, and in such instances there will have been a period of time for review, reanalysis, and reassessment before the attention of mass media is engaged. But it is difficult to know in advance when a complex pre-release procedure is necessary, and when on the other hand it would be superfluous. The volume of social policy research is sufficiently great that review procedures that go beyond the kind of review process for academic publication could never be institutionalised for all but a very few research projects. Yet it is hard to predict just what those will be. For example, if the reports on public-private schools had been released in the Fall, 1980, attention from the mass media would have been unlikely and review procedures beyond those carried out by ... NCES would have been superfluous.

Perhaps a more important aspect of the prior review question concerns the danger of suppression of research results under a cloak of scientific criticism. I know of no general answer to this problem, nor even of a good set of principles that can guide specific cases. Yet any institutionalisation of review processes must be attentive to this problem.

[Who Should Have Access?]

In all that I have said so far, it is assumed that social policy research will be carried out on certain topics, and the central question has been the one of how to insure that the research results (a) get into the public debate and are not suppressed; (b) address questions of interest to all parties affected by the issue; and (c) enter the debate in a fashion that they elevate the level of public debate rather than misinform it or confuse it. Now I want to relax the assumption that policy research should be publicly available, and raise the question whether it should be privately held by the sponsoring government agency, or openly published.

I will begin with an example that illustrates this issue especially well. The example is that of negative income tax (NIT) experiments carried out at various locations in the United States. The first experiment was carried out in New Jersey and analysed by economists at the University of Wisconsin. The analysis focused principally on the question of labour supply: Would the negative income tax (which provided a guaranteed annual income) reduce the amount which people worked, and thus greatly increase the extent of economic dependency in the U.S.? The result was that there was such an effect, but that it was quite small. Those results were openly announced, disseminated, and later when the Carter Administration was attempting to pass a NIT bill, the Department of Health, Education and Welfare [HEW] called research analysts to testify before Congress, thus allaying fears of some Congressmen that there would be a drastic effect in reducing the willingness of people in the lower echelons of the labour force to work.

Another experiment was carried out in Seattle and Denver, and analysed at the Stanford Research Institute (SRI). Sociologists at SRI found a surprising result: The negative income tax sharply increased divorce rates and reduced remarriage rates. These results were treated very differently by HEW. The reports were subjected to extensive challenge, reports were buried rather than disseminated, and HEW did not call the researchers to testify before Congress. The results gained wide attention only after some members of Congress learned of the results and independently called for testimony on the results.

The possible reasons for the differential treatment of these two research results are several. One is institutional: The Institute for Research on Poverty (IRP) at the University of Wisconsin and the Assistant Secretary for Planning and Evaluation (ASPE) at the Department of HEW had very close ties, with some circulating membership; this was not true for the relation between ASPE and the SRI researchers. Thus there was a high level of trust and similarity of viewpoint at IRP and ASPE. A second reason was disciplinary: ASPE and IRP were staffed largely by economists, and the labour supply results were obtained by IRP economists. The SRI researchers were sociologists, and were using mathematical methods of analysis that the IRP and ASPE economists only slowly came to understand and accept.

A third reason, however, and I suspect the most important, had to do with HEW's government policy role: it was the designer and promulgator of the Administration's negative income tax bill. Thus it was interested principally in those research results which showed the benefits of NIT, or allayed fears about its harm. It was not interested in disseminating research results which would help defeat the bill (as in fact the divorce results, once disseminated, did). Thus HEW had a strong interest in preventing open dissemination of certain research results. In short, HEW was interested in the use of research results not primarily to frame policy, but primarily to help sell a policy already designed. This may have led to suppression of those results which were not helpful toward this goal.

This case of social policy research, and social policy research more generally, can be regarded as information feedback to guide social policy. The central question then becomes, who should it be fed back to? Who should have access to this information? Who should see the government-financed report on negative income tax and divorce? Who should see the government-financed report on public and private schools? Who should have access to the data on which these reports are based?

There are two models for feedback processes in a large society which give diametrically opposed answers to these questions. One is the model of society as a cybernetic control system, with government officials as the decision-making agent, and social policy researchers engaged in contract research as the feedback instrument. In this model, the decision-making agent, i.e., the government agency within which direct responsibility for the policy lies, frames the research questions necessary to inform policy, and the social policy researchers carry out the research and report the results back to that government agency. In this conception, it is entirely appropriate that the research reports on the negative income tax experiment go directly to HEW and become the private property of that agency, to use as it sees fit. It is not appropriate for the public to hear the results of government-funded research on private and public schools, nor for the researcher to discuss those results outside government.

This cybernetic conception of society, with social policy research as the feedback link in a sequence of action, has been held up as a spectre of the future by the sociologist Jurgen Habermas. He envisions as a pre-eminent danger a future society with a feedback process from policy effects back to policy makers, bypassing the political process and emasculating the class interests generated by the institutional structure of society. The vision is of societies in which there is "the end of ideology", to use Daniel Bell's imagery, governed by non-political technocrats informed by sophisticated feedback mechanisms.

And the feedback mechanism, of course, is this recent arrival on the political scene, social policy research. Thus in this vision of the future, social policy research undermines the normal political processes by giving the technocratic policy makers that most important weapon: information.

This suggests that social policy research aids the centralisation of power, helping to create a monolithic authority system. There is, however, a second model for feedback processes in a large society. This is a model of society not as one single rational actor, but as many actors. Societal decisions in this conception are not the product of a single decision-making agent, a government agency responsible for a certain area of policy. Rather, they are the outcome of a political process in which a great many actors, the whole spectrum of interested parties, press their interests via the existing political institutions. Some of these interested actors are in government, but most are outside. The policy is an emergent outcome of this political process in which the interests of many actors in society play a part.

In this model, the character of social policy research as a feedback instrument becomes very different from that I described in the other model. The research questions are *not* framed by a government agency; the principal feedback is *not* to a government agency. Rather, the research questions must be those of interest to the variety of parties affected by the policy, the interested parties, being mostly outside government. The feedback must be to that whole set of interested parties, who need that information to press their interests rationally. In this model, the feedback information must be a public good, with the full property of nonexcludability. For if the information can be withheld from any actor in the social system, that actor's interests are not informed. And as an increasing number of social policies come to be made at the national level, and as those policies come to be increasingly complex, rational response increasingly requires systematic feedback from social policy research. Thus interests which are excluded, in either the process of framing the policy research questions or in receiving research results, are increasingly emasculated.

The first of these two models, that of society as a single rational actor and social policy research results as private goods directly fed back to the government policy-making agency, may be termed a cybernetic model of societal decision making. The second, that of society as a multitude of rational actors, with social policy research results disseminated openly to all as public goods, may be termed a pluralistic model of societal decision making.

Often the question is seen as one of openness of inquiry, a question of the rights of the researcher compared to the rights of the policy maker. But I believe the question properly put has nothing to do with the rights of the researcher. It has, rather, to do with the rights of those in direct control of social policy, that is, government agencies, versus the rights of those who have interests in the effects of social policy, that is, those affected by the policy. What Habermas calls the cybernetic model places all information-rights in the hands of the former, the *controlling* parties, and the pluralistic model places all information-rights in the hands of the latter, the *interested* parties.

Some argue that the 'cybernetic' model is wholly incompatible with a democratic society, where information-rights must lie in the hands of the interested parties with social policy research results as a public good. But if that is the stance one takes, there are several points which should be noted. First, social policy research has characteristically not been carried out according to the model of pluralistic policy research. In particular, economists' conception of the role of economic inputs into the policy process is characteristically that of adviser to the prince, implicitly using the cybernetic model of a single decision maker. Nor are sociologists characteristically much closer to the pluralistic model in their policy research, for they ordinarily accept the policy research problem as framed by a government agency; and if they have less often acted in the role of adviser to the prince, it is because the prince has less often found the information they come up with useful.

More generally, if one accepts the model of pluralistic policy research (and I think there are some appropriate caveats to such total acceptance), then it is necessary to recognise that nothing less is being discussed than an augmentation of political rights for the population as a whole, to cope with a social structure that was not originally envisioned by the architects of democratic political theory. While these theorists created constitutions which insured freedom of expression and political representation of interests in government decision making, they did not foresee the information-asymmetry and information-scarcity which could exist in a complex and massive society. Consequently, they neglected to insure representation of interests in the acquisition and dissemination of information relevant to policy. Subsequent institutions have developed to help rectify this omission. In the United States, these are principally the institution of public hearings on proposed legislation by Congressional committees, and public hearings by government policy-making agencies, such as the regulatory agencies. Lobbyists are the principal sources of such information. But with the explosive growth of social policy and the concomitant growth of social policy research, complementary institutions are necessary to insure that the variety of parties affected by a policy not only have an arena for input to policy, but also a means for becoming informed about the potential effects of that policy on them.

James S. Coleman

It is, I suggest, a task of social science, probably consisting of a mixture of social policy researchers and political theorists, to design such institutions. I can only point out that our current conceptions are simplistic and naive. We need to begin from a conception of the political process in which the feedback of systematically gathered information plays a part, and in which information rights are dealt with as explicitly as are voting rights.

It is clear that the task of devising appropriate institutions for protecting citizens' information rights cannot be left to government agencies. To do so would be to give the fox the key to the henhouse. For policy-making agencies in government have an interest in releasing or withholding policy-relevant information to fit their policy goals, that is, in policy-relevant information as a private good. Rather, this is a broader task, one which touches the discipline of social science in two ways: as the technical experts who gather such information and as theorists who conceive of appropriate institutions to insure that information rights are as broadly distributed as voting rights.

References

COLEMAN, J.S., HOFFER, T. and KILGORE, S. (1982). *High school achievement: Public, Catholic, and private schools compared.* New York: Basic Books.

Chapter 11

Reforming Educational Policy with Applied Social Research*

David K. Cohen and Michael S. Garet

Social policy is becoming bigger business. America's drift toward the welfare state has produced a growing number of programs to extend educational opportunity, improve health and housing and establish social security. But as the business has expanded its problems have multiplied. Questions about the impact of social programs have grown. Controversy about the meaning of program effectiveness has mounted. Doubts about the right way to deliver and govern social services have sprung up everywhere.

Responses to concern about the effectiveness, management and control of social policy have run the gamut from administrative reorganization (service coordination is a leading favorite these days) to revised professional training (more emphasis on management, less on client relations) to political change (give clients more authority over the services affecting them). One idea whose importance has increased through all this has been that social policy can be improved by getting better information about it. As a result, applied social research has become a minor growth industry.

The idea that better knowledge produces better decisions is not exactly a political novelty, and the equation of better knowledge with social science is at least 70 years old in the United States (Lyons, 1969, p. 6). But reforming social policy on a large scale by changing the information upon which it is based is a recent development and it is one of considerable proportions....

Characteristically, while lots of money has been spent on policy research, much less has been spent on assessing its consequences. A few

* Abridged from 'Reforming Educational Policy with Applied Social Research' by D.K. Cohen and M.S. Garet, 1975, *Harvard Educational Review*, 45(1), pp. 17–43. (The research reported here was supported by a grant from the Carnegie Corporation of New York to the Center for Educational Policy Research. This essay represents the views of the authors, not the Corporation.)

descriptive accounts and some after-the-fact analyses, however, have shed some light on the issues. In general, efforts to improve decision making by producing better knowledge appear to have had disappointing results. Program evaluations are widely reported to have little effect on school decisions; there is similar evidence from other areas of social policy (see Caro, 1971a; Wholey, Scanlon, Duffy, Fukumoto, and Vogt, 1970; Wholey, White, Vogt, and Zamoff, 1970; Williams, 1971). The recent national experiments in preschool and early childhood education (Head Start Planned Variation and Project Follow Through) do not seem to have affected federal decisions about priorities within such compensatory programs (Elmore, 1972; Lukas, 1973; Williams, 1971; Williams and Evans, 1969). There is little evidence to indicate that government planning offices have succeeded in linking social research and decision making (Williams, 1971).

Our purpose in this essay is to explore these results. In general, we will argue that the impact of applied research seems negligible, odd or surprising because some commonly held assumptions about the relationship between research and policy are misleading.

One assumption is that policies consist of discrete decisions: Social research is expected to affect policy by influencing discrete choices among competing programs and methods. A second assumption is that applied research is more authoritative than ordinary common-sense ideas about social policy: Advances in the methodology of applied research are believed to bring corresponding advances in the authority and relevance of the knowledge available for decision making. Finally, on the basis of these assumptions, it often is argued that applied social research is justified because it provides the state with authoritative and objective evidence concerning the costs and consequences of social policies: Research is expected to improve the effectiveness of social services. Of course, applied social research sometimes is initiated for reasons other than an interest in objective evidence. Critics frequently observe that research can be employed to delay action or to add a veneer of legitimacy to decisions already reached (see Biderman, 1966). The main justification for applied research, however, rests on a belief that research will rationalize social policy.

In the sections that follow, we will consider these assumptions and attempt to assess their validity, particularly in education. On the basis of our review of the assumptions, we will suggest alternative ways of thinking about the relationship between research and social policy. Finally, we will discuss some tentative implications of our analysis for the conduct and justification of applied social research.

Research, Policy and Decisions

The notion that policy consists of discrete decisions is deeply embedded in thought and action. Evaluations, for example, generally are assumed to affect single decisions: Will the program 'go' or 'no go'? (Richardson, 1972; Wholey, Scanlon *et al.*, 1970). Even the language of policy studies is suggestive: books and essays concern 'decisions' and 'decision makers', analyses focus on particular acts of government. Of course, these acts exist. Administrative decisions do occur. Programs go and occasionally they don't.

But decisions are not the same thing as policy. Part of what is meant by social policy is a system of knowledge and beliefs — ideas about the causes of social problems, assumptions about how society works and notions about appropriate solutions (Rein, 1971). In the late 1950s and early 1960s, for example, a national policy concerning educational opportunity began to take shape. It rested partly on the idea that poverty, unemployment and delinquency resulted from the absence of particular skills and attitudes — reading ability, motivation to achieve in school and the like. There was also an assumption that schools inculcated these skills and attitudes and that acquiring them would lead to economic and occupational success. In other words, this policy assumed that doing well in schools led to doing well in life. Finally, the emerging policy, which came to be called compensatory education, assumed that providing schools with more resources would enable and induce them to remedy students' deficiencies.

A policy, then, might be described as a grand story: a large and loose set of ideas about how society works, why it goes wrong and how it can be set right. Such stories make more than mechanical assumptions about society. Compensatory policy accepted the notion that equality meant 'fair' competition within a very unequal social and economic order. It accepted premises about the pathological culture of poor people and minorities. It maintained that the schools, given adequate resources, would assume a positive stance toward the poor.

By characterizing policy as a grand story we do not mean to suggest that policy is fantasy or that it is disconnected from empirical evidence. On the contrary, there was much evidence to support compensatory policy: on the income returns to education, on the relation between delinquency and dropouts, and on the association between occupational status and educational attainment. But this evidence was held together, given meaning and charged with social purpose by larger ideas, assumptions and political judgments which were not empirical in nature.

The other part of what we ordinarily mean by policy has less to do with ideas, theories and assumptions. In this sense, the term denotes a developing set of public acts which have a common theme. Thus compensatory policy refers to the emergence of public pressure for improved schooling for the poor, to the accumulation of particular legislative and executive pronouncements, programs and actions designed to implement those programs, and to the organizational changes — new agencies, offices and citizen organizations — which ensued. In some cases these public acts preceded full articulation of the set of ideas discussed above, and in others they were made possible by a particular vision of social reality. Hence, policy refers as much to a collection of public acts with a common theme as it does to a system of ideas.

Now, if we ask whether applied research has an impact on policy thus conceived, the answer is different than if we ask about the relationship between individual studies and individual decisions. For example, the federal preschool policy which emerged in the early 1960s was premised on the idea that early childhood was a critical time for intervention. The policy emphasized comprehensive educational programs for disadvantaged children on the assumption that if the effects of poverty could be countered early, children would be better prepared to cope with school and adult life. These ideas were expressed first in Head Start and later in other early education programs managed by the Federal Office of Child Development (OCD).

There have been various evaluations of Head Start (see Bissell, 1971; Cicirelli, Evans, and Schiller, 1970; Smith and Bissell, 1970), few of which have affected any particular program or policy decisions. But there is some evidence that taken together these studies have begun to affect early childhood policy. For example, the Westinghouse–Ohio evaluation of Head Start and several smaller studies raised questions about the efficacy of center-based preschool strategies; together, this research seems to have had a role in diversifying OCD's programs. It also gave some impetus to the Head Start and Follow Through Planned Variation experiments, which were designed to test the relative effectiveness of different approaches to early childhood education (Wholey, Scanlon *et al.*, 1970, p. 79). These experiments themselves were major policy innovations, and their results, taken with those of earlier studies, have begun to weaken the assumptions underlying early childhood policy. The Head Start and Follow Through experiments offer relatively gloomy conclusions about the size and stability of Head Start's effects on cognitive ability. The studies gradually have eroded the idea that early intervention is most critical. They have raised serious questions about the idea that cognitive ability is the proper criterion for program success; and they have undermined the idea that preschool intervention can protect children against failure later in school (White, Day, Freeman, Hartman, and Messenger, 1973). . . .

These examples suggest that it makes no more sense to conceive of applied research simply as individual studies than it does to conceive of policy as isolated decisions. Even though individual studies typically affect no particular decisions, research traditions sometimes shape policy. . . .

One moral of this discussion is that the relationship between research and policy in education is often relatively undisciplined. This is evident in a general way in the loose and elusive interaction among applied research, climates of knowledge and belief and public action. One manifestation of this undisciplined relationship is a tendency to assess policies on the basis of fragmentary evidence from evaluations of a few unrepresentative programs....

A second moral of the story is that assumptions about social reality determine what seems to require explanation. Applied researchers and students of decision making generally have thought about the impact of social science on social policy in terms of the relationship between discrete studies and discrete acts of government. The relationship proved to be weak, but because the assumptions used the decision-study categories, attention was focused on explaining the weakness and suggesting ways to repair it. But if policy and research are assumed to be connected by gradual interactions between traditions of inquiry on the one hand and climates of knowledge and belief on the other, then it does not seem terribly important to explain the weak effects of individual studies on individual decisions. It seems much more relevant to explore how research helps to shape policy climates, to understand why the process works as it does, to ask if the results are on the whole desirable and to decide whether there are ways in which the process might be improved.

Methodology and Authority

Most discussions of how applied research will improve social policy begin with a critique. Information ordinarily available to decision makers, the argument goes, is not authoritative (see, for example, Caro, 1971b). It does not provide a believable and consistent basis for social action. One reason for the lack of authority is held to be irrelevance: The only research to which decision makers ordinarily can turn is the basic academic sort, and there is not much of that. This research may be quite valid in a scientific sense, but it is ordinarily quite irrelevant. It is focused on the questions university professors want to answer, rather than on the decisions which officials have to make (Williams, 1971). It also is done to fit professors' schedules rather than to respond to decision makers' needs.

The other reason for the lack of authority is invalidity. The chief information which decision makers have at hand is anecdotal data about programs and projects. This is quite relevant to programs and policies, but it tends to be inconsistent, impressionistic and self-serving. Therefore it is typically not valid (see Houston, 1972). Since the information available to decision makers is generally irrelevant or invalid, either it has little effect on decisions or it is misleading. Or so the critique goes.

Applied research is expected to remedy this problem in two ways. One is to substitute valid scientific evidence for impressions, stories and personal testimony. The other is to substitute research relevant to decisions for research oriented to theories. For these reasons it is assumed that applied research will be more authoritative and more influential in the decision process (National Academy of Sciences, 1969, p. 93).

One can hardly argue with the idea that applied research is more decision oriented, or with the notion that in certain important respects it has greater validity than anecdotal reports. But there are reasons to doubt that relevance and methodological sophistication lead in any regular or consistent way to knowledge which is more authoritative for policy purposes. Often there is no connection between relevance, methodological sophistication and authoritativeness, and sometimes there is a negative relationship.

There are two large reasons for this. One springs from the fact that a great deal of applied research focuses on the outcomes of social action programs. The characteristics of such programs virtually guarantee that evaluation research will be confusing or counterintuitive, or both. The other reason involves the internal logic of applied research. Competing conceptions of methodology and validity ensure conflicting interpretations of the results of applied research. Improvements in methodology often make issues seem increasingly technical and arcane; and the very core of what is to be explained often appears to change in the course of the research.

The Character of Social Action Programs

Most social interventions are broad-aim programs which seek to affect multiple areas of human conduct and social organization (Weiss and Rein, 1970). First, social problems seem broad, and it makes sense that ameliorative programs should reflect this. Second, theories on which social interventions are based are usually not well defined and there is only imprecise evidence about how problems arise, how society works and how particular solutions might help (Warren, 1971). Finally, most social programs are rather weak treatments. That is, they represent only marginal adjustments in established institutions and deeply rooted social systems (Porter, Warner and Porter, 1973, pp. 84–87).

The first of these conditions means that the aims of programs and policies have a paradoxical quality. They are broad and vague and frequently embody conflicting ideas, but they nonetheless have considerable social face validity. Compensatory school programs, for example, are variously thought to be aimed at raising test scores, improving self-concept, getting funds to hard-pressed city schools and reducing racial conflict in education. Most of these goals defy valid measurement and some of them may contradict others. But almost all of them seem plausible.

Given such broad and diverse aims, program evaluations tend to produce confusing or conflicting results. In the case of compensatory education, local project evaluations sometimes reported discouraging results on academic achievement but hopeful results on measures of self-concept. Sometimes they reported the reverse. Sometimes they reported discouraging results on both sorts of measures, but big improvements in students' self-reports of attitudes toward school. Sometimes the results on all such measures were negative, but teachers and parents reported vastly enhanced school-community relations (Cohen, 1975). Each of these outcome areas seemed socially important in itself, and taken all together they had considerable appeal. But the evaluation results were so inconsistent that the net result was confusion — discouragement over negative results on one outcome was always met with assertions that some other outcome may have been better. Rather than providing clear evidence for program decisions, such results tend to discourage the idea that evaluation reports are useful (McLaughlin, 1973).

A second characteristic of social programs that often makes applied research findings seem counterintuitive is that the diagnoses of social problems and the assumptions on which programs rest are themselves often incorrect. There is, for example, a large body of research on efforts to anticipate and treat juvenile delinquency. Studies generally have shown that prediction is not easy, that rehabilitation often does not work and that programs do not seem to be differentially effective. One traditional response to this has been to criticize existing studies for their poor design. Another has been to call for better research. Still another has been to urge greater expenditures on detection, treatment and rehabilitation on the grounds that this would produce sharper program effects. Some investigators, however, have begun to question the definitions of deviance on which delinquency policy rests. They argue that the categories of deviance central to both delinquency policy and research on it are rooted largely in moralistic rejection of lower-class minority cultures (see Platt, 1969).

Research which records the persistent ineffectiveness of various favored social remedies, and which is therefore rejected as nonauthoritative, may therefore be mute evidence for weak assumptions underlying the policy in question. In such instances faulty premises behind the policies rather than methodological defects in the studies make research seem counterintuitive and lacking authority for policy.

The third relevant attribute of most social action programs is their relative marginality. While they often seem like major accomplishments to their sponsors or advocates, such programs generally represent only a modest change at the point of delivery. In education, for example, compensatory programs represented a major national reform but resulted in only small changes at the local level. Compensatory programs certainly were not central to the budgets of most school systems. Organizationally they represented a rather small adjustment to firmly established institutions: Standard operating procedures, established interest groups, and professional and pedagogical routines were little affected (Porter *et al.*,

David K. Cohen and Michael S. Garet

1973). Besides, schools are but one public institution charged with achieving equality in a society dominated by private institutions which do not
share this aim.

The marginality of such social intervention programs means that
evaluations typically reveal no dramatic effects. The effects reported in
most local compensatory program evaluations, for example, were neither
statistically nor educationally significant (Wargo, Campeau and Tallmadge,
1971). While this made sense to analysts after a bit of reflection, it seemed
odd to national program administrators and members of Congress, who
knew perfectly well that Title I of the 1965 ESEA was a major reform in
education, the result of years of painful legislative struggle. As a result
they were irritated by the evaluations and found them in conflict with
common sense (McLaughlin, 1973)....

When compensatory program evaluations seem to show that schooling doesn't make a difference, observers are inclined to think there must
be something wrong with the evaluations. As a result the authority of
the research suffers, rather than (or as well as) the authority of the
programs....

The Nature of Applied Research

The lack of authority of applied research stems not only from the character
of social programs but also from the nature of the research process itself.
One reason for this is that there are strongly competing conceptions of
methodology, and methodologically superior knowledge is often more
complex, arcane and hard to interpret. A second reason is that in the
course of research the very questions addressed seem to change in
unexpected ways.

Methodological diversity is a phenomenon endlessly familiar to
academic researchers, and they know that its basis is partly technical and
partly a matter of what researchers feel it is most important to explain (see
Charlesworth, 1972; White, Bissell and Golenski, 1972). Research on
school effects, for example, has been carried out variously by economists,
sociologists and education researchers (who were mostly trained as
psychologists). Economists are in the habit of asking a particular sort of
question: "All other things being equal, what will be the effect of changing
one influence on a system of production?" They are, of course, addicted to
answering this question in monetary terms whenever possible. Their
approach is particularly suited to calculating the costs and returns associated with one particular course of action or another. In the case of
research on school effects, this question has been translated into a continuing preoccupation with the income returns to schooling. Recently it
has been expressed in a fondness for looking at unstandardized regression

coefficients using school resources as independent variables and academic achievement as the outcome. Such statistics enable economists to estimate the return in test points that increments in each school resource would produce, if other factors were held constant.

Sociologists have a somewhat different research style. They are more concerned with understanding the interplay of forces in complex systems and, as a result, they are fond of asking an equally interesting but substantially less particular question: "What is the relative importance of the influences operating within a given social system?" In recent studies of school effects, sociologists have looked at the same sort of regression analyses economists have used, but they have examined a different statistic, the standardized regression coefficient. Unlike their unstandardized counterparts, which economists use to inspect the heft of individual production factors, the standardized coefficients allow observers to compare the relative importance of different variables to the same criterion, all at the same time. Like returns to schooling, this is hardly a trivial question for those concerned with public policy, but it is not pointed sharply at a particular production factor which managers might want to manipulate. The question is pointed, as it were, at everything.

Thus, we have one fairly sophisticated methodology for analyzing schools' impact on achievement. We have two statistics arising from it which answer two quite different questions. Ordinarily such differences are politely contained within the ivied boundaries of academic departments, with no worse result than snide comments over cocktails. But as James Coleman (1972) has pointed out, when the schools' effect on achievement became a major public issue roughly a decade ago, the result was a veritable Fourth-of-July display of statistical argument and methodological fencing....

As a result, something more is now understood about how schooling affects achievement, income and other outcomes (compare, for example, Sexton, 1961 with Jencks, Smith, Bane, Cohen, Gintis, Heyns, and Michelson, 1972). Still more is understood about how to analyze these issues. But methodological sophistication has not in the least reduced substantive disagreement over the meaning of research results. Quite the contrary. It has refined technical issues, pressed them to higher levels and made at least some people more self-conscious about what the issues imply. This is an advance in knowledge. It is not, however, an advance which has produced any noticeable convergence, either in the sorts of questions being asked, in the techniques with which answers are provided, or in the answers themselves.

In fact, it seems plain that applied research on the effects of schooling is more complex and difficult to interpret now than it was a decade ago. Improving applied research has produced paradoxical results: knowledge which is better by any scientific standard, no more authoritative by any political standard and often more mystifying by any reasonable public standard. Methodological conflict, then, accompanied by growing technical complexity, is one important reason applied research has failed to produce much authoritative knowledge for decisions.

A second reason applied research has not lived up to expectations is that the very questions thought to need scientific explanation and analysis often change in unpredictable ways in the course of research. Consider once again the study of school effects. Midway through the last decade several major research efforts and many compensatory-program evaluations were undertaken. Investigators needed instruments to measure school effects, and usually they needed them very quickly. Nearly everyone thought that existing norm-referenced tests of generalized intelligence and achievement were appropriate for this task. Even when there were doubts, and there were at least a few, there seemed to be no alternatives (Wholey, White *et al.*, 1970). The tests were used.

To the researchers' dismay, these studies indicated that schools and special programs had little impact on achievement. Instead of accepting these findings as the answer to their questions about school effects, researchers began to wonder about the tests themselves. If programs showed poor effects, they reasoned, there must be something wrong with the ways the effects were measured rather than with the way the programs were mounted.

One result was growing doubt that tests could provide any socially useful information about school effects. Standardized tests, after all, were constructed to rank individuals with respect to norms despite curricular variation (see Popham, 1971). Perhaps instruments designed in this way are inappropriate for studies which assess and compare different schools and curricula (Mosher, 1974). Furthermore, one might imagine that good tests would measure things that society finds useful, such as skills that are important to jobs. However, studies show that workers with high test scores are no more productive, no less frequently absent and no more highly rated by their supervisors than workers with low scores (Berg, 1970). Moreover, among people with roughly the same educational attainment, those with higher scores do not wind up with better jobs or more money (Jencks *et al.*, 1972). Finally, there were complaints and some evidence that existing tests were culturally biased (Ells, David, Havighurst, Herrick and Tyler, 1951; Mercer, 1974).

This is a troublesome collection of problems. If tests by design do not reflect curricular differences, how can they be used to assess the relative impact of different curricula? If tests do not measure things important in getting ahead in the world, what in the world do they measure? And if tests are biased against the students which programs are designed to help, how can they give a meaningful estimate of program effects? ...

Thus one result of applied research in this situation was the discovery that previous ways of asking and answering questions about social policy were either doubtful or mistaken. Another was a slow groping toward different questions. What seemed to be the central issues for policy-oriented research in 1966 no longer seem the central issues in 1975. The old issues remain, but the authority of research aimed at resolving them has eroded. Basic questions about an entire field of policy-oriented research have been raised and new lines of inquiry generated, even as the old issues and approaches retain much force. . . .

One moral of this discussion of the authority of applied research is that while such research often produces important learning, it is not authoritative for policy. New insights, better techniques and important findings often bubble to the surface as research churns along in the wake of social action. Sometimes the results are astringent and complicating. Sometimes they are confusing and counterintuitive. Occasionally they are clarifying for action. But in education, at least, it is rare that they provide evidence that is politically authoritative. . . .

The other moral has to do with explaining this puzzle. If, as has generally been the case, we assume that the relevance and methodological soundness of research will influence its authority and usefulness, then it will seem important to explain why there seems to be such a modest relation between good policy-oriented research and decisions. . . .

If, on the other hand, one assumes that the character of applied research and social programs is such that better knowledge typically will not be more authoritative for decisions, then attention will be focused elsewhere, perhaps on the nature of social learning itself. With this in mind, we might ask whether the learning that results from applied research is cumulative, cyclical, or ephemeral. . . .

The Justification of Applied Social Research

To assume that research affects policy by clarifying the basis for particular decisions is to assert that researchers are engaged in the practical business of improving government by illuminating the costs and consequences of public action. The utility of such work seems almost self-evident. To assume that research has its effect mostly on loose systems of knowledge and belief, however, is to assert that researchers are part of a vague and undisciplined process by which inquiry has intermittent and often unforeseeable effects on public purposes. The utility of such work is plainly open to question.

Assumptions about the relationship between research and policy contain or imply ideas about how researchers might explain and justify their work. Most prominent in this connection has been the notion that social science will improve social policy by increasing and improving the objective evidence available to policy makers. In some cases researchers seem to think that their work will reduce conflict; they argue that enlarging the areas of factual agreement about issues will reduce the volume of disputed opinions and ideas (see, for example, Likert and Lippitt, 1953). In other cases researchers are more modest; they believe that policy-oriented research can be expected only to sharpen issues and increase self-consciousness in the decision process (Suchman, 1972). If analysis works as it ought, they argue, all parties to any given decision would be made aware of what their positions mean and what they might imply in practice. Their underlying expectation is that parties will behave more rationally, in the instrumental sense of acting in consonance with their interests, if they are better informed.

In either case, ideas about the importance of research vary considerably: Some proponents of policy analysis maintain that applied research is simply one of many influences on social policy; others give research a more central position (compare Schultze, 1968 with Campbell, 1971). But there is broad agreement that the value of applied research lies in its ability to clarify policy goals and to provide objective evidence concerning the appropriateness of alternative means for achieving chosen ends (see Gouldner, 1968; Weber, 1949).

The operational implications of these ideas are arresting. Most applied research in education is carried out by or for agencies of the state, and with very few exceptions researchers do not view this as questionable or inappropriate. The reason that most research is government sponsored, of course, is that few of the other parties with an interest in social policy have the requisite resources. Organized interest groups sometimes have modest resources to invest in such efforts, but in education the results are not impressive and are often barely professional. The objects of social policy, most of whom are not organized, have no resources to speak of at all, save a few poverty-stricken private organizations and some of the more inventive OEO Legal Services agencies.

Why is it that few within the enterprise regard this situation as curious? The answer, we believe, is that most commentators assume that there is at least broad agreement on the goals of social policy (see, for example, Rivlin, 1971, p. 46). Generally it is thought that there is a division between the political determination of social purposes and the scientific determination of objective evidence. The role of applied research is thought to be primarily technical: the effective articulation of means and ends (Price, 1965, p. 128). Proponents of applied research therefore assume that the appropriate arena for policy analysis is the administrative agency. Analysis is expected to provide objective evidence helpful in agency budgeting and decision making. The idea is that to the extent administrative action can be based on objective evidence rather than an opinion or contending bureaucratic interests, society will benefit.

There is an important difficulty with this view. As we have pointed out, more and better applied research in education has not produced more clarity or any noticeable convergence in policy advice. Rather, it seems to have intensified or sharpened conflicting ideas about policy, research and research method. It has raised these conflicts to new levels of scientific sophistication and difficulty, and it frequently has transformed the issues *en route*. When research has affected public life, it has done so chiefly through its effect on global, diffuse and hard-to-control systems of knowledge and belief.

One wonders, therefore, whether accepted ideas about the social role of applied research are entirely plausible. If applied research has not noticeably increased the authoritative information base for decisions, much less the use of this information in decisions themselves, how can one believe that the justification for policy-oriented research is that it increases rationality by increasing objectivity? Or that there is an unambiguous justification for researchers working principally in the service of the state?

The answer, we think, is that one cannot make either argument with complete plausibility. A justification of applied research solely on the basis of instrumental rationality is illusory, because applied inquiry rarely seems to reduce intellectual conflict about policy issues. Thus, if there is a justification for applied research, it must rest on more than the ability of research to rationalize political life by providing evidence for decisions.

Implications

In summary, then, this essay has questioned several key assumptions underlying the application of social research to social policy. Taken together, attempts to reform social policy with social research assume that better scientific information will improve policy by making decisions more rational. But evidence on these applications, taken together, suggests that mostly they have not had such an effect. There is plenty of evidence that research affects policy, but generally this seems to happen in odd and unexpected ways. This conclusion has important implications for our view of the nature of applied research and for efforts to explain its interaction with policy. It also has implications for efforts to justify the role of social science in public life.

We have attributed the unexpected consequences of applied research to flaws in the assumptions underlying the application of social research to social policy, and we have argued that in order to understand why things turn out as they do, it is necessary to entertain alternative assumptions about the relationship between knowledge and action in social policy:

1 Most policy-oriented research, at least in education, tends to influence the broad assumptions and beliefs underlying policies, not particular decisions.

2 Better methodology and policy relevance in applied research in education have not produced more convergent findings. This is in part because most policy-oriented research concerns programs

135

with broad and conflicting aims, but it is also attributable to methodological conflict among research approaches and to the fact that the advance of applied research tends to complicate and redefine issues. As a result, improving applied research does not tend to produce more authoritative advice about social policy.

3 The justification for applied social research carried out for the state cannot rest on the idea of instrumental rationality, because applied research, at least in education, has not significantly increased the objective information base for decisions.

Of course, these propositions do not cover all aspects of the relation between research and policy, and we have tried to note exceptions and alternative cases along the way. On the basis of these propositions, one might argue that applied research is not a disinterested effort to improve policy, but rather a broad-aim social innovation designed to change the basis for decision making. In education, at least, the enterprise resembles nothing so much as a social action program.

To argue that applied research can be understood as a broad-aim innovation is not necessarily to disparage the enterprise. In a certain sense, this argument simply directs attention to its exploratory character: Applied researchers have been discovering the consequences of their work on the hoof, just as social program administrators do. Instead of being useful for decisions, policy-oriented research on school effects has contributed to a generally negative or skeptical climate of opinion about education. Instead of producing authoritative evidence for decisions, applied research has tended to complicate matters, raise new issues and produce counterintuitive results.

These seemingly odd consequences prompted at least as many doubts about the utility of applied research as about the programs and policies in question (Cohen, 1972, p. 106). Ironically, social research seems prone to the very disorder it was intended to remedy.

This description of the relationship between research and policy suggests two central questions. First, what accounts for the character of the interaction we have described? Our propositions, after all, explain nothing; they offer only a new conception of what needs to be explained. Second, how might the role of applied social research in public affairs be justified? In the course of our study, some ideas about these questions of explanation and justification have emerged, and they might be mentioned by way of suggestion and provocation.

On the first question, our propositions about the relations between research and policy are not laws, nor is it written in heaven that things must remain as they are. For example, it might be possible to maintain a distinction between an evaluation of a program which seems to exemplify a policy and an assessment of the policy itself. This would be difficult, because social policy ordinarily evolves inductively, as an accretion of particular programs; programs are not deduced logically from broad policies. Nonetheless, researchers and administrators might endeavor to keep evaluations of the two distinct.

On the matter of justification, we believe the distribution of analytic resources requires serious consideration. If applied research in general does not improve the administration of social policy by providing objective evidence for agency decision making, then it would appear difficult to justify the fact that most policy research is carried out for the state. Not to consider inequalities in access to research would be to acquiesce in the existing arrangement, which gives government a preponderant advantage in the legitimization of policy through science (Biderman, 1966). To correct this imbalance, government agencies could give grants for policy research to organizations representing relatively powerless elements in the society; or independent research advocacy organizations might be established on the model of local Legal Services offices; or competing views on policy questions might be represented by giving contracts to established research organizations to undertake studies based on multiple approaches.

The questions of explanation and justification are related. An important reason research appears to complicate, change or redefine issues of social policy is that social research is not simply a technical activity. Social inquiry may attempt to achieve successful prediction and explanation; but it is chiefly an effort to interpret and structure the social world by establishing languages and symbolic universes used in comprehending and carrying on social life. The function of policy research is at least as much to describe and discuss the premises and objectives of policy as it is to predict policy effects. In this sense, applied research resembles a discourse about social reality — a debate about social problems and their solutions. Like intelligent discussion or debate, applied research does not necessarily reduce disagreement. Instead, it calls attention to the existence of conflicting positions, sometimes elaborates them, and sometimes generates new issues altogether. Like discourse, it often has a loose and unstable connection with other sorts of social action.

The parallel between applied research and discourse is appealing for it suggests a way of understanding the research process which makes the uncertain relation between applied research and social action less surprising. In addition, this parallel suggests some standards by which the quality and character of applied social research might be assessed. Discourse is possible only when all participants accept certain norms of communication. All interested parties must be able to initiate discussion, to establish or influence the rules of conversation, to put forward statements, to request elaboration and clarification, and to call other statements into question. To the degree applied research resembles discourse, norms of this sort should apply. To the extent they do not, the process may well be deficient.

This involves only one interpretation of applied social research, and only one conception of the analyst's role. If, as we have argued, commonly held assumptions about the relation between research and policy are misleading, the notion of research as discourse may well be worth considering. If it is a plausible metaphor, it should help describe the research process, explain why things work as they do, and offer some rules for evaluating the quality and fairness of the applied research enterprise.

References

BERG, I. (1970). *Education and jobs: The great training robbery*. New York: Praeger.

BIDERMAN, A.D. (1966). Social indicators and goals. In R.A. BAUER (Ed.), *Social indicators* (pp. 102–103). Cambridge, MA: MIT Press.

BISSELL, J.S. (1971). *Implementation of planned variation in Head Start. 1. Review and summary of the Stanford Research Institute interim report: First year of evaluation*. Washington, DC: Department of Health, Education, and Welfare, Office of Child Development, April.

CAMPBELL, D.T. (1971). Methods for the experimenting society. Draft of a paper delivered to the American Psychological Association, Washington, DC, September.

CARO, F.G. (1971a). Evaluation in comprehensive urban antipoverty programs: A case study of an attempt to establish the evaluative research role in a model city program. In F.G. CARO (Ed.), *Readings in evaluation research* (pp. 297–317). New York: Russell Sage Foundation.

CARO, F.G. (1971b). Evaluation research: An overview. In F.G. CARO (Ed.), *Readings in evaluation research* (p. 1). New York: Russell Sage Foundation.

CHARLESWORTH, J.C. (Ed.). (1972). *Integration of the social sciences through policy analysis* (Monograph No. 14). Philadelphia: American Academy of Political and Social Science.

CICIRELLI, V.G., EVANS, J.W. and SCHILLER, J.S. (1970). The impact of Head Start: A reply to the report analysis. *Harvard Educational Review, 40* (February), 105–129.

COHEN, D.K. (1972). The National Institute of Education: What can be expected? Washington, DC: National Institute of Education Planning Unit Report, September.

COHEN, D.K. (1975). The value of social experiments. In A.M. RIVLIN and P.M. TIMPANE (Eds), *Planned variation in education: Should we give up or try harder?* (pp. 147–175). Washington, DC: Brookings Institution.

COLEMAN, J.S. (1972). Integration of sociology and the other social sciences through policy analysis. In J.C. CHARLESWORTH (Ed.), *Integration of the social sciences through policy analysis* (pp. 162–174, Monograph No. 14). Philadelphia: American Academy of Political and Social Science.

ELLS, K., DAVID, A., HAVIGHURST, R.J., HERRICK, V.E. and TYLER, R.W. (1951). *Intelligence and cultural differences*. Chicago, IL: University of Chicago Press.

ELMORE, R.F. (1972). *The politics and administration of an educational experiment: The case of follow through.* Special qualifying paper, Harvard University, Graduate School of Education, Cambridge, MA.

GOULDNER, A.W. (1968). The sociologist as partisan: Sociology and the welfare state. *The American Sociologist, 3* (May), 103–116.

HOUSTON, T.R., Jr. (1972). The behavioral sciences impact-effectiveness model. In P.H. ROSSI and W. WILLIAMS (Eds), *Evaluating social programs: Theory, practice, and politics* (pp. 51–65). New York: Seminar Press.

JENCKS, C., SMITH, M., BANE, M.J., COHEN, D., GINTIS, H., HEYNS, B. and MICHELSON, S. (1972). *Inequality: A reassessment of the effect of family and schooling in America.* New York: Basic Books.

LIKERT, R. and LIPPITT, R. (1953). The utilization of social science. In L. FESTINGER and D. KATZ (Eds), *Research methods in the behavioral sciences* (pp. 618–619). New York: Dryden Press.

LUKAS, C. (1973). *Social experimentation: The case of Head Start planned variation.* Cambridge, MA: The Huron Institute.

LYONS, G.M. (1969). *The uneasy partnership: Social science and the federal government in the twentieth century.* New York: Russell Sage Foundation.

McLAUGHLIN, M.W. (1973). Evaluation and reform: The case of ESEA Title I. Unpublished dissertation, Harvard University, Graduate School of Education, Cambridge, MA.

MERCER, J.R. (1974). A policy statement on assessment procedures and the rights of children. *Harvard Educational Review, 44* (February), 125–141.

MOSHER, F. (1974). *Progress report on the instrumentation study.* Cambridge, MA: The Huron Institute, June.

NATIONAL ACADEMY OF SCIENCES (1969). *The behavioral and social sciences: Outlook and needs.* Washington, DC: National Academy of Sciences.

PLATT, A. (1969). *The child savers: The invention of delinquency.* Chicago, IL: University of Chicago Press.

POPHAM, W.J. (1971). *Criterion-referenced measurement.* Englewood Cliffs, NJ: Educational Technology Publications.

PORTER, D.O., WARNER, D.C. and PORTER, T.W. (1973). *The politics of budgeting federal aid: Resource mobilization by local school districts* (Sage Professional Paper in Administrative and Policy Studies, No. 03–003). Beverly Hills and London: Sage.

PRICE, D.K. (1965). *The scientific estate.* Cambridge, MA: Harvard University Press.

REIN, M. (1971). Social policy analysis as the interpretation of beliefs. *Journal of the American Institute of Planners, 37,* 297–310.

RICHARDSON, E. (1972). (Interview). *Evaluation, 1* (Fall), 9.

RIVLIN, A. (1971). *Systematic thinking for social action.* Washington, DC: The Brookings Institution.

SCHULTZE, C.L. (1968). *The politics and economics of public spending.* Washington, DC: The Brookings Institution.

SEXTON, P.C. (1961). *Education and income: Inequalities of opportunity in our public schools.* New York: Viking Press.

SMITH, M.S. and BISSELL, J.S. (1970). Report analysis: The impact of Head Start. *Harvard Educational Review, 40* (February), 51–104.

SUCHMAN, E.A. (1972). Action for what? A critique of evaluative research. In C.H. WEISS (Ed.), *Evaluating action programs: Readings in social action and education* (pp. 52–84). Boston: Allyn & Bacon.

WARGO, M., CAMPEAU, L. and TALLMADGE, G.K. (1971). *Further examination of exemplary programs for educationally disadvantaged children*. Palo Alto, CA: American Institute for Research.

WARREN, R.L. (1971). The sociology of knowledge and the problem of the inner cities. *Social Science Quarterly, 52*, 469–491.

WEBER, M. (1949). 'Objectivity' in social science and social policy. In *The methodology of the social sciences* (pp. 52–54, E.A. SHILS and H.A. FINCH, Trans.). New York: Free Press.

WEISS, R.S. and REIN, M. (1970). The evaluation of board-aim programs: Experimental design, its difficulties, and an alternative. *Administrative Science Quarterly, 15*, 97.

WHITE, S.H., BISSELL, J.S. and GOLENSKI, J. (1972). Knowledge in education. Paper presented at NIE Symposium on Educational Research and Development, Washington, DC, December.

WHITE, S.H., DAY, M.C., FREEMAN, P.K., HARTMAN, S.A. and MESSENGER, K.P. (1973). *Federal programs for young children: Review and recommendations* (Vol. I). Washington, DC: Department of Health, Education and Welfare.

WHOLEY, J.S., WHITE, B.F., VOGT, L.M. and ZAMOFF, R.B. (1970). *Title I evaluation and technical assistance: Assessment and prospects*. Washington, DC: The Urban Institute.

WHOLEY, J.S., SCANLON, J.W., DUFFY, H.G., FUKUMOTO, J.S. and VOGT, L.M. (1970). *Federal evaluation policy: Analyzing the effects of public programs*. Washington, DC: The Urban Institute.

WILLIAMS, W. (1971). *Social policy research and analysis: The experience in the federal social agencies*. New York: American Elsevier.

WILLIAMS, W. and EVANS, J.W. (1969). The politics of evaluation: The case of Head Start. *The Annals of the American Academy of Political and Social Science, 385* (September), 118–132.

Chapter 12

Social Psychology as History*

Kenneth J. Gergen

... The marked success of the natural sciences in establishing general principles can importantly be attributed to the general stability of events in the world of nature. The [acceleration] of falling bodies or the compounding of chemical elements, for example, are highly stable events across time. They are events that can be recreated in any laboratory, 50 years ago, today, or 100 years from now. Because they are so stable, broad generalizations can be established with a high degree of confidence, explanations can be empirically tested, and mathematical transformations can be fruitfully developed. If events were unstable, if the [acceleration] of falling bodies or the compounding of chemicals were in continuous flux, the development of the natural sciences would be drastically impeded. General laws would fail to emerge, and the recording of natural events would lend itself primarily to historical analysis. If natural events were capricious, natural science would largely be replaced by natural history.

It is the purpose of this paper to argue that social psychology is primarily an historical inquiry. Unlike the natural sciences, it deals with acts that are largely nonrepeatable and which fluctuate markedly over time. Principles of human interaction cannot readily be developed over time because the facts on which they are based do not generally remain stable. Knowledge cannot accumulate in the usual scientific sense because such knowledge does not generally transcend its historical boundaries. In the following discussion two central lines of argument will be developed in support of this thesis, the first centering on the impact of the science on social behavior and the second on historical change. After examining these arguments, we can focus on alterations in the scope and aims of the field suggested by this analysis.

* Abridged from 'Social Psychology as History' by K.J. Gergen, 1973, *Journal of Personality and Social Psychology*, 26(2), pp. 309–320.

Kenneth J. Gergen

Impact of Science on Social Interaction

As Back (1963) has shown, social science can fruitfully be viewed as a protracted communications system. In the execution of research, the scientist receives messages transmitted by the subject. In raw form, such messages generate only 'noise' for the scientist. Scientific theories serve as decoding devices which convert noise to useable information. Although Back has used his model in a number of provocative ways, his analysis is terminated at the point of decoding. This model must be extended beyond the process of gathering and decoding messages. The scientist's task is also that of communicator. If his theories prove to be useful decoding devices, they are communicated to the populace in order that they might also benefit from their utility. Science and society constitute a feedback loop.

This type of feedback from scientist to society has become increasingly widespread during the past decade. Channels of communication have developed at a rapid rate. On the level of higher education, over eight million students are annually confronted by course offerings in the field of psychology, and within recent years, such offerings have become unexcelled in popularity. The liberal education of today entails familiarity with central ideas in psychology. The mass media have also come to realize the vast public interest in psychology. The news media carefully monitor professional meetings as well as journals of the profession. Magazine publishers have found it profitable to feature the views of psychologists on contemporary behavior patterns, and specialty magazines devoted almost exclusively to psychology now boast readerships totaling over 600,000. When we add to these trends the broad expansion of the soft-cover book market, the increasing governmental demand for knowledge justifying the public underwriting of psychological research, the proliferation of encounter techniques, the establishment of business enterprises huckstering psychology through games and posters, and the increasing reliance placed by major institutions (including business, government, military, and social) on the knowledge of in-house behavioral scientists, one begins to sense the profound degree to which the psychologist is linked in mutual communication with the surrounding culture.

Most psychologists harbor the desire that psychological knowledge will have an impact on the society. Most of us are gratified when such knowledge can be utilized in beneficial ways. Indeed, for many social psychologists, commitment to the field importantly depends on the belief in the social utility of psychological knowledge. However, it is not generally assumed that such utilization will alter the character of causal relations in social interaction. We do expect knowledge of function forms to be utilized in altering behavior, but we do not expect the utilization to affect the subsequent character of the function forms themselves. Our expectations in this case may be quite unfounded. Not only may the application of our principles alter the data on which they are based, but the very development of the principles may invalidate them. Three lines of argument are pertinent, the first stemming from the evaluative bias of psychological research, the second from the liberating effects of knowledge, and the third from prevalent values in the culture.

Prescriptive Bias of Psychological Theory

As scientists of human interaction, we are engaged in a peculiar duality. On the one hand, we value dispassionate comportment in scientific matters. We are well aware of the biasing effects of strong value commitments. On the other hand, as socialized human beings, we harbor numerous values about the nature of social relations. It is the rare social psychologist whose values do not influence the subject of his research, his methods of observation, or the terms of description. In generating knowledge about social interaction, we also communicate our personal values. The recipient of knowledge is thus provided with dual messages: Messages that dispassionately *describe* what appears to be, and those which subtly *prescribe* what is desirable.

This argument is most clearly evident in research on personal dispositions. Most of us would feel insulted if characterized as low in self-esteem, high in approval seeking, cognitively undifferentiated, authoritarian, anal compulsive, field dependent, or close-minded. In part, our reactions reflect our acculturation; one need not be a psychologist to resent such labels. But in part, such reactions are created by the concepts utilized in describing and explaining phenomena. For example, in the preface of the *Authoritarian Personality* (Adorno, Frenkel-Brunswik, Levinson and Sanford, 1950) readers are informed that "In contrast to the bigot of the older style, (the authoritarian) seems to combine the ideas and skills of a highly industrialized society with irrational or anti-rational beliefs" (p. 3). In discussing the Machiavellian personality, Christie and Geis (1970) noted: "Initially our image of the high Mach was a negative one, associated with shadowy and unsavory manipulations. However ... we found ourselves having a perverse admiration for the high Mach's ability to outdo others in experimental situations" (p. 339).

In their prescriptive capacity such communications become agents of social change. On an elementary level, the student of psychology might well wish to exclude from public observation behaviors labeled by respected scholars as authoritarian, Machiavellian, and so on. The communication of knowledge may thus create homogeneity with respect to behavioral indicators of underlying dispositions. On a more complex level, knowledge of personality correlates may induce behavior to insubstantiate the correlates. Not so strangely, much individual difference research places the professional psychologist in a highly positive light. Thus the more similar the subject is to the professional in terms of education, socioeconomic background, religion, race, sex, and personal values, the more advantageous his position on psychological tests. Increased education, for example, favors cognitive differentiation (Witkin, Dyk, Faterson, Goodenough and Karp, 1962), low scores in authoritarianism (Christie and Jahoda, 1954), open-mindedness (Rokeach, 1960), etc. Armed with this information, those persons unflattered by the research might overcompensate in order to dispel the injurious stereotype. For example, women who learn they are more persuasible than men (cf. Janis and Field, 1959) may retaliate, and over time the correlation is invalidated or reversed.

While evaluative biases are easily identified in personality research, they are by no means limited to this area. Most general models of social interaction also contain implicit value judgments. For example, treatises on conformity often treat the conformer as a second-class citizen, a social sheep who foregoes personal conviction to agree with the erroneous opinions of others. Thus, models of social conformity sensitize one to factors that might lead him into socially deplorable actions. In effect, knowledge insulates against the future efficacy of these same factors. Research on attitude change often carries with it these same overtones. Knowing about attitude change flatters one into believing that he has the power to change others; by implication, others are relegated to the status of manipulanda. Thus, theories of attitude change may sensitize one into guarding against factors that could potentially influence him. In the same way, theories of aggression typically condemn the aggressor, models of interpersonal bargaining are disparaging of exploitation, and models of moral development demean those at less than the optimal stage (Kohlberg, 1970). Cognitive dissonance theory (Brehm and Cohen, 1966; Festinger, 1957) might appear to be value free, but most studies in this area have painted the dissonance reducer in most unflattering terms. 'How witless,' we say, 'that people should cheat, make lower scores on tests, change their opinions of others or eat undesirable foods just to maintain consistency.'

This critical note underlying these remarks is not inadvertent. It does seem unfortunate that a professional dedicated to the objective and non-partisan development of knowledge should use this position to propagandize the unwitting recipients of this knowledge. The concepts of the field are seldom value free, and most could be replaced with other concepts carrying far different valuational baggage. Brown (1965) has pointed to the interesting fact that the classic authoritarian personality, so roundly scourged in our own literature was quite similar to the "J-type personality" (Jaensch, 1938), viewed by the Germans in a highly positive light. That which our literature termed rigidity was viewed as stability in theirs; flexibility and individualism in our literature were seen as flaccidity and eccentricity. Such labeling biases pervade our literature. For example, high self-esteem could be termed egotism; need for social approval could be translated as need for social integration; cognitive differentiation as hair-splitting; creativity as deviance; and internal control as egocentricity. Similarly, if our values were otherwise, social conformity could be viewed as prosolidarity behavior; attitude change as cognitive adaptation; and the risky shift as the courageous conversion.

Yet while the propagandizing effects of psychological terminology must be lamented, it is also important to trace their sources. In part the evaluative loading of theoretical terms seems quite intentional. The act of publishing implies the desire to be heard. However, value-free terms have low-interest value for the potential reader, and value-free research rapidly becomes obscure. If obedience were relabeled alpha behavior and not rendered deplorable through associations with Adolf Eichmann, public concern would undoubtedly be meager. In addition to capturing the interest of the public and the profession, value loaded concepts also provide an expressive outlet for the psychologist. I have talked with countless graduate students drawn into psychology out of deep humanistic concern. Within many lies a frustrated poet, philosopher, or humanitarian who finds the scientific method at once a means to expressive ends and an encumbrance to free expression. Resented is the apparent fact that the ticket to open expression through the professional media is a near lifetime in the laboratory. Many wish to share their values directly, unfettered by constant demands for systematic evidence. For them, value-laden concepts compensate for the conservatism usually imparted by these demands. The more established psychologist may indulge himself more directly. Normally, however, we are not inclined to view our personal biases as propagandistic so much as reflecting 'basic truths'.

While the communication of values through knowledge is to some degree intentional, it is not entirely so. Value commitments are almost inevitable by-products of social existence, and as participants in society we can scarcely dissociate ourselves from these values in pursuing professional ends. In addition, if we rely on the language of the culture for scientific communication, it is difficult to find terms regarding social interaction that are without prescriptive value. We might reduce the implicit prescriptions embedded in our communications if we adopted a wholly technical language. However, even technical language becomes evaluative whenever the science is used as a lever for social change. Perhaps our best option is to maintain as much sensitivity as possible to our biases and to communicate them as openly as possible. Value commitments may be unavoidable, but we can avoid masquerading them as objective reflections of truth.

Knowledge and Behavioral Liberation

It is common research practice in psychology to avoid communicating one's theoretical premises to the subject either before or during the research. Rosenthal's (1966) research indicated that even the most subtle cues of experimenter expectation may alter the behavior of the subject. Naive subjects are thus required by common standards of rigor. The implications of this simple methodological safeguard are of considerable significance. If subjects possess preliminary knowledge as to theoretical premises, we can no longer adequately test our hypotheses. In the same way, if society is psychologically informed, theories about which it is informed become difficult to test in an uncontaminated way. Herein lies a fundamental difference between the natural and the social sciences. In the former, the scientist cannot typically communicate his knowledge to the subjects of his study such that their behavioral dispositions are modified. In the social sciences such communication can have a vital impact on behavior.

A single example may suffice here. It appears that over a wide variety of conditions, decision-making groups come to make riskier decisions through group discussion (cf. Dion, Baron and Miller, 1970; Wallach, Kogan and Bem, 1964). Investigators in this area are quite careful that experimental subjects are not privy to their thinking on this matter. If knowledgeable, subjects might insulate themselves from the effects of group discussion or respond appropriately in order to gain the experimenter's favor. However, should the risky shift become common knowledge, naive subjects would become unobtainable. Members of the culture might consistently compensate for risky tendencies produced by group discussion until such behavior become normative.

As a general surmise, sophistication as to psychological principles liberates one from their behavioral implications. Established principles of behavior become inputs into one's decision making. As Winch (1958) has pointed out, "Since understanding something involves understanding its contradiction, someone who, with understanding, performs X must be capable of envisioning the possibility of doing not X" (p. 89). Psychological principles also sensitize one to influences acting on him and draw attention to certain aspects of the environment and himself. In doing so, one's patterns of behavior may be strongly influenced. As May (1971) has stated more passionately, "Each of us inherits from society a burden of tendencies which shapes us willy-nilly; but our capacity to be conscious of this fact saves us from being strictly determined" (p. 100). In this way, knowledge about nonverbal signals of stress or relief (Eckman, 1965), enables us to avoid giving off these signals whenever it is useful to do so; knowing that persons in trouble are less likely to be helped when there are large numbers of bystanders (Latané and Darley, 1970) may increase one's desire to offer his services under such conditions; knowing that motivational arousal can influence one's interpretation of events (cf. Jones and Gerard, 1967) may engender caution when arousal is high. In each instance, knowledge increases alternatives to action, and previous patterns of behavior are modified or dissolved.

Escape to Freedom

The historical invalidation of psychological theory can be further traced to commonly observed sentiments within western culture. Of major importance is the general distress people seem to feel at the diminution of their response alternatives. As Fromm (1941) saw it, normal development includes the acquisition of strong motives towards autonomy. Weinstein and Platt (1969) discussed much the same sentiment in terms of "man's wish to to free," and linked this disposition to the developing social structure. Brehm (1966) used this same disposition as the cornerstone of his theory of psychological reactance. The prevalence of his learned value has important implications for the long-term validity of social psychological theory.

Valid theories about social behaviour constitute significant implements of social control. To the extent that an individual's behavior is predictable, he places himself in a position of vulnerability. Others can alter environmental conditions or their behavior toward him to obtain maximal rewards at minimal costs to themselves. In the same way that a military strategist lays himself open to defeat when his actions become predictable, an organizational official can be taken advantage of by his inferiors and wives manipulated by errant husbands when their behavior patterns are reliable. Knowledge thus becomes power in the hands of others. It follows that psychological principles pose a potential threat to all those for whom they are germane. Investments in freedom may thus potentiate behavior designed to invalidate the theory. We are satisfied with principles of attitude change until we find them being used in information campaigns dedicated to changing our behavior. At this point, we may feel resentful and react recalcitrantly. The more potent the theory is in predicting behavior, the broader its public dissemination and the more prevalent and resounding the reaction. Thus, strong theories may be subject to more rapid invalidation than weak ones.

The common value of personal freedom is not the only pervasive sentiment affecting the mortality of social psychological theory. In western culture there seems to be heavy value placed on uniqueness or individuality. The broad popularity of both Erikson (1968) and Allport (1965) can be traced in part to their strong support of this value, and recent laboratory research (Fromkin, 1970, 1972) has demonstrated the strength of this value in altering social behavior. Psychological theory, in its nomothetic structure, is insensitive to unique occurrences. Individuals are treated as exemplars of larger classes. A common reaction is that psychological theory is dehumanizing, and as Maslow (1968) has noted, patients harbor a strong resentment at being rubricated or labeled with conventional clinical terms. Similarly, blacks, women, activists, suburbanites, educators, and the elderly have all reacted bitterly to explanations of their behavior. Thus, we may strive to invalidate theories that ensnare us in their impersonal way.

Psychology of Enlightenment Effects

Thus far we have discussed three ways in which social psychology alters the behavior it seeks to study. Before moving to a second set of arguments for the historical dependency of psychological theory, we must deal with an important means of combating the effects thus far described. To preserve the transhistorical validity of psychological principles, the science could be removed from the public domain and scientific understanding reserved for a selected elite. This elite would, of course, be co-opted by the state, as no government could risk the existence of a private establishment developing tools of public control. For most of us, such a prospect is repugnant, and our inclination instead is to seek a scientific solution to the problem of historical dependency. Such an answer is suggested by much that has been said. If people who are psychologically enlightened react to general principles by contradicting them, conforming to them, ignoring them, and so on, then it should be possible to establish the conditions under which these various reactions will occur. Based on notions of psychological reactance (Brehm, 1966), self-fulfilling prophecies (Merton, 1948) and expectancy effects (Gergen and Taylor, 1969), we might construct a general theory of reactions to theory. A psychology of enlightenment effects should enable us to predict and control the effects of knowledge.

Although a psychology of enlightenment effects seems a promising adjunct to general theories, its utility is seriously limited. Such a psychology can itself be vested with value, increase our behavioral alternatives, and may be resented because of its threats to feelings of autonomy. Thus, a theory that predicts reactions to theory is also susceptible to violation or vindication. A frequent occurrence in parent–child relations illustrates the point. Parents are accustomed to using direct rewards in order to influence the behavior of their children. Over time, children become aware of the adult's premise that the reward will achieve the desired results and become obstinate. The adult may then react with a naive psychology of enlightenment effects and express disinterest in the child's carrying out the activity, again with the intent of achieving the desired ends. The child may respond appropriately but often enough will blurt out some variations of, 'You are just saying you don't care because you really want me to do it.' In Loevinger's (1959) terms, ". . . a shift in parentmanship is countered by a shift in childmanship" (p. 149). In the popular idiom, this is termed reverse psychology and is often resented. Of course, one could counter with research on reactions to the psychology of enlightenment effects, but it is quickly seen that this exchange of actions and reactions could be extended indefinitely. A psychology of enlightenment effects is subject to the same historical limitations as other theories of social psychology.

Psychological Theory and Cultural Change

The argument against transhistorical laws in social psychology does not solely rest on a consideration of the impact of science on society. A second major line of thought deserves consideration. If we scan the most prominent lines of research during the past decade, we soon realize that the observed regularities, and thus the major theoretical principles, are firmly wedded to historical circumstances. The historical dependency of psychological principles is most notable in areas of focal concern to the public. Social psychologists have been much concerned, for example, with isolating predictors of political activism during the past decade (cf. Mankoff and Flacks, 1971; Soloman and Fishman, 1964). However, as one scans this literature over time, numerous inconsistencies are found. Variables that successfully predicted political activism during the early stages of the Vietnam war are dissimilar to those which successfully predicted activism during later periods. The conclusion seems clear that the factors motivating activism changed over time. Thus, any theory of political activism built from early findings would be invalidated by later findings. Future research on political activism will undoubtedly find still other predictors more useful.

Such alterations in functional relationship are not in principle limited to areas of immediate public concern. For example, Festinger's (1957) theory of social comparison and the extensive line of deductive research (cf. Latané, 1966) are based on the dual assumption that (a) people desire to evaluate themselves accurately, and (b) in order to do so they compared themselves with others. There is scant reason to suspect that such dispositions are genetically determined, and we can easily imagine persons, and indeed societies, for which these assumptions would not hold. Many of our social commentators are critical of the common tendency to search out others' opinions in defining self and they attempt to change society through their criticism. In effect, the entire line of research appears to depend on a set of learned propensities, propensities that could be altered by time and circumstance.

In the same way, cognitive dissonance theory depends on the assumption that people cannot tolerate contradictory cognitions. The basis of such intolerance does not seem genetically given. There are certainly individuals who feel quite otherwise about such contradictions. Early existentialist writers, for example, celebrated the inconsistent act. Again, we must conclude that the theory is predictive because of the state of learned dispositions existing at the time. Likewise, Schachter's (1959) work on affiliation is subject to the arguments made in the case of social comparison theory. Milgram's (1965) obedience phenomenon is certainly dependent on the contemporary attitude towards authority. In attitude change research, communicator credibility is a potent factor because we have learned to rely on authorities in our culture, and the communicated message becomes dissociated from its source over time (Kelman & Hovland, 1953) because it does not prove useful to us *at present* to retain the association. In conformity research, people conform more to friends than nonfriends (Back, 1951) partly because they have learned that friends punish deviance in contemporary society. Research on causal attribution (cf. Jones, Davis and Gergen, 1961; Kelley, 1971) depends on the culturally dependent tendency to perceive man as the source of his actions. This tendency can be modified (Hallowell, 1958) and some (Skinner, 1971) have indeed argued that it should be.

Perhaps the primary guarantee that social psychology will never disappear via reduction to physiology is that physiology cannot account for the variations in human behavior over time. People may prefer bright shades of clothing today and grim shades tomorrow; they may value autonomy during this era and dependency during the next. To be sure, varying responses to the environment rely on variations in psychological function. However, physiology can never specify the nature of the stimulus inputs or the response context to which the individual is exposed. It can never account for the continuously shifting patterns of what is considered the good or desirable in society, and thus a range of primary motivational sources for the individual. However, while social psychology is thus insulated from physiological reductionism, its theories are not insulated from historical change.

It is possible to infer from this latter set of arguments a commitment to at least one theory of transhistorical validity. It has been argued that the stability in interaction patterns upon which most of our theories rest is dependent on learned dispositions of limited duration. This implicitly suggests the possibility of a social learning theory transcending historical circumstance. However such a conclusion is unwarranted. Let us consider, for example, an elementary theory of reinforcement. Few would doubt that most people are responsive to the reward and punishment contingencies in their environment, and it is difficult to envision a time in which this would not be true. Such premises thus seem transhistorically valid, and a primary task of the psychologist might be that of isolating the precise function forms relating patterns of reward and punishment to behavior.

This conclusion suffers on two important counts. Many critics of reinforcement theory have charged that the definition of reward (and punishment) is circular. Reward is typically defined as that which increases the frequency of responding: response increment is defined as that which follows reward. Thus, the theory seems limited to *post hoc* interpretation. Only when behavior change has occurred can one specify the reinforcer. The most significant rejoinder to this criticism lies in the fact that once rewards and punishments have been inductively established, they gain predictive value. Thus, isolating social approval as a positive reinforcer for human behavior was initially dependent on *post hoc* observation. However, once established as a reinforcer, social approval proved a successful means of modifying behavior on a predictive basis (cf. Barron, Heckenmueller and Schultz, 1971; Gewirtz and Baer, 1958).

However, it is also apparent that reinforcers do not remain stable across time. For example, Riesman (1952) has cogently argued that social approval has far more reward value in contemporary society than it did a century ago. And while national pride might have been a potent reinforcer of late adolescent behavior in the 1940s, for contemporary youth such an appeal would probably be aversive. In effect, the essential circularity in reinforcement theory may at any time be reinstigated. As reinforcement value changes, so does the predictive validity of the basic assumption.

Reinforcement theory faces additional historical limitations when we consider its more precise specification. Similar to most other theories of human interaction, the theory is subject to ideological investment. The notion that behavior is wholly governed by external contingency is seen by many as vulgarly demeaning. Knowledge of the theory also enables one to avoid being ensnared by its predictions. As behavior modification therapists are aware, people who are conversant with its theoretical premises can subvert its intended effects with facility. Finally, because the theory has proved so effective in altering the behavior of lower organisms, it becomes particularly threatening to one's investment in autonomy. In fact, most of us would resent another's attempt to shape our behavior through reinforcement techniques and would bend ourselves to confounding the offender's expectations. In sum, the elaboration of reinforcement theory is no less vulnerable to enlightenment effects than other theories of human interaction.

Implications for an Historical Science of Social Behavior

In light of the present arguments, the continued attempt to build general laws of social behavior seems misdirected, and the associated belief that knowledge of social interaction can be accumulated in a manner similar to the natural sciences appears unjustified. In essence, the study of social psychology is primarily an historical undertaking. We are essentially engaged in a systematic account of contemporary affairs. We utilize scientific methodology, but the results are not scientific principles in the traditional sense. In the future, historians may look back to such accounts to achieve a better understanding of life in the present era. However, the psychologists of the future are likely to find little of value in contemporary knowledge. These arguments are not purely academic and are not limited to a simple redefinition of the science. Implied here are significant alterations in the activity of the field. Five such alterations deserve attention.

Kenneth J. Gergen

Toward an Integration of the Pure and Applied

A pervasive prejudice against applied research exists among academic psychologists, a prejudice that is evident in the pure research focus of prestige journals and in the dependency of promotion and tenure on contributions to pure as opposed to applied research. In part, this prejudice is based on the assumption that applied research is of transient value. While it is limited to solving immediate problems, pure research is viewed as contributing to basic and enduring knowledge. From the present standpoint, such grounds for prejudice are not merited. The knowledge that pure research bends itself to establish is also transient; generalizations in the pure research area do not generally endure. To the extent that generalizations from pure research have greater transhistorical validity, they may be reflecting processes of peripheral interest or importance to the functioning of society.

Social psychologists are trained in using tools of conceptual analysis and scientific methodology in explaining human interaction. However, given the sterility of perfecting general principles across time, these tools would seem more productively used in solving problems of immediate importance to the society. This is not to imply that such research must be parochial in scope. One major shortcoming of much applied research is that the terms used to describe and explain are often relatively concrete and specific to the case at hand. While the concrete behavioral acts studied by academic psychologists are often more trivial, the explanatory language is highly general and thus more broadly heuristic. Thus, the present arguments suggest an intensive focus on contemporary social issues, based on the application of scientific methods and conceptual tools of broad generality.

From Prediction to Sensitization

The central aim of psychology is traditionally viewed as the prediction and control of behavior. From the present standpoint, this aim is misleading and provides little justification for research. Principles of human behavior may have limited predictive values across time, and their very acknowledgment can render them impotent as tools of social control. However, prediction and control need not serve as the cornerstones of the field. Psychological theory can play an exceedingly important role as a sensitizing device. It can enlighten one as to the range of factors potentially influencing behavior under various conditions. Research may also provide some estimate of the importance of these factors at a given time. Whether it be in the domain of public policy or personal relationships, social psychology can sharpen one's sensitivity to subtle influence and pinpoint assumptions about behavior that have not proved useful in the past.

When counsel is sought from the social psychologist regarding likely behavior in any concrete situation, the typical reaction is apology. It must be explained that the field is not sufficiently well developed at present so that reliable predictions can be made. From the present standpoint, such apologies are inappropriate. The field can seldom yield principles from which reliable predictions can be made. Behavior patterns are under constant modification. However, what the field can and should provide is research informing the inquirer of a number of possible occurrences, thus expanding his sensitivities and readying him for more rapid accommodation to environmental change. It can provide conceptual and methodological tools with which more discerning judgments can be made.

Developing Indicators of Psycho-social Dispositions

Social psychologists evidence a continuous concern with basic psychological processes, that is, processes influencing a wide and varied range of social behavior. Modeling the experimental psychologist's concern with basic processes of color vision, language acquisition, memory, and the like, social psychologists have focused on such processes as cognitive dissonance, aspiration level, and casual attribution. However, there is a profound difference between the processes typically studied in the general experimental and social domains. In the former instance, the processes are often locked into the organism biologically; they are not subject to enlightenment effects and are not dependent on cultural circumstance. In contrast, most of the processes falling in the social domain are dependent on acquired dispositions subject to gross modification over time.

In this light, it is a mistake to consider the processes in social psychology as basic in the natural science sense. Rather, they may largely be considered the psychological counterpart of cultural norms. In the same way a sociologist is concerned with measuring party preferences or patterns of mobility over time, the social psychologist might attend to the changing patterns of psychological dispositions and their relationship to social behavior. If dissonance reduction is an important process, then we should be in a position to measure the prevalence and strength of such a disposition within the society over time and the preferred modes of dissonance reduction existing at any given time. If esteem enhancement appears to influence social interaction, then broad studies of the culture should reveal the extent of the disposition, its strength in various sub-cultures, and the forms of social behavior with which it is most likely associated at any given time. Although laboratory experiments are well suited to the isolation of particular dispositions, they are poor indicators of the range and significance of the processes in contemporary social life. Much needed are methodologies tapping the prevalence, strength, and form of psycho-social disposition over time. In effect, a technology of psychologically sensitive social indicators (Bauer, 1969) is required.

Research on Behavioral Stability

Social phenomena may vary considerably in the extent to which they are subject to historical change. Certain phenomena may be closely tied to physiological givens. Schachter's (1970) research on emotional states appears to have a strong physiological basis, as does Hess's (1965) work on affect and pupillary constriction. Although learned dispositions can overcome the strength of some physiological tendencies, such tendencies should tend to reassert themselves over time. Still other physiological propensities may be irreversible. There may also be acquired dispositions that are sufficiently powerful that neither enlightenment nor historical change is likely to have a major impact. People will generally avoid physically painful stimuli, regardless of their sophistication or the current norms. We must think, then in terms of *a continuum of historical durability*, with phenomena highly susceptible to historical influence at one extreme and the most stable processes at the other.

In this light, much needed are research methods enabling us to discern the relative durability of social phenomena. Cross-cultural methods could be employed in this capacity. Although cross-cultural replication is fraught with difficulty, similarity in a given function from across widely divergent cultures would strongly attest to its durability across time. Content analytic techniques might also be employed in examining accounts of earlier historical periods. Until now, such accounts have provided little except quotations indicating that some great thinker presaged a pet hypothesis. We have yet to tape the vast quantities of information regarding interaction patterns in earlier periods. Although enhanced sophistication about behavior patterns across space and time would furnish valuable insights regarding durability, difficult problems present themselves. Some behavior patterns may remain stable until closely scrutinized; others may simply become dysfunctional over time. Man's reliance on a concept of deity has a long history and is found in numerous cultures; however, many are skeptical about the future of this reliance. Assessments of durability would thus have to account for potential as well as actual stability in phenomena.

While research into more durable dispositions is highly valuable, we should not therefore conclude that it is either more useful or desirable than studying passing behavior patterns. The major share of the variance in social behavior is undoubtedly due to historically dependent dispositions, and the challenge of capturing such processes 'in flight' and during auspicious periods of history is immense.

Toward an Integrated Social History

It has been maintained that social psychological research is primarily the systematic study of contemporary history. As such, it seems myopic to maintain disciplinary detachment from (a) the traditional study of history and (b) other historically bound sciences (including sociology, political science, and economics). The particular research strategies and sensitivities of the historian could enhance the understanding of social psychology, both past and present. Particularly useful would be the historian's sensitivity to causal sequences across time. Most social psychological research focuses on minute segments of ongoing processes. We have concentrated very little on the function of these segments within their historical context. We have little theory dealing with the interrelation of events over extended periods of time. By the same token, historians could benefit from the more rigorous methodologies employed by the social psychologist as well as his particular sensitivity to psychological variables. However, the study of history, both past and present, should be undertaken in the broadest possible framework. Political, economic, and institutional factors are all necessary inputs to understanding in an integrated way. A concentration on psychology alone provides a distorted understanding of our present condition.

References

ADORNO, T.W., FRENKEL-BRUNSWICK, E., LEVINSON, D.J. and SANFORD, R.N. (1950). *The authoritarian personality*. New York: Harpers.

ALLPORT, G.W. (1965). *Pattern and growth in personality*. New York: Holt, Rinehart and Winston.

BACK, K.W. (1951). Influence through social communication. *Journal of Abnormal and Social Psychology, 46*, 9–23.

BACK, K.W. (1963). The proper scope of social psychology. *Social Forces, 41*, 368–376.

BARON, R., HECKENMUELLER, J. and SCHULTZ, S. (1971). Differences in condition ability as a function of race of subject and prior availability of a social reinforcer. *Journal of Personality, 39*, 94–111.

BAUER, R. (Ed.) (1966). *Social indicators*. Cambridge, MA: MIT Press.

BREHM, J.W. (1966). *A theory of psychological reactance*. New York: Academic Press.

BREHM, J.W. and COHEN, A.R. (1966). *Explorations in cognitive dissonance*. New York: Wiley.

BROWN, R. (1965). *Social psychology*. Glencoe, IL: Free Press.

CHRISTIE, R. and GEIS, F.L. (1970). *Studies in Machiavellianism*. New York: Academic Press.

CHRISTIE, R. and JAHODA, M. (Eds). (1954). *Studies in the scope and method of 'The authoritarian personality'.* Glencoe, IL: Free Press.

DION, K.L., BARON, R.S. and MILLER, N. (1970). Why do groups make riskier decisions than individuals? In L. BERKOWITZ (Ed.), *Advances in experimental social psychology* (Vol. 5). New York: Academic Press.

ECKMAN, P. (1965). Communication through non-verbal behavior: A source of information about an interpersonal relationship. In S.S. TOMKINS and C. IZARD (Eds), *Affect, cognition and personality.* New York: Springer.

ERIKSON, E. (1968). Identity and identity diffusion. In C. GORDON and K. GERGEN (Eds), *The self in social interaction* (Vol. 1). New York: Wiley.

FESTINGER, L. (1957). *A theory of cognitive dissonance.* Evanston, IL: Row, Peterson.

FROMKIN, H.L. (1970). Effects of experimentally aroused feelings of undistinctiveness upon valuation of scarce and novel experiences. *Journal of Personality and Social Psychology, 16,* 521–529.

FROMKIN, H.L. (1972). Feelings of interpersonal undistinctiveness: An unpleasant affective state. *Journal of Experimental Research in Personality, 6,* 178–85.

FROMM, E. (1941). *Escape from freedom.* New York: Rinehart.

GERGEN, K.J. and TAYLOR, M.G. (1969). Social expectancy and self-presentation in a status hierarchy. *Journal of Experimental and Social Psychology, 5,* 79–92.

GEWIRTZ, J.L. and BAER, D.M. (1958). Deprivation and satiation of social reinforcers as drive conditions. *Journal of Abnormal and Social Psychology, 57,* 165–172.

HALLOWELL, A.I. (1958). Ojibwa metaphysics of being and the perception of persons. In R. TAGIURI and L. PETRULLO (Eds), *Person, perception and interpersonal behavior.* Stanford: Stanford University Press.

HESS, E.H. (1965). Attitude and pupil size. *Scientific American, 212,* 46–54.

JAENSCH, E.R. (1938). *Der Gegentypus.* Leipzig: Barth.

JANIS, I.L. and FIELD, P.B. (1959). Sex differences and personality factors related to persuasibility. In I. JANIS and C. HOVLAND (Eds), *Personality and persuasibility.* New Haven: Yale University Press.

JONES, E.E., DAVIS, K.E. and GERGEN, K.J. (1961). Role playing variations and their informational value for person perception. *Journal of Abnormal and Social Psychology, 63,* 302–310.

JONES, E.E. and GERARD, H.B. (1967). *Foundations of social psychology.* New York: Wiley.

KELLEY, H.H. (1971). *Causal schemata and the attribution process.* Morristown, NJ: General Learning Press.

KELMAN, H. and HOVLAND, C. (1953). 'Reinstatement' of the communicator in delayed measurement of opinion change. *Journal of Abnormal and Social Psychology, 48,* 327–335.

KOHLBERG, L. (1970). Stages of moral development as a basis for moral education. In C. BECK and E. SULLIVAN (Eds), *Moral education.* Toronto: University of Toronto Press.

LATANÉ, B. (Ed.) (1966). Studies in social comparison — Introduction and overview. *Journal of Experimental Social Psychology, 2* (Suppl. 1).

LATANÉ, B. and DARLEY, J. (1970). *Unresponsive bystander: Why doesn't he help?* New York: Appleton-Century-Crofts.

LOEVINGER, J. (1959). Patterns of parenthood as theories of learning. *Journal of Abnormal and Social Psychology, 59,* 148–150.

MANKOFF, M. and FLACKS, R. (1971). The changing social base of the American student movement. *Journal of the American Academy of Political and Social Science, 395*, 54–67.

MASLOW, A.H. (1968). *Toward a psychology of being.* New York: Van Nostrand-Reinhold.

MAY, R. (1971). Letters to the Editor. *New York Times Magazine*, April 18, p. 100.

MERTON, R.K. (1948). The self-fulfilling prophecy. *Antioch Review, 8*, 193–210.

MILGRAM, S. (1965). Some conditions of obedience and disobedience to authority. In I.D. STEINER and M. FISHBEIN (Eds), *Current studies in social psychology.* New York: Holt, Rinhart and Winston.

RIESMAN, D. (1952). *The lonely crowd.* New Haven: Yale University Press.

ROKEACH, M. (1960). *The open and closed mind.* New York: Basic Books.

ROSENTHAL, R. (1966). *Experimenter effects in behavioral research.* New York: Appleton-Century-Crofts.

SCHACHTER, S. (1959). *The psychology of affiliation.* Stanford: Stanford University Press.

SCHACHTER, S. (1970). The interaction of cognitive and physiological determinants of emotional states. In L. BERKOWITZ (Ed.), *Advances in experimental social psychology* (Vol. 1). New York: Academic Press.

SKINNER, B.F. (1971). *Beyond freedom and dignity.* New York: Knopf.

SOLOMAN, F. and FISHMAN, T.R. (1964). Youth and peace: A psycho-social study of student peace demonstrators in Washington, DC. *Journal of Social Issues, 20*, 54–73.

WALLACH, M.A., Kogan, N. and BEM, D.J. (1964). Diffusion of responsibility and level of risk taking in groups. *Journal of Abnormal and Social Psychology, 68*, 263–274.

WEINSTEIN, F. and PLATT, G.M. (1969). *The wish to be free.* Berkeley: University of California Press.

WINCH, P. (1958). *The idea of a social science and its relation to philosophy.* New York: Humanities Press.

WITKIN, H.A., DYK, R.B., FATERSON, H.F., GOODENOUGH, D.R. and KARP, S.A. (1962). *Psychological differentiation.* New York: Wiley.

Chapter 13

What is the Constructivist Paradigm?*

Egon G. Guba and Yvonna S. Lincoln

Paradigms as Basic Belief Systems

It is useful, by way of introduction, to think of a paradigm as a basic set of beliefs, a set of assumptions we are willing to make, which serve as touchstones in guiding our activities. We daily operate out of many paradigms. For example, our court system is guided by an adversarial paradigm, our churches are guided by a variety of theological paradigms, Wall Street is guided by certain economic paradigms, and so on. Now the crucial thing to note here is that these paradigms are basic *belief* systems; they cannot be proven or disproven, but they represent the most fundamental positions we are willing to take. If we could cite reasons why some particular paradigm should be preferred, then those reasons would form an even more basic set of beliefs. At some level we must stop giving reasons and simply accept wherever we are as our basic belief set — our paradigm. . . .

We [argue] that the constructivist paradigm provides the best 'fit' whenever it is human inquiry that is being considered. We hope to be persuasive on this point even though the basic belief system of constructivism — analogous to the axioms of geometry — may well seem bizarre or even absurd. This basic system is explicated in the next section. Later, we shall extend the [argument] by proposing certain theorems that can be derived from the system, contrasting these with analogous theorems that can be drawn from the conventional paradigm as the axiom set. It will be the reader's task to judge which belief system, and which set of theorems, provides the best fit for his or her own life space.

* Abridged from *Fourth Generation Evaluation* (pp. 80–109) by E.G. Guba and Y.S. Lincoln, 1989, Newbury Park, CA: Sage.

Table 1   *The contrasting conventional and constructivist belief systems*

CONVENTIONAL BELIEFS	CONSTRUCTIVIST BELIEFS
Ontology: A REALIST ONTOLOGY asserts that there exists a single reality that is independent of any observer's interest in it and which operates according to immutable natural laws, many of which take cause-effect form. Truth is defined as that set of statements that is isomorphic to reality.	A RELATIVIST ONTOLOGY asserts that there exist multiple, socially constructed realities ungoverned by any natural laws, causal or otherwise. 'Truth' is defined as the best informed (amount and quality of information) and most sophisticated (power with which the information is understood and used) construction on which there is consensus (although there may be several constructions extant that simultaneously meet that criterion).
Epistemology: A DUALIST OBJECTIVIST EPISTEMOLOGY asserts that it is possible (indeed, mandatory) for an observer to exteriorize the phenomenon studied, remaining detached and distant from it (a state often called 'subject-object dualism', and excluding any value considerations from influencing it.	A MONISITIC, SUBJECTIVIST EPISTEMOLOGY asserts that an inquirer and the inquired-into are interlocked in such a way that the findings of an investigation are the *literal creation* of the inquiry process. Note that this posture effectively destroys the classical ontology-epistemology distinction.
Methodology: AN INTERVENTIONIST METHODOLOGY strips context of its contaminating (confounding) influences (variables) so that the inquiry can converge on truth and explain nature as it really is and really works, leading to the capability to predict and to control.	A HERMENEUTIC METHODOLOGY involves a continuing dialectic of iteration, analysis, critique, reiteration, reanalysis, and so on, leading to the emergence of a joint (among all the inquirers and respondents, or among etic and emic views) construction of a case.

The Basic Belief Systems of the Conventional and Constructivist Paradigms

We begin by laying out the basic beliefs in contrasting form in Table 1. The table is arranged in three levels, which reflect the three basic questions that philosophers have put to themselves for millennia as they have struggled to understand how we come to know what we know:

1   *What is there that can be known?* This is usually called the *ontological* question. Ontology is that branch of philosophy (specifically, of metaphysics) that is concerned with issues of existence or being as such. Another way to phrase the question is this: "What is the nature of reality?"

2   *What is the relationship of the knower to the known (or the knowable)?* This is usually called the *epistemological* question. Epistemology is that branch of philosophy that deals with the

origin, nature, and limits of human knowledge. Another way to
phrase the question is this: "How can we be sure that we know
what we know?"

3 *What are the ways of finding out knowledge?* This is usually called
the *methodological* question. Methodology is a more practical
branch of philosophy (especially of philosophy of science) that
deals with methods, systems, and rules for the conduct of inquiry.
Another way to phrase the question is: "How can we go about
finding out things?"

It would be a mistake to presume that there are only a few ways in
which these questions can be answered. Beginning with Aristotle (and
probably earlier), different formulations have been proposed that are in
effect different paradigms or basic belief systems (Lincoln & Guba, 1985).
It must be clear that there is no way to answer these questions in an
unambiguous and certain way or in a way that is capable of proof. The set
of answers one gives *is* the basic belief system or paradigm.

One set of answers has been dominant for the past several hundred
years — the one that we have called the conventional paradigm but can
also be called, with equal legitimacy, the positivist or scientific paradigm.
The constructivist paradigm, also called the naturalistic, hermeneutic,
or interpretive paradigm (with slight shadings in meaning), has been in
existence for several hundred years as well, but has not been widely
accepted or understood, particularly in English-speaking countries. It has
nevertheless now emerged as a serious competitor to the conventional
paradigm. It is our contention that the conventional paradigm is under-
going a revolution in the Kuhnian sense (Kuhn, 1970), and that the
constructivist paradigm is its logical successor. The reader may wish to
consult our earlier work for references to other paradigms that have been
in vogue at different historical times.

We turn our attention to the ways in which the conventional and the
constructivist paradigms deal with the three questions:

Ontology

The ontological question is answered by adherents of the conventional
paradigm by asserting that there exists an objective reality, 'out there',
which goes on about its business irrespective of the interest that an
inquirer may have in it: a *realist* ontology. In answer to the age-old party
question, "If a tree falls in a wood when there is no one there to hear it,
does it make a noise?" the answer is, "Of course!" The task of science is to
discover nature 'as it really is', and 'as it really works', including its driving
mechanisms. An earlier version of realist ontology, often called *naive*

realism, held not only that reality existed but that disciplined inquiry could eventually converge onto it. This version has been almost universally rejected in favor of another, often called *critical* realism (see, for example, Cook and Campbell, 1979), recently updated as critical multiplism (Cook, 1985). This view holds that it is impossible to discover reality except within some particular, usually disciplinary, perspective. Nevertheless, even the critical realist view does at bottom rest on a belief in a substantial reality; its view is like the blind men discovering the elephant, for there really *is* an elephant.

This reality is not just an inert mass of 'stuff', however. Things go on in that real world, and the *way* in which they go on is determined entirely by certain natural laws (the root belief of which is often called *determinism*). It is because of the existence of such driving laws that science can hope to fulfil its prime directive — to predict and to control. For if there is no order in nature there is no hope that personkind can manage or exploit nature in its own interest.

Many of these underlying laws take the form of cause–effect relationships. Prediction can, after all, be accomplished on purely statistical — correlational — bases. But control requires that natural phenomena be managed — be *made* to act in desired ways. For that to be possible it is necessary for nature itself to be arranged in if–then relationships. It is the discovery of causal laws that represents the bottom line for scientists. Knowing the causes of motion ultimately enables us to send rockets to the moon, knowing the cause of cancer ultimately will enable us to cure it, knowing the causes of the Cold War will ultimately enable us to defrost it, and so on.

The ontological question is answered by adherents of the constructivist paradigm by asserting that there exist multiple, socially constructed realities ungoverned by natural laws, causal or otherwise: a *relativist* ontology. These constructions are devised by individuals as they attempt to make sense of their experiences, which, it should be recalled, are always *interactive* in nature. Phenomena are defined depending on the kind and amount of prior knowledge and the level of sophistication that the constructor brings to the task. Constructions can be and usually are shared, ranging all the way from constructions about subatomic particles to those about cultural mores. That does not make them any more *real* but simply more *commonly assented to*.

It may well be the case, the constructivist might admit, that among things included in a construction are some lawlike attributions. But there is a world of difference between believing that there is some law that one has 'discovered' in nature versus believing that it may be useful for a variety of purposes to think in lawlike terms. Thus it may have utility to imagine that one can cause the lights to go on by flipping the switch, but that is not equivalent to saying that "the cause of the light going on is the switch being flipped", as though that statement asserted something fundamental about nature. If there is no objective reality then there are no natural laws, and cause–effect attributions are simply that — mental imputations.

Given these two very different ontological formulations, it is not surprising that what is taken to constitute truth should also differ. Conventionally, truth is any assertion, whether about entities or their relationships, that is *isomorphic*, that is, that stands in a one-to-one relationship to objective reality. The ultimate test of the validity of any inquiry findings is that they should describe reality *exactly*. On the other hand, "truth" (and note the use of quotation marks to indicate the problematic nature of the term in this case) is defined in the constructivist paradigm simply as that most informed and sophisticated construction on which there is consensus among individuals most competent (not necessarily most powerful) to form such a construction. It is dubious that the constructivist paradigm requires a term like *truth*, which has a final or ultimate ring to it. Multiple constructions that meet the "most informed and sophisticated" criterion *can* exist side by side, a state of affairs well illustrated by the continuing differences of opinion among vanguard thinkers in every field, whether it be economics or physics. Certainly any construction is continuously open to alteration, however it may be treated at some point in time regarding its "truth". As we have already noted, the moral imperative laid upon adherents of the naturalistic paradigm is that they continuously seek out challenging constructions with which to confront their own. Finally, the development of ever more informed and sophisticated constructions should not be understood to mean that they are "truer" constructions; they are simply more informed and sophisticated. They may become harder and harder to challenge, but they can be overthrown in an instant should some really disruptive insight come to light.

Epistemology

How the epistemological question is dealt with depends, in the first instance, on how the ontological question has already been answered. For example, if you assert that there exists an objective reality that goes on about its business despite any interest that an inquirer may have in it, it seems entirely appropriate to require that the inquirer should maintain an objective distance while studying it. Subjectivity would inevitably lead to distortion; the inquirer would not see nature 'as it really is' or 'as it really works' but only through the dark glasses of some bias or prejudice. On the other hand, if you assert that reality consists of a series of mental constructions, objectivity does not make sense; only interactivity can lead to a construction or its subsequent reconstruction. Taking either a realist or a relativist posture with respect to ontology places constraints on the ways in which the epistemological question can be answered.

The epistemological question is answered by adherents of the conventional paradigm by asserting, first, that it is possible to maintain an objective, 'exteriorized' posture, a dualism, with respect to the phenomenon being studied, and, second, that it is possible to exclude, as part of this dualism, the values held by the inquirer or any other individual, including clients or sponsors of investigations or (need we say it?) stakeholders. It is this posture that provides a warrant for asserting that scientific data must be absolutely accepted, for if they were properly obtained, they are free of any possible taint of subjectivity, bias, or disjunctive values. Inquiry can, in short, be both objective and value-free.

The epistemological question is answered by adherents of the constructivist paradigm by asserting that it is impossible to separate the inquirer from the inquired into. It is precisely their interaction that creates the data that will emerge from the inquiry. Since this is so, the constructivist position effectively eliminates the ontology–epistemology distinction. For if what-there-is-that-can-be-known does not exist independently but only in connection with an inquiry process (which need not be formalized, of course), then it is not possible to ask the questions, "What is there that can be known?" and "What is the relationship of the knower and the known?" independently.

Furthermore, an inevitable element in the inquiry mix is the values of the inquirer and a whole variety of other persons in and around the inquiry. Inquirers are human, and cannot escape their humanness. That is, they cannot by an act of will set aside their own subjectivity, nor can they stand outside the arena of humanness created by the other persons involved. The values of the inquirer (and of those who influence him or her, especially funders, sponsors, and professional peers) inevitably enter the inquiry in connection with the whole series of decisions involved in designing, mounting, and monitoring. The values of involved individuals, especially those from whom information is solicited (whom we much prefer to call *respondents* rather than *subjects*) also exert influence, not only if they are given some modicum of control over the inquiry, but also because inquiries always take place in value contexts. Values are reflected in the theory that may undergird the inquiry (for example, a theory of reading), in the constructions that the inquirer and others bring to the inquiry, and in the inquiry paradigm itself. Moreover, all of these values may be disjunctive — for example, there may be a value conflict between the theory undergirding an inquiry and the paradigm that guides it.... For all these reasons, say the constructivists, values cannot be ignored; their very influential role in all inquiry must be acknowledged.

Methodology

Just as the response to the epistemological question depends on the prior response given to the ontological question, so the response to the methodological question in turn depends on the other two. Having assumed a realist ontology and an objectivist epistemology, it would make sense to adopt a methodology that might include covert observation and misleading instructions to subjects in order to eliminate reactivity and make 'real' behaviors apparent, for example. On the other hand, having assumed a relativist ontology and an interactive epistemology, the use of covert or misleading techniques would be exactly counterproductive; one could not hope to ascertain or to influence constructions by hiding the nature of the desired response from the respondents.

The methodological question is answered by adherents of the conventional paradigm by asserting that inquiry must be mounted in ways that strip the context of possible contaminating influences (confounding variables) so that 'the way things really are' and 'the way things really work' can emerge — an *interventionist* methodology. Structuring the inquiry so as to be able to discover (or test presumptions about) causal mechanisms is especially important. The ultimate pragmatic criterion of the methodology is that it must lead to successively better means for predicting and controlling phenomena. The key process is *explaining*: making clear the cause or reason for something. In order to reach unequivocal conclusions about causes or reasons, inquiries must be *controlled*. Either physical or statistical controls may be instituted, but both require intervention to accomplish.

The methodological question is answered by adherents of the constructivist paradigm by asserting that the inquiry must be carried out in a way that will expose the constructions of the variety of concerned parties, open each to critique in the terms of other constructions, and provide the opportunity for revised or entirely new constructions to emerge — a hermeneutic methodology. The ultimate pragmatic criterion for this methodology is that it leads to successively better *understanding*, that is, to *making sense* of the interaction in which one usually is engaged with others. In order to carry out such an inquiry, a process must be instituted that first iterates the variety of constructions (the sense-makings) that already exist, then analyzes those constructions to make their own elements plain and communicable to others, solicits critiques for each construction from the holders of others, reiterates the constructions in light of new information or new levels of sophistication that may have been introduced, reanalyzes, and so on to consensus — or as close to consensus as one can manage. The process is *hermeneutic* in that it is aimed toward developing improved (joint) constructions, a meaning closely associated with the more traditional use of the term to denote the process of evolving successively more sophisticated interpretations of historical or sacred writings. It is dialectic in that it involves the juxtaposition of conflicting ideas, forcing reconsideration of previous positions.

These then are the basic beliefs undergirding the conventional and constructivist paradigms, stated in very truncated form. It is surely the case that the belief system of the conventional paradigm will sound much more 'right' to those reared in Western culture (although constructivism may sound more familiar to the oriental reader, especially with a Buddhist background; see Zukav, 1979). Nevertheless, we plead for a suspension of disbelief . . . until we have had the opportunity to demonstrate what a shift to the constructivist paradigm might mean, regardless of the apparent absurdity of its basic belief system. . . .

Some Theorems

[We use Euclidean geometry as a metaphor to help the reader to understand implications of both the conventional and constructivist positions. The answers to the three basic questions above are analogous to Euclid's axioms — basic beliefs taken for granted, such as that a straight line can be drawn connecting any two given points — while the statements below are analogs to Euclid's theorems — consequences deduced from the axioms or basic beliefs that guide the application of the belief system to practical problems. In addition, Euclid's geometry illustrates the fact that axioms are arbitrary and need not appear valid on their face to be useful.]

We have a twofold purpose in mind in introducing the metaphor of Euclidean geometry. . . . First, we want to make the point that, while the basic beliefs of constructivism might sound bizarre to anyone heavily socialized to the scientific paradigm (as everyone in our culture has been), that fact alone ought not be sufficient warrant to reject constructivism without giving it a fair hearing. Second, we have in mind to extend the metaphor by proposing certain parallel and constrasting theorems derivable from the basic axioms that further illustrate the great gap between those belief systems, and suggesting the implications that ensue from following each. We will take up a discussion of such theorems now.

We [should however] stress that our use of the term *theorem* is different from that of Euclidean geometry. The latter theorems have all been shown, by a formal deductive process, to be logically derivable from, and dependent on, the axioms. The theorems we propose here have not undergone such a rigorous test; we hope, however, that they will appear to be consistent with their respective paradigms on their face. The reader obviously has the right to take exception to that claim. . . .

1 *Inquiry problematic*
   Conventional. Scientific inquiry *is not* problematic; it is the naturally sanctioned way to determine the definitive and enduring truth about states of affairs.

Constructivist. Constructivist inquiry *is* problematic; it is the humanly devised way to entertain constructions about states of affairs that are subject to continuous refinement, revision, and, if necessary, replacement.

Comment. This theorem follows directly from the basic ontological assumption of an objective reality, on the one hand, and of socially constructed realities, on the other.

2 *Nature of truth*

Conventional. The truth of any proposition (its factual quality) can be determined by testing it empirically in the natural world. Any proposition that has withstood such a test is true; such truth is absolute.

Constructivist. The "truth" of any proposition (its credibility) can be determined by submitting it semiotically to the judgment of a group of informed and sophisticated holders of what may be different constructions. Any proposition that has achieved consensus through such a test is regarded as "true" until reconstructed in the light of more information or increased sophistication; any "truth" is relative.

Comment. Both forms of this theorem follow logically from the separate ontological propositions. Tests are carried out empirically, that is, by experience or experiment, on the one hand, but semiotically, that is, via signs and symbols, usually language, that permit sharing of a construction among multiple parties, on the other. Scientific truth represents things as they really are; constructivist "truth" represents tentative agreements or consensus among qualified persons who find the proposition credible.

3 *Limits of truth*

Conventional. A proposition that has not been tested empirically cannot be known to be true. Likewise, a proposition incapable of empirical test can never be confirmed to be true.

Constructivist. A proposition is neither tested nor untested. It can only be known to be "true" (credible) in relation to and in terms of informed and sophisticated constructions.

Comment. This theorem follows from Theorem 2 above.

4 *Measurability*

Conventional. Whatever exists exists in some measurable amount. If it cannot be measured it does not exist.

Constructivist. Constructions exist only in the minds of constructors and typically cannot be divided into measurable entities. If something can be measured, the measurement *may fit* into some construction but it is likely, at best, to play a supportive role.

Comment. The conventional form of this theorem undergirds all measurement theory. It is often used as a rationalization for asserting that data must be quantified to be meaningful. The constructivist form admits a much wider range of information, including *quantitative*, but does not assign quantitative information the same central position.

5   *Independence of facts and theories*

Conventional. Facts are aspects of the natural world that do not depend on the theories that happen to guide any given inquiry. Observational and theoretical languages are independent.

Constructivist. "Facts" are always theory-laden, that is, they have no independent meaning except within some theoretical framework. There can be no separate observational and theoretical languages.

Comment. The constructivist's claim that there can be no separate observational and theoretical languages follows from the presumption that realities are mental constructions. Thus their elements ("facts") and their organizational structure cannot be independent. The conventionalist's claim rests on a realist ontology. The maintenance of the fact/value distinction is crucial to the conventional argument, however, since Theorem 2 above has no meaning without it.

6   *Independence of facts and values*

Conventional. Facts and values are independent. Facts can be uncovered and arrayed independently of the values that may later be brought to bear to interpret or give meaning to them. There are separate factual and valuational languages, the former describing 'isness' and the latter "oughtness."

Constructivist. "Facts" and "values" are interdependent. "Facts" have no meaning except within some value framework; they are value-laden. There can be no separate observational and valuational languages.

Comment. The claim for independence of facts and values rests, for the conventionalist, on the assertion of an objective epistemology. It is, the constructivist avers, an absurd claim in view of the assertion of an interactive epistemology.

7   *Causation*

Conventional. Every observed action (effect) has a cause, and every cause has an effect.

Constructivist. Any observed action is the instantaneous resolution of a large number of mutual, simultaneous shapers, each of which is constantly shaping, and being shaped by, all other shapers.

Comment. The conventional version of this theorem follows from the ontological presumption that nature is driven by certain immutable laws. The metaphor is one of a great machine in which everything is linked; the action of any part inevitably induces an appropriate counteraction (effect) in some other part(s). The constructivist version argues from the base of continuous reconstruction; anything that happens provides new information or provides a press for increased sophistication. But such reconstruction does not occur in simple linear pathways.

8   *Root causes*

Conventional. It is always possible, *in principle*, to determine the root cause of any observed action (although that may prove to be virtually intractable in practice).

Constructivist. One or several mutual simultaneous shapers may be singled out *arbitrarily* for some specific purpose.

Comment. If the metaphor for nature is that of a great machine, then it is possible to follow linkages back and forth to discover that linkage which has produced or resulted in the action in which the inquirer is interested. The constructivist avers that such singling out, itself a mental imputation, is arbitrary, meaningful only for given, limited purposes. So for example, a new curriculum (an evaluand) may be taken to be the dominant shaper of learning by a curriculum developer, while a school ethnographer may instead single out the school's peer culture for that honor.

9   *Successful inquiry*

Conventional. The determination of root causes is the basis for scientific prediction and control. The success of a science can be judged on whether it displays ever-increasing ability to predict and control its phenomena (the ultimate pragmatic criterion for scientific inquiry, Hesse, 1980).

Constructivist. The positing of a shaper or shapers as key in some action provides a basis for purposively simplifying an otherwise very complex field. The success of constructivist inquiry can be judged on whether it displays ever-increasing understanding of its phenomena (the ultimate constructivist criterion for naturalistic inquiry).

Comment. The ability to isolate and identify root causes makes it possible for the conventional scientist to view increasing prediction and control as the most useful criterion for judging the success of inquiry efforts across an area or discipline. On the other hand, the constructivist cannot define such a key role for what are at best only simplifying decisions. However, in some context, if simplification leads to better understanding, it is useful.

10   *The genesis of problems*

Conventional. Phenomena, including problems, scientifically identified are real and have widespread significance, that is, they will be noted in many contexts, and they are generalizable.

Constructivist. Phenomena, including problems, exist only within some construction(s) and have no meaning except in that context in which they are identified and described.

Comment. If science is the way to discover how things really are and the way things really work, then the products of science, including problems, have reality. And if problems exist, they must have a cause, and if they have a cause, that cause can be responded to. The constructivist rejects such a line of reasoning, arguing that if problems are embedded in constructions, it is the construction that must receive attention.

11 *Applicability of problem solutions*

Conventional. Scientifically devised problem solutions have widespread applicability.

Constructivist. Problem solutions devised through reconstruction have local applicability only.

Comment. Both of these positions depend on the respective beliefs regarding generalizability (the existence of universal truths).

12 *Stability of problem solutions*

Conventional. Problem solutions are stable; when these solutions are introduced into specific contexts they will maintain their characteristics over time.

Constructivist. Problem solutions change; when these solutions are introduced into specific contexts they will be at least as much affected (changed) by those contexts as they are likely to affect them.

Comment. This theorem follows from Theorems 7 and 11, above. The conventionalist sees solutions as scientifically designed and developed to be responsive to certain problems; once they are put into place they will continue to deliver whatever curative, restorative or ameliorative power they have. The constructivist realizes that the processes of reconstruction go on continuously, so that any constructed solution is likely to be itself radically changed over time, with its putative, curative, restorative, or ameliorative power also altered, redirected, eliminated, or even reversed.

13 *The change process*

Conventional. Change is a process that must be stimulated by outside forces. The natural state of affairs is at best to maintain the status quo and at worst to disintegrate to the lowest organizational/energy level possible (entropy). Change is a process that must be managed.

Constructivist. Change is a continuously ongoing process that requires neither outside stimulation nor direction, even though at times such intervention may be useful. Outside management may often impede change rather than promote it.

Comment. The mechanistic model of the universe persuades the conventionalist that humans, like machines, can run only if there is some outside source of energy continuously provided. Left to their own devices humans will always take the path of least resistance. The constructivist argues that the actions people take depend in the last analysis on the constructions they hold. If there is to be outside stimulation it is most usefully applied in the form of information/sophistication that leads to reconstruction.

14 *Implementing the change process*
Conventional. Change is a linear process that moves through stages from research (basic inquiry) through development (applied inquiry) through diffusion to adoption. Each stage looks to the preceding one for its inputs and provides output to the following stage.

Constructivist. Change is a nonlinear process that involves the infusion of new information and increased sophistication in its use into the constructions of involved human constructors. The infusion received from constructivist inquiry is but one kind that will be and probably should be taken into account.

Comment. The conventionalist appropriately organizes the change process into stages that begin with the 'discovery' of scientific information (which might include the needs of target audiences). The information is then put through a cycle of development to produce whatever the scientific information indicates is needed. That developed product is then disseminated (creating awareness in target audiences and making the product available for adoption), and, finally, adopted. The constructivist focuses not on scientifically justified products but on changed constructions, noting that not all information that enters into constructions can or should be information gleaned from some kind of disciplined inquiry.

References

COOK, T.D. (1985). Postpositivist critical multiplism. In L. SHOTLAND and M.M. MARK (Eds), *Social science and social policy*. Beverly Hills, CA: Sage.

COOK, T.D. and CAMPBELL, D.T. (1979). *Quasi experimentation: Design and analysis issues for field settings*. Chicago: Rand McNally.

HESSE, M. (1980). *Revolutions and reconstructions in the philosophy of science*. Bloomington: Indiana University Press.

KUHN, T.S. (1970). *The structure of scientific revolutions* (2nd ed., enlarged). Chicago: University of Chicago Press.

LINCOLN, Y.S. and GUBA, E.G. (1985). *Naturalistic inquiry*. Beverly Hills, CA: Sage.

ZUKAV, G. (1979). *The dancing Wu-Li masters*. New York: Bantam.

Part 3

Knowledge Generation and Knowledge Distribution

Chapter 14

The Many Meanings of Research Utilization*

Carol H. Weiss

This is a time when more and more social scientists are becoming concerned about making their research useful for public policy makers, and policy makers are displaying spurts of well-publicized concern about the usefulness of the social science research that government funds support. There is mutual interest in whether social research intended to influence policy is actually 'used', but before that important issue can profitably be addressed it is essential to understand what 'using research' actually means.

A review of the literature reveals that a diverse array of meanings is attached to the term. Much of the ambiguity in the discussion of 'research utilization' — and conflicting interpretations of its prevalence and the routes by which it occurs — derives from conceptual confusion. If we are to gain a better understanding of the extent to which social science research has affected public policy in the past, and learn how to make its contribution more effective in the future, we need to clarify the concept.

Upon examination, the use of social science research in the sphere of public policy is an extraordinarily complex phenomenon. Authors who have addressed the subject have evoked diverse images of the processes and purposes of utilization. Here I will try to extract seven different meanings that have been associated with the concept.

The Knowledge-Driven Model

The first image of research utilization is probably the most venerable in the literature and derives from the natural sciences. It assumes the following sequence of events: basic research — applied research — development — application. The notion is that basic research discloses some

---

* Reprinted from 'The Many Meanings of Research Utilization' by C.H. Weiss, 1979, *Public Administration Review*, 39(5), pp. 426–431.

opportunity that may have relevance for public policy; applied research is conducted to define and test the findings of basic research for practical action; if all goes well, appropriate technologies are developed to implement the findings; whereupon application occurs (Havelock, 1969, chap. 1).

Examples of this model of research utilization generally come from the physical sciences: biochemical research makes available oral contraceptive pills, research in electronics enables television to multiply the number of broadcast channels. Because of the fruits of basic research, new applications are developed and new policies emerge (cf. Comroe and Dripps, 1976).

The assumption is that the sheer fact that knowledge exists presses it toward development and use. However well or poorly this model describes events in the natural sciences, in the social sciences few examples can be found. The reasons appear to be several. Social science knowledge is not apt to be so compelling or authoritative as to drive inevitably toward implementation. Social science knowledge does not readily lend itself to conversion into replicable technologies, either material or social. Perhaps most important, unless a social condition has been consensually defined as a pressing social problem, and unless the condition has become fully politicized and debated, and the parameters of potential action agreed upon, there is little likelihood that policy-making bodies will be receptive to the results of social science research.

I do not mean to imply that basic research in the social sciences is not useful for policy making. Certainly many social policies and programs of government are based, explicitly or implicitly, on basic psychological, sociological, economic, anthropological, and political scientific understandings. When they surface to affect government decisions, however, it is not likely to be through the sequence of events posited in this model.

Problem-Solving Model

The most common concept of research utilization involves the direct application of the results of a specific social science study to a pending decision. The expectation is that research provides empirical evidence and conclusions that help to solve a policy problem. The model is again a linear one, but the steps are different from those in the knowledge-driven model. Here the decision drives the application of research. A problem exists and a decision has to be made, information or understanding is lacking either to generate a solution to the problem or to select among alternative solutions, research provides the missing knowledge. With the gap filled, a decision is reached.

Implicit in this model is a sense that there is a consensus on goals. It is assumed that policy makers and researchers tend to agree on what the desired end state shall be. The main contribution of social science research is to help identify and select appropriate means to reach the goal.

The evidence that social science research provides for the decision-making process can be of several orders. It can be qualitative and descriptive, e.g., rich observational accounts of social conditions or of program processes. It can be quantitative data, either on relatively soft indicators, e.g., public attitudes, or on hard factual matters, e.g., number of hospital beds. It can be statistical relationships between variables, generalized conclusions about the associations among factors, even relatively abstract (middle-range) theories about cause and effect. Whatever the nature of the empirical evidence that social science research supplies, the expectation is that it clarifies the situation and reduces uncertainty, and therefore, it influences the decision that policy makers make.

In this formulation of research utilization, there are two general ways in which social science research can enter the policy-making arena. First, the research antedates the policy problem and is drawn in on need. Policy makers faced with a decision may go out and search for information from preexistent research to delimit the scope of the question or identify a promising policy response. Or the information can be called to their attention by aides, staff analysts, colleagues, consultants, or social science researchers. Or they may happen upon it in professional journals, agency newsletters, newspapers and magazines, or at conferences. There is an element of chance in this route from problem to research to decision. Available research may not directly fit the problem. The location of appropriate research, even with sophisticated and computerized information systems, may be difficult. Inside experts and outside consultants may appear to be out of date or not generalizable to the immediate context. Whether or not the best and most relevant research reaches the person with the problem depends on the efficiency of the communications links. Therefore, when this imagery of research utilization prevails, the usual prescription for improving the use of research is to improve the means of communication to policy makers.

A second route to problem-solving use is the purposeful commissioning of social science research and analysis to fill the knowledge gap. The assumptions, as with the search route, are that decision makers have a clear idea of their goals and a map of acceptable alternatives and that they have identified some specific informational needs to clarify their choice. This time they engage social scientists to provide the data, analytic generalizations, and possibly the interpretations of these generalizations to the case in hand by way of recommendations. The process follows this sequence: definition of pending decision — identification of missing knowledge — acquisition of social science research — interpretation of the research for the decision context — policy choice.

The expectation is that research generated in this type of sequence, even more than research located through search procedures, will have direct and immediate applicability and will be used for decision making. In fact, it is usually assumed that the specific study commissioned by the responsible government office will have an impact and that its recommendations will affect ensuing choices. Particularly the large-scale government-contracted policy study, tailored to the specifications set by government staff, is expected to make a difference in plans, programs, and policies. If the research goes unused, the prescription to improve utilization that arises from this imagery is to increase government control over both the specification of requested research and its conduct in the field. If the research had actually met decision-makers' information needs, it is assumed, it would have been used.

Even a cursory review of the fate of social science research, including policy research on government-defined issues, suggests that these kinds of expectations are wildly optimistic. Occasional studies have direct effect on decisions, but usually on relatively low-level, narrow-gauge decisions. Most studies appear to come and go without leaving any discernible mark on the direction or substance of policy. It probably takes an extraordinary concatenation of circumstances for research to influence policy decisions directly: a well-defined decision situation, a set of policy actors who have responsibility and jurisdiction for making the decision, an issue whose resolution depends at least to some extent on *information*, identification of the requisite informational need, research that provides the information in terms that match the circumstances within which choices will be made, research findings that are clear-cut, unambiguous, firmly supported, and powerful, that reach decision makers at the time they are wrestling with the issues, that are comprehensible and understood, and that do not run counter to strong political interests. Because chances are small that all these conditions will fall into line around any one issue, the problem-solving model of research use probably describes a relatively small number of cases.

However, the problem-solving model remains the prevailing imagery of research utilization. Its prevalence probably accounts for much of the disillusionment about the contribution of social science research to social policy. Because people expect research use to occur through the sequence of stages posited by this model, they become discouraged when events do not take the expected course. However, there are other ways in which social science research can be 'used' in policy making.

Interactive Model

Another way that social science research can enter the decision arena is as part of an interactive search for knowledge. Those engaged in developing policy-seeking information not only from social scientists but from a variety of sources — administrators, practitioners, politicians, planners, journalists, clients, interest groups, aides, friends, and social scientists, too. The process is not one of linear order from research to decision but a disorderly set of interconnections and back-and-forthness that defies neat diagrams.

All kinds of people involved in an issue area pool their talents, beliefs, and understandings in an effort to make sense of a problem. Social scientists are one set of participants among many. Seldom do they have conclusions available that bear directly and explicitly on the issue at hand. More rarely still do they have a body of convergent evidence. Nevertheless, they can engage in mutual consultations that progressively move closer to potential policy responses.

Donnison describes this interactive model of research use in the development of two pieces of legislation in Great Britain. He notes that decisions could not wait upon completion of research but had to be made when political circumstances compelled.

> Research workers could not present authoritative findings for others to apply; neither could others commission them to find the "correct" solution to policy problems: they were not that kind of problem. Those in the four fields from which experience had to be brought to bear [politics, technology, practice, and research] contributed on equal terms. Each was expert in a few things, ignorant about most things, offered what he could, and generally learnt more than he could teach. (Donnison, 1972, p. 527)

In this model, the use of research is only part of a complicated process that also uses experience, political insight, pressure, social technologies, and judgment. It has applicability not only to face-to-face settings but also to the multiple ways in which intelligence is gathered through intermediaries and brought to bear. It describes a familiar process by which decision makers inform themselves of the range of knowledge and opinion in a policy area.

Political Model

Often the constellation of interests around a policy issue predetermines the positions that decision makers take. Or debate has gone on over a period of years and opinions have hardened. At this point, decision makers are not likely to be receptive to new evidence from social science research. For reasons of interest, ideology, or intellect, they have taken a stand that research is not likely to shake.

In such cases, research can still be used. It becomes ammunition for the side that finds its conclusions congenial and supportive. Partisans flourish the evidence in an attempt to neutralize opponents, convince waverers, and bolster supporters. Even if conclusions have to be ripped out of context (with suppression of qualifications and of evidence 'on the other hand'), research becomes grist to the mill.

Social scientists tend to look askance at the impressment of research results into service for a position that decision makers have taken on other grounds. They generally see it as an illegitimate attempt to 'use' research (in the pejorative sense) for self-serving purposes of agency justification and personal aggrandizement. Using research to support a predetermined position is, however, research utilization, too, in a form which would seem to be neither an unimportant nor improper use. Only distortion and misinterpretation of findings are illegitimate. To the extent that the research, accurately interpreted, supports the position of one group, it gives the advocates of that position confidence, reduces their uncertainties, and provides them an edge in the continuing debate. Since the research finds ready-made partisans who will fight for its implementation, it stands a better chance of making a difference in the outcome (Weiss, 1973).

One of the appropriate conditions for this model of research use is that all parties to the issue have access to the evidence. If, for example, bureaucrats monopolize research that would support the position of clients, then equity is not served, but when research is available to all participants in the policy process, research as political ammunition can be a worthy model of utilization.

Tactical Model

There are occasions when social science research is used for purposes that have little relation to the substance of the research. It is not the content of the findings that is invoked but the sheer fact that research is being done. For example, government agencies confronted with demands for action may respond by saying, "Yes, we know that's an important need. We're doing research on it right now." Research becomes proof of their responsiveness. Faced with unwelcome demands, they may use research as a tactic for delaying action ("We are waiting until the research is completed . . .").

Sometimes government agencies use research to deflect criticism. By claiming that their actions were based on the implications and recommendations of social science research studies, they may try to avoid responsibility for unpopular policy outcomes. Or support for a research program can become a tactic for enhancing the prestige of the agency by allying it with social scientists of high repute. Some agencies support substantial amounts of research and in so doing, build a constituency of academic supporters who rally to their defense when appropriations are under Congressional review. These are illustrations of uses of research, irrespective of its conclusions, as a tactic in bureaucratic politics.

Enlightenment Model

Perhaps the way in which social science research most frequently enters the policy arena is through the process that has come to be called "enlightenment" (Crawford and Biderman, 1969; Janowitz, 1972). Here it is not the findings of a single study nor even of a body of related studies that directly affect policy. Rather it is the concepts and theoretical perspectives that social science research has engendered that permeate the policy-making process.

There is no assumption in this model that decision makers seek out social science research when faced with a policy issue or even that they are receptive to, or aware of, specific research conclusions. The imagery is that of social science generalizations and orientations percolating through informed publics and coming to shape the way in which people think about social issues. Social science research diffuses circuitously through manifold channels — professional journals, the mass media, conversations with colleagues — and over time the variables it deals with and the generalizations it offers provide decision makers with ways of making sense out of a complex world.

Rarely will policy makers be able to cite the findings of a specific study that influenced their decisions, but they have a sense that social science research has given them a backdrop of ideas and orientations that has had important consequences (see, for example, Caplan, Morrison and Stambaugh, 1975). Research sensitizes decision makers to new issues and helps turn what were non-problems into policy problems. A recent example is child abuse (Weiss, 1976). Conversely, research may convert existing problems into non-problems, e.g., marijuana use. Research can drastically revise the way that policy makers define issues, e.g., acceptable rates of unemployment, the facets of the issue they view as susceptible to alteration, and the alternative measures they consider. It helps to change the parameters within which policy solutions are sought. In the long run, along with other influences, it often redefines the policy agenda.

Unlike the problem-solving model, this model of research use does not assume that, in order to be useful, research results must be compatible with decision-makers' values and goals. Research that challenges current verities may work its way into official consciousness (Aaron, 1978) and, with support from dissident undergrounds, overturn accustomed values and patterns of thought.

The notion of research utilization in the enlightenment mode has a comforting quality. It seems to promise that, without any special effort, truth will triumph; but the enlightenment process has its full share of deficiencies. When research diffuses to the policy sphere through indirect and unguided channels, it dispenses invalid as well as valid generalizations. Many of the social science understandings that gain currency are partial, oversimplified, inadequate, or wrong. There are no procedures for screening out the shoddy and obsolete. Sometimes unexpected or sensational research results, however incomplete or inadequately supported by data, take the limelight. As an environmental researcher has noted, "Bad science, being more newsworthy, will tend to be publicized and seized on by some to support their convictions" (Comar, 1978). The indirect diffusion process is vulnerable to oversimplification and distortion, and it may come to resemble 'endarkenment' as much as enlightenment.

Moreover, the enlightenment model is an inefficient means for reaching policy audiences. Many vital results of social science research never penetrate to decision-making centers. Some results take so long to come into currency that they are out of date by the time they arrive, their conclusions having been modified, or even contradicted, by later and more comprehensive analysis.

Finally, recent reviews of research on poverty, incomes, unemployment, and education suggest that social science research has not led to convergent conclusions (Aaron, 1978; Cohen and Weiss, 1977). As more studies are done, they often elaborate rather than simplify. They generate complex, varied, and even contradictory views of the social phenomena under study, rather than cumulating into sharper and more coherent explanation. The effect may be to widen and enrich our understanding of the multiple facets of reality, but the implications for policy are *less* simple and clear-cut. When the diverse research conclusions enter the policy arena, the direction they provide for policy is confused. Advocates of almost any policy prescription are likely to find some research generalizations in circulation to support their points of view.

Research as Part of the Intellectual Enterprise of the Society

A final view of research utilization looks upon social science research as one of the intellectual pursuits of a society. It is not so much an independent variable whose effects on policy remain to be determined as it is another of the independent variables, collateral with policy — and with philosophy, journalism, history, law, and criticism. Like policy, social science research responds to the currents of thought, the fads and fancies, of the period. Social science and policy interact, influencing each other and being influenced by the larger fashions of social thought.

It is often emerging policy interest in a social issue that leads to the appropriation of funds for social science research in the first place, and only with the availability of funds are social scientists attracted to study of the issue. Early studies may accept the parameters set by the policy discussion, limiting investigation to those aspects of the issue that have engaged official attention. Later, as social science research widens its horizons, it may contribute to reconceptualization of the issue by policy makers. Meanwhile, both the policy and research colloquies may respond, consciously or unconsciously, to concerns sweeping through intellectual and popular thought ('citizen participation', 'local control', spiraling inflation, individual privacy). In this view, research is one part of the interconnected intellectual enterprise.

These, then, are some of the meanings that 'the use of social science research' can carry. Probably all of them are applicable in some situations. Certainly none of them represents a fully satisfactory answer to the question of how a polity best mobilizes its research resources to inform public action.

An understanding of the diversity of perspectives on research utilization may serve many purposes. For one, it may help to overcome the disenchantment with the usefulness of social science research that has afflicted those who search for use only in problem-solving contexts. For another, it may enable us to engage in empirical study of the policy uses of research with better awareness of its diverse and often subtle manifestations; if immediate impact of a specific study on a specific decision is only one indicator of use, we will have to devise more complex but more appropriate modes of study.

Finally, we may need to think more deeply about the proper role of social science in public policy making. There has been much glib rhetoric about the vast benefits that social science can offer if only policy makers paid attention. Perhaps it is time for social scientists to pay attention to the imperatives of policy-making systems and to consider soberly what they can do, not necessarily to increase the use of research, but to improve the contribution that research makes to the wisdom of social policy.

References

AARON, H. (1978). *Politics and the professors*. Washington, DC: Brookings Institution.

CAPLAN, N., MORRISON, A. and STAMBAUGH, R. (1975). *The use of social science knowledge in policy decisions at the national level*. Ann Arbor, MI: Institute for Social Research.

COHEN, D.K. and WEISS, J.A. (1977). Social science and social policy: Schools and race. In C.H. WEISS (Ed.), *Using social research in public policy making* (pp. 67–83). Lexington, MA: Lexington/D.C. Heath.

COMAR, C. (1978). Bad science and social penalties. *Science, 200* (June 16), 1225.

COMROE, J.H. Jr. and DRIPPS, R.D. (1976). Scientific basis for the support of biomedical science. *Science*, April 9, 105–111.

CRAWFORD, E.T. and BIDERMAN, A.D. (1969). The functions of policy-oriented social science. In E. CRAWFORD and A. BIDERMAN (Eds), *Social scientists and international affairs* (pp. 233–243). New York: Wiley.

DONNISON, D. (1972). Research for policy. *Minerva, 10*(4), 519–536.

HAVELOCK, R.G. (1969). *Planning for innovation through dissemination and utilization of knowledge*. Ann Arbor, MI: Institute for Social Research.

JANOWITZ, M. (1972). Professionalization of sociology. *American Journal of Sociology*, 78, 105–135.

WEISS, C.H. (1973). Where politics and evaluation research meet. *Evaluation*, 1(3), 37–45.

WEISS, J.A. (1976). Using social science for social policy. *Policy Studies Journal*, 4(3), 236.

Chapter 15

Knowledge Creep and Decision Accretion*

Carol H. Weiss

The conventional title for this article would be "Knowledge Utilization in Decision Making". I have chosen the mangled terminology to make a point — in fact, two points. The first is that knowledge, at least the subcategory of knowledge that derives from systematic research and analysis, is not often 'utilized' in direct and instrumental fashion in the formulation of policy. Only occasionally does it supply an 'answer' that policy actors employ to solve a policy problem. Instead, research knowledge usually affects the development and modification of policy in diffuse ways. It provides a background of empirical generalizations and ideas that *creep* into policy deliberations. Its influence is exercised in more subtle ways than the word 'utilization' — with its overtone of tools and implements — can capture.

The second point is that many policy actions, even those of fateful order, are not 'decided' in brisk and clear-cut style. The term 'decision' implies a particular set of events: A problem comes up, a set of people authorized to deal with the problem gather at particular times and places to consider options for coping with it, they weigh the alternative options (with more or less explicit calculation of costs and benefits), and they choose one response. That becomes the decision — a set of rules or guidelines, the funding or not funding of a program, the reorganization of a structure, leaving the situation as is, or whatever. But in large organizations, policies often come into being without such systematic consideration. No problem (or opportunity) is identified as an explicit issue, no identifiable set of authorized decision makers meets, no list of options is generated, no assessment is made of relative advantages and disadvantages, no crisp choice is made. Yet the onrushing flow of events shape an accommodation — and a pattern of behavior — that has widespread ramifications. It may in time be ratified by conscious policy action, but in

---

* Abridged from 'Knowledge Creep and Decision Accretion' by C.H. Weiss, 1980, *Knowledge: Creation, Diffusion, Utilization*, *1*(3), pp. 381–404.

the crucial formative stages, it just seems to happen. Without conscious deliberation, the policy *accretes*.

That decisions often take shape gradually, without the formality of agenda, deliberation, and choice, helps to explain the lack of direct utilization of research and analysis. When decisions accrete through small uncoordinated steps taken in many offices — by staffs who have little awareness of the policy direction that is being promoted or the alternatives that are being foreclosed, there is scant opportunity for deliberate application of research information to the task. But staff base their ongoing actions on the sum of their knowledge and judgment. To the extent that research has entered into their understanding of the nature of problems and of feasible responses, they draw upon it as they carry on their work.

These are the basic themes of the paper. They developed out of research that Michael Bucuvalas, Laurie Bauman, and I did at Columbia University on the usefulness of social science research to officials in federal, state, and local mental health agencies. We interviewed 155 people who held high-level positions in these organizations about their responses to research (Weiss, 1977; Weiss and Bucuvalas, 1977, 1980). Among the questions we asked them were:

> Do you consciously use the results of social science research in reaching decisions on your job? In what ways do you use social science research on your job?
>
> Do you seek out research information when you're considering policy or program alternatives? Under what circumstances do you seek research?

The first pair of questions obviously asks about the *conscious use* of social science research, not about the circuitous percolation of research ideas into people's construction of social reality. Yet it was from answers to this set of questions that we came to understand much about the amorphous process that I have here labeled "creep".

The second pair of questions refers not only to conscious use but to *active search*. It sets the search in a frame of decision making in the traditional sense, assuming that high-ranking officials "consider policy or program alternatives" and that they need information to help them in their consideration. Again the interview takes a relatively hard line, setting a context of rational choice, and again some respondents managed to circumvent the implicit imagery and describe the very different world they inhabit. Their responses stimulated a reconceptualization of the decision-making process in bureaucratic organizations and speculation about the antecedents and consequences of diffuse decisions. . . .

Varieties of Research Use

[Answers given to our questions suggest] that social science research serves many functions for holders of upper-level bureaucratic positions. They use it on occasion as a direct input to decisions to help them make difficult choices. Particularly when the decisions are momentous in scope or consequence, they may attend to research results. Somewhat more often, they use research as general guidance, finding evidence of needs and problems and gaps or shortcomings in existing services, and identifying successful strategies as a model for future efforts. Some research use is ritualistic, a ceremony to satisfy requirements for rational procedure or scientific gloss. Officials are engaged by the concepts of social science, which contribute to their understanding of the nature of social problems, the range of possible options for addressing problems, and the context in which remedies must be applied. In new program areas, where officials lack first-hand experience, such orienting perspectives are particularly valuable. They use research ideas, too, to rethink old program assumptions and as scaffolding for building new formulations.

Another major use of social science research is as continuing education to enable officials to maintain their professional expertise. Research is, among other things, a medium of news about needs, services, promising approaches, obstacles and pitfalls, and the most up-to-date knowledge about human behavior. It offers information about the issues and ideas that are engaging the attention of social scientists and about current directions in intellectual thought. Even when officials are not consciously using research, the perspectives they have absorbed from the social science literature influence which features of the environment they accept as 'given' and unchangeable, which aspects are candidates for intervention, and their understanding of the interconnections among social phenomena.

There are times when officials use these insights to challenge and clarify their own thinking. Sometimes they derive the warm comfort of reassurance that their judgments are sound and have support and reinforcement in systematic investigation. They use research, too, to buttress their position and promote their case in dealing with colleagues and superiors and to convince others to accept their viewpoints, programs, and budgets. They speak the language of social science research to make their arguments convincing. By adopting its symbols and its grammar, they may find their positions subtly influenced by the structure of its rules.

Our research, like other recent empirical studies of the use of social science research in organizations (Alkin, Daillak and White, 1979; Berg, Brudney, Fuller, Michael, and Roth, 1978; Caplan, Morrison and Stambaugh, 1975; Knorr, 1977; Patton, Grimes, Guthrie, Brennan, French and Blyth, 1977; Rich, 1977), converges on the conclusion that public officials use research more widely than previous laments on the subject have suggested. But they do not often use it by considering the findings of one study in the context of a specific pending decision and adopting the course of action recommended by (or derived directly from) the research. That kind of instrumental 'utilization' is what many observers have expected and looked for in vain. Failing to find it, they have concluded that research is ignored. Instrumental use seems in fact to be rare, particularly when the issues are complex, the consequences are uncertain, and a multitude of actors are engaged in the decision-making process, i.e., in the making of *policy*. The further restriction that many observers have imposed on their definition of research utilization — that the research *change* the decision from what it would have been in the absence of research — makes the frequency of 'utilization instances' in policy making rarer still. But when we recognize the many and diverse ways in which research contributes to organizational action, we get a much more positive view of the influence of research.

I am particularly impressed by the numbers of people in our study who had a strong sense that social science research mattered. Even when they could not cite *any* conscious use of research, they believed that they had assimilated generalizations, concepts, and perspectives from the social sciences that inevitably colored their understanding and shaped their actions. As Lindblom (1977) has written: "Fact, analysis, idea, and misinformation achieve their effects even when influence is unintended, simply because all of us constantly react to our perceptions of the world around us" (p. 52). Social science, by helping to structure people's perceptions of social reality, seems to have pervasive effects. It provides an underlying set of ideas, models of the interaction of people, conditions, and events, which enter into our images of how the world works. The respondents in our study underscored this indirect kind of knowledge creep.

The Diffuse Decision

But however pervasive the general effects of social science research may be, and I have come to believe that they are substantial, we must still confront the question of the specific effects. Why don't the social science research studies, evaluations, and analyses that are specifically funded to help decision makers decide have more discernible effect? Why can't people in positions of organizational authority cite particular studies that have influenced particular decisions?

In all fairness, I must report that we asked our respondents to name a study they had found useful for their work and 72% produced a citation. (In all, 39% gave a full reference, and 33% gave a somewhat fuzzy one, i.e., lacking the name of the author or the title of the study or the journal/publisher.) However, most of them had great difficulty in identifying a particular publication that had been useful; some arbitrarily pulled a title out of their heads or off the bookshelf; and many of them objected that the question was meaningless: They could not disentangle the special contribution of any one study. Given the amount of research in mental health that the government supports for the ostensible purpose of affecting policy and program decisions, why don't more applications of research to decisions show up?

We know many of the reasons. Scholars over the years have cited a series of disjunctures between research and decision that limit the use of research. Research does not fit the exact circumstances within which decisions are made, research is not ready on time for decisions, research conclusions are not unambiguous or authoritative enough to provide direct guidance, research reports do not reach the right audience, decision makers do not understand or trust research findings or understand how to interpret and apply them, the lessons from research are outweighed by the combination of competing interests, agency self-protection, and individual career concerns. These and other obstacles block the route to application.

Officials in our study give a measure of support to several of these explanations. But the undertext of their responses adds a further insight into the nature of the problem. When we listen to them carefully, we recognize that a salient reason why they do not report the use of research for specific decisions is that many of them *do not believe that they make decisions*.

The people we interviewed held responsible positions. At the federal level, they were bureau chiefs, division directors, or higher-level administrators in the National Institute of Mental Health, the National Institute of Drug Abuse, the National Institute of Alcohol Abuse and Alcoholism, and the parent agency, the Alcohol, Drug Abuse, and Mental Health Administration. At the state level, they held the tier of positions just below the commissioner or director of mental health, with titles such as deputy director of mental health, director of community programs, or director of addiction services. At the local level, they were directors of mental health centers and mental health hospitals or chiefs of services within those agencies. Their titles and their statutory responsibilities suggest considerable authority. Yet a great many of them indicated that decision making was an inappropriate concept for their work.

In our pretest interviews, we had a question asking respondents to describe the kinds of decisions they made on their jobs. Discomfort with the question was so prevalent and acute that in the final version of the interview we discarded the "decision" wording and asked instead about "the main functions of your job". Only one question in the interview retained the word "decision", i.e. the question about conscious use of social science research "in reaching decisions on your job". Even this scaled-down version drew frequent disclaimers. For example: "I don't know what it means when you say 'reaching decisions.' I decide to answer or not answer various pieces of correspondence. . . . Let's leave decisions out and talk about action." The idea that they made decisions about policy, programs, budgets, allocations, or services was widely disconcerting. If officials do not give the label decision to their actions, even the highly consequential actions they take, if they do not perceive their acts as decisions or as part of decision making, then they can hardly identify research that influences their decisions.

Review of the responses suggests that three conditions mainly account for the disavowals of decision-making authority: (a) the dispersion of responsibility over many offices and the participation of many actors in decision making, so that no one individual feels that he or she has a major say; (b) the division of authority among federal, state, and local levels in the federal system; and (c) the series of gradual and amorphous steps through which many decisions take shape.

Obviously in large organizations, decisions on complex issues are almost never the province of one individual or one office. Many people in many offices have a say, and when the outcomes of a course of action are uncertain, many participants have opportunities to propose, plan, confer, deliberate, advise, argue, forward policy statements, reject, revise, veto, and rewrite. In addition, legislative action is often required for major shifts in direction, and legislative appropriations are needed for a major increase in activities. The operational staffs in the agencies are sensitive to the preferences and expectations of the legislature. However influential their own proposals and actions turn out in fact to be, they are conscious of the recurrent approvals and sign-offs that must be obtained within the department and the modifications that may be introduced during the legislative process. In fact, they seem to be more conscious of the power of others — whether or not it is exercised — than they are of the influence of their own actions.

Given the slow and cumbersome process through which proposals often travel, many organizational members are not fully aware of the influence they have. They make proposals and see nothing happen for months. Even if the proposal is eventually adopted with only minor modifications, they may lose sight of the connection between what they proposed and what eventually happens. And when a series of adaptations is made, they seem to conclude that they have little power in the system.

Officials at the top echelon can be equally convinced that they do not make decisions. At the top of the hierarchy, it often looks as though they are presented with a *fait accompli*. Accommodations have been reached and a decision negotiated by people in the many offices below, and they have little option but to accept it. Only rarely, and with the expenditure of a considerable amount of their political capital, can they change or reject it. To them, the job often looks like rubber-stamping decisions already made. Thus, the division of authority leaves each participant largely unaware of the nature and extent of his contribution.

The federal system adds further indeterminacy. During the interviewing in our study, we were told by people at each governmental level that 'real' decisions were made elsewhere. Federal officials said that Congress passed the law and determined the appropriations, and all they did was write guidelines to carry out congressional intent and pass the money down to the agencies, which made real decisions about services. State officials said they were a conduit. They received federal funds hedged about by congressional requirements and . . . guidelines [of the Department of Health, Education, and Welfare], along with state funds restricted by requirements of the state legislature. Their main job was not to decide but to do the paperwork to move the money to operating agencies. To local agencies, it looked as though funds came ringed around by tight constraints — legislative provisions, federal guidelines, state plans and regulations — and extra regulations for funds received from city, county, and third-party payers. They saw little latitude for local 'decisions.' They did what they were allowed to do under the weight of rules.

Thus, fragmentation of authority for decisions is not only horizontal but vertical. For a decision to take effect requires cooperation at every level. What the federal agency 'decides' can be distorted or undone by action (or inaction) in state and local agencies. What the care-giving agency 'decides' is so hemmed in by requirements of other bodies that it feels it has little discretion. Again, people at every point are more conscious of the limits to their authority than of the latitude available.

The final set of reasons why the concept of decisions is inapt derives from the nature of bureaucratic work. Many problems and issues are dealt with simultaneously, and consideration of each one goes on over a protracted period. Responsible officials only rarely convene at one time and one place to make a decision. The image of decision making represented by President Kennedy and his group of advisers thrashing out the nation's response to the Cuban missile crisis is inappropriate to most of daily bureaucratic life. Much more commonly, each person takes some small step (writes a memo, answers an inquiry, edits the draft of a regulation) that has seemingly small consequences. But over a period of time, these many small steps foreclose alternative courses of action and limit the range of the possible. Almost imperceptibly a decision has been made, without anyone's awareness that he or she was deciding.

Many moves are improvisations. Faced with an event that calls for response, officials use their experience, judgment, and intuition to fashion the response for the issue at hand. That response becomes a precedent, and when similar — or not so similar — questions come up, the response is uncritically repeated. Consider the federal agency that receives a call from a local program asking how to deal with requests for enrollment in excess of the available number of slots. A staff member responds with off-the-cuff advice. Within the next few weeks, programs in three more cities call with similar questions, and staff repeat the advice. Soon what began as improvisation has hardened into policy. Bauer (1963) writes of this type of decision making:

> It is ordinarily assumed that *important* decisions are made most deliberately and ordinarily with the least constraint of other considerations. But this is not always the case. For example, it has long been a complaint of our State Department that the ordinary problems get explicit attention and overall policy is made by default. There is a familiar phrase used to describe this: "Policy is made on the wires," that is, in the cabled responses to specific problems arising in the field. (p. 59)

Kissinger (1979) recently explained how an action, taken for a considered purpose, can be repeated unthinkingly under conditions for which it was not designed. Writing about the "double-bookkeeping" that kept the bombing of Cambodia secret, he said:

> The method of reporting was set up for the first (and we then thought only) strike on March 18, 1969. . . . What was originally conceived as a one-time response to the North Vietnamese offensive became a continuing practice about two and a half months later — after Hanoi had turned down a new peace offer. The double-bookkeeping set up for a single attack was then repeated by rote and without a special new decision. This may have been mindless. (p. E19)

Repetition is only one route to the accretion of policy without decision. Some decisions take shape through a series of actions and reactions. An inside or outside event triggers a move, which sets off the next move, which leads to the next — until the unconcerted series of well-advised or bumbling moves has shifted the direction of policy. (Through such a series of disastrous moves, the great powers stumbled into World War I.) The many independent accommodations and contests led to a result that no one anticipated.

Probably even more common is the decision that 'happens' as a side effect of other decisions. Nobody is paying explicit attention to the issue at hand, but the unintended consequences of actions taken for other purposes effectively set policy. A town that adopts strict environmental regulations to preserve open spaces, coastline, and water in effect limits the influx of new residents. Without conscious consideration, it 'decides' to keep out lower income and minority families. Or a state agency with insufficient office space moves to an available suburban location that happens to be poorly served by public transit. In so doing, it in effect 'decides' to reduce the number of inner-city employees, even while its equal opportunity office is trying to increase minority representation on staff.

Much of the literature on organizational decision making assumes that a set of officials with authority for an issue-arena exists, that this set of officials becomes aware of a problem or opportunity within its jurisdiction requiring action, that it generates options for dealing with the situation, considers the advantages and disadvantages of each option, and makes a conscious choice. In such a process, research and analysis (as well as other information) can be formally taken into account. But under many conditions, each one of the assumptions breaks down. Many decisions 'happen' without the (a) acknowledged responsibility, (b) boundedness of time and events, (c) purposiveness, (d) calculation, or (e) perceived significance assumed in this image of decisions.

The respondents in our study tended to view their work as a stream of ongoing activities. They rarely thought of it as making discrete decisions but rather as "doing their job." They planned and recommended and administered, but these were not time-specific, choice-determining events. As Barnard (1962) wrote about an order to move two telephone poles across the street:

It can, I think, be approximately demonstrated that carrying out that order involves perhaps 10,000 decisions of 100 men located at 15 points, requiring successive analyses of several environments, including social, moral, legal, economic, and physical facts of the environment, and requiring 9,000 redefinitions and refinements of purpose, and 1,000 changes of purpose. If inquiry be made of those responsible, probably not more than half-a-dozen decisions will be recalled or deemed worthy of mention.... The others will be 'taken for granted', all of a part of the business of knowing one's business. (p. 198)

People in high organizational positions similarly compress dozens of large and small decisions into the category of knowing their business and doing their work. In consequence, the conscious use of research to guide specific choices is a relatively uncommon event. On the other hand, drawing upon the stock of knowledge that they have absorbed from social science research is highly compatible with the manner in which they conceptualize (and perform) their jobs. What they do is conditioned by what they know. The integration of social science generalizations and concepts into their *Weltanschauung* can have pervasive — if ultimately unmeasurable — effects. To the extent that their viewpoints are shaped by information, misinformation, and ideas from the social sciences, their policies will bear the imprint.

References

ALKIN, M., DAILLAK, C.R. and WHITE, P. (1979). *Using evaluations: Does evaluation make a difference?* Beverly Hills, CA: Sage.

BARNARD, C.I. (1962). *The functions of the executive.* Cambridge, MA: Harvard University Press.

BAUER, R.A. (1963). Problem-solving behavior in organizations: A functional point of view. In M.M. HARGROVE, I.H. HARRISON and E.L. SWEARINGEN (Eds), *Business policy cases — With behavioral science implications.* Homewood, IL: Irwin.

BERG, M.R., BRUDNEY, J.L., FULLER, T.D., MICHAEL, D.N. and ROTH, B.K. (1978). *Factors affecting utilization of technology assessment studies in policy making.* Ann Arbor: Center for Research on Utilization of Scientific Knowledge, University of Michigan.

CAPLAN, N., MORRISON, A. and STAMBAUGH, R.J. (1975). *The use of social science knowledge in policy decisions at the national level: A report to respondents.* Ann Arbor: Center for Research on Utilization of Scientific Knowledge, Institute for Social Research, University of Michigan.

KISSINGER, H.A. (1979). America's role in Cambodia. *New York Times*, September 23, E19.

KNORR, K.D. (1977). Policy makers' use of social science knowledge: Symbolic or instrumental? In C.H. WEISS (Ed.), *Using social research in public policy making.* Lexington, MA: D.C. Heath.

LINDBLOM, C.E. (1977). *Politics and markets.* New York: Basic Book.

PATTON, M.Q., GRIMES, P.S., GUTHRIE, K.M., BRENNAN, N.J., FRENCH, B.D. and BLYTH, D.A. (1977). In search of impact: An analysis of the utilization of federal health evaluation research. In C.H. WEISS (Ed.), *Using social research in public policy making.* Lexington, MA: D.C. Heath.

RICH, R.F. (1977). Uses of social science information by federal bureaucrats: Knowledge for action versus knowledge for understanding. In C.H. WEISS (Ed.), *Using social research in public policy making.* Lexington, MA: D.C. Heath.

WEISS, C.H. (1977). Introduction. In C.H. WEISS (Ed.), *Using social research in public policy making.* Lexington, MA: D.C. Heath.

WEISS, C.H. and BUCUVALAS, M.J. (1977). The challenge of social research to decision making. In C.H. WEISS (Ed.), *Using social research in public policy making.* Lexington, MA: D.C. Heath.

WEISS, C.H. and BUCUVALAS, M.J. (1980). *Social science research and decision making.* New York: Columbia University Press.

Chapter 16

The Use of Social Research Knowledge at the National Level*

Nathan Caplan

Knowledge utilization of any kind does not occur in a vacuum. The utilization of scientific information in the formulation of public policy, even under ideal conditions, is the result of a complex and often seemingly capricious set of circumstances. Some of these vicissitudes, however, are foreseeable, and it is my purpose to discuss certain of these factors and conditions on which social science knowledge utilization is contingent at the upper levels of governmental power and responsibility in the United States. . . .

[The ideas I will discuss here are based on the findings of a study in which 204 upper-echelon administrators in the executive branch of the United States government were asked to volunteer instances in which they used social research knowledge for making policy decisions.] Further details of the study, procedures for analysis, and results can be found in Caplan, Morrison, and Stambaugh (1975). . . .

If one were to step back and take an overview of the data collected in this study of federal executives, a number of findings emerge as particularly important to successful utilization. At the risk of oversimplification, utilization is most likely to occur when:

1   The decision-making orientation of the policy maker is characterized by a reasoned appreciation of the scientific and the extra-scientific aspects of the policy issue.
2   The ethical-scientific values of the policy maker carry with them a conscious sense of social direction and responsibility.
3   The policy issue is well defined and of such a nature that a 'best' solution requires research knowledge.
4   The research findings share the following characteristics: (a)

* Abridged from *Using Social Research in Public Policy Making* (pp. 183–197) edited by C.H. Weiss, 1977, Lexington, MA: D.C. Heath.

they are not counterintuitive; (b) they are believable on grounds of objectivity; and (c) their action implications are politically feasible.

5 The policy maker and knowledge producers are linked by information specialists capable of coupling scientific inputs to policy goals and objectives.

The Decision-Making Orientation

The ways in which policy makers process information appear to have different consequences in determining the amount and kinds of knowledge used in arriving at a policy decision even after variables such as rank and department are statistically controlled. Seventy percent of the respondents could be classified in one of ... three information-processing styles — clinical, academic, or advocacy — on the bases of their descriptions of how they used knowledge pertaining to the scientific and the extrascientific aspects of the policy issue under consideration. The remaining 30% did not fall into these categories because either it was impossible to classify them, or they straddled two or more categories. Those who adopted the clinical style used empirically based knowledge to the greatest extent; those with an academic orientation exhibited the next highest level of use; and those who adopted the advocacy style exhibited the lowest level of utilization....

The Clinical Orientation

The federal officials who expressed this style, approximately 20% of those interviewed, are the most active users of scientific information. They combine two basic approaches to problem solving. First they gather and process the best available information they can obtain to make an unbiased diagnosis of the policy issue. They use knowledge in this way to deal with the 'internal logic' of the problem. Next they gather information regarding the political and social ramifications of the policy issue to deal with the 'external logic' of the problem. To reach a policy decision, they finally weigh and reconcile the conflicting dictates of the information.

The Academic Orientation

The largest group of social science information users, approximately 30% of those interviewed, processes information with an academic orientation. They are often experts in their fields and prefer to devote their major attention to the internal logic of the policy issue. They are much less willing, however, to cope with the external realities that confound this type of problem. Considerations of the external logic of the problem are likely viewed as a menace to the prestige and standing of their expertise. Consequently, they use scientific information in moderate amounts and in routine ways to formulate and evaluate policies largely on the basis of scientifically derived information.

The Advocacy Orientation

Comprising another 20% of the federal officials is the advocacy-orientation group, which is much at home in the world of social, political, and economic realities. Their use of social science information is limited, but when used, its use is almost exclusively dictated by extrascientific forces to the extent that the group will at times intentionally ignore valid information that does not fit the prevailing political climate. The preoccupation is with the external logic of a policy issue, and the function of scientific knowledge when used in that context is largely to rationalize a decision made on extrascientific grounds.. . .

The Ethical-Scientific Values

An important characteristic of the more frequent users of social research is a quality of mind or what might be called a 'social perspective', which, put simply, involves a sensitivity to contemporary social events and a desire for social reform: They react as if what is happening in the larger society were indistinguishable from what is happening within themselves.

It is evident to a large extent that many respondents failed to distinguish between objective social science information and subjective social sensitivity. Thus, most of the examples they offered to illustrate knowledge applications really involved the application of secondary source information, organized common sense, and social sensitivity, which as a mixture, might be called a 'social perspective'.

The importance of this social perspective is particularly evident from responses to the following item: "On the basis of your experiences in the federal government, can you think of instances where a new program, a major program alternative, a new social or administrative policy, a legislative proposal or a technical innovation could be traced to the social sciences?" The 82% of the respondents who replied "yes" to this question were asked to be specific and provide examples.

Among the approximately 350 examples given, the policy areas represented ranged widely and were as likely to be technological or medical issues as the more strictly social policy issues. To illustrate, the following decisions were offered as examples: to establish water and sewer construction assistance programs and highway construction projects such as the interstate system; to go to an all volunteer army; to select particular diseases such as sickle cell anemia and cancer for major governmental research funding; to establish the lead-base paint prevention program, compensatory educational programs, the Environmental Protection Agency, manpower and development programs, the GI Bill, consumer information programs, revenue sharing, and major programs to 'humanize' management in government operations. All of these and many more programs involving governmental actions of considerable national importance were in some way traced by these respondents to the social sciences.

As respondents cited these examples, what seemed especially crucial in the decision-making process was the application of a value-laden appraisal of the possible social consequences of the policy decisions. This is not to deny that many respondents provided citations to specific social science information, particularly research, and emphasized its importance to the decision making process. But such 'hard' knowledge (research based, quantitative, and couched in scientific language) was usually only of some instrumental importance, and the final decision — whether or not to proceed with a particular policy — was more likely to depend upon an appraisal of 'soft' knowledge (nonresearch based, qualitative, and couched in lay language) considerations of the possible social consequences of the policy decisions. Further, regardless of whether or not the relevant information was 'hard' or 'soft', these respondents were eclectic in their use of information sources and relied on newspapers, TV, and popular magazines as well as scientific government research reports and scientific journals sources. In fact, one gets the overall impression that social science knowledge, 'hard' or 'soft', is treated as news by these respondents — allowing its users to feel that their awareness of social issues does not lag behind the rest of society or the professionals who deal with the policy-maker's field. . . .

The Policy Issue

Our third finding — that the policy issue is well defined and of such a nature that a 'best' solution requires research knowledge — is a situation that is best understood if viewed from the standpoint of the policy maker and the insetting which he operates. Put simply, the policy maker dealing with macrolevel problems often finds himself beset with an overwhelming number of bewildering and complex responsibilities. This is especially true in social problem areas where terms suffer from considerable ambiguity and have accumulated a number of different meanings. Persons in such positions, particularly if they are political appointees and new to the job, often find themselves in a serious need of help to identify and understand the problem issues they face and the options available to deal with them. Often research is sponsored to help the policy maker find his way out of this conceptual mudhole; the purpose of such research, however, is rarely made explicit to the researcher.

It is conceivable that social scientists might be useful to help policy makers if the real purpose of the research were made explicit and if empirical data were really needed. But, without knowledge of the policy-makers' difficulties, the researcher is unlikely to provide the policy maker with relevant and useful information. In the absence of a clear definition of the purposes to which the research will be addressed, the researcher creates his objectives, for no other reason than to carry on within a framework in which he can operate.

This point is aptly illustrated by research in two areas representing major efforts to supply policy makers with useful knowledge; they are (a) the collection of social indicators and (b) program evaluation studies. My purpose here is not to go out of my way to fault the research efforts going on in these areas, but to argue that underutilization may result from a failure to clearly define research purposes in two areas where the federal government and the social science community have been most actively involved in efforts to increase the utility of social research.

In the present study, nine out of ten respondents reported that an index of social well-being was a good idea and that it represented a major opportunity for social science to contribute significantly to policy formulation. They were also able to name several measures relevant to their own operations that they would like to see included in such an index. But, when asked what use they would make of such data, the responses were so rambling and diverse that it was impossible to derive empirically-based coding categories for purposes of quantification.

It is my opinion that this uncertainty results from the fact that a logically prior step in the policy formulation is lacking, namely, social indicators research would probably proceed more efficiently and its potential for policy use [would] increase greatly, if the collection of data were based upon some previously agreed upon notion of what purposes were to be served by such indicators. But, instead, we witness a widespread and often desultory collection of data conducted with the implicit hope that, somehow, from this pragmatic but goalless effort, there will evolve some notions about what is the good life and how responsible government may help to achieve it. In short, the idea of social indicators and all of the activity currently associated with it is desirable and will probably result in a considerable amount of useful information. But it really cannot be considered to be an efficient activity simply because it started as and continues to be an activity where the 'facts' are expected to provide answers to larger, essentially nonempirical issues. . . .

Perhaps evaluation research provides even better examples of these conceptual problems that hamper knowledge utilization. Here the criteria against which success and failure of program goals and strategies assessed by the evaluation researcher may bear little reference to what the sponsor 'had in mind' and therefore, the findings, while not meaningless, may be viewed as irrelevant. The difficulty here appears to arise from the failure of research sponsors to be explicit with respect to the nature of the problems to be attacked, the nature of the treatment variables, or the criteria for evaluation. The research sponsor may well 'know' what he means by mental health, and the like, but conceptualizing and then communicating that conceptualization may be difficult, and what he implicitly considers to be important may ultimately be quite different from the operational definitions imposed by the researcher for the purposes of obtaining measurable independent and dependent variables.

Many examples in the data show that well-conducted evaluations were judged useless by policy makers because the researchers' understanding of what was to be evaluated was not what the sponsor 'had in mind'. Often, however, the sponsor was unclear in his own mind about what he wanted, or was intentionally nonexplicit if he intended the research to serve latent political or administrative functions — evaluation objectives that the typical researcher would not likely assume if left to his own devices.

Some seriously disturbing consequences may have resulted from evaluations of Head Start and similar compensatory education programs. The original goals of these programs were far more broad based than allowed for by the scope of the measuring instruments used to evaluate their success. Initially, it was intended that social and emotional development were to be major components of efforts to increase academic adjustment among children from families in the lower economic ranges. This, however, was not made explicit to evaluators, who assumed the 'obvious' and derived oversimplified characterizations of the program treatment and objectives. These researchers then went about evaluation almost exclusively in terms of intellective functioning and gave little more than passing attention to the broader issues. In consequence, as evaluations accumulated over time, policy makers and research evaluators lost sight of the original intent of the programs, and soon issues of race and intelligence replaced questions of emotional deprivation, sociological 'damage', and educational achievement. . . .

It is difficult enough to do policy relevant research without losing the sense of the problem even when we have explicit knowledge of the issues under investigation. But if the problem is not made explicit and if the kind of knowledge needed is beyond the range of social science research and analysis, then the conduct of research is very likely to be a wasteful and futile exercise.

Characteristics of the Research Findings

Counterintuitive Findings

Many respondents who rejected policy-relevant information did so because they found the result to contradict what they considered to be true. For example, they were impressed with the concepts of democratic leadership and organizational management and the data supporting these ideas, but given the nature and pressures of their situation, many upper-level officials were convinced that such approaches to management would probably fail. To illustrate further, although the evaluation of some governmental programs showed failure, program administrators and sponsors remained convinced that the programs had succeeded. Similar examples in research on criminal justice, welfare, work satisfaction, and education could be cited to illustrate the fact that officials are willing to accept findings that coincide with their beliefs, but unwilling to accept findings that are counterintuitive to their beliefs, quite apart from issues of scientific objectivity and political feasibility.

An additional finding is worth mentioning here. When asked about how worthwhile intuition is in understanding social behavior, the respondents who were high knowledge users answered differently from those who were low knowledge users. Low users were more likely than high users to agree that "a sensitive or intuitive person can know as much about social behavior as the social scientist can by doing research". Not only did respondents provide examples of the rejection of information because it was counterintuitive, but of equal concern were examples that indicated they often uncritically accept information that is intuitively satisfying.

Intuitive feelings about the correctness of social science research is probably a less important factor than either the issues of objectivity or political feasibility, but it nonetheless plays an influencing role in utilization. Surely one of the difficult tasks ahead for persons interested in advancing the use of social science information in the formulation of social policy is to find ways to increase the acceptability of counterintuitive findings and decrease the acceptability of findings simply because they are intuitively agreeable. It should also be added that many findings are counterintuitive not because they run contrary to the beliefs of a single person who occupies a policy position, but because they appear contrary to many of the sacred beliefs of society. A public official would be reluctant to defend actions premised on such information, even if it were politically feasible to do so. The supporting evidence for his actions would have no prima facie plausibility since the public would not be likely to be persuaded by any decisions made under these conditions and would interpret such information as political deception.

Objectivity

The following question was asked each respondent: "Have you for any reason purposely disregarded or rejected relevant social science information in making or influencing a policy decision?" Forty-four percent of the respondents indicated that they had intentionally chosen not to use certain social science information relevant to a policy issue. If they responded "yes," they were then asked to describe the rejected information and the circumstances under which it was disregarded. It was found that, first, there appeared to be no failure on the part of respondents to understand the meaning or relevance of their social science information policy. Indeed, in some instances it was clear that rejection arose because they understood only too well. Second, one of the most frequent reasons given for rejection was lack of objectivity, both in terms of methodology and interpretation.

Objectivity becomes an issue when the data base is viewed as weak and the study design as poor, or if in general the respondent is of the belief that objectivity is so lacking in the social sciences that valid findings are indiscernible from invalid findings especially when two studies in the same subject produce opposite findings. But perhaps more than for other reasons, careless, irresponsible, and shoddy program evaluations were cited by respondents to discredit social science research.

Evidence for objectivity as a factor affecting utilization is supported in other questionnaire items as well. The respondents were asked to rate various scientific disciplines on the basis of their objectivity, and it was found that the heavier users of social science information consistently rated the social science items higher than less frequent users or nonusers. These differences in ratings across utilization score levels were sizable and statistically significant.

Political Feasibility

The ultimate test of data acceptability is political, particularly in the area of domestic social policy. The reason given most frequently for rejecting relevant social science information is that the implications are politically unfeasible. Rarely are data in their own right of such compelling force as to override their political significance. While this issue is an ancient one, and much has been written on it, it remains important. We should note, however, that while operative in some way in almost all policy decisions, political considerations are rarely the sole basis for sponsoring research or for deriving action implications from its results. Moreover, we have found few instances where research was deliberately misused to serve political ends. The framework in which the policy maker seeks social science help is not, for example, one that simply looks for the 'best' way to deal with welfare, but how to deal with it in such a way that what benefits recipients must also benefit the political givers.

Simply on ideological grounds it would be difficult for researchers to operate within such a framework. Moreover, even where no ideological conflicts exist, political events change at such speed that they would outpace the ability of researchers to orient themselves in accordance with the needs of policy makers who want relevant information quickly.

In fairness it should be pointed out that much of what is interpreted here as 'political' would be interpreted 'organizational' if this study had been conducted outside of a governmental setting. Which of these powerful and overriding 'political' factors truly involve issues of political ideology and which involve considerations necessary for the management and survival of any large bureaucratic organization is difficult to say. This distinction is important, but a difficult one to make on the basis of empirical data and, in consequence, many factors labeled as 'political' influences on utilization are probably more organizational than really political in that they operate in any large organization, irrespective of its goals and objectives.

The Policy Maker and Knowledge Producers

In preparation for the interviews with the federal executives, a review of the literature on utilization and policy making was conducted in order to frame questionnaire items specifically to test the most commonly held theoretical positions on the use and nonuse of scientific knowledge. Briefly, it was found that the most prevalent interpretations could be ordered into one of three classifications: (a) knowledge-specific theories, in which the essential idea is that the main reasons for nonutilization are the ways such information is gathered or the behaviors of the social scientists themselves; (b) two-communities theories, in which the argument is similar to the one C.P. Snow makes in *The Two Cultures* to explain the gap between the humanities and the hard sciences; and (c) policy maker-constraint theories, in which the chief idea is that nonutilization results mainly because of the constraints under which the policy maker operates.

Accordingly, one section of the interview was devoted to three sets of items, each of which represented one of these classifications of utilization theories. A multivariate analysis was conducted to determine the relationship between the attitudes of respondents to these theoretical positions and their self-reported use of social science information. In this process, the data were not simply aggregated by item to determine the degree of consensus among respondents about each classification of theories, but rather, to determine the relationship between the utilization scores of respondents and their responses to each of the three sets of items. The purpose was to determine the amount of variance, or utilization score differences, accounted for by the sets of items as they represented three different theoretical positions.

It was found that the items representing knowledge-specific and policy maker-constraint theories accounted for far less variance reduction than the items representing the two-communities theories. The attitudes of respondents toward the two-communities theories accounted for 14% of the variance compared with only 6% of the variance accounted for by the items representing the other two theoretical positions combined. Thus the set of items representing the two-communities theories clearly accounts for the largest proportion of explained variance.

The implication of this analysis is that theories of underutilization with the greatest degree of explanatory power are those emphasizing the existence of a gap between social scientists and policy makers due to differences in values, language, reward systems, and social and professional affiliations. More generally, it suggests that the factors responsible for the gap between the humanities and the hard sciences play a similar role in keeping the social science knowledge producers and knowledge users apart.

These three classifications of utilization theories are, of course, not meant to be mutually exclusive; it is likely that many factors work together to determine what use is made of social science information. But if the attitudes of these respondents accurately represent their experiences and their efforts to understand utilization, then these findings would strongly suggest that social scientists would be well advised to pay particularly close attention to the utilization theories that stress the lack of interaction among social scientists and policy makers as a major reason for nonuse.

Reference

CAPLAN, N., MORRISON, A. and STAMBAUGH, R. (1975). *The use of social science knowledge in policy decisions at the national level*. Ann Arbor, MI: Institute for Social Research.

Chapter 17

Research and Policy Making in Education: Some Possible Links*

T. Neville Postlethwaite

But I dare say sustained thinking is a minority occupation amongst Ministers, though I've always found it helpful. (Crosland, in Kogan, 1971, p. 157)

Various experiences on the international scene in the last two decades have played a key role in forming my views on the relationship between researchers and policy makers. I shall recount some experiential anecdotes and then extract some principles which I think important.

Some Experiences

First Experience

In 1960, I undertook a study which could loosely be described as social–psychological in nature. The focus of the study was the working conditions and attitudes of 'au pair girls' in England. Whether or not au pair girls were 'exploited' was a frequently occurring theme in the newspapers at the time. The results of the research were discussed by a pressure-group, and were widely reported in the media. The results were used in preparing new legislation in Parliament.

Second Experience

In 1965, I had been invited to a celebratory retirement party for an eminent professor of education in a bilingual West European country. The Director General of Education for that country drove me back to the

* Abridged from *Educational Research and Policy: How Do They Relate?* (pp. 195–206) edited by T. Husén and M. Kogan, 1984, Oxford: Pergamon Press.

capital after the party. I had just completed an analysis examining sex differences in mathematics achievement according to whether the boys and girls were in separate schools, mixed schools but with boys and girls taught in separate classes, or mixed schools with mixed classes. The results indicated that the more the segregation the wider the difference in mean scores and the more mixed the closer the mean scores.

The country in which I was had many separate schools and provided one of the country's data sets which I had used in the analysis. I asked the Director General, by way of making conversation, if there was any problem with having so many sex-segregated schools. His reply was that there was no problem whatsoever. However, I further elicited from him that he was not in favour of large sex differences in achievement. This was, for me, a puzzling situation. I continued to quiz the Director General and by the time we reached the capital city it became clear to me that a 'problem' only existed for my kind policy-making driver if it had been raised in the Parliament, or by a teachers' union, or in the media or by vocal parents' groups. I then told him the results of my analyses and we parted. I never heard from him.

Third Experience

In the early 1970s a friend of mine told me the following episode which he had experienced. He had been a member of a multinational agency's team to review the French national system of education. At that time grade repetition was frequently practised in primary schools in France. Indeed, it was said that by the age of 10 about 70% of an age group had repeated at least one class. In reporting to the Minister of Education, the team had pointed out that grade repeating produced a larger spread of achievement than an age promotion system, and also cost more — if children had to stay in school to complete the minimum number of grades. The Minister replied "*Messieurs, je vous le crois mais qu'est ce que vous voulez que je fasse. Le redoublement, c'est une tradition de la France!*"

I have pondered much on this reply. My interpretation is that education is a very national business in that the voters (and in many cases the decision makers, too) are victims of the education they themselves experienced and they often think that 'theirs' is the best educational system in the world because they are unaware of the alternatives which exist.

To change attitudes towards an educational system — such as towards automatic promotion instead of grade-repeating — requires a powerful propaganda campaign. And an effective propaganda campaign can often take a long time, a longer time than before the next election! In this case, the reviewers (some of whom were researchers) communicated well with the policy makers, but the policy makers saw difficulties in implementing a reform. I was also told that teacher trade unions were in favour of grade-repeating.

Fourth Experience

In 1973, the first sets of results of the IEA[1] Six Subject Survey appeared. The Minister of Education in an East-European country held meetings with the researchers from the national institute participating in the IEA research. The Minister first of all inspected the mean scores in his country compared to the mean scores of other countries. His country was well above the international mean in general but he was struck that in one subject area it was below the international mean. He quizzed his researchers and subject matter experts on the adequacy of the tests. Having been reassured that the tests were adequate he sent school inspectors into the schools. They reported that certain aspects of the curriculum in that subject matter were not being adequately covered in that there was insufficient time being allocated. Within a short space of time, legislation had been enacted to ensure more time coverage. In this case, there was a direct link between the researchers and the top policy maker, and the policy maker was in a position to take direct action.

Fifth Experience

After the IEA Six Subject Survey had been completed and two years had passed, I was constantly asked about the 'effect' of the studies. Had they really improved educational practice in the participating countries? I talked with the heads of the IEA National Centres. Of the 21 countries, something in terms of impact on legislation, curricular guidelines or policy action had happened in 15 of them and nothing had happened in the other 6. My general assessment of the reasons for this dichotomy was that in the countries where nothing had happened the researchers had no links with policy makers and had also made no attempt to forge such links. Again, my impression was that the researchers were either poor communicators with policy makers (or were too junior to attempt to forge such links) or were very good academic researchers and disdained the notion of communicating with mere 'administrative' policy makers. Sometimes, the enormous task of communicating with policy makers, where each of the hundreds of school districts is autonomous, was a major deterrent. In these cases, the research publication ended up as the proverbial 'yet

---

[1] [Since the early 1970s the International Education Association has been conducting comparative research on educational achievements in various countries.]

another dusty report on a dusty shelf'. In some instances, it might have been the case that the policy makers just did not want to know the results or had not any established channel for receiving data which they, themselves, had not requested.

Of those who did 'something' there were various types of 'somethings' which they did and in some cases facilitating circumstances existed. Some researchers deliberately forged links with policy makers from the beginning of the research project. A typical tactic was to include on a 'national committee' for the research one or more key persons from the Ministry of Education and in one case the Director General of Education was on such a committee. Indeed, the Director General was impatient for the results and was forever phoning the data processors for them. The key persons on the national committee reviewed all instruments and often helped with the translation of items and questions, and wrote special national questions for extra information which they wanted from a national probability sample of children or schools. . . .

From Personal Experiences to Promulgation of Practice

The experiences given above exemplify key points. They have covered two themes: the links or communication between researchers and policy makers, and policy makers' reactions or non-reactions.

Before drawing the points together it should be mentioned that all decisions for implementation are political in that not only should policy makers take into account research findings but they must take into account the funds required and the attitudes/desires of the various pressure groups within and outside government in the country. However, in many cases it is clear that the political decisions are taken first and the policy makers *post hoc* search for evidence to legitimize their decisions. The alternative logical approach is to identify that problem, collect *all* information available — including extant research results and commissioning new research — and then taking the policy decision(s).

In what I shall present below I shall make the optimistic assumption that it is the latter approach which is being taken.

1. Facilitating circumstances. Where the problem being researched is widely discussed in the media and is emphasised by pressure groups within the country, and where the various levels of policy makers are motivated to have research results, then the probability is high of good links between researchers and policy makers and of subsequent action being taken. But even under these circumstances it may be necessary for the researchers to make the effort to forge links with the policy makers. So often one cannot take on board the ultimate objectives to the policy makers because these are determined by values and ideologies which are unknown to the researchers or not shared by them.

2. Which links with which level of policy makers? One proposition which I would like to make is 'the more links the better'. Where research is being undertaken at the state or national level and achievement in one or more subject areas is one of the variables being measured, it is, to my mind, usually desirable to involve the appropriate persons responsible for curriculum development in these subject areas. This is at a level where action is usually fairly quick. When objectives are poorly achieved curriculum developers usually examine the materials they are producing and make modifications. This is also a link which has been under-utilized.

Another major link was that between the researchers and the central unit responsible for curriculum development in the country. Since all six subject studies produced accurate estimates of the percentage of the target population children answering an item it was very important for the curriculum developers to know which objectives were being well or poorly achieved. This link was useful for the revision of curricular materials.

A third link was to the teacher unions. In some countries deliberate efforts were made to arrange lecture and discussion groups with the major teacher associations. In general, these were successful for spreading the results.

A fourth link which occurred was a direct link from the researchers to the teachers. Pamphlets were written about the results in language understandable to teachers and distributed to teachers in schools. In one country in which I visited schools, I was most impressed to discover that IEA was a household word among teachers.

The message of this experience for me was twofold: First of all it is very important that researchers forge or strengthen links with the policy makers from the inception of a major national research project; the second was that there are different levels of policy makers from the Minister through to the Director General, the various divisions within a ministry, the curriculum developers, the teacher unions and associations, and the school principals and teachers. It is important to have links with all. In some countries this is becoming a necessity in that to undertake research in any school a series of prior permissions are required. In the country where I work, researchers must obtain permission from the state school authorities and then for each school from the school principal, teachers, parents and students. In effect, this means that the research team needs one more or less full-time person for 'public relations'. This person can also be responsible for feeding the results back to the various groups who have participated in the research.

Sixth Experience

In the mid-1970s I was working in a curriculum centre in an East African country. It became clear that the curriculum centre needed close links with the examinations centre to ensure that the new curriculum fed into the examinations being prepared for the end of the school year after the new curriculum had been introduced. At the same time, links were also needed to the teacher training colleges. Even though the Director General of Education understood the problem and its urgency very well, it still took two years to establish the links. It was the slowness of the bureaucracy and the power play within it which caused the delay.

A similar experience was in a small Asian country where I was also working in the curriculum centre. There was no link between the curriculum centre and the university department of education where all pre- and in-service training took place. The teacher trainers in the university had no motivation or intention of changing the content of their teaching despite the Ministry's desire to implement new curricula in the schools. The university and curriculum centre were both financed by the Ministry. The Minister, when asked to intervene, was unwilling to take any action because although the university was financed by the Ministry, the university was 'constitutionally autonomous'! To what extent research results have affected educational practice through teacher training institutes is debatable.

Seventh Experience

In 1975, I was the chairman of a seminar consisting of senior educational planners from a West European country with some senior Ministry of Education officials from neighbouring countries. We were discussing research results pertaining to organisational factors of schools and their 'effects' on achievement. Two points became clear to me: the first was that only a handful of the planners had any knowledge at all of how empirical research is undertaken, of the terminology of research (for example, the concept of a standard error was completely new to them) or of what criteria could be used to judge the quality of a research study put in front of them; the second was that, in general, they were blind to the alternatives which existed for a particular mode of organisation in their schools. They knew only what had been discussed and tried out in their own countries. They had very little idea of how other countries dealt with the same problem. This ignorance was in part due to language. Many major research findings are published in English and in certain countries senior administrators are reluctant to read in English. Of course, we also have the problem that many researchers write their reports in an excruciatingly complex way. In the country where I now work there is a saying "*Warum soll man es einfach sagen, wenn es kompliziert gesagt werden kann!*" Many academics — and researchers are usually academics — truly believe that complicated language is necessary in order to make a research report academically respectable!...

It might be that I am taking too much for granted when advocating that close links are desirable. It can be argued that researchers should be independent, and be able to critique freely — even the policies of the decision makers. Given close links, the researchers may come under funding threats and political pressures. Some would advocate that perhaps an arm's length relationship is desirable (perhaps with an occasional hug!).

3. *What forms should the links take?* Ideally, the more the junior policy makers can be involved in the practical work of the project the better. This can be in the form of curriculum content analysis, writing test items, deciding on indicators for variables, making *a priori* decisions on which variables form a latent variable, etc.

If this is not possible, every attempt should be made to involve the appropriate policy makers in the organisational structure of a project; for example, on the overall steering committee or an instrument subcommittee. At worst, the researchers should attempt to have regular meetings with the appropriate policy makers — say, every three months.

Once the results are known and an estimate has been made of how much credence one can have in the results, full discussions should be held on the practical consequences of the results.

4. *Forms of language to be used.* Too often researchers use jargon. I often admire the mathematical training of researchers but am uneasy about their training in the clear and parsimonious use of their mother tongue. Occasionally, some of them have an attitude of disdain towards those not versed in technical details. This is unfortunate. Often the people with whom one has to deal in life are technically ignorant but not stupid.

Researchers must learn to express their ideas in non-technical language and learn to use policy makers where they can help. On the other hand, policy makers not versed in research concepts and methods should attempt to learn some of the critical concepts.

The Dissemination of Results

It is rare for Ministers of Education to be interested in the detailed results of research studies or even in research itself, except where it has evaluated the relative efficacy of two or more ways of achieving a particular aim.

When discussing the use of research in decision making (such as before deciding to encourage Local Education Authorities to implement comprehensive schools) Anthony Crosland who had been the Secretary of State (same as Minister) said some years later:

... this argument (i.e. the use of research) had a natural attraction for an ex academic like myself. But as soon as I thought the thing through I could see it was wrong. It implied that research can tell you what your objectives ought to be. But it can't. Our belief in comprehensive reorganisation was a product of fundamental value-judgments about equity and equal opportunity and social division as well as about education. Research can help you to achieve your objectives.... But research can't tell you whether you should go comprehensive or not — that's a basic value judgement. (Kogan, 1971)

Thus, when I talk about senior policy makers, I do not mean the Minister or top permanent civil servant but rather the senior persons in each division within a Ministry.

One technique often employed is what I call the Churchillian technique — the important results and implications for practice are all written down on to one sheet of paper to be handed to the Director General or Minister. I find this an almost impossible task. As a rule caveats have to be entered into findings. A large study is virtually impossible to summarize on one sheet of paper. However, I do believe that most research studies can be summarized in some three to ten pages (depending on the richness of results and caveats to be made).

A technique sometimes used is that of discussions. It is usually possible to have a small group of top policy makers meet for half a day or, in exceptional cases, for a whole day. The strategy I suggest here is that the researchers carefully summarize their findings together with their perceived implications for changes in practice. A discussion then ensues. It is my hope for the current IEA research studies that small two-day regional meetings will be held for Directors General from three or four nations. It is my belief that if these discussions are well-planned and conducted they can be highly influential in improving the decision maker's information bases.

The dissemination of results to curriculum developers is relatively easy, but the feedback should not overburden the developers with statistics and should not be seen as a chastisement of the developers. Ugly scenes have occurred when the feedback has not been handled with sensitivity!

Finally, the dissemination to teachers is very important. The "'SET' research information to teachers" mechanism used in New Zealand and Australia seems to me to be an excellent mode of dissemination. It does, however, require an editor who is skilful in transforming research reports into highly readable synopses for teachers. And, it requires a very good distribution system from the national educational research centre to schools. Apart from this direct form of dissemination, teacher newspapers and magazines can also be used.

Figure 2   A tentative model

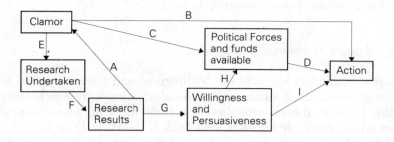

The Beginnings of a Model

Research studies now exist in abundance and speculation based on experience can be tested empirically. Many (major) research studies provide data and the unit of analysis is a research study. It is the variance between studies which is analyzed.

As with any model there are always one or more alternatives. The model presented (Figure 2) is to initiate the idea in the hope that it will induce others to produce better models. It is only a beginning and, for example, one can imagine different models according to whether the project is initiated by one interested group for their consumption only or whether the results are for general debate on public policy.

In this model the unit of analysis is, as mentioned above, research projects. They can *either* be many different types of research projects in different countries or within a country *or* the same project (as in IEA) but in different countries. For example, the IEA Second Science Project has some 40 countries participating in it and, since it is just beginning, data about relationships could be collected in each country as the study proceeds....

What Would the Links Be?

Clamor

If clamor arose, it could be because research results had become available which created the clamor (A). In this case, the link B could occur where the reform did not involve extra money (as, for example, in my au-pair-girl study or where the reform might involve changing the content of in-service teacher training but not the number of days spent by teachers at in-service courses). Or the links C → D → Action could occur.

On the other hand, clamor could occur which would result in research being undertaken (E) and results being made available (F). At that point, A → B or A → C → D could occur. Or G → H → D, or, in the case of no extra money being required, G → I.

Agency Sponsored Research

The agency (which is basically the 'Willingness and Persuasiveness' box in the model) could itself initiate research culminating in research units (G), but this term in the reverse direction from the case mentioned under clamor which could then either feed back G → H → D or G → I. This would be what Coleman has called the "Prince" model. Or, it could go A → C → D or A → B, both of which, as I understand it, would be the Coleman "People" model.

How Do the Experiences Mentioned Earlier Fit with the Model?

Experience 1   A → B
Experience 2   The research results existed but link A did not occur and neither did G.
Experience 3   Link A did not occur. Link G occurred but there appeared to be an unwillingness to go either H or I. In fact, grade repeating is much less frequent in France now, so that in the period 1970 to 1980 something must have happened. It would be interesting to know whether H or I were used or whether there was another route — perhaps involving extra constructs.
Experience 4   G → H → D.
Experience 5   Either G → H → D or nothing. In other words, the "Prince" model was tacitly assumed. Hence, some of my points refer to introducing or strengthening A.
Experience 6   In both cases H and I never occurred.
Experience 7   The Willingness construct was weak and no links involving research were used.

Development of Model

It must be remembered that this model is concerned with situations where research occurs and where 'policy making' does or does not occur. Of course, policy making occurs without research at all but that is a different model.

It is also clear that the model probably needs more [development]. By taking further examples, it should be possible to improve and extend the model. Or it could lead to the point where the model is abandoned and replaced by another. Finally, it is to be noted that it is a so-called 'linear model' and it may be that another type of model (e.g. catastrophe theory model) may be more appropriate. What is clear is that complementing the existing qualitative data with quantitative data should help our understanding of the relationship(s) between researchers and policy makers.

Reference

KOGAN, M. (1971). *The politics of education* (Education Specials). Harmondsworth: Penguin.

Chapter 18

If Dissemination is the Solution, What Is the Problem?*

Jack Knott and Aaron Wildavsky

No matter what other differences there may be about public policy, there appears to be universal acceptance of dissemination. What could be wrong with transferring knowledge about public policy from those who have it to those who do not? Yet the chorus of acclaim should be enough to warn us that the term may be vacuous, a convenient excuse for failures that may be attributed to the lack of this essential ingredient, whatever it is supposed to be. The lore of policy analysis, which warns us that no instrument is good for every purpose, should provide pause when confronted with universal nostrums. Are there no conditions under which dissemination might be counter-productive, the less done the better? The interests of senders may not necessarily coincide with those of receivers. Certainly this is the theme of safety regulations from drugs to airplane disasters. Like any proverb, 'Dissemination in time saves nine' may be countered with 'Disseminate today and be sorry tomorrow!' The injunction to disseminate is no better than crying 'charge!' in a crowded policy environment, when you are more likely to be trampled to death than to get where you want to go.

A world following a single decision rule — disseminate everything! — would be as comforting as it was uninteresting. Dissemination stands for unresolved conflicts. One is between undersupply and overload: Is there too little or too much information being transferred? Once overload is admitted into the discussion, so that not everything can be sent, it is apparent that there must be rules for selection. Immediately another potential conflict arises between knowledge and ignorance, so that the quality of information is crucial. Do we know anything worth transmitting or would we do less harm by taking a vow of silence? Maybe the targets of these dissemination opportunities know more than their would-be men-

* Abridged from *The Knowledge Cycle* (pp. 99–136) edited by R.F. Rich, 1981, Beverly Hills, CA: Sage.

tors. Rules of relevance require that such knowledge as exists be appropriate according to the special circumstance of the time and place. At each stage of utilization there is a different need for information. Certainty gives way to contingency. And the task becomes one not of the wholesale force-feeding of ignorant policy makers by knowledgeable disseminators but of the discovery of those types of transfer that are worthwhile under varying conditions. . . .

Dissemination Unlimited

Dissemination is viewed by many as having a potentially unlimited domain of applicability. It works in agriculture, the argument goes, so why can it not also be successful in other policy areas? Perhaps we have trouble developing better public housing policies, health delivery systems, or educational practices because no mechanism connects new ideas in these areas to those policy makers who could put them to good, practical use. This concern makes dissemination, which is based upon the notion of linking policy makers to research potentially useful to them, so attractive.

Numerous government agencies besides the Department of Agriculture have developed programs to disseminate information. The National Institute of Education, for example, now spends 23% of its budget (up from 5% in 1973) on dissemination of educational research materials to the classroom (McNeely & McNett, 1975). Some of the techniques that are used include information exchanges, newsletters, "policy studies abstracts", and computer retrieval services. The stated purpose of these efforts is to "get as much information as possible out of the educational journals, laboratories, and centers and into the minds and hands of those who work directly with school children".

The most basic argument for establishing these dissemination programs goes: Successful policies are out there somewhere, though these ideas are unknown in many specific areas where they could be put to good use. One cause of this gap between demand for policies and awareness of existing supply may be that old solutions have been forgotten. If such old programs were disseminated, they supposedly could be used to good effect. Another cause might be the unequal distribution of policy-maker resources for searching out and applying policy-relevant information. Dissemination might remedy this inequity by providing at no cost what poor policy makers lack, namely, knowledge.

But the rationale for dissemination can also be reversed: Rather than not enough information, policy makers are seen as having too much. Dissemination becomes a tool to free policy makers from the burden of an overwhelming influx of studies, facts, and figures. This overload problem requires that dissemination be more than the mere provider of knowledge; it demands in addition that disseminators should 'simplify!'; 'clarify!'; 'pass through only relevant knowledge within the policy-maker's field of view.' In this rationale, disseminators are to be the translators, interpreters, and gatekeepers for government decision makers.

Yet beyond the transfer of knowledge, dissemination is often proposed as a 'change agent' strategy to right wrong policies, and thus becomes a mask for policy advocacy. Under the guise of spreading knowledge, disseminators try to make changes which policy makers perceive as unnecessary or, when a performance gap is perceived, to promote their own policy to the exclusion of others. Rather than information about what works and might be done, dissemination is an effort to tell policy makers what should be done. Glennan, Hederman, Johnson, and Rettig, for instance, see demonstration projects as possible substitutes for politically unacceptable regulatory or tax policies that place undesirable burdens on certain groups and interests. The demonstration project thus buys state and local government support for federal policy priorities when other political strategies run into opposition. Despite the many known obstacles to success, and in order to circumvent the political liabilities of other policies, demonstrations become the "best (alternative) policy instrument available" (Glennan *et al.*, 1977, p. ix). Even skepticism can be corrupted into dogma.

For some people, finally, dissemination is nothing more than a synonym for the desire to have policy making work better to solve public problems. It would be good if policy-related knowledge existed; better if decision makers know about it or understood it; still better if it were applied to problems and could thereby influence chosen alternatives; best of all, if such knowledge led to a program that actually was implemented and had the desired impact on people. But, of course, if the injunction 'Disseminate!' means only 'Improve!' or 'Succeed!' then the solution called dissemination is but a restatement of problems it was supposed to solve.

Dissemination is in danger of becoming a catch-all term for a series of unsupported allegations — policy relevant knowledge exists, it can be transported, a market for it is in place — and careless conclusions — what is knowledge in one place will be so in another, if only there were disseminators to connect suppliers with demanders. 'Have policy will travel' may be the slogan but, as we shall see, there is reason to believe that what little knowledge there is may not travel well.

Evidently, there is more than one rationale for dissemination, and they work at cross-purposes. A lack of awareness of existing solutions is not quite the same as being overloaded with them. Advocacy is not exactly objectivity. The difficulty with dissemination is that it serves to cover up conflicts instead of illuminating them.

What to do? Delimit a domain of applicability in which certain strategies of dissemination may be effectively used to improve policy. How? By hypothesizing that dissemination is an inappropriate solution for most problems most of the time, we place the burden of proof on dissemination to justify itself. This is not only more satisfactory scientifically, focusing on rejection rather than acceptance of a hypothesis — but also aesthetically more pleasing, permitting us to puncture overblown pretensions. By desegregating the multiple concepts of dissemination, submerged conflicts may also be brought to the surface, so that it is possible to ask which modes of dissemination are (in)appropriate for what purposes under various conditions. . . .

Undersupply or Overload?

What might cause available knowledge not to be used? The assumption underlying many federal demonstration projects and other dissemination activities is that policy makers are unaware of knowledge that is out there somewhere. Although policy makers crave relevant knowledge for making decisions, according to this view, they do not know how to find it or, in some cases, they cannot interpret what is there because of its complexity.

How likely is it that policy makers want knowledge but cannot get it? What evidence there is, at the very least, casts doubt on the proposition. In [a] Rand study of educational innovations, the authors "saw no real evidence that the lack of information or the perceived absence of well-developed technology were important barriers to innovation at the local level" (Berman and McLaughlin, 1977, p. 68). King (1977, p. 8), based on his experience in the U.S. Department of Housing and Urban Development technology transfer programs to local governments, says something similar: "In most cases managers and operating officials are well informed regarding available tools and techniques. They put them to use selectively when the time is right." In their assessment of government-sponsored demonstrations projects, Baer, Johnson, and Merrow conclude:

> Dissemination of information from demonstration projects has generally not been a serious problem. . . . One might conjecture that some projects contain good ideas that somehow do not get into the hands of potential adopters because of inadequate information dissemination links. In our sample, however, this seems not to be true. The projects that failed to achieve diffusion success did so not because of weaknesses in the information network . . . past experience suggests that if the results are good, diffusion is likely to take place. If the results are poor, diffusion will not take place — and for good reasons. (1977, p. 956)

The second argument given for policy makers' ignorance is the opposite: policy makers do not lack knowledge or information; they already have too much. With the enormous volume of research and analysis being carried out these days, how can policy makers sift through this material and make sense out of it for their own purposes? One answer is to set up knowledge brokerage houses — groups of disseminators who interpret and pass through only that material which is relevant to their clients. Rather than see dissemination as the partial cause of this overload problem, proponents see dissemination as the solution to it (see Greenberger, 1977).

Great we say. The trouble is that the disseminators themselves (rather than the policy makers) must now locate and select targets and choose strategies. How suited are they for these tasks? Disseminators do not participate directly in policy making but must interpret internal needs from an outside perspective. But, not infrequently, analysis units within public organizations have difficulty clarifying and influencing critical decisions. How are outside disseminators to fare any better? Similarly, disseminators must depend on scientists for judging scientific research. Even then, scientists disagree among themselves over competing theories and adequate tests. Consequently, disseminators do not necessarily avoid overload. In danger of becoming caricatures of their own worst problems, they drown in data that once overwhelmed the policy makers.

Despite these general arguments against the proposition that dissemination is the solution to the problem of ignorance, there are circumstances which may prevent policy makers from obtaining sufficient knowledge even though they have a demand for it. One such situation is the emergence of a new policy issue. The salience of the issue requires that policy makers do something, yet old routines and solutions do not seem appropriate. Would a dissemination effort at this time help to solve the problem?

Since the policy issue is new, probably little is known about it. The best that can be hoped for is the availability of theoretical studies. No one, more likely, has had the time or the opportunity to conceptualize the possible relationships between policy variables and effects. There may be a time during the emergence of a policy issue when there is absolutely nothing to disseminate except bits of data useless to both sender and receiver. The problem is not how to disseminate information or knowledge but rather how to develop a policy-relevant theory for organizing the data that do exist.

But it is precisely at this time of emergence that the demand for dissemination grows. The demand too often seems to be insistent upon solutions whether they exist or not. Recall the energy crisis of 1973: in his study of the use of opinion surveys in seven federal agencies, Rich found that the demand for and use of survey data diverged sharply between the energy-related policy area and the other policy areas. He offers the explanation that, "Upper-level policy makers [in the energy-related problem area] were interested in receiving any information that could potentially be relevant to their vast and immediate decision-making responsibilities and needs" (1977, p. 207). Apparently, one would just say 'dissemination', and the data would provide their own meaning. When Billy Batson cried "shazam!" he turned into Captain Marvel, but we doubt that an analogous procedure will convert data into information. . . .

Spreading the Wrong Word

Is it change or the absence of it that is characteristic of our time? Sometimes new information appears to spread with ease; policy makers jump over one another to be the first to try it out. Rivlin (1971) reports that the inventors of individually prescribed instruction were swamped with requests for the new method even before the first project had been adequately evaluated. Management techniques, such as PPBS of the 1960s and the budget balancing amendments of the 1970s, have also spread so rapidly as to raise the eyebrows of even the most cynical disseminators. What accounts for this apparent ability of some new ideas to defy the laws of organizational inertia?

Much of what is disseminated is not knowledge in the sense we have been speaking of but is instead policy-relevant information. Rather than showing what does not work, disseminated information purports to tell policy makers how to improve policy. This is because policy makers are generally not content to restrict their efforts to detecting policy errors. Solving problems is more appealing. Policy makers must frequently take actions whether adequate knowledge is available or not. Political demand thus creates a need for information about new policies and techniques. But as the individually prescribed instruction and PPBS examples indicate, the demand for the best information in general is weaker than the demand for policy-relevant information in particular.

Policy makers do not only want to receive information in order to improve policy; they are also interested in controlling choices (Wildavsky, 1972). Policy makers may use data, therefore, in ways which disseminators do not like and for purposes they do not support. It is this manipulation of information that policy analysts lament when they see their factual arguments sacrificed as ammunition in bargaining salvos and their tentative conclusions used aggressively to give technical respectability to decision-makers' policy preferences. . . .

Dissemination is only indirectly related to utilization but is repeatedly urged as a solution. Perhaps current dissemination efforts, viewed by many as inchoate, provide scapegoats for more unresolvable causes of underutilization. Researchers do not like to admit that what they are producing is not policy-relevant information; they more readily believe that decision makers have not yet received their products or do not understand the material. Decision makers likewise do not like to accept the charge that they pay no attention to relevant information but more easily convince themselves that relevant material is still out there somewhere. Finding the main causes of underutilization — insufficient knowledge, weak demand, and faulty implementation — too intractable and the solutions too unpalatable, researchers and decision makers alike turn to dissemination as the way of improving performance.

Since producing knowledge where none exists cannot be assured, the emphasis shifts to distributing whatever is produced, whether worthy or not: New roles and institutions can be developed; dissemination plans for government contracts can be required; joint seminars and conferences between users and producers can be organized. This 'premature programming' of a solution to the problem of underutilization substitutes dissemination means for the utilization end. In the words of Landau and Stout, procedures are employed that are "in error, irrelevant to the issue under attack, or inappropriate as a valid basis for action" (1979, p. 148). Proponents frequently recommend mandatory dissemination procedures for policy areas regardless of the knowledge base.

Premature dissemination occurs when the results of demonstration projects are routinely promoted into technology transfer programs. The results are presumed ready for standard distribution to a wider range of policy makers. But if they rest on nontransferable technologies, their standard distribution merely contributes to overload. Similar premature efforts occur when dissemination plans are required for government contracts or seed money is routinely spent on projects that cannot be replicated elsewhere. Participants are easily led to believe that their task is complete when they have drawn up the plans and spent the money, even though the requisites for utilization are not available.

At the reception stage, the impact of dissemination is not upon the physical receipt of knowledge itself but upon how the knowledge is perceived once it arrives. Premature dissemination increases the certainty of physical reception but decreases the likelihood of cognitive awareness of what is sent. By enlarging the volume of material that goes to any given set of policy makers, premature dissemination exacerbates the overload problem; its net effect is to decrease reception of research by decision makers while creating the appearance of a more widespread distribution. Knowledge dispersion is retarded at the same time that it appears to be advanced.

At the adoption stage, premature dissemination runs the risk of a growing cynicism. Crying 'wolf' too often reduces the impact of a real alarm signal. How are disseminators to 'sell' a product that is in fact superior if all the others were also presented in that manner? Before it can be adopted, a really worthwhile innovation may first have to overcome the cynicism generated by earlier, less fortunate, dissemination efforts. Some local school districts have routinely come to suspect the applicability of demonstrated educational reforms, believing their purported success to be due to especially favorable circumstances. The irony of using seed money to ensure adoption may very well be that the value of the project for others is vitiated because they recognize the importance of the subsidy for the project's success.

If a technique is lavishly advertised as capable of reducing costs or improving planning, policy makers are also tempted to adopt it for electoral gain or administrative reputation. Premature dissemination, therefore, may actually enhance the adoption of inaccurate information that caters to a favorable political environment.

The effects of premature dissemination are most clearly seen during the implementation stage of the policy process. The adoption of prematurely disseminated information, because it rests on a weak knowledge base, inevitably leads to either unsuccessful implementation, disappointing results for citizens, or both (Berman and McLaughlin, 1977, p. 20).

If policy-relevant information does not reach decision makers, who is to say that dissemination is at fault? The fact that in many areas policy-relevant information is slow in developing is as plausible an explanation as the failure to disseminate. The identification of particular clienteles whose special circumstances prevent them from obtaining information even when it is available more accurately eliminates those utilization problems that are benefited by a dissemination solution.

Dissemination by Design

A dilemma for dissemination is that policy makers are often able to learn about policy-relevant knowledge through ordinary interchanges, thus making extra efforts unnecessary. These inter changes occur when people with common interests interact socially and professionally. Doctors exchange ideas about medications and surgical techniques as they meet with one another in their work and in organizations devoted to medicine (Rogers, 1971). Teachers share new approaches to learning and collective bargaining through professional associations and on the job. The common interests among group members and their interaction result in the exchange of information and the diffusion of ideas within the groups. The doctor may be a teacher; the legislator, an environmentalist. Such multiple memberships lead to the cross-fertilization of ideas between groups. In public policy, multiple memberships lead to the transmission of information from one government to another. A California legislative staff member may not know that analysts in Rhode Island already have studied the very policy problem he confronts. Then he attends a meeting of the American Economic Association in Boston where he encounters the economists working on the issue in Rhode Island and exchanges notes. The California staff member's role as an economist has led to the diffusion of policy information from one end of the nation to the other.

The concept of dissemination, as used in public policy, denotes something in addition to this diffusion of ideas in the market place. Webster defines the verb "to disseminate" as "to spread abroad as though throwing a seed". "Throwing a seed" connotes more than the spontaneous diffusion of ideas; it implies a deliberate act to accomplish a purpose. This more deliberate and centrally organized process is captured by Havelock's questions: "Who sees to it that knowledge gets to the user? Who is charged with the responsibility of retrieving basic or applied knowledge . . . and distributing it to people who need and can use it?" (1969, pp. 7–20). Dissemination is not to be spontaneous but is to be controlled and administered.

Proponents of dissemination apparently believe that weeds alone are growing where flowers ought to bloom; thus they advocate dissemination by design. A larger government role is "needed to coordinate effort, to plan, and to provide support" for dissemination in most policy areas, observes Havelock (1969). Even those who recognize many of dissemination's limitations are not immune to the lure of planned dissemination. Lynn (1979) recommended, for example, "more systematic efforts" to disseminate research findings to state and local governments. Agencies also feel obliged to act. The Research Task Force of the National Institute of Mental Health has objected that the institute lacks "a purposeful, coordinated, and planned effort to make research findings known" (Segal, 1975, p. 396). Just as dissemination can be prematurely programmed in the absence of relevant knowledge, so dissemination can be overly administered in the presence of an existing market. . . .

Strategies of Dissemination

Relating the stages of utilization to specific strategies is difficult. It is easier to criticize than to say what should be done, especially when so many factors must be considered at each level. The crux of the matter is that planned dissemination should be employed when diffusion processes fail. Yet not all failures are amenable to planned solutions. Dissemination is a reasonably economical solution only in cases of emerging new issues and recall of old policies. Other types of failure involve either inattention/ resistance or geographic isolation/poverty. The former situation raises the dilemma of advocacy versus objectivity; the latter, cost and capacity. Disseminating to private business gets around this second problem because new techniques promise increased productivity which should lead to greater revenues. This is the lesson of the Agricultural Extension Service. In social policy areas, however, in which monetary savings are not forthcoming, dissemination is turned into subsidization. The problem of advocacy versus objectivity involves a fine line between helping policy makers overcome sunk costs so that they can adopt new policies and force feeding them policy preferences of the disseminators. . . .

Reprise

What is the problem to which dissemination is the solution? Dissemination can be a solution to the problem of underutilization if knowledge is disseminated to particular clienteles under specific circumstances. The trouble is that premature dissemination in the absence of knowledge contributes to information overload, thus making dissemination a cause of underutilization rather than a cure. Dissemination should not substitute for supply when diffusion is already cheap and effective. When markets for policy items are strong, it is preferable to support them rather than to create new administrative structures.

A major concern is to keep from inundating policy makers with ever more data. In general, therefore, passive exchanges, in which the initiative and costs of obtaining material are left to the policy makers, are to be preferred to active exchanges that place responsibility on the disseminators. We also prefer an emphasis on information exchanges such as clearinghouses, regional depositories, data banks, computer services, journals, and the like. If people are to be moved, once again the initiative should reside with the policy makers to take the responsibility for getting to know a helpful staff member at the information exchange. By giving policy makers more discretion in choosing information, passive information exchanges also allow them more skepticism in assessing results. Undoubtedly they will at times miss important material, but more frequently they will avoid irrelevant data.

The urge to disseminate should be combined with analysis that aims at better screening. The Institute of Medicine's recent review of HEW's Research Planning Principles calls attention to this issue. Expressing concern for the "premature dissemination of developments" in health care, the Institute applauded HEW's decision "that studies on risks and benefits especially [be] required before the widespread introduction of a new procedure throughout the health care system" (U.S. Department of Health, Education and Welfare, 1979, p. 37). Dissemination of the idea that more data can be something other than an unalloyed good should be encouraged. . . .

Delimiting a role for dissemination demands that a connection be made between the problems of utilization and specific strategies that contribute to their solution at reasonable cost. Three difficulties stand out: (a) pretensions to knowledge, which makes many dissemination efforts premature; (b) dissemination by design (or the Newcastle syndrome) substitutes unnecessarily for the market spread of knowledge; and (c) the Matthew effect, in which those policy makers who are the most in need of dissemination are also the ones who are the least able to process and apply what is sent. Preventing dissemination from doing harm while trying to ensure that it also does some net good is the task confronting analysis. And if the latter is not likely, then the Hippocratic Oath is as good a guide as any.

References

BAER, W.S., JOHNSON, L.L. and MERROW, E.W. (1977). Government-sponsored demonstrations of new technologies. *Science, 196* (May 27).

BERMAN, P. and MCLAUGHLIN, M. (1977). *Federal programs supporting educational change: Vol. VII: Factors affecting implementation and continuation* (Rand report to the U.S. Office of Education, Contract No. HEW-OS-73-216). Santa Monica, CA: Rand Corporation.

GLENNAN, T., JR., HEDERMAN, W.F., JOHNSON, L.L. and RETTIG, R.A. (1977). *The role of demonstrations in federal R & D policy* (RAND/WN-10014-OTA). Santa Monica, CA: Rand Corporation.

GREENBERGER, M. (1977). Modelers and decision makers. *EPRIJ, 8* (October), 3–16.

HAVELOCK, R.G. (1969). *Planning for innovation through dissemination and utilization of knowledge.* Ann Arbor: University of Michigan, Center for Research on the Utilization of Scientific Knowledge.

KING, J. (1977). *Improving local government capacity: An odyssey.* Paper presented at the conference on Transferring Science Technology and Innovation in the Public Sector, SRI International, Menlo Park, Ca, December.

LANDAU, M. and STOUT, R. (1979). To manage is not to control: Or the folly of type II errors. *Public Administration Review*, March–April, 148–156.

LYNN, L.E., JR. (1979). Studies in management of social R and D: Selected policy areas. In L.E. LYNN, JR. (Ed.), *Study project on social research and development, Vol. 3.* Washington, DC: National Academy of Sciences.

MCNEELY, M. and MCNETT, I. (1975). Spreading the latest word. *American Education, 11*, 9.

RICH, R.F. (1977). Uses of social science information by federal bureaucrats: Knowledge for action versus knowledge for understanding. In C.H. WEISS (Ed.), *Using social research in public policy making.* Lexington, MA: Lexington Books.

RIVLIN, A. (1971). *Systematic thinking for social action.* Washington, DC: Brookings Institution.

ROGERS, E.M., with SHOEMAKER, F.F. (1971). *Communication of innovation: A cross cultural approach.* New York: Free Press.

SEGAL, J. (Ed.). (1975). *Research in service of mental health: Report of the research task force of NIMH* (U.S. Department of Health, Education and Welfare, National Institute of Mental Health). Washington, DC: Government Printing Office.

U.S. DEPARTMENT OF HEALTH, EDUCATION AND WELFARE (1976). *HEW News.* Washington, DC: Government Printing Office.

WILDAVSKY, A. (1972). The self evaluating organization. *Public Administration Review*, 509–520.

Chapter 19

Research Models: Insiders, Gadflies, Limestone*

Patricia Thomas

[I conclude then] that government policy making only occasionally takes conscious account of social research. It is one of many influences that may shape policy. Not a great deal of research which is directly influential is carried out independently of government funding. Almost all the civil servants interviewed said or implied that the government of the day can look after its own research needs through in-house or commissioned work. Others, outside government, may claim that government has research needs which it does not recognise, that disinterested parties are in a better position to draw attention to a problem of which policy makers are only dimly aware or to suggest a range of policy options and their likely consequences. There is logical force in the argument that government is not necessarily the best and only judge of its research needs, but it would be difficult to persuade any government to be directly influenced by the results of externally sponsored research.

There are usually mechanisms in government departments for taking note of outside research and informing the administrators, though some systems seem rather rudimentary. In most departments it is someone's job to — at the least — list relevant research and circulate the list to administrators. Officials in research divisions often said that they would expect administrators themselves to keep up with research findings in their own fields. In fact it is doubtful whether policy makers do normally read the literature on their subjects in any systematic way. They are busy people, preoccupied with their day-to-day tasks, likely to stay in their posts for only about three years. . . .

It should be stressed that the author recognises many roles for social research other than the direct promotion of policy change and many

---

* Abridged from *The Aims and Outcomes of Social Policy Research* (pp. 97–114) by P. Thomas, 1985, London: Croom Helm.

functions for the ESRC[1] and the foundations other than supporting policy research. If this [essay] seems unduly sharp in deflating the notion that externally-sponsored research will have a direct effect on social policy, the pessimism should not be seen as applying to social research as such.

If government sees itself as capable of looking after its own research needs and therefore able to turn a deaf ear to research supported by other bodies, are there nevertheless circumstances in which it can be forced to hear or in which the research will become influential indirectly? There are certain models of research which yield results to which the policy makers will pay attention (which is not to say that, having listened, they will act). Conclusions about these models are in general drawn from the evidence collected from interviews, but the author has not stopped short at the evidence when logic and personal experience have suggested that the argument could be taken further.

In any discipline people undertake research for a variety of reasons and a wish to bring about social change through research does not rule out other motives such as disinterested search for truth, the desire to be promoted and to win and retain the respect of one's peer group, or indeed pleasure in the research itself. Similarly, applicants for grants or people otherwise in a position to have their research supported have preferences about funding which do not bear solely on the optimum use of the finished research. A grant from the ESRC may carry with it a certain academic cachet lacking in a contract from a government department. A grant from a foundation may be relatively free of bureaucratic difficulties. An ESRC or a foundation grant may allow the researcher more freedom both in the conduct of his research and in the publication of the findings and may give the researcher knowledge and a track record that enable him subsequently to do directly influential work for government. For many people, however, to negotiate and accept a government contract involves a compromise they are not prepared to make.

Despite the clear message that to stand the best chance of having a direct influence on government policy, a researcher should be funded by a government department, policy researchers are not deserting the ESRC and the foundations. (They may of course be successively funded and enjoy the advantages of both types of funding.) But to be government-financed is only the starting point on a difficult journey. It is not so much that the path is strewn with obstacles, but rather that it has a tendency to fall away on either side. Whoever funds the research, there are certain minimum conditions which must be fulfilled if it is to be used by policy makers in a direct way, and we will return to these in the discussion of the Gadfly and the Insider Models. If the conditions are fulfilled, the chances of having a direct and evident influence still remain rather small, and

---

[1] [The Economic and Social Research Council, the governmental authority presently responsible for supporting basic social research in Britain.]

chance plays a large part, but government-commissioned research has the advantage that some of the minimum conditions are built into the system.

[The Limestone Model]

It is possible to have an indirect influence on policy without fulfilling these conditions and perhaps it is worth exploring first a model which relies on indirect or cumulative interest, since it is the one to which a great deal of policy research most closely conforms. The effect of this kind of research has been described by Robin Guthrie, Director of the Joseph Rowntree Memorial Trust, as like "the action of water through limestone. You may know where the water falls on the limestone, but there is no means of knowing what route it will take down the various levels or where it will emerge through unexpected fissures" (Guthrie, 1979). We shall call this the Limestone Model. It is the only one that requires no action other than undertaking academic research and presenting the findings (which may or may not include recommendations for action) in a publication which is as likely to be directed towards an academic audience as towards policy makers. If various circumstances (many of them outside the control of the researcher) permit, the research, probably in combination with other research with a similar tale to tell, will seep into the public consciousness, almost without people being aware that their views are being subtly altered, thus changing the parameters within which the public and the policy makers conduct debates on or discussions of the issues. It can focus concern on matters which had not hitherto been seriously considered. The existence of a Limestone Model is a seductive notion, but in its pure form it is not a model to which policy research is usually expected to conform. It is unlikely that current problems can be solved by the application of the Model in this form and it is difficult to predict the problems of the future. Moreover, in seeking to exert this kind of influence, researchers are in competition with a number of other powerful forces, not the least of which is journalism: Investigative journalism is quick (compared with research); it follows a different and rather freer ethical code than that usually employed by academic researchers; and journalists write in a style that can easily be read and understood by the general public. The impact of investigative journalism is immediate and the message often provocative. Research may be more authoritative, more painstaking and more accurate than journalism; its influence may be no greater than even a hastily put together item in the popular press. There is a sense in which all public actions, writings and utterances have an effect on public opinion. This is not to deny the validity of the Limestone Model; merely to suggest that there is more permeating the limestone than research and some of the liquid is finding more direct paths.

[The Gadfly Model]

The Limestone Model assumes that bringing about specific policy change in the short term is not the top priority of the researcher. The Limestone Model may, as we shall see, be adapted in a way that causes the research results to flow more directly to the policy maker; and the researcher may apply a pure or an adapted version of the Model while acquiring enough knowledge and track record to be able to exert a more direct influence on policy. But if and when he wants a more direct and immediate effect on policy, the prudent researcher will adopt a quite different approach and he will set about fulfilling the minimum conditions which make for implementation of research findings. Although it is argued that, left to itself, government is usually impermeable to direct and immediate influence from outside research, there are modes by which one can set about influencing government in a purposeful way. Here two quite different models apply. Both can be subverted by chance events but both rely for their success on the exploitation of chance. The first of these we will call the Gadfly Model. Far more researchers aspire to become Gadflies than succeed. It is not enough to tease and provoke the system, even when proclaiming the truth, for being a successful Gadfly is a serious business. The role is not usually best undertaken by the inexperienced because a sound knowledge of the workings of the government machine and of its strong and weak points is essential. It is important, too, to establish a relationship with administrators at several levels and preferably to be of some use to them. The relationships are likely to be somewhat tense at times, but the tension can be constructive so long as it does not generate into hostility.

The Gadfly, at least in his pure form, is unlikely to be commissioned by government (and might feel compromised if he were), but may be supported by the ESRC or, perhaps more likely, by a private foundation. He will not feel constrained by the political feasibility of his recommendations, though he will know enough to be conscious of political limitations. He is usually radical in his thinking and his conclusions may be more palatable to one party than to another (even though there may be nothing of a party political nature in his research). When research findings begin to emerge the Gadfly will set up meetings with interested parties of all kinds, inside government and without. Publications will be sent to all those who might either be influenced by the research or use it to influence others; the press and other media will be alerted; influential friends and acquaintances will be telephoned and, where appropriate, benevolent members of Parliament will ask questions in the House.

Thus the Gadfly perceives the research itself as only part of a process and the communication of the results of the research as vital as the inquiry itself. A characteristic response by administrators to the work of a Gadfly is to attack it on methodological grounds, because it is too insistent to be ignored, and there are few social scientists whose methodology cannot be faulted on some point of detail. It is unusual for changes in policy to be attributed to the endeavours of a Gadfly but there may be a consonance over the years between his recommendations and the changes that have taken place. Michael Zander, professor of law at the London School of Economics and legal correspondent of the *Guardian*, has vividly described the process of promoting change in this way in his inaugural lecture delivered at the LSE (Zander, 1979).

> In order to be effective it is often necessary to go to the trouble to take the next step. Many people, and especially perhaps academics, find this uncongenial. They regard their function as completed when they have written the original proposal and put it into circulation in a book or article. But this is to leave everything to chance. It assumes that those who have the power to do something about a proposal will receive the book or article, that they will read it, that having read it, they will not only agree with the writer's view but will feel moved to do something about it, and to such an extent that they will 'carry the ball' in the face of the opposition that is bound to develop soon enough from one quarter or another. This is to pile improbability on improbability. The danger, in other words, is not so much that one's proposal may be opposed as that it may not even be noticed.
>
> The innocent in public affairs tends to assume that those in authority will automatically get to hear of any new facts or ideas within their area of competence. This is far from being the case. If one believes one has new facts or ideas it is normally necessary to peddle them around before anyone will pay the slightest attention.
>
> One should send the original article to the lay and professional press. Copies should also be sent to the relevant officials and bodies concerned with the problems. If this includes a government department it is often sensible to send copies both to the Minister and to the relevant civil servants. If there are several levels of civil servant concerned with the matter, one does well to send copies to the junior as well as to the senior man. It should never be assumed that one will pass a letter to the other. It is usually sensible to send copies at the same time to others who are more peripherally concerned but who may be interested and who will have occasion in the ordinary course of things to see and talk to those more directly involved. A casual word in the corridors of power by one denizen to another sometimes advances things marvellously. It may help to get an MP to table a parliamentary question directing the Minister's and thereby possibly the press's attention to the matter. Often it is essential or at least desirable to

mobilise other organisations or individuals to add their support for the proposal.

[The Insider Model]

The third model in the series is the Insider Model. The Gadfly makes occasional forays into government, but he is as likely to meet his government contacts in a pub or at a party as to visit them in their offices. He remains aloof from the day-to-day business of government, and is quite untainted by his friendships within government circles. The Insider, on the other hand, makes it his business to burrow into the corridors of power. He may already have or have had a post as consultant ... or have once been a full-time official.... If not he may subsequently be offered a post.... Like the Gadfly he knows the government machine; unlike the Gadfly he may be prepared in some circumstances to reach an accommodation with government, by steering clear of conclusions that are not politically feasible or adapting his research to cover topics which are a matter of government concern. He wants to be helpful. Because a process of negotiation might be useful to both parties he may welcome a government research contract, which will in addition facilitate access to data and a continuing dialogue with administrators. It is recognised that elements of Gadfly and Insider may exist in one person. An individual may act the role of Gadfly for a project or series of projects and take on the attributes of the Insider for others. Successful Insider research of this kind is seldom supported by the ESRC or the foundations, though there is a great deal of willingness on the part of these bodies to support the Insider, and the Insider will often work on a series of projects, some financed by departments and some by the ESRC and/or foundations. The ESRC supports some Insiders, but not as many as its policy of the pursuit of relevance implies. To secure maximum direct influence for a given study the Insider will choose to be supported by government, but such a choice may curtail his freedom to publish (though some departments have a liberal attitude to publication), even if it does not condition, in the early days of his project, the direction in which the project is allowed to move.

David Donnison, in his *Minerva* article (1972), describes a different kind of Insider, who relies on networks which he has established or of which he is already a part. Such a variant still fits the model rather well. The person who can exploit networks of influential friends and acquaintances inside and outside government will not need to work as hard as the average Insider to achieve the same ends; a telephone call may be substituted for a seminar. On the other hand it is arguable that the kind of eminent person Donnison describes relies less on research projects as such than on a distillation of wisdom (their own and that of others) which may have been derived only in part from research.

[The Pressure Group]

Another model, which often includes elements of the Gadfly and the Insider Models, is one in which the investigator simply undertakes a research project and allows (or encourages) some other body to take up the findings and press for their implementation. Thus research findings are frequently taken up by pressure groups with or without the full consent and approval of the researchers.... The relationship between research and pressure groups may be institutionalised as some pressure groups (which cannot normally be supported by the ESRC or charitable foundations) have separate sister organisations which are eligible for such support because their remit is research. An example is the pressure group, the National Council for Civil Liberties, which is closely allied to the research organisation, the Cobden Trust. If the Pressure Group Model is to work satisfactorily for the researcher, he will need to work fairly closely with the pressure group concerned. Although the model relieves the investigator of the trouble of ensuring that his findings reach the attention of policy makers, he runs the risk (if he does not take preventive measures) that his research may be misinterpreted or otherwise used for a purpose which he did not foresee and would not have approved had he foreseen it, for, once research is published, the investigator has little or no control over the way in which it is used for policy purposes. Both the Insider and the Gadfly will have taken some precautions to ensure that the apropriate people know of their research, but they cannot control the use of their data, whether qualitative or quantitative. The academic who actively desires that his work should be used by a pressure group may risk no more than a compromise: His findings may be used to present a more dramatic picture than he had intended. If it is simply fortuitous that his results are used in this way, and he has played no part in securing its use, a real distortion may appear — not necessarily because the pressure group intends to distort: The case may appear quite differently if it is repre-sented in a simplified form. Obviously research which is capable of use is also capable of misuse, but the investigator can take steps to maximise the use: These steps, if successful, can mitigate any damage caused by misuse.

These last three models, the Gadfly, the Insider, and the Pressure Group, require a degree of effort on the part of the investigator that is seldom considered by funding bodies and also a set of skills which are only tenuously related to the ability to carry out a rigorous research project and write a well-argued book. A comfortable myth exists that good ideas travel on their own legs. There is little evidence to suggest that findings relevant for policy will travel of their own accord, in the vast majority of cases, further than the bookshelves of fellow academics.

There are examples of social research being taken up with enthusiasm by government policy makers, even when the research had not been primarily intended to promote policy change and when the investigator has made little or no effort to fulfil the conditions implicit in these models. Such examples occur when researchers have perfectly caught the tide of ministerial thinking (which sometimes, though not always, reflects the mood of an informed public). There is absolutely no way of knowing at the outset of a three-year project how that tide will run in, say, four years' time when a publication emerges. There are no safe bets for this category of research, though it is fair to say that research which points towards a method of saving public expenditure *in a way that is acceptable to the government of the day* stands a high chance of political acceptability. Such enthusiastic take-up is difficult, if not impossible, to plan in advance, however, since there are still few examples of social research in which saving public money is a prime objective in the early stages of the research.

Sometimes it is easier to speak to the party in opposition in the hope that the research's message will still be timely when the party returns to power. Ministers and perforce their civil servants are at their most alert for new ideas at that stage, as well as for research findings that legitimise their policies. The Educational Priority Area research, where the message of positive discrimination, translated into that of selective benefits, made it acceptable to the new Conservative administration, is an example. It is worth noting, however, that [the person responsible for this research,] Professor [A.H.] Halsey conformed closely to the Insider Model. To set out to catch the tide without working hard to make one's name and one's work familiar to Whitehall and to other relevant groups of powerful persons is to offer oneself as a hostage to a most capricious fortune.

Corridors of power shift. At different times social scientists who wished to influence policy were considered to be in an advantageous position if they were research consultants to Royal Commissions, or enjoyed a special relationship with a Cabinet Minister, or — in more optimistic days — were appointed to senior research posts within the Civil Service. Nowadays research advisers to Select Committees of the House of Commons seem especially influential and the Committees, following in many cases the evidence presented by these advisers, have brought out reports which are notable for taking a radical view which is based on the doctrine of neither major political party. How long the Committees' practice can survive a system of confrontation politics it is impossible to predict. If they survive they are unlikely to exert a direct influence on policy — backbenchers seldom do so — except by being sufficiently well-informed to embarrass the government of the day. It is not self-evident that such views are necessarily objective and reliable, as nobody and no group has a monopoly of the truth, but it is already apparent that the public will more readily accept opinions which are not divided along party political lines and which have the appearance of impartiality, even if this may be somewhat illusory at times.

References

DONNISON, D. (1972). Research for policy. *Minerva, 10*(4), 516–536.

GUTHRIE, R. (1979). Research and social policy. Paper delivered at the Conference of Researchers in Violence in Marriage, Bristol, September.

ZANDER, M. (1979). Promoting change in the legal system. *The Modern Law Review, 42*(5: September), 489–507.

Part 4
Research, Ideology and Educational Impact

Chapter 20

Brown vs. Board of Education*

Irving Louis Horowitz and James Everett Katz

This [famous] Supreme Court decision marked [an early and] significant utilization of social science inputs into the direct transformation of domestic policy. On May 17, 1954, the Supreme Court of the United States handed down a ruling that announced the beginning of full citizenship for the country's largest minority. On that day the Court ruled that segregation in the nation's schools was unconstitutional. Twenty-one states that either permitted or required separate school systems for blacks and whites were told that "separate but equal" was no longer the law of the land. "Separate educational facilities are inherently unequal", declared Chief Justice Earl Warren for the unanimous Court.

The school decision was bound to be controversial, for in spite of a score of rulings against higher-education segregation in the nation's highest courts, the principle of "separate but equal" as enunciated in *Plessey vs. Ferguson* had never been challenged. It is probable that those Southerners who were watching the pattern of decision making in the courts expected that, sooner or later, segregation would have to come to an end. But it is likely that they expected an incremental step; the sweeping nature of the pronouncement — which, after all, was made by a court comprised of three Southerners and a brand-new chief justice with very little judicial background — fueled the outrage with which it was greeted in the South.

It was a surprising decision, not especially because it ruled for the black appellants but because of the apparent basis of the decision. The court made virtually no effort to argue from legal precedent. The basis of the decision was, in effect, that times had changed: Modern sociological and psychological evidence showed separate educational facilities to be damaging to blacks. The courts quoted with favor the finding of the Kansas case court:

* Abridged from *Social Science and Public Policy in the United States* (pp. 125–146), by I.L. Horowitz and J.E. Katz, 1975, New York: Praeger.

Segregation of white and colored children in public schools has a detrimental effect upon the colored children. The impact is greater when it has the sanction of the law; for the policy of separating the races is usually interpreted as denoting the inferiority of the negro group. A sense of inferiority affects the motivation of a child to learn. Segregation with the sanction of law, therefore, has a tendency to retard the educational and mental development of negro children and to deprive them of some of the benefits they would receive in a racially integrated school system (cf. Clark and Kamisar, 1969, p. 330).

The social science evidence presented and discovered through its own research, the Court stated, led the Court to conclude that the plaintiffs were, by reason of segregation, "deprived of the equal protection of the law guaranteed by the Fourteenth Amendment". The decision to a significant degree represented and, more importantly, was perceived as a shift from judicial decision based primarily (if not exclusively) on legal precedent to one based on presumed facts of social change. That perception had no disastrous consequences for the Court or the decision but it ushered in a period of intense criticism from conservative sectors that argued that the Court was acting as a policy-making body by using nonlegal evidence to reach its decision, that social science was an improper form of evidence, and that if the evidence used was invalid the decision must also be invalid (cf. Garfinkel, 1959; LaFarge, 1953).

Social scientists themselves were not entirely confident of the worth of the evidence submitted in the school segregation cases. The argument went that since the Court itself has criticized the introduction of nonlegal evidence on numerous occasions, and of social science evidence in particular, a decision based on such evidence was clearly erroneous. There was also some effort to impugn the integrity of the experts called upon to testify: Kenneth Clark was said to be biased since he was employed by the [National Association for the Advancement of Colored People], Gunnar Myrdal was called a Socialist who had been unforgivably critical of the United States in the work cited (*An American Dilemma*). The attempt overall was clearly to attack both the use of social science in general and the quality of the social science cited. A third tactic is suggested by a speech by Strom Thurmond after the implementation decision. "We might do well," he said, "to adopt the tactics of our opponents. If propaganda and psychological evidence are effective for our opponents they can be effective for us. Our worthy objective of preserving the Constitution justifies the method" (Thurmond, 1955, pp. 29–32).

In other words, if one cannot prove that social science is not a legitimate form of evidence in the courts and that the social science used was poor social science, one should present one's own social science evidence to the contrary. A concerted effort was mounted in the period after 1955 to persuade the Court to reverse itself and to gain support among the public for the idea that blacks are inherently inferior. After the school desegregation decisions, an attempt was made to formulate a scientific defense for segregated education. The evidence for segregation usually took the form of investigations of comparative racial intelligence, psychological test results, and the relative intellectual capacity of whites and blacks. Research also began to appear on the psychic traits and personality characteristics of the races and the extent to which they are transmitted by heredity or dictated by environment. The debate has persisted to this day, despite the legislative success of the advocates of civil rights, and many of those who argue the case for innate racial differences have been taken quite seriously. Arthur Jensen and Robert Herrnstein are ... recent examples.

The attempt to set up a countervailing body of popular opinion, buttressed by the expert opinion described above, was reinforced by supporters who, whether or not they agreed with the decision, were concerned about some of its implications. Advocates of states' rights felt that the decision granted too much power to the federal government and that it represented a fundamental interference with the right of a state to educate its children in accordance with the majority of its citizens' wishes. Strict constitutionalists felt that it signified an imbalance of power in the judiciary, and judicial conservatives worried about the implications of the use of something so temporal as social science. Unlike legal evidence, it was argued, social science evidence may change with the frame of mind of the researcher. It is very close to opinion and is certainly not a 'science' such as physics, for example. This attitude, which was far from uncommon, suggests a fundamental misunderstanding about the nature of social science. Because social scientists could not point to a body of social science 'law', some laymen concluded that it could not be taken seriously. Some social scientists were not certain that they liked social science being used as advocacy. The 1950s were, after all, the heyday of functionalism, which advocated that social scientists strive toward a value-free orientation. Social science research, according to this school of thought, should not be contaminated by anything so demeaning as politics. Even some liberals were nervous about the implications of the political use of social science research (Berger, 1957, pp. 471–477). The Court had used the social science evidence presented by the plaintiffs to show that they had suffered damage to their personalities as a result of segregation. What if, some social scientists wondered aloud, this became legal precedent, and one had to prove damage to ensure equality under the law? The right to equality should be protected, it was argued, even if it made no difference to an individual or even if it were not harmful to another party. Some lawyers who supported the decision fretted about the poor quality of logic exhibited in the decision and regretted that the decision was not more firmly based on legal precedent (cf. Cahn, 1955, pp. 150–159).

Once the school desegregation decision was made, other political factors came into play. The administration's low-key reaction to southern indignation in the wake of the decision was, perhaps, designed to avoid fanning the flames by involving President Eisenhower in the controversy; the civil rights actions taken on behalf of blacks through administrative directive were accomplished quietly — and slowly. At worst, the Eisenhower administration's inaction resulted from the President's own tepid feelings about civil rights. But whatever the motivation, the result of the lack of administration support was that the Supreme Court's decision became vulnerable to attack; lacking any legitimacy ascribed to it by the executive branch, it had to stand or fall on the prestige of the Court.

The decision was scrutinized for flaws. Many of the arguments made by the appellees in the argument before the Court began to appear in the popular media and found their way into speeches by southern congressmen and southern sympathizers. Critics fastened on the social science aspect because that was the most novel element of the decision. Both the decision's critics and its supporters perceived that the use of social science in this new and, to some, radical way made the decision vulnerable. Yet, as the arguments presented by the critics shifted from 'all social science is inexact and therefore inadmissible evidence' to 'this particular social science research is wrong, and here is the evidence to the contrary', in short, as the critics began to use social science to *refute* the social science presented in the Brown case, they gave up the battle. For in so doing, prosegregationists were accepting the legitimacy of social science as evidence; in adopting the genre of evidence used by opponents of segregation, they were conceding the validity of social science advocacy. Today, no one questions whether or not social science may legitimately be used by any court to reverse a legal precedent; in a recent discussion of a forthcoming Supreme Court ruling on busing, Christopher Jencks listed three possible bases upon which the Court could reverse busing precedents, and one of them was social science evidence (Jencks, 1972, p. 41).

The quality of the social science evidence presented in the school segregation decision remains to be discussed. In all frankness, it was not very high. The most superior evidence was presented by Kenneth Clark, and, as the counsel for South Carolina was quick to point out, there were serious problems in the formulation of Clark's conclusions. He could not, for example, convincingly account for the higher incidence of "negative self-identification" on the part of northern blacks. One-third of the social scientists sampled by Isidore Chein, who said they felt that segregation was harmful to both black and white children, also said that they based that decision upon their own research, and two-thirds gave others' research as the primary influence. Yet since very little research on the effects of segregation had been published in the academic journals, and, in any case, since the Court could not evaluate the research to which it referred, its response constituted opinion, nothing more. In fact, research on black/white differences did not really begin in earnest until after the Supreme Court decision, which itself stimulated great interest in and emphasis upon research on blacks. After 1955 a number of journals and newsletters began to appear that published regular reports on such research and where it was being conducted. Prior to the decision virtually the only major research done had been commissioned by the NAACP or appeared in special-interest publications, such as the *Journal of Negro Education*. Funding for such work was simply not easily available. Aside from civil rights organizations, Jewish organizations, and some foundation sponsorship there was little money around for such research; certainly no government funding was available.

The criticism of the social science evidence presented before the Supreme Court by the proponents of segregation had a great deal of validity. The empirical evidence for integration was hardly conclusive. Moreover, the works cited by the Court appear to have been almost arbitrarily selected, as critics have charged. The Court did not make an extensive or systematic effort to find out on its own what social science had to say about the subject. On the contrary, there is a random quality to its citations of social science evidence; less important authors and less relevant works of important authors are cited, and fundamental works and authors are omitted. The social science research that had been done prior to the *Brown* decision by no means *proved* that segregation caused the educational and mental retardation of black children; that variable has simply not been isolated. Furthermore, except for Clark's tests, very little evidence had been presented to show conclusively that damage had actually been done to the educational and mental development of black children[1] (cf. Pasamanick & Knobloch, 1958).

This is not to argue that the decision should not or could not have been made. The point is, instead, that the Court made its decision on the basis of its sense of the effect of segregation and the requirements of the Fourteenth Amendment. Members of the Court may been swayed by the testimony presented by the social scientists; Clark's tests were said to have been particularly convincing. Two NAACP staff members, Herbert Hill and Jack Greenberg, assessed the effect of oral testimony very highly: "The experts were cross-examined, and their testimony was subject to rebuttal; this gave the defendants (arguing for the legality of segregation) a certain opportunity but it enhanced the persuasiveness of the testimony if it could not be shaken" (Greenberg & Hill, 1957, p. 474).

But social science was not the *foundation* of the decision; it was used to lend weight to what the justices clearly were persuaded was true: that segregated education is unequal education. The problem that the

---

[1] In fact, recent research on desegregation and its effects has indicated that the questions and answers are considerably more complex than would be supposed from the 1954 decision (cf. Jencks, 1972, p. 120).

proponents of segregation faced was not that social science led the Court down an erroneous path; rather it was that the time had come in the judgment of the Court — and, judging from the initial media response, in the opinion of many opinion makers — for the black to take his place as a full-fledged U.S. citizen. Given the widespread faith in education as a panacea for all social ills, the hope was that equal opportunity in education would be enough (cf. Sutherland, 1954). Certainly, no one foresaw the massive social revolution that was loosed by the *Brown* victory. The segregationists held a bad deck; but the Court had to find a way to reverse *Plessey* without seeming to do so. The solution was the argument that the situation in 1954 was no longer what it was in 1896, that times have changed: "In approaching this problem, we cannot turn the clock back to 1868 when the Fourteenth Amendment was adopted or even to 1896 when *Plessey v. Ferguson* was written. We must consider public education in the light of its full development and its present place in American life throughout the Nation (cf. Clark and Kamisar, 1969, p. 329; see also Clark, 1955).

The Supreme Court is, then, a policy-making body, and like any such body it recognizes that there is no truth or untruth, no right or wrong, that there are only degrees of each. Perhaps the Court is less swayed by political winds than are other branches of the government (the justices are, after all, appointed for life, or until retirement), but though it has no constituency, it does respond, as is clear in the *Brown* case, to its sense of the needs of the body politic, as well as to its awareness of its own limitations. It is also clear that the Court is not above internal politics; recent studies (by social scientists) of voting behavior on the Court have subjected it to the same scrutiny given any other branch of the government (cf. Schmidhauser and Berg, 1972). It is now recognized — if it was not before — that the appointment of a Supreme Court justice is a political act; that justices vote along distinguishable lines of judicial conservatism or liberalism, strict constructionism or activism (cf. Glick, 1971).

Social science can play an important role in the process of judicial policy making, just as it has contributed to the formulation of policy by other branches of government. The important point is that social science has little discernible influence unless it is taken up and exploited for political reasons. We have only to look at the lack of positive reaction by political figures when social science research does not come up with the expected or desired answers; hence, the sad fate of the presidential commission on drugs, the rejection of the president's commission on obscenity and pornography, and the dismissal of the Population Council's recommendations for liberalized abortion laws and wider dissemination of birth-control devices. Despite the claims of critics of and participants in the decision alike, the role of social science in the school desegregation cases was not decisive. By the 1953 argument the Court asked its 'five questions', because it had not found the information presented in the 1952 brief conclusive and was searching for another basis for decision. When neither side was able to present an airtight historical or constitutional case, the Court was forced to turn back to the social science argument. But even then the strongest statement for social science in the decision originated in the Kansas case and was merely quoted by the Supreme Court. Moreover, the Court was not consistent in its reliance on social science evidence; otherwise, it would have been more sanguine about the possibilities for peaceful integration, even in the South, and would have given a more vigorous order to integrate.

Though, in fact, the role of social science in the school segregation cases may be more modest than has been claimed, the cases represented a significant advancement for the social sciences. For the first time social science played a role in judicial advocacy that resulted in a significant policy decision and initiated what Bayard Rustin has characterized as the decade in which "the legal foundations of racism in America were destroyed" (cf. Rainwater and Yancey, 1967, p. 9). Brandeis had used social science to prevent a conservative judiciary from holding back progress; now the Court was taking an active role in molding a social consensus. In the process the social sciences acquired new legitimacy, even though under severe attack, and within and outside the social science profession their powerful and potential influence began to be taken seriously (cf. Curtis, 1973).

References

BERGER, M. (1957). Desegregation, law and social science. *Commentary, 23* (5: May), 471–477.

CAHN, E. (1955). Jurisprudence. *New York University Law Review, 30.*

CLARK, K.B. (1955). *Prejudice and your child.* Boston: Beacon Press.

CLARK, K.B. and KAMISAR, Y. (1969). *Argument; The oral argument before the Supreme Court in Brown v. Board of Education of Topeka 1952–1955.* New York: Chelsea House Publishers.

CURTIS, M.E. (1973). Social science and the law: An analysis of the school segregation decisions of the Supreme Court. Unpublished manuscript, Rutgers University, Department of History, New Brunswick, NJ.

GARFINKEL, H. (1959). Social science evidence and the school segregation cases. *Journal of Politics, 21*(1), 37–59.

GLICK, H.R. (1971). *Supreme Courts in state politics: An investigation of the judicial role.* New York: Basic Books.

GREENBERG, J. and HILL, H. (1957). A citizen's guide to desegregation. (Cited in M. Berger, Desegregation, law and social science. *Commentary, 23* (5: May) 471–477.

JENCKS, C. (1972). Busing — the Supreme Court goes north. *The New York Times Magazine,* 19 November.

LaFARGE, J. (1953). Judgment on racial segregation. *America, 90* (December 12), 289–291.

PASAMANICK, B. and KNOBLOCH, H. (1958). The contribution of some organic factors to school retardation in negro children. *Journal of Negro Education*, 27(1), 4–9.

RAINWATER, L. and YANCEY, W.L. (1967). *The Moynihan report and the politics of controversy*. Cambridge, MA: MIT Press.

SCHMIDHAUSER, J.R. and BERG, L.L. (1972). *The Supreme Court and Congress: Conflict and interaction 1945–1968*. New York: The Free Press/Macmillan.

SUTHERLAND, A.E. (1954). The Supreme Court and the public school. *Harvard Educational Review, 24*, 71–85.

THURMOND, S. (1955). The Constitution and the Supreme Court. *Vital Speeches, 22* (7: October 15), 29–32.

Chapter 21

Special Commissions and Educational Policy in the U.S.A. and U.K.*

Maurice Kogan and J. Myron Atkin

The crisis of legitimation in society and in educational policy has affected the ways in which certain traditional instruments of government are used. In the United Kingdom and in the U.S.A., Royal Commissions, special committees and commissions, and the so-called 'blue ribbon' committees have had a venerable history. Their purposes and functions are now in doubt....

The classic Commission of Enquiry was developed in the 19th century and became a device common in education policy formulation (and many other fields) not only in Britain but also in most of the British commonwealth countries, the United States, and, perhaps most effectively of all, in Sweden. It must now compete with such developments as think tanks, Congressional and Parliamentary Committees, specialist bodies that assist legislatures such as the General Accounting Office and Congressional Budget Office, the single-person study, and the different varieties of ombudsmanship and other forms of equity audit in many countries.

In examining the changing fortunes of blue-ribbon enquiries and committees, and in thinking about additional or substitute ways in which those involved in educational governance seem to be able to improve their knowledge and their ways of operating, we have attempted to identify some of the factors in contemporary education that seem to be hastening the development of new mechanisms. Traditionally, government has been expected to be stable, reliable, and equitable. Political figures were expected to articulate the norms of the society that they served and search for policies that would reflect the broadest identifiable consensus. These desiderata have not been entirely dissolved by contemporary turbulence and the challenge to conventional modes of legitimation. But parallel, if

* Abridged from *Legitimating education policy: The use of special committees in formulating policies in the U.S.A. and the U.K.* (Project Report No. 82–A17, pp. 1–17, 82–97) by M. Kogan and J.M. Atkin, 1982, Stanford, CA: School of Education, Center for Educational Research at Stanford.

not conflicting, impulses demand that government also be receptive to a far wider range of interests and groups than those who have traditionally been regarded as stakeholders in educational policy. It must be encompassing rather than discrete, expressive and even declamatory, and not solely analytic. . . .

[Early Perspectives on Commissions]

There is a large literature on commissions of enquiry concerned mainly with substantive areas other than education. Over time there has been a shift in emphasis in this writing from mainly historical and approving descriptions of such traditional models as British Royal Commissions (e.g., Clokie and Robinson, 1937; Hanser, 1965) to sharp critiques of the ways in which it is alleged that American Presidential and city commissions on race riots, or violence, or pornography (e.g., Platt, 1971; Komarovsky, 1975; Lipsky and Olson, 1977) have contrived to assimilate social discontent into the consensus seeking procedures of a society wrongly assumed to be pluralist.

The consensual assumption was generally strong in the traditional literature. In the view of Sir Arthur Salter (Vernon and Mansergh, 1940): "The proper use of Advisory bodies is the right answer of representative democracy to the challenge of the Corporate State." Such a claim would now be refuted directly by those who see these instruments as a collusive and confirmatory instrument of the Establishment.

> Radical changes are usually initiated from outside the Government service and, on all the more complicated and social problems, exploration by a Royal Commission is the usual preliminary to legislative action. . . . In social change, enquiry is so generally a preliminary of legislation as to have become almost a part of the legislative process.

These developments, Salter thought, might affect beneficially the very processes of government:

> The utilization of advice from outside . . . does involve the introduction of a new element as a part of official technique. The consideration of outside opinion is a means of effecting a continuous penetration of the machinery of government by the spirit of democracy.

Other, all earlier, American authors (e.g., Clokie and Robinson, 1937) referred to the Royal Commission in such terms as "a notable example of the wise combination of fact finding and policy forming in the state." They also concluded, however, that "the Golden Age of Royal Commissions is past and that new devices and processes are rapidly superseding them". There is Hanser's view that the Royal Commission is "the best of its kind ever developed . . . its findings of fact are accepted by the knowledgeable as definitive; its policy directives almost invariably guided societal evolution" (1965). From Britain, there is Pinker's (1971) observation of how, in the years following the Poor Law Amendment Act (1834), "a growing number of social investigations led to the accumulation of a body of evidence on our social conditions. This evidence provided the substantial basis of what is now termed 'blue book' sociology." Many have remarked how Marx himself made exhaustive use of many of the major reports that were prepared by the great social investigators of the early and mid-19th century and that he paid testimony to their value.

Although the impact made by Commissions is a matter for dispute, they have certainly not been an art form neglected by policy makers. [An earlier] British work (Kogan & Packwood, 1974) analyzed the operation and consequences of 28 commissions and committees in education, and had to draw quite severe boundaries around the subject area for many more could have been included. Similarly, Rhodes (1975), in coping with the same subject over the whole field of governmental action in Britain, after anxious thought about how to define his subject, restricted his study to 170 committees or commissions appointed by the central government between 1959 and 1968. In the U.S.A., between 1945 and 1968, Presidents appointed 66 advisory commissions. "By a somewhat broader classification, fully 132 boards and commissions were appointed to advise the President, Congress and various executive agencies in the three-and-a-half-year period from 1965 through the summer of 1968." Johnson ('The Great Commissioner') appointed Presidential Advisory Commissions at the rate of four a year (Lipsky and Olson, 1977, ch. 3).

Some of the earlier evaluations were more skeptical than those quoted above (e.g., Laski, 1938; Webb, 1948; or Wilson, 1964), . . . [but] the moderate and traditional view of them is summarized by Rhodes. They enable a problem to be looked at in depth by other than those officially concerned with the issue. The independent outsider carries more weight when proposing change. If they help to focus on a policy issue it is not because of what they recommend but, in Vicker's (1965) view, the way that they focus or change the appreciation of an issue. Rhodes sees them as part of a policy-making process which is gradual and unsystematic: "Reexamination of policy rarely takes place out of the blue. There will almost certainly be in any given situation pressures for a change in policy, weak or strong, internal or external, which have to be accommodated in the perpetual process of policy making." He recognizes their implicitly negotiative and collusive nature. In some, "The representation of interests and the element of negotiation are as prominent, if not more so, as the element of enquiry." . . .

Rhodes also confirms other views that the acceptance of reports might predicate a predisposition towards the proposals on the part of Ministers who create and receive the results of a commission's work. The U.K. case of the Robbins Committee on Higher Education (1963) stands out here (Boyle, 1971). The government assumed that higher education should be greatly expanded. Another instructive point emerges from Robbins. The government accepted the Committee's recommendations on access to higher education and the general social and economic arguments for expansion. But nothing was done to pursue the recommendations on curriculum and course organization. Nor did government like to be told how to govern: the proposals about departmental responsibility for higher education — Robbins wanted a separate Ministry — were soon abandoned. Impact and acceptance might thus be analyzed in terms of the type of issue raised. In education it is possible to differentiate among educational content and curriculum; social issues and access; organizational and structural issues (such as selection for secondary education); and the degree of control of government itself in an area of policy. Receptivity of a report will depend on the dimension of education to which the study and recommendations are directed. Some issues are hugged close to the bosom of Whitehall or the White House and recommendations on them are not welcomed.

More Recent Perspectives

[About two decades ago], critical sociological eyes [began to be] focused on the subject. Katz (1965), in a review of the assumptions underlying British educational reports, maintains that they carry forward without challenge the assumptions that comprise the core of the British educational tradition. They avoid the resolution of uncomfortable dilemmas. Katz's critique is based on a sensitive reading of the reports, although others (Kogan and Packwood, 1974) believe that he underestimates the extent to which they were ahead of the schools in the "traditional" doctrines which they communicated. Smith and Stockman (1972) attempted to clarify the extent to which the official reports "propose a description of the world" and "embody a causal model", and the extent to which the causal model may be consistent and supported by evidence. In 1979, Burton and Carlen asked, "Why do government reports take the form they do?" and make excursions into what their publishers describe as "linguistics, psychoanalysis, and Marxism" in an effort to produce a "theoretical reconstruction and elaboration of a specific ideological practice". They subjected British enquiries into police and judicial procedures to an analysis which can be taken as representing the extreme of the critical statements about enquiries. They asserted how in the 19th-century commissions were developed to help meet the

> requirement of the ascendant capitalist class to control the social contradictions produced by an unstable and potentially revolutionary situation.... Their main function was to provide and to publicly propagate knowledge of social conditions that would shape the technology of social engineering ... a clearly dual function of not only creating information but manipulating its proper reception....

They were "a pedagogy of reform based on inductive enquiry and public propaganda". "They are seen as representing a system of intellectual collusion whereby selected, frequently judicial, intelligentsia transmit forms of knowledge into political practices." Burton and Carlen declare enquiries to be "affirmatory texts that announce the professional functionaries" competence' and that they are concerned with the "exoneration of the system". These authors thus raise points, in an extreme form, which many other observers concerned with issues of law and order make, if with more recourse to evidence.

Virtually the whole of recent American commentary on the use made of committees of enquiry has been critical, perhaps because much of it has been concerned with commissions on deeply distressing and divisive events in recent American history: race riots, violence, the growth and potential control of pornography. The appraisals are virtually silent on the mass of Presidential and other enquiries, often instigated by philanthropic foundations, which are nearer the predominant British mode in assuming that consensually minded people will examine a problem ruminatively and on the basis of evidence, or negotiate differences through the committee medium.

What are the main points made in the American political and sociological analyses? First, those with a governmental origin are assumed to obey what Popper (1970) called "the iron law of presidential appointment" in that "representatives of major sectors of American society participate collectively in arriving at consensus on policy". To some extent this is the predominant British view, but it will be recalled that both Laski and Salter thought British commissions helped policies to be tested and changed by nonofficial intervention, and Graves thought they were an antidote to bureaucratic dominance. The allegations about inbuilt conformity, made sardonically and without too much care for facts in such writing as Elizabeth Drew's *On Giving Oneself a Hot Foot: Government by Commission* (1968), have been refuted by Martha Derthick: "If presidential commissions articulate a consensus, the common denominator of opinion about the nature of a social problem, then they serve an important political function" (1971). Indeed, Robert Nisbet's (1970) complaint that the Commission on Campus Unrest was not good social science but merely "pieties" misses the whole point of committees that have anything more than a merely technical remit: they are appointed to form judgments and not to produce academic treatises. In fact, the critique of committees as consensus assuming is contained in the very title of a leading book on the subject: Lipsky and Olson's *Commission Politics* which is subtitled *"The Processing of Racial Crisis in America"* (1977).

The second general finding concerns the different ways of using data. In particular, social scientists have been interested in the role of social science in these exercises. At minimum, many of the data collected have been thought useful for students of the subjects covered. But the use made has varied. The Committee on Obscenity and Pornography (Larsen in Komarovsky, 1975) "had more input from sociologists and other social scientists than any other commission in government history ...". But, Larsen thought, if there is a movement to adopt the commission's findings, it will not be won by reference to the data collected or the logic created. In another case the commission decided to include one and exclude another social science contribution and thus biased the findings. Larsen felt that the Obscenity and Pornography Commission was too scholarly. It should have made empirical studies of the policy options which could then have shaped the scholarly contributions. The Commission on Population Growth and the American Future (Westoff) made use of social science on demography and fertility which greatly affected its findings. But it avoided the far more value-saturated issues that might have been generated by studies of social structure. And, then, there is the ambivalence of social scientists on whether they should draw close to the policy setting system. American commentators feel that many social scientists do not share the willingness and ability of the lawyers to come in without demur and make decisive recommendations with little analysis of philosophical assumptions.

Thirdly, as part of the consensus setting function, the commissions develop different degrees of public display. Some members cannot tolerate the discretion and quiet that reflective and impartial work might demand and break loose of the collective discipline. Other commissions deliberately engage in what Skolnick (in Komarovsky, 1975) calls "a form of theater". The Commission on Obscenity and Pornography adopted the first course and Katzenbach's Commission on Law Enforcement and the Administration of Justice the latter. On issues of extreme distress and division, some commissioners see themselves as using theater in a therapeutic fashion to allow the afflicted and the concerned to have their say and thus assure the world that there is study going on which will bear their problems in mind. As we [note elsewhere], the use of publicity can [also] be a deliberate means of enhancing impact, as in the Kerr Commission. . . .

[The Decline of Commissions]

Educational commissions in both the United States and the United Kingdom are less in favor now than in previous decades. Even in Sweden where they have been a virtually indispensible part of policy formation there is no longer universal acceptance of their ability to ensure wide enough participation in policy making. The committees as a device are less the victim of their own deficiencies than of the far more complex political and social environment in which they now operate. There is a lack of consensus about educational policy, about, for example, egalitarianism or the efficacy of education in enhancing the economy or advancing social reform. Officially appointed committees as an outcrop of the public administrative system share the lack of faith in government which is also a universal phenomenon and which has led to the election, by large majorities, of governments with declared antistatist policies. 'Disengagement' is a slogan of the times. There is, as well, ... a decline in confidence in the power of disciplined enquiry to identify problems and help solve them. Within public bureaucracies there is a sapping of the self-confidence of permanent officials which reflects a deterioration in the relationships between permanent civil servants and their elected masters. There is, most potently of all, and associated with the lack of consensus about policy and lack of faith in the elected political and appointed administrative system, the growth of new forms of political action, often to be found at the community level, causing or agitating for change ... or raising demands for different modes of social control and resource distribution, ... all claiming not only a legitimacy for their actions but denouncing the lack of legitimation of the authorized political structure.

There is also reduced faith in the power of social science to identify and solve problems. Government in the 1950s and 1960s was prepared to pay for research and other forms of systematic enquiry which would not only produce immediately usable data but also sometimes fundamental criticism of society and comment on its functioning and its dysfunctions. Increasingly, governments now ask the scholarly community to undertake short-order enquiries that will provide precise information in answer to questions of limited dimension. Hence government might be prepared to finance short-contract research or think-tank operations but not the longer-term enquiry that allows much scope for the academic unit.

The reasons for disenchantment with social science are not too difficult to find. Some social scientists have directed criticism at the authority of scholarship and of higher education at large. Other social scientists seeking to be helpful to society have been associated with some of its most serious blunders: high-rise flats which have divorced families from their original communities; highway systems that emphasize mobility rather than continuity and recreation; developments in the theory of deviance which have seemed to undermine the rightness and possibility of forms of social control; unsuccessful attempts to predict and manage economic behavior. The list can be long. Perhaps it is unfairly drafted. Compared, however, with the relative certainties of medicine or engineering, the social scientists' debut into the world of practical affairs in the 50s and 60s is not considered by many observers to have been highly successful.

[Commissions and other Agencies]

Yet government, if limping a bit on its uncertain legitimacies, still seems to need resources for reflection and critique outside itself. So, far from there being a foreclosure on alternative instruments and modes of analysis, there has been a proliferation of them.... We briefly enumerate some of them before concluding with some thoughts on the relative legitimacy of each.

First, we have already remarked that it is unlikely that committees and commissions will simply fade away. The criticisms made of them do not automaticallly dispose of their merits, and in many countries, for example, Australia, Canada, New Zealand, and Sweden, they remain a strong and important part of the policy-making process.

They have been displaced in part by institutions that are not all that different. In Britain, for example, the specialist Committee on Education, a committee of the House of Commons, has developed more effective modes of enquiry into policy zones. The model is that of the U.S. Congressional Committee, although British Parliamentary Committees have no power to block or modify budgets. The Education Select Committee relies upon its ability to summon witnesses, mount enquiries, and publish reports which can then stimulate debate on the floor of the House of Commons. It is developing stronger relationships with the Department of Education and Science in mounting its enquiries, and it uses more sustained methods of enquiry than its predecessor subcommittees of the Expenditure Committee. The earlier committees lasted for one Parliamentary session only; the present committee, initiated in 1979, continues throughout the life of a Parliament. Its main limitation is that its membership consists only of MPs. MPs possess, of course, a particular legitimacy and strength of their own. But they cannot draw in, as could the DES in appointing central advisory councils, the whole range of expertise that might be needed. The committees consist wholly of back benchers. In the past, ministers never appeared before them but only their senior officials. That has now changed. Although [a recent] Chairman, Mr. Christopher Price, declared himself against "traditional" academics, he [did] employ a staff of academics, presumably all non-traditional, and other consultants who presumably, like the staff officers to

Congressional committees, [began] to develop styles, and policy orientations, and institutional memories of their own.

A third developing instrument is that of the think tank. In Britain there is no such institution for educational policy alone. Within the Cabinet Office there is the Central Policy Review Staff established by a Conservative Prime Minister in 1970. Its job is to examine current policy issues which either cut across departmental boundaries, or are in danger of being overlooked by the departments, or are simply thought to need a second view beyond that of the department. The term "think tank" is used somewhat casually. As we understand it, it is an institution for systematic enquiry, which can be either long term or short term, related to policy. In the U.S.A., the most important think tanks are in fact independent of government, although some of their money might come from public sources in return for work deemed useful, or the private foundations. In the U.S.A., different think tanks have acquired different political orientations and followings. In Britain, too, there are politically related analytic groups. For example, the Institute of Economic Affairs and the Centre for Policy Studies are associated with Conservative policy making. Others, however, such as the Policy Studies Institute are studiously impartial and are likely to produce policy analyses for education that have no particular political orientation.

[A fourth instrument constitutes] single-person enquiries. These have developed in the last two years under the Conservative government in Britain and embody recent assumptions about the value of external enquiry. In the U.S.A. such one-man studies as those conducted by James Conant in the 1950s and 1960s were not officially commissioned but were, all the same, important contributions to public opinion on the American high school. In Britain, the present government selects individuals to undertake enquiries because of some impatience with the slower and more consensual model embodied in the education committee style. The appointment of a single person assumes, indeed, that the central value judgments are already made and do not need, therefore, the process of vetting and agreement among a disparate group with legitimate interests in the issue. Instead, the individual can go straight from assumed value positions to technical judgments on such subjects as the organization of the Schools Council, or the efficiency of the civil service, or the usefulness or otherwise of 'quangos' (quasi non-governmental organizations — mainly committees set up by government departments to advise them).

Again with the traditional mode, in both countries there are enquiries mounted by private foundations.... [One need only cite] the Carnegie and Bundy enquiries to show how important they might be in the American context. In Britain, there have been few of these in education although some of the more famous general social enquiries such as those financed by Rowntree at the turn of the century (into poverty) were outstandingly important contributions to policy formation. More recently, the Leverhulme Foundation has aided initiative in collaboration with the Society for Research in Higher Education and Lancaster University creating a policy formulating seminar on higher education policy.

A particular form of one-man enquiry is the forensic tribunal of the kind best exemplified by the Auld enquiry. The forensic enquiry illustrates the way in which no particular mode of public investigation has simple effects. The single person sitting in judgment on the behavior of teachers in a particular school reaches conclusions about which management might take action. It is, therefore, quasijudicial and the singleness of the judgment is, indeed, the equivalent to that of a judge in court. At the same time, however, again like judges in court, the single-person enquiry will produce *obiter dicta* which might prove to be significant discussion of matters of wide policy importance. This was patently the case with the Auld enquiry. The motives of government in choosing between committees and single-person enquiries are, therefore, varied and are likely to produce varied results.

Finally, the political parties have increasingly provided themselves with tools for analyzing policies. In Britain, the starting points are historic. The Fabian Society for a long time provided an analytic capacity for the Labour Party. The Conservative Research Office furnished the post-1945 Conservative government with an entirely new approach to the welfare state under the guidance of some of its most prominent and able politicians. All parties now have their research departments but, more significantly, they also have policy committees which put together the outlines of policy that will be approved by party conferences and will form the basis of party manifestoes and, perhaps, legislative programs when the parties are in office. Somewhat separately from these internal procedures are the activities of political advisers who are associated with ministers once they are in office. These were used much more generally by the recent Labour government than by the present Conservative government in Britain. The political advisers, it should be noted, were not necessarily expert in the substantive policy issues but were just as likely to be competent at giving advice on political tactics and helping with the contacts between ministers and their supporting groups.

Acting within this range of institutions or as individuals, there are the contributions of the academic community. The government machine at many levels, and in both countries, has been able to derive knowledge and concepts relevant to policy from the work of academics. In educational policy, for example, in Britain, the creation of selection examinations at 11+, and their abolition, were both the products of academic work. The arguments for the expansion of higher education were forged in academic workshops before and during the lifetime of the Robbins Committee. The theories selected by ministers and their advisers in steering the economy in both countries are the products of academic economists. These contributions of social science to educational policy making have, however, come from what one might call the free range academy. Tenured academics have had freedom within which to develop studies and to lead research teams that might be financed by government. In recent years the contribution of academic institutions to policy formation has become more strongly institutionalized. Major research funding has come from both Washington and Whitehall to universities and to research institutes. And many leading universities, particularly in the U.S.A., have responded by taking contracts and producing work. At the same time, interchange between government and the academic world in the U.S.A. has been vigorous since the time of Franklin D. Roosevelt and has grown in Britain where the economists since the 1910s have been recruited by government for short-term appointments.

We have already observed that the longer-range work of academics is now in less favor by government, at least as far as policy issues are concerned. In education in both countries there is a turning away from the results of research. The more short-term findings of academics still, however, find their place and again, as we have observed, this may well lead to a resumption of relationships on longer-term research before too long.

[Establishing Legitimacy]

What might be the conditions under which any or all of these devices are regarded as legitimate? We might observe, first, that legitimation has dual characteristics. Legitimacy remains predominantly based upon the power of elected government in both the United States and the United Kingdom. Those devices that are created by government to help it reflect upon its own policy developments are legitimated by virtue of their dependence upon the democratically appointed system. But, as recent history has shown, the criticism of government is that it will too comfortably listen to the echoes of its own voice and appoint those to advise it who will share its own preconceptions. Legitimation is thus denied by those in opposition to government to those forms of analysis which are not able to start from different perspectives and represent groups other than those in power. This denial of government legitimacy has become all the more potent as the life of government becomes shorter, as has been the case in so many western European and Third-World countries. At the same time, the continuity of ruling ideologies has been weakened. The changes in policies between one government and the next are now extremely wide. So the groups which are characterized as disenfranchised can say, with some justification, that what is deemed legitimate by the ruling system in one year may find itself in opposition in the next.

To achieve legitimacy where there can be no consensus among

different groups in society requires, therefore, particularly strong efforts. The devices adopted for norm setting must be more open to more groups in society, or there must be a sufficiently wide number of them so that, in all, they will be capable of exploring a desirable range of opinions and methods.

The first of these possibilities has not proved useful in the past. What has been referred to earlier as the "Noah's Ark" device, whereby every member of a committee represents some interest and is matched with a constrasting partner from some opposing interest, is thought to create a mode of indecisive negotiation producing a weak and camouflaging consensus rather than useful analysis and progress. The other possibility, of using the whole of the range that we have described, is what we in fact prefer. But if that were to happen, it must be assumed that government is prepared to be open and eclectic in that which it is prepared to encourage. Governments must be prepared to sponsor, and therefore pay for, their own antibodies or counter analysis. If they do so, however, a new set of difficulties will arise. Donald Schon in *Beyond the Stable State* (1971) observed how "outsiders" who become engaged in decision making then become, unsurprisingly, the insiders.

We ought not to leave our subject before indicating some of the different uses to which the different device might be put. Some issues require relatively long reflection with a corresponding lead time for research and enquiry and reflective deliberation leading to consensus. This kind of operation, exemplified by the work of the traditional education committee, might particularly apply to areas which are not sharply contentious but where the time is ripe for action. In Britain, the recent Warnock Committee on special education (1978) is a good example.

Issues which have political potency but which also need an authoritative collation of multiple opinions are suitable for the legislative style of enquiry. No other group has the authority with which to challenge, for example, a government's plans for revamping a higher education system. The short-term, expert, perhaps forensic or managerial style enquiry is best suited to work by the single person. In such a case, we have remarked, government has made up its mind on the basic policy and needs help with elucidating the operational consequences. The think tanks are, potentially, the most flexible of the instruments. They can respond, because of their contractual conditions for their staff, to short-order requests for analysis. In the U.S.A., however, some of them have produced quite fundamental work on methods of social enquiry. They are not, however, value setters, they are as able as the legislative enquiry or the blue-ribbon commission to pick up the range of opinions from the larger society and help confirm or change the norm. They are essentially technocratic institutions, whereas the Parliamentary or Congressional committee exploits technocratic work for the purposes of determining values. Some think tanks, it is true, which are directly associated with political ideologies, will start with the affirmation and elucidation of a value position before moving on to the technical problems of its implementation.

In concluding this paper, we note how the study of legitimation in education, as exemplified by the record of the education committees, has led us to contemplate the whole range of consultative, advisory, and analytic bodies in education. Many of the components of the total system of which they form part cannot be treated here: legislative activities, or the ways in which individual practitioners in the schools might improve professional practice, for example. But we hope we have produced enough evidence to show that legitimation does not automatically or permanently adhere to any particular device. For that reason we urge the need to sustain as many options as possible in the ways in which educational policies can be created, refreshed, and changed.

References

BOYLE, E. (1971). In M. KOGAN, *Politics of education*. Harmondsworth: Penguin Books.

BURTON, F. and CARLEN, P. (1979). *Official discourse*. Boston: Routledge and Kegan Paul.

CLOKIE, H.M. and ROBINSON, J.W. (1937). *Royal commissions of inquiry: The significance of investigations in British politics*. Stanford, CA: Stanford University Press.

DERTHICK, M. (1971). On commissionship — presidential variety. *Public Policy*, 19, 624–638.

DREW, E.B. (1968). On giving oneself a hot foot: Government by commission. *Atlantic Monthly, 221* (5: May).

HANSER, C.J. (1965). *Guide to decision: The Royal Commission*. Totowa, NJ: Bedminster Press.

KATZ, M.B. (1965). From Bryce to Newsom: Assumptions of British education reports, 1895–1963. *International Review of Education, 11*, 287–290.

KOGAN, M. and PACKWOOD, T. (1974). *Advisory councils and committees in education*. Boston: Routledge & Kegan Paul.

KOMAROVSKY, M. (Ed.). (1975). *Sociology and public policy — The case of presidential commissions*. New York: Elsevier.

LASKI, H.J. (1938). *Parliamentary government in Britain*. London: Allen and Unwin.

LIPSKY, M. and OLSON, D.J. (1977). *Commission politics: The processing of racial crisis in America*. Brunswick, NJ: Transaction Books.

NISBET, R. (1970). An epistle to the Americans. *Commentary, 50*(6), 40–45.

PINKER, R.A. (1971). *Social theory and social policy* (ch. 2). London: Heinemann.

PLATT, A. (1971). *The politics of riot commissions, 1917–1970: A collection of official reports and critical essays*. New York: Macmillan.

POPPER, F. (1970). *The President's commission*. New York: Twentieth Century Fund.

RHODES, G. (1975). *Committees of enquiry*. London: Allen and Unwin.

SCHON, D. (1971). *Beyond the stable state*. New York: Random House.

SMITH, G. and STOCKMAN, N. (1972). A sociological approach to the study of government reports. *Sociological Review*, 20(1), 59–77.

VERNON, R.V. and MANSERGH, N. (Eds). (1940). *Advisory bodies: A study of their uses in relation to central government*. London: Allen & Unwin.

VICKER, G. (1965). *The act of judgement*. New York: Chapman and Hall.

WEBB, B. (1948). *Our partnership*. Cambridge: Cambridge University Press.

WILSON, H. (1964). Speech at the Trades Union Congress. (Quoted in R.A. CHAPMAN (Ed.) (1973). *The role of commissions in policy making*. London: Allen and Unwin.)

Chapter 22

Some Historical Facts about IQ Testing*

Leon Kamin

> If . . . the impression takes root that these tests really measure
> intelligence, that they constitute a sort of last judgment on the
> child's capacity, that they reveal "scientifically" his predestined
> ability, then it would be a thousand times better if all the intelli-
> gence testers and all their questionnaires were sunk without warn-
> ing in the Sargasso Sea. (Walter Lippmann, 1922)

Binet and the Early Testers

The first widely used intelligence test was created in France, in 1905, by
Alfred Binet. The public school authorities in Paris had asked Binet to
devise a method that might pick out in advance those children who were
not likely to learn much from the teaching methods and curriculum of
ordinary schools. Those children could then be placed in special classes.

The test pieced together by Binet put different sets of questions to
children of different ages. The questions depended on the child's general
fund of knowledge, and some were intended to measure how well the
child could reason and how sound his judgment was. The basic idea was
that, on average, older children are able to answer more difficult questions
than younger children. Thus any given child could be assigned a 'mental
age,' depending upon what questions he could answer. Pierre, for example, would be given a mental age of 8 if he could answer questions passed
by the average 8-year-old, but could not answer questions passed by the
average 9-year-old. Whether Pierre was said to be retarded, average, or
bright depended upon the relation between his mental age and his
chronological age. Thus an 11-year-old with a mental age of 8 was clearly

---

* Abridged from *The Intelligence Controversy* (pp. 90–97) by H.J. Eysenck and L.
Kamin, 1981, New York: John Wiley & Sons.

retarded, but a 5-year-old who could answer the same questions was obviously bright.

To Binet's great satisfaction, performance on his brief test correlated with teachers' judgments about which children seemed bright in school and which seemed dull. The fact that test scores were related to success at school work was thought to demonstrate that the test in fact measured 'intelligence.' This relation, which depended upon Binet's use of school-like questions, is what made his test more useful and more influential than the so-called 'mental tests' with which earlier psychologists had experimented.

Galton and the Eugenics Movement

Earlier interest in mental tests had stemmed largely from the work in the 1860s of Francis Galton, who founded the eugenics movement. Galton believed firmly in the inheritance of mental ability and of just about everything else. The purpose of eugenics was to improve the human breed by encouraging the genetically superior to have many children, and by discouraging (or preventing) the genetically inferior from reproducing at all. To accomplish such a result, however, it would be necessary to devise tests and measurements that could identify the genetically superior and inferior. Hence the interest of Galton and his followers in measuring physical and psychological differences between individuals and between races.

The earliest 'mental testers', following Galton's lead, concentrated on obtaining precise measurements, preferring tests of the kind used in laboratories to the kind used in schools. Laboratory tests make it possible, for example, to determine a person's reaction time to a fraction of a second by measuring how long it takes him to press a telegraph key in response to the sound of a buzzer. To the early experimenters it seemed reasonable that quickness in such simple 'mental reactions' might be related to 'quick-wittedness' in general, or to 'intelligence'. It soon became apparent, however, that precisely measured performances in such laboratory tasks did not even correlate with each other — far less with school grades, or other assumed indices of intelligence. The experimental tests inspired by Galton's interest in eugenics came to a dead end. But Binet, whose motives were practical and humanitarian, provided the Galtonians with fresh ammunition.

Binet's Ideas Misused

The IQ test, in Binet's view, was not a measure of 'innate' or 'inborn' intelligence. Binet thought of his test as a diagnostic instrument which made it possible to pick out children whose intelligence was not developing properly, who could then be given courses in what he called "mental orthopedics." The point of such courses was to *increase* the intelligence of children who had scored low on IQ tests. Binet's attitude is clear: He firmly rebuked those who believed that "the intelligence of an individual is a fixed quantity, a quantity that one cannot augment. . . . We must protest and react against this brutal pressimism" (Binet, 1913).

Early Racism

Those who first translated and used Binet's test, both in the United States and in England, were convinced Galtonians, however. They *knew*, even before data had been collected, that intelligence had to be largely hereditary. Thus Lewis Terman, who introduced the Stanford–Binet test to the United States in 1916, wrote that IQs in the 70 to 80 range were "very, very common among Spanish–Indian and Mexican families of the Southwest and also among negroes." He continued:

Their dullness seems to be racial, or at least inherent in the family stocks from which they come. . . . The whole question of racial differences in mental traits will have to be taken up anew. . . . The writer predicts that when this is done there will be discovered enormously significant racial differences in general intelligence, differences which cannot be wiped out by any scheme of mental culture.

Children of this group should be segregated in special classes. . . . They cannot master abstractions, but they can often be made efficient workers. . . . There is no possibility at present of convincing society that they should not be allowed to reproduce, although from a eugenic point of view they constitute a grave problem because of their unusually prolific breeding. (Terman, 1916)

There was no doubt in Terman's mind that differences in the IQ scores of different racial groups were produced by genetic differences between the races. And IQ differences *within* a particular racial group were also determined by genes. Terman believed that members of the upper social and economic classes possessed superior genes, which they passed on to their children. The same point of view was clearly expressed by another early translator of Binet's test, Henry Goddard, in 1920. "The fixed character of mental levels", Goddard argued, caused the unending plight of the degenerate poor and of the unemployed. This "fixed" mental level was said to be measured by Binet's test — a view entirely opposed to Binet's own.

In England, the early mental testers made extravagant claims about the hereditary basis of test performance even before they became acquainted with Binet's test. As early as 1909 Cyril Burt administered a set of crude tests to two very small groups of schoolchildren in the city of Oxford. The children at one school were the sons of Oxford dons, Fellows of the Royal Society and such like, while at the other school they were the sons of ordinary townspeople. Burt maintained that the children of higher social class did better on the tests — and that this demonstrated that intelligence was inherited. By 1912 Burt could write that "the evidence is conclusive" for the inheritance of mental capacities. The fact that parents provide children with their environments, as well as with their genes, seems to have made no impression upon Burt or upon Terman and Goddard.

Sterilisation Laws

The uncritical belief in the power of heredity, linked to the advocacy of eugenic ideas, was already widespread when Binet's test appeared. More than 30 American states followed the lead taken by Indiana in 1907 in passing eugenic sterilisation laws which provided for the compulsory sterilisation of, among others, criminals, idiots, imbeciles, epileptics, rapists, lunatics, drunkards, drug fiends, syphilitics, moral and sexual perverts, and "diseased and degenerate persons". The laws declared as a matter of legal fact, that the various defects of all these offenders were transmitted through the genes. The wholly unscientific fantasies of the eugenicists encouraged the naive claim that sterilisation of offenders would eliminate these undesirable traits from the population. Fortunately, the sterilisation laws were not often enforced. When they were, the victims were poor.

Immigration Quotas

In the hands of eugenicists like Henry Goddard, the new science of mental testing was also employed to reduce unwanted immigration into the United States by the peoples of southern and eastern Europe. Goddard administered Binet's test in translation, together with some 'nonverbal' or 'performance' tests, to a number of 'average immigrants' arriving at New York. His results claimed to show that 83% of Jews, 87% of Russians, 80% of Hungarians, and 79% of Italians were "feeble-minded". There was no doubt in Goddard's mind — or in the minds of other American mental testers — that tests producing such results measured 'innate ability'.

This naive belief had far-reaching consequences. During the First World War, the American army administered the new mental tests — basically modifications of Binet's pioneer procedures — to literally millions of men. After the war the National Academy of Sciences published the average scores of immigrant soldiers from different European countries. The highest scorers were immigrants from England, Scotland, Canada, and Scandinavia, the lowest from Russia, Italy, and Poland. Mental testers concluded that "Nordics" were genetically superior to the "Alpine" and "Mediterranean" races. The claim was confidently repeated, this time by Brigham (1923) and others, that the tests measured 'native, inborn intelligence'. The Army data were cited repeatedly in congressional and public debates which led to the passage in 1924 of the overtly racist 'national origin quotas' designed to reduce immigration by the genetically inferior peoples of southern and eastern Europe.

The Educational Scrap-heap

The IQ test has also played an important part in the American school system — especially in assigning lower class and minority children to dead-end classes for the 'educable mentally retarded.' The fact that a child has a low IQ score has been misinterpreted to mean that the child does not have the capacity to learn school subjects. The IQ test played an even more central role in England, where it formed the basis for the selective education system introduced after the Second World War. On the strength of Cyril Burt's enthusiastic argument that a test given to a child at the age of 11 could measure its 'innate intelligence', it was decided to use the results of tests administered to 11-year-olds to 'stream' children into one of three separate — and far from equal — school systems.

"Intelligence" Burt wrote in 1947,

> will enter into everything the child says, thinks, does or attempts, both while he is at school and later on.... If intelligence is innate, the child's degree of intelligence is permanently limited. No amount of teaching will turn the child who is genuinely defective in general intelligence into a normal pupil.

This pessimistic claim — so antithetical to Binet's point of view — was later put into even plainer language when Burt equated intelligence with "educable capacity". "Capacity", he stated in 1961, "must obviously limit content. It is impossible for a pint jug to hold more than a pint of milk; and it is equally impossible for a child's educational attainments to rise higher than his educable capacity permits." In other words, an IQ test could measure a child's capacity for education, and it was obviously nonsensical to try to force more education into the child's head than could be fitted in, as indicated by his score.

The notion that a so-called intelligence test can somehow measure innate 'capacity' or 'potential' was considered and explicitly rejected in 1975 by a committee of testing experts appointed by the American

Psychological Association's Board of Scientific Affairs. The Cleary Commit-tee declared:

> A distinction is drawn traditionally between intelligence and achievement tests. A naive statement of the difference is that the intelligence test measures capacity to learn and the achievement test measures what has been learned. But items in all psycholo-gical and educational tests measure acquired behavior.... An attempt to recognize the incongruity of a behavioral measure as a measure of capacity is illustrated by the statement that the intelli-gence tests contain items that everyone has an equal opportunity to learn. This statement can be dismissed as false.... There is no merit in maintaining a fiction.

Politics and the Nature–Nurture Debate

The points made by the Cleary Committee seem so obvious that it is hard to understand how any psychologist could believe that IQ tests measure innate intelligence. Perhaps we should look at a scientist's social and political beliefs, for they are likely to influence the way he interprets IQ data. Pastore (1949) has shown that eminent scientists who stressed the 'nature' side of the nature–nurture controversy tended to be politically conservative, while those who stressed the 'nurture' side tended to be liberal.

We have seen that the pioneers of IQ testing in the United States were enthusiastic advocates of eugenic policies, and believers in the innate basis of IQ test scores, even before they collected data. The 1903 notebook of Cyril Burt, then a 20-year-old Oxford undergraduate, contains the following neatly handwritten entry: "The problem of the very poor — chronic poverty: Little prospect of the solution of the problem without the forcible detention of the wreckage of society ... preventing them from propagating their species" (Hearnshaw, 1979). With beliefs of that sort, it is not surprising that Burt could interpret the fact that slum children did poorly on Binet's test as a sign of their genetic inferiority — and as proof that the test miraculously measured inborn ability.

The Hereditarian Argument

There are, of course, a number of facts cited by hereditarians to support their claim that IQ is largely determined by the genes. To begin with, it is clear that IQ scores tend to run in families. Parents with high IQs tend to have children with high IQs, just as parents with low IQs tend to have low-IQ children. The closer the biological relationship between two members of a family, the more they are likely to resemble each other in IQ. Children of different socio-economic classes have different average IQs. Children of manual workers tend to have lower IQs than children of professors and executives — a fact that has convinced some professors that they are genetically superior to manual workers. To some theorists, the fact that blacks in the United States have a lower average IQ than do whites is still further evidence that tests must be measuring inborn ability.

The most recent wave of interest in the genetic basis of IQ was largely provoked by concern over racial questions in the United States. Professor Arthur Jensen argued in an influential article in 1969 that American 'compensatory education' programmes — aimed primarily at improving the scholastic performance of poor black children — had not worked. The failure of such programmes was, in his view, inevitable, for the data of Cyril Burt, described by Jensen as "the most satisfactory attempt' to measure the heritability of IQ, had indicated that about 80% of the variation in whites" IQs was genetic. It was plausible to suppose, therefore, Jensen argued, that the difference in average IQ between blacks and whites was caused by the genetic inferiority of blacks. Finally, the argument went, differences with a highly heritable basis could not be eliminated by environmental treatments such as compensatory education.

Fallacious Logic

[Unfortunately, for the argument,] the evidence used to demonstrate the high heritability of IQ among whites ... is extraordinarily weak. Indeed, what was thought to be the clearest evidence — Burt's — is now recognised to be fraudulent. We should note at the outset, however, that even if the claim that IQ is highly heritable among whites were true, the remaining steps in Jensen's argument are entirely fallacious. Though it may seem intuitively correct to assert that a highly heritable trait cannot be changed by environmental treatment, it is simply not the case. Weak eyesight, for example, may be highly heritable, but it is easy to correct with spectacles, and we do not regard an eye test as measuring some fixed and unchangeable 'capacity to see'. And take the case of phenylketonuria, a rare form of extreme mental retardation which is caused by the inheritance of a single gene. The defective gene results in a metabolic defect which in turn affects development of the brain and nervous system. Yet it is simple to prevent mental retardation from occurring in a child born with the gene by feeding it a special diet with as little phenylalanine as possible. There is no reason, then, to believe that the role of genes — whatever it may be — in *producing* a trait is in any way related to the ease (or difficulty) of *modifying* that trait by environmental methods.

Leon Kamin

The Concept of Heritability

There is an unfortunate tendency for many readers — and for some scientific writers — to misunderstand the technical concept of 'heritability'. To assert that the heritability of IQ is 0.80 is *not* to assert that 80% of John Smith's IQ is inherited, while 20% is produced by environment. Rather, it is to claim that — in some particular population, at some point in time — about 80% of the variation in IQ, or IQ *differences* among individuals, is determined by genetic differences. Note, for example, that the heritability of two-eyedness in human populations is close to zero. That does *not* mean that the possession of two eyes is not determined by our human genes. What it means is that there is very little *variation* among us in the number of eyes we possess, and that any such variation is not related to individual genetic differences. The vast majority of people with only one eye, or none, have lost eyes through environmental accident, and not through transmitted genetic defect.

The heritability of a trait in a human population is, to say the least, very difficult to estimate, some would say impossible. When an estimate is made, it applies at best to a particular population at a particular time. The heritability of the same trait may be very different in other human populations, or in the same population at later (or earlier) times. The heritability of a trait is not some 'law of nature'. It is a population statistic, rather like the death rate in Madagascar during the fourth century — which tells us nothing about the death rate in North America today.

The Elementary Confusion in Jensenism

Finally, it is important to realise that even if the heritability of a trait is high *within* each of two populations, that in no way allows us to conclude that a difference in the average value of the trait *between* the two populations is genetically caused. This elementary confusion lies at the root of what the *New York Times* christened "Jensenism". The basic claim by Jensen was that the 'fact' of high IQ heritability *within* both the white and black populations made it likely that the 15-point difference in average IQ *between* the two groups was caused by the genetic inferiority of blacks. The fallacy in this claim — even if Jensen's alleged 'fact' were true — has since been pointed out by many geneticists and psychologists. The fallacy can be made obvious by a simple example.

We fill a white sack and a black sack with a mixture of different genetic variations of corn seed. We make certain that the proportions of each variety of seed are identical in each sack. We then plant the seed from the white sack in fertile Field A, while that from the black sack is planted in barren Field B. We will observe that within Field A, as within Field B, there is considerable variation in the height of individual corn plants. This variation will be due largely to genetic factors (seed differences). We will also observe, however, that the average height of plants in Field A is greater than that in Field B. That difference will be entirely due to environmental factors (the soil). The same is true of IQs: Differences in the average IQ of various human populations could be entirely due to environmental differences, even if *within* each population all variation were due to genetic differences!...

Many of the key 'facts' asserted by Jensen, Eysenck, and other hereditarian IQ theorists are simply not true. Perhaps more important, it should be clear at the outset that even if the asserted facts were true, the implications drawn from them do not follow logically. We are entitled to conclude that today, as in the past, untrue facts and fallacious conclusions tend to reflect the social and ideological biases of the theorists.

References

BINET, A. (1913). *Les idées modernes sur les enfants*. Paris: Flammarion.

BRIGHAM, C.C. (1923). *A study of American intelligence*. Princeton, NJ: Princeton University Press.

BURT, C. (1912). The inheritance of mental characteristics. *Eugenics Review, 4*, 168–200.

BURT, C. (1947). *Mental and scholastic tests* (2nd ed.). London: Staples.

BURT, C. (1961). Intelligence and social mobility. *British Journal of Statistical Psychology, 14*, 3–24.

CLEARY, T.A., HUMPHREYS, L.G., KENDRICK, S.A. and WESMAN, A. (1975). Educational uses of tests with disadvantaged students. *American Psychologist, 30*, 15–41.

GODDARD, H.H. (1920). *Human efficiency and levels of intelligence*. Princeton, NJ: Princeton University Press.

HEARNSHAW, L.S. (1979). *Cyril Burt: Psychologist*. Ithaca, NY: Cornell University Press.

JENSEN, A.R. (1969). How much can we boost IQ and scholastic achievement? *Harvard Educational Review, 39*, 1–123.

LIPPMANN, W. (1922). (Quoted in 'The abuse of the tests.' In N.J. BLOCK and G. DWORKIN (Eds). (1976). *The IQ controversy*. New York: Pantheon.)

PASTORE, N. (1949). *The nature–nurture controversy*. New York: Columbia University Press.

TERMAN, L.M. (1916). *The measurement of intelligence*. Boston, MA: Houghton-Mifflin.

Chapter 23

Does Evaluation Make a Difference?*

Marvin C. Alkin, Richard Daillak and Peter White

What can now be said about utilization? Earlier ... we raised two questions about utilization and indicated that they would be addressed through the case studies and the subsequent analysis. The first of these questions — does evaluation make a difference? — arises from the confrontation between two evaluation utilization positions. On the one hand, guided by the 'mainstream' point of view, one might contend that utilization seldom occurs and evaluation makes little difference. From the competing, 'alternative' viewpoint, the contention would be that utilization is common and evaluation does indeed make a signifcant difference. Which viewpoint is correct?

Does Evaluation Utilization Occur?

As we [have suggested], a disagreement over definitions may underlie the debate on evaluation utilization. The mainstream perspective employs a rather narrow definition of utilization that stresses a rapid decisive impact of the evaluation on major program activities and decisions. The alternative perspective softens these rather stringent requirements, broadening the concept of utilization to include impacts which are more subtle and impacts which are not felt for a period of time.

In our case studies we employed a methodological perspective sensitive not only to mainstream utilization but also to those more elusive instances of utilization that fit the broader, alternative definition. Rather than arguing the merits of one definition over the other, it may be useful to consider separately the two classes of utilization as we address the question of whether evaluation utilization occurs.

---

* Abridged from *Using Evaluations: Does Evaluation Make a Difference?* (pp. 223–261) by M.C. Alkin, R. Daillak, and P. White, 1979, Beverly Hills, CA: Sage.

Mainstream Utilization

One of the case studies, [that for] Rockland [School], readily fits the pattern of mainstream utilization. A specific identifiable program was evaluated; comparison groups were established; students were tested in both the experimental program and in the comparison programs; an evaluation report was written; the findings were negative; and the program was dropped. Rockland, then, is almost a textbook case of mainstream utilization.

None of the other case studies provides as pure an instance of this sort of utilization, although it is possible to identify several additional instances where evaluation had impact upon a program in ways which *approach* the mainstream ideal either in clarity of impact or in emphasis upon measures of program outcomes. Along these lines, the Garrison case provides an example of evaluation outcome data having clear impact, but impact upon community attitudes rather than upon formal program decision making. Specifically, the first year evaluation report, bolstered by the prestige and credibility of the evaluator, allayed the fears of the community about bilingual education and convinced them that a bilingual program could help their children.

Later in the history of the bilingual program in Garrison, utilization of a different kind occurred as the cumulative weight of positive program outcome data became an important factor in the fight to obtain continued funding. This might seem an example of mainstream utilization were it not for the fact that the funding decisions at first *went against* the program despite the favorable data results. Only after the political maneuvering of program partisans, such as the principal, Rose Franklin, was funding secured. While positive evaluation results were central to the arguments advanced by these partisans, the force of their position resulted more from the skill with which the data were employed.

Clayburne also furnished examples of evaluation impact close, but not quite equal, to mainstream utilization. Achievement outcome data from the annual evaluations of the career high school program in Clayburne had little or no influence on global decisions about the program during the first two years of its operation. Then, at the end of the third year of operation, the mediocre cumulative test results appeared to have been an important determiner in the state's decision not to grant continuation funding. Thus, seemingly, evaluation results accumulated over three years of program operation had a delayed impact on a major summative decision. In an interesting twist, process-focused data collected by the evaluator, and used for ongoing program fine tuning (a nonmainstream use), appear to have cumulatively had a major influence on the other summative decision taken, that is, the district's decision to continue the career high school using local district funds (the epitome of mainstream impact).

Thus, Rockland, Clayburne, and Garrison all provide evidence that evaluation can have major influence on critical program decisions — albeit not always immediately and sometimes in an unexpected fashion. Our data show that evaluation can make a difference in truly important decisions of the mainstream type. Possibly, the most interesting point to extract from these data, however, is the indication that cumulative influence — perhaps two or three years down the line — may be more important to look for than the immediate impact so cherished in the evaluation texts. The search for mainstream evaluation impact must be sensitive to the cumulative influence of evaluation data.

Alternative Utilization

Besides the instances described above, the case studies furnish numerous examples of evaluation influence which fit the broader, alternative conception of utilization. In Rockland, there is the gradual development of an evaluation data system which was found useful by the program director in monitoring the Title I effort. In Bayview, the usefulness of the evaluation data on instructional individualization stands out, along with a general trend toward frequent consulting with the evaluator. The achievement test data in Valley Vista were fed back into the system and did have some influence there. Clayburne provided a striking example of intense evaluator involvement in a multitude of program activities. Garrison, while involving primarily summative evaluation and political impact, did include some instances of evaluation data being provided and influencing program operation.

What is Utilization?

While providing valuable insights into understanding evaluation utilization, the mainstream and alternative conceptions of utilization as we have described them, have not attended to defining rigorously what is meant by 'utilization'. Rather than following the course of least resistance and leaving the definition comfortably ambiguous (as seems to be the practice in most writing on evaluation utilization), we have chosen to deal with this question head-on. The issue, then, is, how do we know a utilization when we see one? Or alternatively, how do we define a utilization occurrence?

One simplistic solution to this dilemma would be to say that anytime that anyone uses anything from the evaluation for any purpose *that* is utilization. Such a definition is clearly stacking the deck so that utilization would almost certainly be noted in every situation. Alternatively, a very restrictive definition of evaluation utilization might require that a single intended user make a specific decision immediately following the receipt of an evaluation report and solely based upon the findings of that report.

270

The two definitions just given represent opposite ends of a continuum, and might be thought of as caricatures of the alternative and mainstream conceptions of utilization. Neither of the above descriptions is workable; neither is realistic. As we have seen from the case study examples presented in the previous pages, instances of utilization are far more complex and fall between these extremes.

Given this complexity, can we arrive at a definition that is flexible enough to encompass the variety of types of utilization that actually occur without also capturing inconsequential spin-off effects of the evaluation? Perhaps the best course may be to try to isolate the essential components of utilization. First, for example, some kind of evaluation information must be communicated as a prior step, else there is nothing to be utilized. Second, the information should be used by what we designate (and will define further) as an 'appropriate user'. Third, there are different ways in which this information may be used, e.g., as a single input or as one of several information inputs. Finally, this evaluation information should be *used* — whether in making decisions, substantiating decisions or actions, or altering attitudes. Let us consider each of these elements in greater detail.

Evaluation 'information' can take many shapes and can be presented in any of several ways. It might include quantitative test results, accounts of interviews, budget analyses, implementation checks or vignettes on important program aspects. Perhaps the most important points to make are that (a) quantitative outcome data are not the only important information produced by evaluation, and (b) written evaluation reports are not the only, or even necessarily the most important, means by which information is presented. The evaluator's qualitative observations about program processes communicated in a conversation with the program director at midyear just might turn out to be the most important and influential information transmitted during the evaluation.

Once the information is 'on the table', someone must make use of it for utilization to have occurred. Of course, not every user or use is truly admissible. Suppose, for example, an evaluator used a particularly novel analytical procedure, which was reported in a subsequent journal article. Use of this procedure by other evaluators who had read the article would, in our minds, hardly count as an instance of 'evaluation utilization'. This is an extreme case but it does draw our attention to the need to limit our definition of admissible users and uses so that such tangential uses are not counted as instances of utilization.

A starting point in defining just who may be an admissible user is the formal authority structure in the evaluation situation. There is almost always some group of persons within the district or program who are explicitly authorized to oversee the evaluation. We refer to this group as *clients*. (It should be noted that not all of this group, even though authorized to do so, will actively concern themselves with the evaluation.)

Members of the client group could include among others the program director, the principal of the school within which the program is housed, a district-office level administrator, or the school board.

Other admissible users would certainly include those within the program whose use of evaluation information is sanctioned by those persons we have designated as clients. For example, teachers at a school, even though they are not authorized to oversee the evaluation, might make use of evaluation information to improve classroom instruction. This sort of use ordinarily does not require an official sanctioning by clients but is nevertheless viewed as an appropriate action.

The case studies provide examples of both clients and sanctioned users. In the Garrison case study, the school principal, Mrs. Franklin, was responsible for hiring the evaluator, Quijano, and it was well understood that she would supervise the work of the evaluator. Throughout the evaluation, Franklin maintained her position as the primary client. Other less involved clients in Garrison included the district director of special projects, several levels of administration above Franklin, and the school board. Franklin, in addition to her active client role, was also the most active user of the evaluation. However, Dr. Valles and Dr. Aguilar, the project directors, also assumed user roles.

Clients at Bayview included the project director (a staff person at the district office), the site project coordinator (Vice-Principal Dexter) and various levels of school administration beginning with the McNaught principal. Of these, the site coordinator took the most active role in supervision of the evaluation and was an important user of the evaluation information. As the evaluation progressed, a second McNaught staff person, the counselor Robert Harris, assumed an equally important user role *vis-à-vis* the evaluation. Harris was assigned full-time to project MORE (while Dexter had other administrative responsibilities), had an office within the classroom complex assigned to the project, and, as counselor, had a central role in working with students and teachers and reviewing the progress of the program. As a result, the evaluator worked extensively with Harris and also was able to devote considerable attention to the project's small staff of teachers. Thus Harris and the teachers were sanctioned users since Dexter approved of the evaluator's attention to these other individuals.

Up to this point, we have emphasized school district, or program users — program administrators, staff, and so forth — who use evaluation in their roles as program officials. Of course, there are sometimes other persons whose use of the evaluation information could appropriately be counted as 'utilization' by the researcher. For example, federal education personnel could make various uses of nation-wide data; or, the local data could be used by a graduate student performing a secondary analysis for his own research purposes. However, such a broad specification of admissible users is problematic. The difficulty is in establishing some threshold of salience; at some point, the user and the use become so attenuated from the program as to seem insignificant.

We have chosen, in this research, to consider as admissible only those external users who have influence upon the operation or funding of the local program itself. Thus, state-level decisions to continue or discontinue funding are important to the local program people; therefore, users concerned with influence on such decisions are defined as admissible. Those state level administrators who aggregate evaluation data into routine reports to the U.S. Office of Education probably would not be included as admissible users. More concretely, in the Garrison case study, the state Title IV review committee made critically important funding decisions; its use of evaluation data certainly would constitute utilization. Furthermore, the barrio community — whose fears about bilingual education were to be allayed — constituted another important and admissible user of evaluation information, because its attitude toward the school program could have great influence on its future development.

In our prior discussion of admissible users, we have referred to the 'use' of information without rigorously defining what is meant by 'use'. One rather idealized mode of use is as the sole (i.e., one and only) input to a program decision. Of course, there is never really only one input to action; people do not live in a world devoid of all stimuli save for evaluation — although many naive evaluators sometimes act under the assumption that they do. Certainly, a more common mode of use would be either as the dominant influence upon action or as one of multiple influences. In the Rockland study, the evaluation findings seemed to have a dominant influence on subsequent decisions. In most instances, however, the evaluation information is but one of many influences with information from other sources, contextual factors, political considerations, and so forth, constituting other important influences. The Bayview and Valley Vista case studies both provide illustrative instances of this latter mode of utilization, as when the evaluation data on instructional individualization in Bayview were combined with the program staff's own subjective assessments. . . .

Even more complex is when several elements of evaluation information have influence *cumulatively*, along with other nonevaluation inputs, such as program costs, district resources, etc. Often this occurs when evaluation findings presented at a number of different points in time together constitute a stimulus for action. In Clayburne, for example, our evidence indicates that none of the evaluation reports was so spectacular by itself that it could have led to a decision by the district to have funded the program. However, the reports — which convincingly portrayed a program being modified, improved, and having value for its constituents — did cumulatively influence the district's decision to continue the career high school program. Of course, the need to use existing physical facilities and the interest of the district in maintaining a strong vocational program undoubtedly influenced the decision, too.

The preceding discussion of the role of evaluation information relative to other influences still does not define the uses that will be made of information. In particular, we must more clearly examine the purposes to be served in considering the information and the issues to be addressed.

While decision making is the prototypical use of evaluation information, it is not the only purpose that might be served by such information. Sometimes there is no real decision to be made. Often the important decisions (for example to establish a program) have already been made, and the only real purpose of evaluation is to substantiate the prior decisions or actions. At other times, there may be no pressing need to make any program decisions, but the evaluation information can be used to alter the attitudes or climate of opinion surrounding a program. . . .

Ann Marie Stuart's use of the 1971–1972 Title I evaluation data to discontinue the Norton Music Program in Rockland kindergartens is an archetypical example of evaluation conducted specifically to aid in making a decision. At her behest, Dr. Harvey built into the more general Title I evaluation additional measures that focused exclusively on the learning effectiveness of Norton. Stuart intended these measures to provide her with a definitive picture of the component's worth, and when the data clearly indicated no appreciable effects, she quickly moved to eliminate Norton. Interestingly, the same year's evaluation in Rockland also illustrates the uses of evaluation for purposes of substantiating previous decisions or actions. Several years of favorable experience with the K-LEAD diagnostic approach had established the program as an integral part of Rockland's Title I effort; the 1971–1972 evaluation data confirmed K-LEAD's effectiveness and thereby substantiated, *ex post facto* the original decision to include it under Title I.

Finally, evaluations can be used at the local level to establish or to alter attitudes about a program. Rose Franklin's hiring of Dr. Quijano and the later dissemination of the first-year Title IV-C reading scores at McNair were both astute moves intended to alter the community's initial opposition to a bilingual program.

Clearly there is a variety of issues about which one might make or substantiate decisions or alter attitudes. The case study data indicate that these issues range across all aspects of a program, from questions of funding to the day-to-day operational concerns and to the winning of community acceptance. Further, most admissible users will identify more than one issue on which they wish to focus the evaluation's information. . . .

The Garrison case provides an example of establishing or altering attitudes about community acceptance. The Rockland case, on the other hand, entailed a specific issue of concern: continuance of a program

Figure 3   Utilization defined

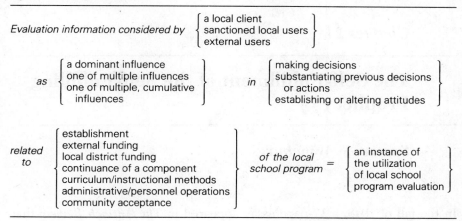

component. The Valley Vista case provides another instance in which the issues of concern were fairly limited; Erica Law used evaluation primarily in the program area most familiar to her, the IGE's curricular and instructional methods. In Clayburne the evaluation influenced several issues; the principal Warner directed Gerry's evaluation to external funding questions, district funding decisions, and, within Edison High, to Warner's immediate interests in curricular and administrative aspects of program operations.

We have, in summary, presented and discussed the essential aspects of our concept of evaluation utilization. Fitting these component elements together, we obtain the following definition of utilization (see Figure 3).

This definition helps to clarify the somewhat oversimplified approaches to utilization presented earlier in the chapter. Posing the utilization dilemma — does utilization occur? — as a dialectic between two conflicting points of view has enabled a new definition to emerge. The initial assertion that utilization does, in fact, occur is still maintained, but there is greater clarity as to the specific characteristics of a situation that would allow it to be categorized as an instance of utilization....

Chapter 24

The Self-Fulfillment of the Self-Fulfilling Prophecy*

Samuel S. Wineburg

In the fall of 1948, a 17-page essay appeared in *The Antioch Review* that altered how we speak about social life. It did so by inventing a term to describe a widespread yet poorly understood social phenomenon. The man who coined the term was Robert K. Merton; the term was also the title of his paper, "The Self-Fulfilling Prophecy."

What began as a neologism of theoretical sociology has become common parlance. Sportswriters hurl the self-fulfilling prophecy from their columns; legislators issue it from the rostrums of Congress; and even a President has been known to invoke it, hoping thereby to find a verbal tonic for an ailing economy (Richard Nixon, 1971, quoted in Merton, 1981). Thousands of scholarly papers employing the term have appeared in sociology, social psychology, economics, political science, anthropology, public administration, and social work. But the self-fulfilling prophecy has wielded greatest influence — and doubtless stirred the most controversy — in education.

In its original form, the self-fulfilling prophecy scarcely seemed controversial. The notion that a false but widely believed prediction could become true simply because enough people believed in it was neither new nor original. Merton, in fact, saw the term as convenient shorthand for W.I. Thomas's famous dictum that "If men define situations as real, they are real in their consequences." But the idea predated Thomas, finding roots in Bishop Bossuet's defense of Catholic orthodoxy in the 17th century; in Marx's critique of the Hegelian dialectics of change; and in Freud's work in places too numerous to count.

The self-fulfilling prophecy was a uniquely social idea with no corollary in the physical or natural sciences. Predictions of earthquakes may set Californians on edge, but words do not make the ground tremble. But in

---

* Abridged from 'The Self-Fulfillment of the Self-Fulfilling Prophecy' by S.S. Wineburg, 1987, *Educational Researcher*, 16(9), pp. 28–37.

the social sphere, self-fulfilling prophecies abounded. So, for example, rumors about the insolvency of banks, when widely believed and acted upon, brought doom to otherwise flourishing financial insititutions. Although the term "self-fulfilling prophecy" was new, the idea was not, and Merton wove it into his text with no claim of originality. Indeed, he abjured pretenses of innovation: "So common is the pattern of the self-fulfilling prophecy that each of us has his favored specimen" (1948, p. 105).
. . .

The Self-Fulfilling Prophecy, Desegregation, and Teachers' Expectations

America on the eve of the 20th century was a land that had grown accustomed to its social institutions, especially its system of separate schools for children of different colors. But by this century's midpoint much had changed, and claims that the 'necessary institutions' of separate schools were no more than 'mere customs' — and inhumane customs at that — were heard with greater frequency. Separating children on the basis of skin color, claimed critics, flouted the ideals of a democratic society. This was not all. Segregation's effects extended beyond institutional spheres — more was at stake than inequality of *social* opportunity. Segregation, according to these claims, caused *psychological* damage to its victims, engendering maladaptive internal states that left the personality scarred. These were new and serious charges, and their documentation became a social priority. Society looked to the universities for evidence, and the universities looked to the social sciences.

The research program of Kenneth B. Clark stands out above the rest. In Clark's work (e.g. Clark, 1955/1963; Clark and Clark, 1939) black youngsters between the ages of 3 and 7 were presented with two dolls, one black and one white, and asked by an adult experimenter which doll they wanted to play with. At each age level, the majority of children rejected the black doll. Sometimes youngsters showed extreme reactions, as did one little girl who, after choosing the white doll, called the black one "ugly" and "dirty." This girl sobbed uncontrollably when the researcher asked her to identify herself with one of the two dolls. Clark, a black social psychologist then at the City College of New York, summarized the implications of such an episode:

As minority-group children learn the inferior status to which they are assigned and observe that they are usually segregated and isolated from the more privileged members of their society, they react with deep feelings of inferiority and with a sense of personal humiliation. . . . Like all other human beings, they require a sense of personal dignity and social support for positive self-esteem. . . .

Under these conditions, minority-group children develop conflicts with regard to their feelings about themselves and about the values of the group with which they are identified. (1955/1963, p. 63)

Not fleeting or easily healed, this feeling of inferiority was "enduring or lasting as the situation endured, changing only in its form and in the way it manifested itself" (*Brown V. Board of Education*, 1954, pp. 89–90). Taught by society to be inferior, black children learned to feel and act inferior. Aided by the mechanism of the self-fulfilling prophecy, the effects of racism moved from 'out there' in society to inside people's heads, and became, in Clark's terms, "embedded in the personality" (1955/ 1963, p. 50)....

In a report describing this research (Clark, 1963), the term 'self-fulfilling prophecy' first appeared in the educational literature. Fore-shadowing controversies that would rage a few years later, the term appeared in the context of a discussion of IQ tests. The argument was straightforward. Because teachers thought minority children were dumb, they didn't waste their time on them, and teachers' expectations were later borne out by students' low test scores. Clark wrote:

If a child scores low on an intelligence test because he cannot read and then is not taught to read because he has a low score, then such a child is being imprisoned in an iron circle and becomes the victim of an *educational self-fulfilling prophecy* [italics added]. (p. 150)...

A Finding in Search of Data

By the mid-1960s, the notion that teachers' expectations for minority students caused them to do poorly in school was well established in people's minds. But one problem remained. If children who did poorly in school were expected by their teachers to do poorly, it could always be argued that expectations were based, not on self-fulfilling prophecies, but on students' past performance. Thus viewed, the educational self-fulfilling prophecy became a chicken or egg problem, something to be puzzled over endlessly but never known with certainty. That is, unless this alternative hypothesis could be ruled out....

[The stage was thus set for the research of Robert Rosenthal, recently appointed to the Harvard faculty.] Rosenthal (1966) had earned a reputa-tion for a series of ingenious experiments that demonstrated how researchers influenced the results of their seemingly dispassionate investigations. By 1963, Rosenthal had already begun to wonder if the expectancy effects he discovered with psychology students and albino rats

(Rosenthal and Fode, 1963) might not also operate with doctors and their patients, psychotherapists and their clients, bosses and their employees, and teachers and their students. As Rosenthal (1985), in a retrospective essay on the course of his research program, put it, "If rats became brighter when expected to then it should not be farfetched to think that children could become brighter when expected to by their teachers" (p. 44).

Rosenthal's idea to test the self-fulfilling prophecy in a school, rather than in a hospital, a factory, or a mental health clinic, was not wedded, it seems, to any deep educational interest. Among the requests he received for a copy of an article on experimenter effects was one from Lenore Jacobson, an elementary school principal in South San Francisco. Rosenthal sent her the article along with a stack of unpublished papers and "thought no more about it" (Rosenthal, 1985, p. 44). But Lenore Jacobson did. She dashed off a second note to the Harvard psychologist and in it presented a challenge. "If you ever 'graduate' to classroom children," she wrote, "please let me know whether I can be of assistance" (p. 44). From this challenge *Pygmalion in the Classroom* was born.

Rosenthal and Jacobson's experiment was unabashedly simple, elegant, and arch. Their research site was the "Oak School," located in a low-income south San Francisco neighborhood, and, in order for the experiment to work, the researchers had to violate the good faith of teachers. First, children in this elementary school were administered a little-known IQ test. Rosenthal described the procedure: "We had special covers printed for the test; they bore the high-sounding title 'Test of Inflected Acquisition.' The teachers were told that the testing was part of an undertaking being carried out by investigators from Harvard University" (Rosenthal and Jacobson, 1968c, p. 21). An information sheet given to the teachers explained that the "Harvard Test of Inflected Acquisition" could identify children who could be expected to "bloom", or experience an intellectual growth spurt, during the ensuing academic year. The test was actually Flanagan's Test of General Ability (TOGA), a group administered IQ test. The "bloomers" had been chosen by means of a table of random numbers.

The subject of the "bloomers" was brought up casually at a faculty meeting during which each teacher was given a list of about 2–7 "bloomers" in each classroom as identified by the "Harvard Test of Inflected Acquisition." Four months later, and again at the end of the school year, the test was readministered. The findings of the study, as reported in the full-length book about it, were striking. "We find increasing expectancy advantage as we go from the sixth to the first grade; the correlation between grade level and magnitude of expectancy advantage ($r = -.86$) was significant at the .03 level" (1968a, p. 74). Elsewhere, Rosenthal and Jacobson wrote, "The results indicated strongly that children from whom teachers expected greater intellectual gains showed such gains" (1968b, p. 22).

The finding of "an increasing expectancy advantage as we go from the sixth grade to the first grade" seemed to mean two things: First, that the treatment conferred an "advantage" upon the children who received it (the bloomers) and, second, that there was some kind of progression in the data, with the magnitude of effect decreasing linearly as children became older. But did the data support this claim? Not exactly. [Their data] showed statistically significant results (or "expectancy advantages") only for children in the first and second grades. In the other four grades, the treatment either conferred a statistically nonsignificant advantage (4th grade), no difference at all (3rd grade), or a statistically nonsignificant *disadvantage* (5th and 6th grades). In other words, the null hypothesis could not be ruled out in 66% of the grade levels.

Odd, then, were statements like "when teachers expected that certain children would show greater intellectual development, those children did show greater intellectual development" (Rosenthal and Jacobson, 1968a, p. 82). The lack of qualifications in the assertions was even more striking in light of the mixed results of a replication experiment in two Midwestern schools by Evans and Rosenthal (1969). Described in a footnote on page 96 of *Pygmalion*, the results of this study showed that in these two schools, control-group girls gained about 15 points on the reasoning subscale of the IQ test, whereas the treatment-group girls gained just over 5 points, a statistically significant advantage in favor of the control-group girls.

[Claims and Criticisms]

Rosenthal and Jacobson's assertions about the effects of expectations on IQ did not go unnoticed by the research community. Scholarly reviews of the book appeared in the American Psychological Association's review journal, *Contemporary Psychology*, and in AERA's main publication, *American Educational Research Journal*. Neither took kindly to *Pygmalion*.

Writing in *Contemporary Psychology*, Richard Snow, a differential psychologist at Stanford University, pointed out that TOGA was in-adequately normed for children in the youngest grades. In one classroom, a group of 19 normal children had a mean IQ score of 31 on the reasoning subscale of the test (Rosenthal and Jacobson, 1968a, p. 189). Like most IQ tests, TOGA was normed to have a mean of 100. Thus, the 19 children in the 'C' track of the first grade were hardly the type of children one would expect at this run-of-the-mill school. Snow asked pointedly, "Were these children actually functioning at imbecile and low moron levels?" "More likely", he hypothesized, "the test was not functioning at this grade level ... to obtain IQ scores as low as these, given reasonably distributed ages, raw scores would have to represent random or systematically incorrect responding" (Snow, 1969, p. 198). In other words, even if some students marked their tests at random the raw scores would have been higher than those obtained. In order to score so low, some students must have refused to put pen to paper. Snow criticized other features of the book, such as the fact that additional mental ability information (readily available at the school) was not used in the analysis, the reliance on simple gain scores "even though many mean pretest differences between treatment groups equal or exceed obtained posttest differences" (p. 198), and the use of "microscopic scales to overemphasize practically insignificant differences" (p. 199). Snow concluded: "*Pygmalion*, inadequately and prematurely reported ... has performed a disservice to teachers and schools, to users and developers of mental tests, and perhaps worst of all, to parents and children whose newly gained expectations may not prove quite so self-fulfilling" (p. 198).

Robert Thorndike, an expert in educational and psychological testing at Columbia University and the coauthor of a widely used IQ test, was no kinder to *Pygmalion*. Like Snow's criticisms, Thorndike's had less to do with the theory behind the study or even with the design employed, than with an IQ test that produced uneven and wildly unpredictable results. Thorndike (1968) questioned the validity of a measure that would yield a mean of 150.17 among the six "bloomers" in class 2A, an extraordinarily high score that could only be obtained if most students received a perfect score on the subtest. But because the standard deviation for these six scores was 40 points, Thorndike wondered about the students who fell about the mean. *Pygmalion*, he wrote, "is so defective technically that one can only regret that it ever got beyond the eyes of the original investigators!" (p. 708).

Not only did *Pygmalion* get past the eyes of the original investigators but, even before the book hit the streets, headlines about it splashed over the front page of the August 14, 1967 *New York Times* (Leo, 1967). (Details of the experiment's failure to replicate, however, received a scant column inch in the continuation of the story on page 20.) Robert Rosenthal appeared on national television telling the *Today Show*'s Barbara Walters that "teachers shouldn't be allowed to teach students who they know won't learn" (NBC, May 28, 1969). And reviews of *Pygmalion* in the media hailed it as a major contribution to understanding the problems of disadvantaged students.

Robert Coles, a Harvard psychiatrist, writing in the *New Yorker* (Coles, 1969), declared that *Pygmalion*'s lesson was clear: "All sorts of young children did very much better in school than others like them, presumably because their teachers *expected* them to become "bloomers", and TOGA's putative prophecy was fulfilled so conclusively that even hard-line social scientists were startled "(p. 174). Who were these "startled" social scientists, and in what forum did they shake their heads in wonderment? Coles did not say, but it was certainly not at the 1966 American Psychological Association symposium in which Rosenthal presented the study and listened to his discussant, N.L. Gage, a Stanford University expert on teaching methods, criticize it roundly (Gage, 1966). Equally reticent was Coles on the fact that in four of six grade levels there were no statistically significant differences between the bloomers and the regular pupils; nor did he have anything to say about the failure of the experiment to replicate. Although these points eluded Coles's analysis, the opportunity to point his finger at the real culprits in the American educational system did not: "The prejudices of teachers — and the effects the prejudices have on learning — come across on almost every page of this book" (p. 175).

The reports of *Pygmalion* in the press showed how the study came to stand for whatever people wanted it to, regardless of the original research questions asked by Rosenthal and Jacobson. *Pygmalion* tested the hypothesis that teachers who believe their students are due for an intellectual growth spurt will, in fact, score higher on an IQ test than a group of comparable students for whom no expectations are held. But an article in *Time* reported that "a new book called *Pygmalion in the Classroom*" demonstrated that "many children *fail to learn* simply because their teachers do not expect them to" (September 20, 1968, p. 62, emphasis added). Not only was such an effect not documented, it was never even addressed in Rosenthal and Jacobson's study. *Time* went on to claim that the findings of *Pygmalion* "raise some fundamental questions about teacher training" and "cast doubt on the wisdom of assigning children to classes according to presumed ability" (p. 62).

One might think that only writers in the popular press would leap so quickly from the findings of a field-experiment to questions of reforming teacher education and the organization of schooling. But the idea that *Pygmalion* had direct implications for teacher training, compensatory education, and the ways in which this nation dealt with its poorest students was not the media's invention. Rosenthal and Jacobson themselves set the stage by forging links between *Pygmalion*'s findings and questions about how to train our teachers and run our schools.

Writing in the *Scientific American* (1968c), they questioned the wisdom of federal programs that had been trying to come up with ways to overcome the educational handicaps of disadvantaged children. They argued that such programs rested on the assumption that disadvantaged children possessed some problem, or deficit, that must be remedied. Rosenthal and Jacobson asserted that such thinking was, at best, misguided:

> Our experiment rested on the premise that at least some of the deficiencies — and therefore at least some of the remedies — might be in the schools, and particularly in the attitudes of teachers toward disadvantaged children. In our experiment nothing was done directly for the child. There was no crash program to improve his reading ability, no extra time for tutoring, no

program of trips to museums and art galleries. The only people affected directly were the teachers. (p. 23)

What conclusions were readers to draw from such statements? That compensatory education had been a waste? That changing teachers' expectancies might prove more cost-effective than programs sponsored under the Elementary and Secondary Education Act? "More attention in educational research should be focused on the teacher," the authors continued. And once researchers learned how the Oak School teachers were able to accomplish what they did, training packages could be designed so that "other teachers could be taught to do the same." This might even lead to the development of psychological instruments for earmarking teachers who could produce similar effects and weeding out those unable to do so. *Pygmalion* would thus play a role in the "sophisticated selection of teachers" (p. 23). Given enough time, it seemed, *Pygmalion*'s findings would revolutionize American education. . . .

Pygmalion Reconsidered in Educational Research

Pygmalion's influence on educational research is nothing short of remarkable — since the original study there have been, by one estimate (Meyer, 1985), between 300 and 400 published reports related to the educational self-fulfilling prophecy (for reviews see Brophy, 1983; Brophy and Good, 1974; Cooper and Good, 1983; Dusek, 1975, 1985). A research tradition that began by inducing teachers to form false expectations based on experimental manipulation quickly progressed to the study of expectations as they naturally occurred in ordinary classrooms. In the course of this work, researchers built and refined elaborate models for the communication of expectations (Brophy and Good, 1974; Cooper, 1979; Cooper and Good, 1983; West and Anderson, 1976) and developed finely-tuned observation systems for analyzing complex classroom interactions (Brophy and Good, 1970b).

Brophy and Good (1970a) were among the first to study naturally occurring expectations. They asked four 1st-grade teachers to rank their students in order of expected achievement and then observed high- and low-expectation students in their respective classrooms. Interesting patterns emerged. High-expectation students volunteered more answers, initiated more contacts with their teachers, raised their hands more often, and had fewer reading problems than their low expectation peers, findings which led Brophy and Good to the realization that many 'teacher expectation effects' are best understood as student effects on teachers. But other findings were less easy to explain this way. For instance, when low-expectation students gave wrong answers they were less likely to receive specific feedback, and when they gave right answers they were less likely to receive praise. Although all four teachers in this study displayed relatively similar behavior patterns, a follow-up study (Evertson, Brophy and Good, 1972, cited in Brophy and Good, 1974) yielded less uniform results. Here, only three of nine teachers resembled those in the first study; three others displayed few differences in their interactions with high- and low-expectation students; and the final three showed the opposite pattern from the first — often seeking out lows for extra help and giving them more of a chance to get the right answer. These early studies set the tone for much of the research that followed — expectations in the classroom were phenomena far more complex and multi-dimensional than most had imagined (Dusek, 1985).

As research on teacher expectancies began to accumulate, teachers looked less like the villains portrayed in the earlier studies. True, some teachers ignored information from students and hewed to rigid expectations, distributing turns unfairly in reading groups (Allington, 1980), criticizing some students more harshly than others (Brophy and Good, 1970b; Good, Sikes and Brophy, 1973), and smiling at some while reacting coolly to others (Babad, Inbar and Rosenthal, 1982). Every profession includes those who do it a disservice, and teaching is no exception. But for the most part, teachers' expectations proved to be based on the best evidence in their possession (Borko, Cone, Russo and Shavelson, 1979; Shavelson, Cadwell and Izu, 1977), and most teachers were willing to abandon initial expectations when more dependable evidence became available. Indeed, a recent study suggests that those *least* acquainted with classroom life are often most influenced by the background information they receive about students (Carter, Sabers, Cushing, Pinnegar and Berliner, 1987). Experienced teachers tend to disregard such information, preferring to form judgments based on their own firsthand experience with students. Summarizing much research over the years on educational self-fulfilling prophecies, Brophy (1983) concluded:

> Although there are relationships between teacher expectations, teacher-student interaction, and student achievement, most of these are more accurately construed as student effects on teachers rather than as teacher expectation effects on students. Most differential teacher expectations are accurate and reality-based, and most differential teacher interaction with students represents either appropriate, proactive response to differential student need, or at least understandable reactive response to differential student behavior ... although the potential for teachers' expectations to function as self-fulfilling prophecies always exists, the extent to which they actually do so in typical classrooms is probably limited ... (p. 634)

One might assume that somewhere amidst all of these subsequent studies lay the vindication of *Pygmalion*, proving once and for all that teacher expectations boost (or lower) students' IQs.... [Unfortunately,] years of replications and follow-up studies have shown that strong claims about the relationship between expectations and intelligence were unwarranted. For example, Rosenthal and his associates tried several times to replicate the expectation-IQ linkage they reported in *Pygmalion*. Evans and Rosenthal (1969) found no significant differences in total IQ after a year between the treatment and control groups. A study by Conn, Edwards, Rosenthal, and Crowne (1968) yielded no statistically significant differences between the treatment and control groups in total IQ after 4 months (though there was a 1.46 point gain score advantage to the bloomers). After three semesters the effect faded in total IQ, with slight nonsignificant differences favoring the control groups. In another study, Anderson and Rosenthal (1968) manipulated the expectations of counselors at a day camp for retarded boys and administered an IQ test at the beginning and end of the eight-week experimental period. The only significant IQ change was a *decrease* on the reasoning subscale for the boys who were expected to bloom, a finding that clearly ran contrary to predicted results. In a meta-analysis based on 18 studies, Raudenbush (1984) found a small mean effect size in IQ-expectation studies ($\Delta = .11$), a finding that either achieved or failed to achieve statistical significance depending on the test employed. In Smith's (1980) meta-analysis, sizeable effects were found for teacher expectancies on student achievement, class participation, and social competence. But a meta-analysis of 22 teacher expectancy/IQ studies showed that the "effect of teacher expectations on pupil IQ was quite low. ... Pupil intellectual ability is minimally affected by the labelling information about this intellectual potential" (p. 54).

Yet such evidence often does little to dislodge beliefs about the expectation/intelligence linkage. Thus, when *Pygmalion*'s critics (e.g., Snow, 1986) try to refute claims that the self-fulfilling prophecy is responsible for enduring intellectual gains (Jones, 1986), their letters to the editor are rejected for 'lack of space'. Perhaps this response is understandable given the almost mythic proportions *Pygmalion* has assumed in some college textbooks. When material from the study appeared in a chapter on "Prejudice and Discrimination" in Kenneth and Mary Gergen's *Social Psychology* (1981), the data for grades 3, 4, 5, and 6 (the grade levels in which there were no significant effects) mysteriously vanished, leaving a chart containing only the *positive* effects for grades 1 and 2. It seems that, in *Pygmalion*'s old age, she doesn't develop wrinkles — but loses them.

Pygmalion as a Cultural Ideal

Most new ideas in education have a pitifully short half-life, but occasionally an idea captures the popular imagination and takes hold. In one form or another, the self-fulfilling prophecy had been in the educational literature since the late 1950s, but it wasn't until *Pygmalion in the Classroom* that its popularity soared. Why?

Pygmalion represented not merely an idea, but an *ethos*, a uniquely American way of looking at ourselves and understanding what we saw. *Pygmalion* used empirical research to document what we believed as a people: that not our social class, our previous experiences, or even the test scores in our academic files limited our ability to bloom. An ad in *Reader's Digest* put it thus: "Self-Fulfilling Prophecy — A key to success. Actual experiments prove this mysterious force can heighten your intelligence, your competitive ability, your will to succeed. The secret: Just make a prediction" (quoted in Good and Brophy, 1977, p. 383). In intelligence, as in so many other spheres of American life, the road to success was paved with the power of positive thinking.

Not only was *Pygmalion* born in the right country, but her timing was impeccable. Bewildered by a far-off war and rocked by the civil rights movement, busing, and racial disturbances at home, America readily laid blame. Teachers, sufficiently powerless and disorganized, were convenient candidates. Graphic portrayals of teacher negligence poured from all quarters — especially from bookstores where Jonathan Kozol's *Death at an Early Age* (the 1967 National Book Award winner) and Herbert Kohl's *36 Children* (1967) became bestsellers. Reviewing *Pygmalion* for the *New York Review of Books*, Kohl (1968) claimed the book's findings were consistent with what critics of schools had long been saying. Indeed, before the nation had ever heard of the Oak School or the Harvard Test of Inflected Acquisition, the educational self-fulfilling prophecy was a *social truth*, a familiar explanation of how schools undermined the intellectual performance of the disadvantaged. By the time *Pygmalion* arrived, her numbers were of less importance than her message. Her data did not substantiate a theory as much as a theory substantiated her.

Events within the educational community also spread *Pygmalion's* popularity. By the late 1960s, Arthur Jensen's ideas about the heritability of IQ were being noted (Jensen, 1969). Jensen proposed that the average difference in "IQ scores between black and white people may be attributable as much to heredity as environment" (1973, p. 80). To these claims, *Pygmalion* provided a powerful counter, asserting that intelligence was as much a function of our social situation as anything in our genes. For years, Arthur Jensen and Robert Rosenthal squared off in perennial, sometimes acrimonious debates (e.g., Edson, 1969; Jensen, 1969, 1980; Rosenthal, 1980, 1985; Rosenthal and Rubin, 1971). But divisiveness between two psychologists is of less interest to us here than the impressions about this conflict picked up by the popular press and the public. *Pygmalion*, matching the beliefs of jurists, journalists, and the public at large, came to symbolize the American ideal (cf. Cronbach, 1975). As the cover of the

May, 1970, *Family Circle* proclaimed: "Your Child's IQ Can Be Improved — New Findings."

Educational researchers are naturally drawn to studying variables they can control, and obviously teachers' expectations are much easier to manipulate than students' social class or parents' educational attainments. In *Pygmalion's* trail, teacher expectations became an educational growth industry. The "Teacher Expectancy and Student Achievement" (TESA) training program of the Los Angeles County Unified School District (cf. Columbus Public Schools, 1982; Kerman, 1979) has emerged as one of the most widely distributed inservice programs in this country, in addition to its distribution in Western Europe, Puerto Rico, England, Panama, Australia, and Saudi Arabia (Kerman, personal communication, June 15, 1987). Workshops that bring teachers' biases to the surface and heighten their awareness of classroom behavior can only be viewed positively. But when distinctions between what expectations can and cannot do become blurred, when all differences among students are cast as a function of their teachers' expectations, a dangerous trend is set. As Fein (1971) noted of such thinking:

> [It] makes educational quality seem much easier to attain. No longer are we required to worry centrally about . . . environmental disadvantage; simply create a system which can provide teachers who will say to their students, in effect, that they are getting better in every way, every day and, eureka, the gap will vanish. (p. 114)

Training programs and courses in teacher education programs notwithstanding, the painful gap in school performance between children of different colors and social classes remains. This is not to dismiss the contributions made by research on the educational self-fulfilling prophecy. But *writ large*, the attempt to solve the ills of American schools by changing the expectations of teachers diverts attention from basic social inequities by claiming that the central, if not the entire, cause of school failure rests in the minds of teachers.

The process by which schools inherit the responsibility for social inequity is not well understood. Yet one thing is certain — creating high expectations for school children costs less than building new housing or funding new jobs. The omnipotence of schooling is a compelling idea in a democracy, but sometimes popularity obscures falseness. Ironically, in the same article in which Robert Merton (1948) introduced the self-fulfilling prophecy, he expressed doubts about education's ability to solve the problems caused by it: "The appeal to 'education' as a cure-all for the most varied social problems is rooted deep in the mores of America. Yet it is nonetheless illusory for all that" (p. 197).

References

ALLINGTON, R. (1980). Teacher interruption behaviors during primary-grade oral reading. *Journal of Educational Psychology*, 72, 371–377.

ANDERSON, D.F. and ROSENTHAL, R. (1968). Some effects of interpersonal expectancy and social interaction on institutionalized retarded children. *Proceedings of the 76th Annual Convention of the American Psychological Association*, 3, 479–480.

BABAD, E.Y., INBAR, J. and ROSENTHAL, R. (1982). Pygmalion, Galatea, and the Golem: Investigations of biased and unbiased teachers. *Journal of Educational Psychology*, 74, 459–474.

BORKO, H., CONE, R., RUSSO, N. and SHAVELSON, R. (1979). Teachers' decision making. In P. PETERSON and H. WALBERG (Eds), *Research on teaching: Concepts, findings, and implications*. Berkeley, CA: McCutchan.

BROPHY, J.E. (1983). Research on the self-fulfilling prophecy and teacher expectations. *Journal of Educational Psychology*, 75, 631–661.

BROPHY, J.E. and GOOD, T.L. (1970a). Teachers' communication of differential expectations for children's classroom performance: Some behavioral data. *Journal of Educational Psychology*, 61, 365–374.

BROPHY, J.E. and GOOD, T.L. (1970b). The Brophy–Good dyadic interaction system. In A. SIMON and E. Boyer (Eds), *Mirrors for behavior: An anthology of observation instruments continued* (1970 supp., Vol. A). Philadelphia: Research for Better Schools.

BROPHY, J.E. and GOOD, T.L. (1974). *Teacher–student relationships: Causes and consequences*. New York: Holt, Rinehart, and Winston.

BROWN V. BOARD OF EDUCATION (1954). 347 U.S. 483.

CARTER, K., SABERS, D., CUSHING, K., PINNEGAR, S. and BERLINER, D.C. (1987). Processing and using information about students: A study of expert, novice, and postulant teachers. *Teaching & Teacher Education*, 3, 147–157.

CLARK, K.B. (1955/1963). *Prejudice and your child*. Boston: Beacon Press.

CLARK, K.B. (1963). Educational stimulation of racially disadvantaged children. In A.H. PASSOW (Ed.), *Education in depressed areas*. New York: Columbia University, Teachers College, Bureau of Publications.

CLARK, K.B. and CLARK, M. (1939). Development of consciousness and the emergence of racial identification in Negro children. *Journal of Social Psychology*, 10, 591–599.

COLES, R. (1969). What can you expect? (Review of *Pygmalion in the Classroom*.) *The New Yorker*, April, pp. 169–177.

COLUMBUS PUBLIC SCHOOLS (1982). *TESA News*, 1(1).

CONN, L.K., EDWARDS, C.N., ROSENTHAL, R. and CROWNE, D. (1968). Perception of emotion and response to teachers' expectancy by elementary school children. *Psychological Reports*, 22, 27–34.

COOPER, H.M. (1979). Pygmalion grows up: A model for teacher expectation communication and performance influence. *Review of Educational Research*, 49, 389–410.

COOPER, H.M. and GOOD, T.L. (1983). *Pygmalion grows up: Studies in the expectation communication process*. New York: Longman.

CRONBACH, L.J. (1975). Five decades of public controversy over mental testing. *American Psychologist*, 30, 1–14.

Dusek, J.B. (1975). Do teachers bias children's learning? *Review of Educational Research, 45,* 661–684.

Dusek, J.B. (1985) *Teacher expectancies.* Hillsdale, NJ: Lawrence Erlbaum Associates.

Edson, L. (1969). Jensenism, N. The theory that I.Q. is largely determined by the genes. *New York Times Magazine,* August 31, pp. 10–11, 40–45.

Evans, J.T. and Rosenthal, R. (1969). Interpersonal self-fulfilling prophecies: Further extrapolation from the laboratory to the classroom. *Proceedings of the 77th Annual Convention of the American Psychological Association, 4,* 371–372.

Fein, L.J. (1971). *The ecology of the public schools: An inquiry into community control.* New York: Pegasus.

Gage, N.L. (1966). Discussion of the symposium on 'Teachers' expectations as an unintended determinant of pupils' intellectual reputation and competence.' Paper presented on the program of Division 15 and 8 of the American Psychological Association, New York, September.

Gergen, K.J., and Gergen, M.M. (1981). *Social psychology.* New York: Harcourt Brace, Jovanovich.

Good, T.L. and Brophy, J.E. (1977), *Educational psychology: A realistic approach.* New York: Holt, Rinehart, & Winston.

Good, T.L., Sikes, J. and Brophy, J. (1973). Effects of teacher sex and student sex on classroom interaction. *Journal of Educational Psychology, 65,* 74–87.

Jensen, A.R. (1969). How much can we boost IQ and scholastic achievement? *Harvard Educational Review, 39,* 1–123.

Jensen, A.R. (1973). The differences are real. *Psychology Today,* December, 80, 86.

Jensen, A.R. (1980). *Bias in mental testing.* New York: Free Press.

Jones, E.E. (1986). Interpreting interpersonal behavior: The effects of expectancies. *Science, 234,* 41–46.

Kerman, S. (1979). Teacher expectations and student achievement. *Phi Delta Kappan, 60,* 716–718.

Kohl, H. (1967). *36 Children.* New York: New American Library.

Kohl, H. (1968). Great expectations (Review of *Pygmalion in the classroom.*) *The New York Review of Books,* September 12, p. 31.

Kozol, J. (1967). *Death at an early age.* New York: Houghton Mifflin.

Leo, J. (1967). Study indicates pupils do well when teacher is told they will. *New York Times,* August 8, pp. 1, 20.

Merton, R.K. (1948). The self-fulfilling prophecy. *Antioch Review, 8,* 193–210.

Merton, R.K. (1981). Our sociological vernacular. *Columbia: The magazine of Columbia University,* November.

Meyer, W.J. (1985). Summary, integration, and prospective. In J.B. Dusek (Ed.), *Teacher expectancies* (pp. 353–370). Hillsdale, NJ: Lawrence Erlbaum Associates.

Raudenbush, S.W. (1984). Magnitude of teacher expectancy effects on pupil IQ as a function of the credibility of expectancy induction: A synthesis of findings from 18 experiments. *Journal of Educational Psychology, 76,* 85–97.

Rosenthal, R. (1966). *Experimenter effects in behavioral research.* New York: Appleton-Century-Crofts.

ROSENTHAL, R. (1980). Error and bias in the selection of data. *The Behavioral and Brain Sciences, 3*, 352–353.

ROSENTHAL, R. (1985). From unconscious experimenter bias to teacher expectancy effects. In J.B. DUSEK (Ed.), *Teacher expectancies* (pp. 37–65). Hillsdale, NJ: Lawrence Erlbaum Associates.

ROSENTHAL, R. and FODE, K.L. (1963). The effect of experimenter bias on the performance of the albino rat. *Behavioral Science, 8*, 183–189.

ROSENTHAL, R. and JACOBSON, L. (1968a). *Pygmalion in the classroom: Teacher expectation and pupils' intellectual development.* New York: Holt, Rinehart, and Winston.

ROSENTHAL, R. and JACOBSON, L. (1968b). Self-fulfilling prophecies in the classroom: Teachers' expectations as unintended determinants of pupils' intellectual competence. in M. DEUTSCH, I. KATZ, and A.R. JENSEN (Eds), *Social class, race, and psychological development* (pp. 219–253). New York: Holt, Rinehart, and Winston.

ROSENTHAL, R. and JACOBSON, L. (1968c). Teacher expectations for the disadvantaged. *Scientific American, 218*, 19–23.

ROSENTHAL, R. and RUBIN, D.B. (1971). Pygmalion reaffirmed. In J.D. ELASHOFF and R.E. SNOW (Eds), *Pygmalion reconsidered* (pp. 139–155). Worthington, OH: Jones.

SHAVELSON, R., CADWELL, J. and IZU, T. (1977). Teachers' sensitivity to the reliability of information in making pedagogical decisions. *American Educational Research Journal, 14*, 83–97.

SMITH, M.L. (1980). Teacher expectations. *Evaluation in Education: An International Journal, 4*, 53–55.

SNOW, R.E. (1969). Unfinished Pygmalion (Review of *Pygmalion in the Classroom.*) *Contemporary Psychology, 14*, 197–200.

SNOW, R.E. (1986). Letter to the editor of Science. Unpublished manuscript, Stanford University, Stanford, CA.

THORNDIKE, R.L. (1968). Review of *Pygmalion in the classroom. American Educational Research Journal, 5*, 708–711.

WEST, C. and ANDERSON, T. (1976). The question of preponderant causation in teacher expectancy research. *Review of Educational Research, 46*, 185–213.

Chapter 25

The Manchester Statistical Society and the Foundation of Social Science Research*

R.J.W. Selleck

... I must ask you to allow yourself to be transported to the north of England, to Manchester, in the early 1830s, and to two different scenes which took place at about the same time and which featured a young physician, Dr. James Phillips Kay. (He was later to be known as Sir James Phillips Kay-Shuttleworth, having acquired a knighthood, his wife's maiden name as part of an arrangement made when they married, and fame as a major figure in the foundation of the British public elementary school system.) The first scene took place in 1832. For some months at the beginning of that year Manchester seemed to believe that it had escaped the cholera epidemic which was raging elsewhere in England (*Manchester Guardian*, 1832). It had not — as the 27-year-old Kay discovered when he visited a dying Irishman in a house on a loop of the polluted Medlock River below the Oxford Road. Kay suspected that cholera had caused the death and, fearful of what "the excitable Irish population" among whom the man had lived might do, he arranged for a cholera van to remove the body while the man's widow and their three children, one of them a baby, were taken to hospital — the hospital was a disused cotton factory stripped of its machinery and filled with iron bedsteads. Having assured himself that the family were comfortable Kay left them sitting around a fire in a gloomy ward in order to get something to eat. When he returned later that night the baby had died and, having tried to comfort the terrified and anguished mother, Kay went home to snatch some sleep. He came back to the hospital at 6:00 next morning to find one child with severe cramps. It died as he stood by its bedside, and later the same day the third child and the mother died, each manifesting the characteristic symptoms of cholera (Bloomfield, 1964, pp. 9–10).

This experience and his work for the Board of Health established to

---

* Abridged from *Melbourne Studies in Education: 1987–88* (pp. 53–63) edited by D. Stockley, 1989, Bundoora, Victoria: La Trobe University Press.

fight the epidemic led Kay to look anew at the city in which he lived. The Industrial Revolution had brought turbulent Manchester extraordinary growth and wealth, but Kay had observed beneath the surface of society "the habits and manners of the poor, stripped of disguise" (Kay, 1834a, p. 4). In *The Moral and Physical Condition of the Working Classes Employed in the Cotton Manufacture in Manchester*, written with speed and passion in 1832, he expressed his shock at the disruption of family life and the physical and moral dislocation caused by the new conditions of labour, at the long hours of unremitting toil for men, women and children in the cotton mills which Dickens and other writers were to attack, and at working classes who were inadequately fed, prone to drunkenness, profligacy and prostitution, and who lived (occasionally accompanied by their pigs) in houses, basements, cellars and garrets which were dirty, grossly overcrowded, damp and unsewered. Kay had confronted the middle classes with what they did not wish to see and, though his pamphlet was dismissed as "a malicious libel" (Gaulter, 1833, p. 2) his descriptions remained to haunt social commentators throughout the 19th century.

The second scene occurred on 2 September 1833 when Kay was mixing with a very different group of people from those dying in the cholera hospital. The group had gathered at Claremont, the home of Benjamin Heywood, a leading banker, where they took up a collection to finance the Manchester Statistical Society which they were in the process of founding. The society was established for "the discussion of subjects of political and social economy, and for the promotion of statistical enquiries, to the total exclusion of party politics". To highmindedness they added social exclusiveness and self-satisfaction, declaring themselves to be "gentlemen accustomed for the most part to meet in private society, and whose habits and opinions are not uncongenial". [This] first British society for social and educational research ... was a men's club. The importance these Mancunians placed on "agreeable social intercourse" became obvious a few months later when, confronted with financial difficulties, they considered expanding their membership but decided to raise money in other ways, in case the society's "social character" was disrupted by the influx of new members. For all their self-satisfaction, they tackled their task with earnestness, being motivated by a "strong desire ... to assist in promoting the progress of social improvement in the manufacturing population by which they are surrounded" (Manchester Statistical Society, 1834a, 1834b).

"By which they are surrounded...." There is a hint of a threat to the congenial company in the comfortable room, and certainly James Kay, haunted by what he had seen in Manchester's back streets, pondered "the fearful strength of that multitude of the labouring population, which, for the present, lies like a slumbering giant" (Kay, 1831, p. 14). But the company at Claremont had much beside fear to unite them. They shared, most of them, liberal politics, Unitarianism, the occupations of the cotton trade, banking or medicine, in many cases an Edinburgh education, membership of many other philanthropic and intellectual societies — so many, in fact, that on occasions they might have wondered which one it was they were attending — and, through a remarkable network of marriages, family links (Elesh, 1972).

They also shared a particular view of statistics. For William Rathbone Greg, a cotton manufacturer and one of the society's founding members, statistics, far from being "a dry collection of figures and tables, possessing no interest, and leading to no result" were of "surpassing interest and moment." Expressing sentiments which social scientists have repeated for the last 150 years, he insisted: "Without accurate data on which to ground our enquiries we can never attain to any adequate knowledge of the various influences which modify the Social State." Any political philosophy not based on a statistical foundation was "speculative and uncertain and can never attain the dignity and the value of a *Science*" (Greg, 1833). The London Statistical Society, founded only a little later than its Manchester counterpart, expressed the faith which underlay both institutions. Its "first most essential rule" was "to exclude carefully all *opinions* from its transactions and publications — to confine its attention rigorously to facts — and, as far as it may be found possible, to facts which can be stated numerically and arranged in tables" (Manchester Statistical Society, 1834c).

We are present at an important moment in English intellectual history. Kay, Greg and the London and Manchester Statistical Societies had decided that a *social* science was possible, that the techniques of detached observation and experiment which had been so fruitful in other 'scientific' fields would have similar successes if applied to moral and social problems, particularly if their application could be expressed in quantities. Previously, James Kay announced, people had relied on "an approximation to truth" with results which were "never so minutely accurate to those obtained from statistical investigations". Now, Kay had decided, he need not use evidence founded on "general opinion" or dependent "merely on matters of perception"; instead, he would draw chiefly on evidence which admitted of "a statistical classification". Or as he said: "It is necessary that all the information collected should be presented in a statistical form and that vague generalizations and personal impressions should, as much as possible, be avoided" (Kay, 1832a, 1834b). Detachment, clarity, objectivity, precision — those pre-eminently scientific virtues were being extolled. Perhaps the Council of the London Statistical Society might be left to make a final link between the social and the physical sciences. In 1838 it concluded:

It is indeed truly said that the spirit of the present age has an evident tendency to confront the figures of speech with the figures of arithmetic; it being impossible not to observe a growing distrust of mere hypothetical theory and *a priori* assumption, and the appearance of a general conviction that, in the business of social science, principles are valid for application only inasmuch as they are legitimate induction from facts, accurately observed and methodically classified.... (Ashton, 1934; also see Abrams, 1968)

As it happened Manchester, even in the midst of an epidemic, was an appropriate place to nourish such beliefs for it housed a mighty symbol and exemplar of the power of science. From the early 19th century John Dalton had worked in the town and as he developed his atomic theory he read his papers not at international congresses nor in the lecture rooms of the somnolent universities — Oxford and Cambridge were still the preserves of gentlemen being taught the classics to prepare them to rule the empire which their fathers were acquiring — but to the Manchester Literary and Philosophical Society, a provincial institution composed of the aspiring commercial, industrial and professional middle class. Dalton had been president of the society since 1817, and from 1829 Kay was a member and exposed to the discussions of Dalton's work and of many less important scientific issues (Manchester Literary and Philosophical Society, 1896). Significantly it is about this time that the meaning of the word 'science' began to change ... Previously 'science' had denoted knowledge at large — comprehensive, accurate and coherent knowledge ("not having hitherto reduced politics into a science"). In the 1830s this connotation gave way to the narrower modern meaning in which one particular form of knowledge has captured the word. And it seems that in 1834, just as the Manchester Statistical Society was getting under way, the word 'scientist' was first proposed to describe the practitioner of the new knowledge: a new word to delineate a new and powerful figure (Ross, 1962).

Though it was a pioneer of new intellectual ways, the Manchester Statistical Society's originality should not be exaggerated. It was itself an expression of a growing interest in statistical work, which has led an historian of the movement to describe the 1830s and 1840s as "the era of enthusiasm" (Westergard, 1969, p. 36). In France and particularly in Germany there was considerable activity and the writings of the Belgian statistician, Adolphe Quetelet, were most important. In 1835 he published *Sur l'homme* in which he wrote of "the average man" around whom he grouped measurements of human traits in accord with the normal probability curve. England had conducted censuses each decade from 1801, actuarial statistics especially as they related to life insurance and annuities had advanced reasonably rapidly, medical statistics were improving, national criminal statistics, driven in part by a controversy over capital punishment, began to be published by the Home Office in 1810, and some statistics were being collected on education and the health of factory children (see Cullen, 1975, pp. 8–16). In 1833, the year the Manchester

Statistical Society was begun, the Board of Trade, then a small department, was driven partly by a desire to get accurate information on trade
and manufacturing from the provinces (Brown, 1958, pp. 76–98; Cullen,
1975, pp. 19–27). The Manchester Statistical Society was part of a new
and exciting intellectual movement.

What did they do, these sociable and scientifically inclined men who
had gathered to establish the first statistical society in England? Apart
from trying to get agreement on the society's rules, their first activity was
a study of the working population in Manchester. Benjamin Heywood
commissioned an agent, an "intelligent Irishman" (Heywood chose the
adjective) who was to conduct a house-to-house survey in a predominantly
working-class district of Manchester. In what was one of the first pieces of
survey research he was given questions on the country of origin of the
people in the district, their religion, the condition of their accommodation, the ages of their children, their educational history, stages of literacy
and occupations. The results of the survey were expressed in tabular form
(which would have pleased the London Statistical Society), and Heywood
reported them to the Statistical Section of the British Association for the
Advancement of Science in Edinburgh in 1834 (British Association for the
Advancement of Science, 1835, pp. 690–691; also see Manchester Statistical Society, 1835a).

Today's sophisticated researchers might permit themselves the flicker
of a smile if they were to examine the study's crude methodology or to
reflect on the serious simple-mindedness with its results were reported.
They would be unwise, because not only was this a pioneering study, but
in it the Manchester Statistical Society, over 150 years ago, had hit upon
a durable research strategy: choose a trendy topic which involves working
with people of low socio-economic status, design a questionnaire, hire a
research assistant, use him (now, it would probably be her) to do the
fieldwork, appropriate the results with the minimum of acknowledgement,
turn them into statistical tables, and deliver the findings as a paper to a
learned society.... The Manchester Statistical Society got all this right,
first time, in 1834, with the help of an intelligent Irishman.

Even the manner of reporting has a familiar ring. The agent,
"research assistant", had trouble getting answers — some people refused
him admittance to their homes and others were absent when he called.
Heywood was undaunted — though "the return was not as complete as we
would wish" there was "no reason to dispute its correctness". It was a "fair
and impartial" account of 4,102 families from "the poorest class of the
labouring population of Manchester" (Manchester Statistical Society,
1835a). Again Heywood got it right: the measured tone, the qualification
made then put aside, the reassuring objectivity, the solid conclusion. All
that is missing is the jargon, but Heywood was a primitive in social science
research and wanted to communicate his results rather than to mystify his
audience.

What the Manchester Statistical Society was attempting to do can be understood more fully if we look at two proposals. The first was developed by Kay in order to study the "habitations" of the poor. Taking a district containing houses of a particular rental, Kay sought to discover the number, age, sex, employment and wages of each family member, the number in the family who were unemployed or on poor relief, the condition of their dwellings, the literacy of the adults, the nature of their amusements, and whether or not they were members of a benefit society or subscribed to a mechanics institute. He then proposed to use this information to make comparisons with districts of higher or lower rental, and to classify the houses according to the occupations of those who lived in them (Kay, 1834b). He outlined this plan in more detail than can be given here, but sufficient has been said to show that, however tentative and undeveloped, it is recognizably modern. We can, in Kay, catch off guard the new social scientist trying to create objective numerical data, not discovering but devising the evidence from which he could derive a picture of the lives of the poor. Very clearly, in this its beginnings, we can see social science constructing its own vision of reality, making its own truth, and using words which hide its operations from itself. Data, that which are given, material independent of the researcher, a bank of convenient facts to be raided in search of conclusions — yet as Kay's proposal shows data, despite the derivation of the word, are not given; they are made.

The second project, one of the most important of the society's early investigations, was a study of education in Manchester which acted as a model for similar studies in other places (see Butterfield, 1974). The agent employed by the society, James Riddall Wood, was particularly effective and his door-to-door survey showed that an earlier parliamentary investigation chaired by the Earl of Kerry had underestimated the number of children receiving some form of education in Manchester. Despite the satisfaction which Kay and his colleagues gained by preparing a report which corrected the earlier work, they came to the conclusion that schooling was still inadequately provided and of poor quality. Though the requisite tables of statistics appeared, the bulk of the report was taken up with a discussion, unsupported by statistical analysis, of the *quality* of the education offered in the various types of schools. The report was contemptuous of the education provided by the dame schools and, though allowances must be made as the investigation was conducted by a man reporting to an all male audience, the study was equally contemptuous of what male teachers were doing in the common day schools. The agent reported one master who claimed a wide expertise in hydraulics, hydrostatics, geography, geology, etymology and entomology. More surprised than impressed, Wood asked:

Do you teach Reading and Writing — Yes! Arithmetic? Yes! Grammar and Composition? — Certainly! French? Yes! Latin? —

Yes! Greek? — Yes, yes! Geography? — Yes, etc. and so on till the list of Queries was exhausted answering every question in the affirmative. As he concluded the visitor remarked, "This is *multum in parvo* indeed" to which the Master immediately replied, "Yes, I teach that; you may put that down too." (Manchester Statistical Society, 1835b)

For all their superiority and their failure to adhere to their own standards these early studies were of critical importance in the history of educational and social research. They established a belief in the power of scientific detachment and objectivity and, through that belief, masked a fundamental ambiguity typical of many social scientists ever since. James Kay believed that the social system which produced the industrial revolution had advanced commerce and enriched and diffused civilization and therefore could not be inconsistent with "the happiness of the *great mass of the people*" (Kay, 1832a, p. 78). Yet at the same time he had to admit, had in fact insisted, that many in the working class were morally and physically degraded. How could they resolve that contradiction? Kay and most early social scientists did it indirectly: By concentrating attention and research on the working classes, Kay, by implication, identified them as the source of society's problems. It was with them that the difficulties lay, they who had to be understood, their behaviour which had to be changed, while the aristocracy and the middle class, who actually possessed political power, were left without scrutiny. The lack of power, not power or the getting of power, became, and for the most part has remained, a fundamental problem for social scientists. Over the last 150 years enquiries into poverty have been commonplace, but you may like to reflect on what happened recently when an enquiry into wealth was suggested. If that had gone ahead it might have changed the nature of the problem.

And by their problems you shall know them. The invocation of objectivity, though made sincerely, even excitedly, had a valuable political effect: It invested the questions which Kay asked with a cloak of scientific detachment which disguised the political impact of his choice of problem and the political assumptions he had made. Despite the information these early social scientists collected, despite the tables they filled with statistics (or, to put it more accurately, because of the tables they filled with statistics) they had made an unexamined assumption that the poor were the source of Manchester's problems. The interests of the merchants and manufacturers, determined to preserve a recently obtained and hard won power, slipped out of sight. The poor were to be offered improvements in public health, provident societies, and education; the powerful had statistics, the collection of quantified information, knowledge that helps to define and control. Social science, educational research, was born into a power struggle and does itself bad service when it forgets its origins.

Kay's political objectives were typical of those of his Statistical Society colleagues — the breaking of the power of the Church and aristocracy. "We do not love lords," he proclaimed, "because they give us races in their parks, and lectures on the dignity of the aristocracy at our dinners." In 1831, writing in support of the struggle for parliamentary reform, he bitterly attacked the giving of seats to young gentlemen because "they were accomplished in the simpering tactics of the drawing room"; he did not wish to be represented by "a member of the party self-styled '*conservative*'; but which is always the advocate of *rottenness* and *corruption*." Manchester and Liverpool in the past had been small and powerless; now the energies of their large populations had become absorbed

> in the production of those great commercial changes of which this country had been the scene — one invention had succeeded another — each scheme of successful enterprise had prompted a bolder — the day had appeared too short for its duties, and night had continually witnessed the exertions of the restless state of its inhabitants.

Manchester should be represented in Parliament, and not by Tories, aristocrats, younger sons who had gained a prize for Greek at Oxford, "exquisites," half-pay colonels or superannuated generals. "Our representatives," Kay said, "shall be upright, independent, sagacious merchants, too rich to accept a bribe, and too astute to be deceived" (Kay, 1831, pp. 6–21). Members of the Manchester Statistical Society, in other words.

Kay also captures the dilemma of his class, for in the struggle to shrug off the power of the Church and King, the new capitalists needed the support, but also had to contemplate the fearful strength, of that multitude of the labouring population which lay like a slumbering giant at their feet. He had heard of "the turbulent riots of the people — of machine breaking — of the secret and sullen organization which has suddenly lit the torch of incendiarism, or well nigh uplifted the arm of rebellion in the land" (Kay, 1832a, p. 77). In a telling image, Kay, who had himself seen "mobs" gutting mills, destroying machinery and burning factories, wrote of "the dense masses of the habitations of the poor, which stretch out their arms, as though to grasp and enclose the dwellings of the noble and wealthy" (Kay, 1832a, p. 11). Despite their protestations that politics had been put aside, despite their assertions of objectivity and neutrality, and despite the suffering, poverty and neglect Kay and his colleagues saw when they looked at the homes of the poor, they also saw a slumbering giant which might suddenly awaken, or powerful arms which might enclose and crush them. The schools they pressed upon the poor were in part the response of a class which had wrested some economic and political power from the Church and the aristocracy and did not wish to see it vanish into the hands of the labouring population.

Hence the significance of their swift decision to embark on educational research. Through schooling they believed, in an extraordinary act of faith which revealed their debt to the rationalism of the Enlightenment, that the working classes might be taught to respect order and authority, their order and authority. Absence of education, Kay assured his readers, was like the absence of cultivation in a garden — "the mind untutored becomes a waste, in which prejudices and traditional errors grow as rankly as weeds." "Alarming disturbances of social order generally commence with *a people only partially instructed*. The preservation of *internal peace*, not less than the improvement of our national institutions, depends on the education of the working classes." Or, in a display of uncompromising confidence: "That good government may be stable, the people must be so instructed, that they may love that *which they know to be right*" (Kay, 1832a, pp. 93–95). Members of the Statistical Society knew what was right, and through their social research they hoped to find ways of convincing others to share their views and values. The education they studied carefully in their first researches was both the subject of their study and its cause: They studied it because they had made a prior judgement that it was a social weapon they wished to wield more effectively.

What made that interest in power and statistics more fascinating was the link the Statistical Society immediately established with government. Charles Poulett Thomson was elected to represent Manchester in 1832 and was Vice-President of the Board of Trade which had recently established its own statistics department. Kay, who was a political activist, had worked hard to secure Poulett Thomson's election and it is not surprising that late in 1833 he met with the Statistical Society which had sprung up in his electorate (Kay, 1834b). In March 1833, six months before the society was formed, Kay and his Parliamentary representative had been in touch about statistical matters, and Poulett Thomson wrote congratulating Kay on the establishment of the society almost as soon as it had been founded, pointing out that the deficiency in the system for collecting statistics could only be made up from "private undertakings such as that which you have instituted at Manchester" (Thomson, 1833). He repeated these sentiments when he met with the society, arguing somewhat ominously that the government could not develop a scheme for obtaining statistical information throughout the country, partly because of the expense but mainly because "the organization requisite for such a system would be more difficult in a free than in a despotic state". Enquiries from government would be considered "inquisitorial", and it would need a long course of legislation "to reconcile the people to such enquiries into their condition as would alone be useful to the state". However, these enquiries (so Poulett Thomson thought) would be regarded with much less suspicion if run by voluntary associations. He made clear his strong support for the society and his hope that its work might draw attention to "the great economical interests of this part of the country, and to a question of paramount inportance[,] the best means of ameliorating the social condition of the labouring classes" (Kay, 1834b).

Thus, in these very first days of statistical research in England, a lasting concern of social scientists and educational researchers in particular, was made explicit: The researchers set themselves to meet the wishes of government, even if these were not made public. Apparently scientific detachment was not compromised by working on problems chosen by the powerful.

The social and political assumptions of those in the Manchester Statistical Society who placed so much emphasis on education can be illuminated still further. For Kay, again a representative figure of his class in Manchester, the social order was ultimately rational. It was like a clock, or planetary motion, or the circulation of the blood, or the behaviour of gases — if you could understand the laws which governed society, you could control and direct it in sensible and productive ways. So Kay opened his study of Manchester with the laborious but revealing comment that the physical and moral evils of society "may be more easily avoided when we are directly conscious of their existence," and the virtues and health of society could be preserved "when we are acquainted with the sources of its errors and diseases". However, unlike the human body (it is *Dr.* Kay speaking), where illness is made evident by pain, society has no sure indicator of disorder. In fact a knowledge of evils affecting one part of society was often conveyed so slowly to another that efforts at relief might be delayed until the evils "threaten to convulse the whole social constitution" (Kay, 1832a, pp. 17–18). Statistics were a way of making up for that slowness — they represented a disciplined attempt to understand society. When confronted by tension, by political tumult, by poverty or disease, Kay's response was to seek for information, for facts which would lead to understanding — fundamentally society was a rational entity.

This view had great political advantages. Kay need show no surprise that evils existed in society without its rulers being aware of them; few of the aristocracy lived near the large provincial towns, their time was spent in "an unbroken quiet, gentle amusements," and in the care of their estates. The working classes did not enter their parks. So ignorance had led the aristocracy to deny that the people were miserable or to attribute "popular tumults" simply to the instigation of unprincipled leaders. Once they had been shown the facts, things would be different: "The public welfare will be most powerfully promoted by every event, which exposes the condition of the people to the gentry England." The merchants were deeply involved in "the anxious and harassing pursuits of commerce" and could not be expected "to become personally acquainted with the state of the population, much less to expose the evils which they suffer". The manufacturers had been so divided from the working classes by industrial conflict that they saw them as objects of anger not of comprehension (Kay, 1832a, pp. 8–9).

These failings, however serious, could not be, so Kay believed, the fault of the economic arrangements. "The evils here unreservedly exposed, so far from being the necessary consequences of the manufacturing system, have a remote and accidental origin, and might, by *judicious management*, be entirely removed" (Kay, 1832a, p. 15). Once he had decided that the social system was not at fault, or not fundamentally at fault, and made his assumption that social behaviour could in principle be explained scientifically, Kay was driven irresistibly to search for explanations. Having come to the irrational conclusion that society was amenable to balance and reason, he and his colleagues at the Manchester Statistical Society set out to acquire the basic social knowledge which would enable them to control it.

There were times when Kay felt a shiver of doubt. Writing in November 1832 about the reception of his pamphlet, he remarked that

the inconsiderate hostility which was at first raised by a few of those capitalists, who considered themselves *attacked* (!) in my first edition, is now almost entirely assuaged, and in its room is springing up a most healthful disposition to do all that is possible for the remedy of evils whose existence cannot be denied.

Kay believed that this change of heart would be permanent and "issue in some practical results" (Kay, 1832b). In fact the change of heart was brief while the anger he had stirred endured, as he was to discover a few years later when conservative forces blocked his appointment as an honorary physician to the Manchester Infirmary.

Had he not been so optimistic, Kay might have learned from the first ungenerous reaction of the Manchester capitalists a lesson which Engels taught through an anecdote: He had spoken to a member of the Manchester bourgeoisie "of the bad, unwholesome method of building, the frightful condition of the working-people's quarters," and asserted that "I had never seen so ill-built a city." The man listened quietly to the end, and said at the corner where he parted from Engels: "And yet there is a great deal of money made here; good morning, sir" (Engels, 1958, pp. 301–302). The assumptions of the new social scientists, and especially their belief in a society which was ultimately amenable to reason, meant that they did not confront the implications of irreconcilable class interests or of the ruthless struggle for power.

The first social scientists, these early educational researchers, these imaginative and intellectually ambitious members of the Manchester Statistical Society, were bound within their own insular world of values, the more certainly because it never occurred to them that they were. Protected by the opinion that theirs was privileged work, done with the authority of science, they were as partial, as prejudiced, as passionately opinionated, as the poets or philosophers they often affected to despise. . . .

Modern social scientists are, of course, quite different? Perhaps we should remember how unerringly the Manchester Statistical Society, in the first piece of research it commissioned, anticipated procedures which became commonplace. And we might reflect how researchers still approach policy makers, governments, national bodies of one kind or another, offering to help solve their problems. In education, social work, or health (familiar fields indeed for Manchester men) today's scientists endeavour to conduct research which will provide acceptable data upon which policies can be based — social scientists endeavouring to produce knowledge for the policy makers to put to use. . . .

The biases, political judgements and social assumptions of the early educational researchers in Manchester are easy for us to see, but it would be "a strange effect of narrow principles and short views," to borrow Jonathan Swift's words, if we considered our own judgements and assumptions any the less obvious. Sounder, they may be, more enlightened and subtle, but they are no less grounded on value judgements and unexamined beliefs — they are equally open to challenge and controversy, they are betrayed, just as the Manchester Statistical Society's were, by our choice of subject, and they shelter, just as uneasily, behind a particular version of the scientific tradition.

There is another comparison with the Manchester of the 1830s which may be worth making. We are getting too self-conscious to use words like 'the subject' to describe those on whom our research is being done. Yet when we study the unemployed, the disadvantaged, ethnic groups, women, youth in transition from school to work, aborigines, early leavers, are we not, like those earnest middle-class Manchester men, seeing these as victims in our society, and (so often) finding that if they are to 'improve' they will have to change their behaviour in certain ways, especially to become more like us?

A final reflection: the word 'statistics' itself. G.M. Young described the transformation in Victorian England of the treatment of social affairs from a polemical to a statistical basis, as a transition "from Humbug to Humdrum." He may be right, but the humdrum word 'statistics' once meant a wide ranging study of the state, often comparatively — its population, forms of government, exports, economy, etc. Then just as 'science' narrowed, 'statistics' came to mean "numerical facts systematically collected," to use the present definition of the *Concise Oxford Dictionary*. In its origin, however, the word is connected to the process of government, to 'state', 'stat-istics'. The Manchester Statistical Society embodied that link when it volunteered to do the Board of Trade's work for it. Social scientists (and not just statisticians) are continuing that embrace. In this country a government with particular social and economic policies is striving to bring educational institutions into closer accord with those politics. In the struggle it proposes to reward those who do 'relevant' research, that is, research on the topics it chooses, the topics it believes will most advance its policies. There is nothing new in that, though the scale of the present enterprise is remarkable, as is made clear by recent changes in research funding arrangements, the mechanistic use of performance indicators, and the commercialization of research — putting research contracts out to tender increases the client's control over the research worker. . . .

We might ponder those eager members of the Manchester Statistical Society protesting their scientific objectivity while they rushed to ascertain the wishes of their political masters. They at least have the excuse that they were making the history from which it seems we might fail to learn.

References

ABRAMS, P. (1968). *The origins of British sociology: 1834–1914.* Chicago: University of Chicago Press.

ASHTON, T.S. (1934). *Economic and social investigations in Manchester, 1833–1933.* London: P.S. King and Son.

BLOOMFIELD, B.C. (Ed.) (1964). *The autobiography of Sir James Kay-Shuttleworth.* London: University of London, Institute of Education Library.

BRITISH ASSOCIATION FOR THE ADVANCEMENT OF SCIENCE (1835). *Report of the fourth meeting of the British Association for the Advancement of Science; held at Edinburgh in 1834.* London: Author.

BROWN, L. (1958). *The Board of Trade and the free-trade movement 1830–42.* Oxford: Clarendon Press.

BUTTERFIELD, P.H. (1974). The educational researches of the Manchester Statistical Society, 1830–40. *British Journal of Educational Studies, 12*(3), 340–359.

CULLEN, M.J. (1975). *The statistical movement in early Victorian Britain: The foundation of empirical social research.* New York: Barnes and Noble.

ELESH, D. (1972). The Manchester Statistical Society: A case study of a discontinuity in the history of empirical social research, part 1. *Journal of the History of the Behavioral Sciences, 8,* 280–287.

ENGELS, F. (1958). *The condition of the working class in England* (W.O. HENDERSON & W.H. CHALONER, Trans. and Eds.). Oxford: Basil Blackwell. (Original work published 1844)

GAULTER, H. (1833). *The origin and progress of the malignant cholera in Manchester.* London: Longman, Rees, Orme, Brown, Green, and Longman.

GREG, W.R. (1833). *Brief memoir on the present state of criminal statistics,* October 16 (Papers of the Manchester Statistical Society, PMSS, No. 2). Manchester, Archives Department, Manchester Central Library.

KAY, J.P. (1831). *A letter to the people of Lancashire.* London.

KAY, J.P. (1832a). *The moral and physical condition of the working classes employed in the cotton manufacture in Manchester.* London: J. Ridgway.

KAY, J.P. (1832b). November 21. Chalmers Collection (CHA 4, 183.4). New College, Edinburgh.

KAY, J.P. (1834a). *Defects in the constitution of dispensaries, with suggestions for their improvement.* London and Manchester.

KAY, J.P. (1834b). Untitled paper in James Phillips Kay's handwriting (Papers of the Manchester Statistical Society, PMSS, No. 5). Manchester, Archives Department, Manchester Central Library.

MANCHESTER GUARDIAN (1832), February 4 & 11.

MANCHESTER LITERARY AND PHILOSOPHICAL SOCIETY (1896). *Complete list of members and officers of the Manchester Literary and Philosophical Society.* Manchester: Author.

MANCHESTER STATISTICAL SOCIETY (1834a). *First report of the Statistical Society, Manchester,* July (Papers of the Manchester Statistical Society, PMSS, No. 11). Manchester, Archives Department, Manchester Central Library.

MANCHESTER STATISTICAL SOCIETY (1834b). *Report of the committee appointed to revise the rules of the Manchester Statistical Society,* October 15 (Papers of the Manchester Statistical Society, PMSS, No. 20). Manchester, Archives Department, Manchester Central Library.

MANCHESTER STATISTICAL SOCIETY (1834c). *Prospectus of the objects and plan of operation of the Statistical Society in London,* April 23 (Papers of the Manchester Statistical Society, PMSS, No. 8). Manchester, Archives Department, Manchester Central Library.

MANCHESTER STATISTICAL SOCIETY (1835a). *Report of the fourth meeting of the British Association for the Advancement of Science; held at Edinburgh in 1834* (Papers of the Manchester Statistical Society, PMSS, Nos. 17–19, 21). Manchester, Archives Department, Manchester Central Library.

MANCHESTER STATISTICAL SOCIETY (1835b). *Report of a committee of the Manchester Statistical Society on the state of education in the Borough of Manchester* (Papers of the Manchester Statistical Society, PMSS, No. 49). Manchester, Archives Department, Manchester Central Library.

ROSS, S. (1962). Scientist: The history of a word. *Annals of Science, 18*(2), 65–85.

THOMSON, C.P. (1833) November 6. Kay-Shuttleworth Papers (No. 91). Manchester, John Rylands Library.

WESTERGARD, H. (1969). *Contributions to the history of statistics.* New York: A.M. Kelley.

YOUNG, G.M. (1961). *Portrait of an age.* London: Oxford University Press.

Name Index

Subject Index

Action Research, 16–17
American Educational Research Association, 84, 280
Applied Research, 8, 23–30, 98, 100, 123–139, 152

Behavioral Research, 87–101
Basic Research, 8, 23–30, 32–38, 98, 103–111
applications, 34, 104–106
effects on educational policy, 106–109
effects on professional preparation, 109–111
in psychology, 153
unanticipated consequences, 36

Causal Explanation, 45–46, 89–91
Commissions of Inquiry, 16, 245–257
decline of, 251
use of social science, 250
Compensatory School Programmes, 128–130
Conflicts of Interest, 14, 77
Constructivist Paradigm, 158–170
Counterintuitive Findings, 199

Decision Accretion, 183
Decision-making, 183–191, 194–196
Department of Health, Education and Welfare (USA), 119, 223
Desegregation of Schools, 237–243

Dissemination, 15, 119, 209–210, 214–223
by seepage, 36, 227
in medicine, 33
Determinism, 161

Economic and Social Research Council (UK), 226
Education, 3
Educational Change, 16
Educational Policy, 72
Educational Priority Area, 232
Education Research, 39–42, 70–84
characteristics, 75
definition, 73
disjunction with policy, 75–76
lack of financial support, 83
lack of political support, 80–82
methods, 74–75
proposals, 40
Empiricism, 93
Epistemology, 47, 162–163
Ethnographic Research, 12
Eugenics Movement, 260, 262
Evaluation Research, 16, 268–275
Experiment, 89
Explanations, 11

Feedback, 119–122, 142
Freedom of Information Act (USA), 116
Funding, 2, 36–37, 65, 83

Government Research, 225–227

311